T0393243

Firsting in the Early-Modern Atlantic World

For centuries, historians have narrated the arrival of Europeans using terminology (discovery, invasion, conquest, and colonization) that emphasizes their agency and disempowers that of Native Americans. This book explores firsting, a discourse that privileges European and settler-colonial presence, movements, knowledges, and experiences as a technology of colonization in the early modern Atlantic world, 1492–1900. It exposes how textual culture has ensured that Euro-settlers dominate Native Americans, while detailing misrepresentations of Indigenous peoples as unmodern and proposing how the western world can be un-firsted in scholarship on this time and place.

Lauren Beck holds the Canada Research Chair in Intercultural Encounter and is Professor of Hispanic Studies at Mount Allison University.

Routledge Research in Early Modern History

The Peace of Augsburg and the Meckhart Confession
Moderate Religion in an Age of Militancy
Adam Glen Hough

Social and Cultural Relations in the Grand Duchy of Lithuania
Microhistories
Edited by Richard Butterwick and Wioletta Pawlikowska

Spain, Rumor, and Anti-Catholicism in Mid-Jacobean England
The Palatine Match, Cleves, and the Armada Scares of 1612–1613 and 1614
Calvin F. Senning

Firsting in the Early-Modern Atlantic World
Edited by Lauren Beck

Early Modern English Noblewomen and Self-Starvation
The Skull Beneath the Skin
Sasha Garwood

Maurits of Nassau and the Survival of the Dutch Revolt
Comparative Insurgences
Nick Ridley

The Economic Causes of the English Civil War
Freedom of Trade and the English Revolution
George Yerby

Edwin Sandys and the Reform of English Religion
Sarah L. Bastow

For more information about this series, please visit: https://www.routledge.com/Routledge-Research-in-Early-Modern-History/book-series/RREMH

Firsting in the Early-Modern Atlantic World

Edited by Lauren Beck

NEW YORK AND LONDON

First published 2020
by Routledge
52 Vanderbilt Avenue, New York, NY 10017

and by Routledge
2 Park Square, Milton Park, Abingdon, Oxon, OX14 4RN

Routledge is an imprint of the Taylor & Francis Group, an informa business

First issued in paperback 2021

Library of Congress Cataloging-in-Publication Data
A catalog record for this book has been requested

ISBN: 978-0-367-33468-0 (hbk)
ISBN: 978-1-03-209206-5 (pbk)
ISBN: 978-0-429-32000-2 (ebk)

Typeset in Sabon
by Apex CoVantage, LLC

Contents

Figures

Acknowledgments

I owe the development of this book to conversations about firsting with Andrew Nurse and Robert LeBlanc, both of whom helped to shape this project during its chrysalis.

Introduction

Firsting and the Architecture of Decolonizing Scholarship on the Early-Modern Atlantic World

Lauren Beck

Firsting is the process through which an act or accomplishment, a circumstance or phenomenon generated by man, is represented as having occurred for the first time. Firsting necessarily implies *seconding* and *lasting* as concomitant processes that help structure historical exchanges. Firsting also involves complex issues that conflict our present, including those of race and ethnicity, gender and sexuality, religion and language, and place of origin. These issues inform firsting within scholarship devoted to a diverse range of fields, from classics and Ottoman studies, to Australian and African studies, in addition to transatlantic scholarship, which is the focus of this book.

Scholarship on historical transmigration and exchanges between peoples tends to participate in firsting one way or another, a problem acknowledged by J.B. Harley and David Woodward thirty years ago in their introduction to the now-seminal *History of Cartography*.[1] Firsting manifests itself in scholarship through declarations, such as "The first Europeans to discover America came from the lands of the north. Called Vikings or Norsemen, they were the terror of Europe,"[2] or by not acknowledging the presence of Indigenous peoples when discussing the activities of Europeans in the Americas. Comparably greater interest in European activities rather than those of Indigenous and non-European peoples exemplifies the deep-rooted nature of firsting and how it continues to subvert ethnic and gender equality today.

Firsting can be detected in language that supports overtly or incidentally the doctrine of discovery, or renders secondary those who came after (such as enslaved Africans and African Americans, and immigrants from other parts of the world who willingly came).[3] This taxonomy of arrivals manifests itself in socio-political and economic contexts, as Jean M. O'Brien recently observed in her important book, *Firsting and Lasting: Writing Indians out of Existence in New England* (2010). Lasting, or un-firsting through the effacement and extinction of Indigenous peoples, is attracting increased scholarly scrutiny throughout the Americas. Advances in democratic liberalism in most settler-colonial contexts have involved the explicit and violent oppression of Indigenous populations and have resulted in either the real or constructed erasure of their presence.[4] Lasting involves the real or fictional disappearance of Indigenous languages, spiritual beliefs and practices, territories, and sovereignty, which gives rise to a sense of loss or absence rather than presence in scholarship on the early-modern period. The phenomenon of the "last Indian" is nowhere more apparent than in the titles of scholarly and popular works on this subject, which range from Theodore L. Kazimiroff's *The Last Algonquin* (1982) to the hit film, based on the novel by James Fenimore Cooper, *The Last of the Mohicans* (1992).

Preventing scholars from engaging properly with Indigenous perspectives on the early-modern Atlantic world, and their reception of Europeans, is a subject pursued by Theodore Binnema in *Common and Contested Ground* (2001). Binnema reminds his reader that posing the same type of question—for instance, European-settler impact on Indigenous cultures and ways of life—has ensured that the same lacunae in scholarship have remained the last number of decades. He adds that "Euroamericans became influential but not powerful participants in the ancient, dynamic, and complex patterns of trade, diplomacy, and warfare in the region."[5] Binnema decenters this period of Indigenous-European interaction so that the Euro-settler is not the powerful actor with agency overcoming that of the Indigenous peoples with whom he met. Instead, he encourages his reader to view Indigenous peoples as powerful in their own right and as agents who impacted their own lives as well as those of the settlers with whom they occasionally interacted. The perception that a wave of white men spread out across the continents that comprise the Americas, moving toward the west, southwest, and northwest from points east and south, contrasts with the reality that much of the American and Canadian mid-west and west remained unpopulated by white people until about two centuries ago, and Spanish settlement in the southwestern parts of South America remained difficult until the eighteenth century. Indigenous peoples lived productively without this interaction. Occasionally choosing to harness western technologies and products—horses and guns, for example—without interacting regularly with Euro-settlers demonstrates the degree to which their trade networks went unnoticed by settler-colonizers. Binnema and others publishing in the early twenty-first century signal a change in how anthropological, ethnohistorical, and historical research is being done and the types of questions and information that would emerge from this re-centering of contact and interaction between Indigenous peoples and Euro-settlers.

Beyond framing the book's primary themes, this introductory essay outlines firsting as a scholarly and historiographical paradigm, and proposes ways through which it can be mitigated, eliminated, or counteracted. In tandem, critical background for English, French, and Spanish contact with the Americas will be re-positioned in light of firsting, particularly through the elevation of Indigenous, as opposed to Euro-settler, firsts, to echo what Jodi Byrd has recommended Indigenous peoples do in order to fortify their claims to territory, resources, and sovereignty.[6] This approach models and points to progressive scholarship that eschews firsting practices or otherwise empowers Indigenous peoples as first peoples who experienced firsts just as much as Europeans did during the early-modern period; it will allow us to understand how firsting can impact individuals differently according to their gender, social class, education, economic means, race, and religion. An exploration of the contested vocabularies for racialized and Indigenous peoples will furthermore demonstrate how firsting discourse activates the armature of Euro-settler colonization within western scholarship on the early-modern Atlantic world. This case study is urgently required because conflicting and variable terminology for Native-American peoples continues to be used in scholarship, and it will be encountered throughout this book. Finally, the gendered nature of firsting remains an area that requires addressing with the objective of calling upon scholars to actively disengage from masculinist scholarly practices, such as firsting, while pointing to new ways of performing scholarship that welcome perspectives and experiences beyond those of white Euro-settler men. This last aim involves a summary of the findings and remedies developed in the chapters that follow the introduction, which have been crafted by an interdisciplinary array of scholars specializing in the disciplines of history, literature, ethnography, and Indigenous studies.

As we will see throughout this book, many terms for racialized and racially mixed peoples evidently emphasize skin color in ways that are no longer embraced today, and for historical reasons as well as differences in scholarly practices across the world, we have chosen to explore these nuances rather than unify all Native Americans with the term Indigenous, for example. Terms for racially mixed individuals (i.e. Peruvian-Japanese man, African-Canadian woman) point to the origin of the mixed-blooded person's parents and possibly the person's region of birth, which have geographic implications that require context in light of the phenomenon of firsting. Christopher Columbus (1451–1506) and his contemporaries understood the differences between people not so much in terms of nationality and skin color—although these are factors that arise in some racial typologies of the period—but rather geographic place of origin.[7] Racial typologies of this nature had long been part of Christian eschatology. According to that tradition, Noah's sons inherited the three continents, and scholars during the medieval period racialized geographies according to Noah's most and least favored sons (Japheth, who received Europe, and Ham, who received Africa); these alignments were used to justify the apparatus of enslaving African peoples for European economic and social benefit.[8] Asia, sometimes called India in medieval geographical works, went to Shem, whose descendants, along with those of Ham, would serve those of Japheth. This geographic hierarchy structures humanity in a way that privileges Europe and its peoples, and provides the framework for firsting even before Columbus set his eyes on the Caribbean.

Racialized terms, such as black (*negro*) in Spanish, were not as common in the medieval period as epithets such as moor (*moro*), which could apply to a mixed-blood person as easily as someone from the Arab world or from Africa, whether Christian or Muslim.[9] This flexibility allows its diminutive derivative, *morisco* (little moor), which emerged around 1492 to describe Christian converts in Spain, to appear in references to Indigenous peoples of the Americas. Hernán Cortés (1485–1547), after all, described seeing mosque minarets in Tenochtitlan on the eve of it falling in 1521, which synchronizes these peoples as collective enemies of Catholic Spain whose cultural signifiers could slide from one to the other.[10] In many ways, finding Indians in the Caribbean was no different than finding white moors in Spain; the deracination of the name from any place of origin becomes an important means through which peoples could be dispossessed of their lands, culture, and even identity.[11] These terms today are antiquated and even considered offensive, which bathes light on how racialized vocabularies can cause offense while they also assign and construct identity in ways that can even build allegiances between the name and the named. An example of this practice can be found in the place name Oklahoma, coined by Choctaw chief Allen Wright (1826–1885) to replace Indian Territory; *okla* (people or nation) and *homa* (red) became his way of making the lands assigned to Indigenous peoples such as him his own.[12]

The elasticity of racialized terms denoting non-whiteness or non-Europeanness dovetails in the early-modern period with increasing interest in cultivating a civilizing discourse that creates an opposition between the metropole and the country, technology and the lack of mechanization, the refined and the barbaric, the Christian and the non-Christian, the modern and the ancient, the known and the unknown, and the white Christian and nonwhite of any religion.[13] As José Rabasa has shown, a significant symptom of European self-eminence emerges through the map as a powerful technology through which lands were created, claimed, and conquered in ways that expose these oppositions.[14] Medieval-era maps in the west centered on Jerusalem and featured the tripartite division of the world according to Noah's children. Sixteenth-century maps, however, abandoned this locus so significant to Christianity and instead re-centered on Europe and the Atlantic Ocean while detailing the newest knowledge about the remaining parts of the world, which itself compelled the production of new maps and generated an entire industry around the enterprise of constructing a new worldview in an era of European imperialism.[15] While theories about civilization and race emerge in fully fleshed out form in the eighteenth and nineteenth centuries, we can detect that early moderns including Columbus and his analogs from Britain, France, and Portugal, increasingly were subscribing to these civilizing dichotomies that inherently advanced European interests and undergirded the architecture of colonization.

Columbus and his contemporaries believed that Asia lay to their west. According to the *Capitulaciones de Santa Fe* signed by Isabel and Ferdinand months before he departed Spain, Columbus was traveling "per maria oçeana ad partes Indie" (across the ocean to parts of India).[16] The Americas and its inhabitants were named quite previous to Columbus's voyage, which was not uncommon. The Portuguese monarchs during the latter half of the fifteenth century awarded their explorers terms similar to those outlined in the *Capitulaciones*; they, too, underlined their expectation that most lands explored and claimed by Portuguese men in Africa and later in Brazil would be inhabited.[17] This insight into what comprises a discovery allows us to conclude that Europeans during this period were aware that others already knew about these far-away lands and their contents. Claims to territory become, as Ashley Glassburn Falzetti determines, "a willful insistence that the most recent conquest defines which people count, resulting in a refusal to acknowledge the histories of those who lived in a place before that moment."[18]

While considering how to address the deeply engrained issue of firsting in scholarship on the early-modern period, which itself builds upon firsting discourses expressed in primary sources and the logic underpinning European expansion, let us also consider the language employed by Columbus in his letter to the Catholic kings about his arrival to the Caribbean region. He often used the verb *hallar* (to observe one's location or to perceive a place) in the original letter published by Pero de Posa in Barcelona in 1493. Like the Romans when they invaded Spain, he believed that he knew where he was—somewhere in eastern Asia, the precise location to be determined later. His contemporaries who later published the letter characterized the lands as "nuper inventis" (recently found),[19] which translators and editors subsequently termed "nuper repertis" (popularly translated as "recently discovered").[20] Were he in Asia, as most contemporaries believed possible at the time, the matter of discovery in the sense that it is used today is not logical. An examination of early-modern dictionaries demonstrates that the verb "to discover" at the dawn of the sixteenth century was associated with concepts and facts that could be apprehended and thus acquired, and the legal term remains in the English lexicon today.[21] Viewed in this way, discovery, once associated with land, becomes an act of acquisition, not one of simple observation or perception. Firsting enabled Columbus and his successors to make discovery an acquisitive act and a means of claiming a land possessed or occupied by someone else.[22]

The *Capitulaciones* also accord the Genovese man a territory as-yet unlocated, the *almirantazgo*, which like a *condado* (a count's territory) and a *reino* (a king's territory) comprised the regions that the admiral would control, if he found any.[23] In a letter to a royal official prepared in

February 1493 and published two months later, Columbus notes how he gave the present-day Bahamian Watling Island the name "San Salvador, a conmemoración de su Alta Majestad, el cual maravillosamente todo esto ha dado: los indios la llaman Guanahani" (San Salvador in commemoration of his Highness, to whom all of this has been given: the Indians call it Guanahani).[24] His admission that San Salvador was not the first name of this island, and that it had a preexisting one given by its inhabitants, tends to be overshadowed by the performance of staking his claim and the ensuing possession of the territory also unfolding within the letter, especially his argument that claiming these lands was valid because the inhabitants, who in this case were Taíno, did not contradict his proclamation. Without a common language, it would have been difficult to contradict Columbus's verbalized intentions.

The earliest European visualization of the lands described by Columbus during his first three voyages demonstrates how Spaniards and their contemporaries rendered the lands vacant, in what has been termed *terra nullius*. Lands thus described were occupied by no people or nation recognized by European powers, or when occupied, the inhabitants supposedly were not making adequate use of their resources, making the lands ripe for acquisitive discovery.[25] The view that Native Americans were less capable than Europeans to even govern themselves remains apparent in legal structures impacting Indigenous claims to territory and ways of life in place today across the Americas and whose origins are European.[26] Terra nullius also remains an active colonizing discourse today throughout the Americas. Importantly, terra nullius as a term emerged only in the nineteenth century as a means of describing this firsting rhetoric employed for centuries by Euro-settlers and especially by lawyers and scholars. As Anthony Pagden observes, "terra nullius became the argument of final appeal in most of the American colonies," and elsewhere in the world; it was paired with a second legal process, prescription, which allowed authorities to give retrospective rights to land and resources to settlers who lived in the Americas (de facto occupation).[27] Throughout the Spanish Americas, the inducement to settle and occupy lands and the promise to benefit from their wealth enticed Spanish men to bring their families across the Atlantic while fortifying efforts at colonization through their presence.[28]

Columbus and his successors paired a prototypical version of terra nullius with their lack of knowledge about the landscape of the Americas. Having read either news about his third voyage or witnessed the man's remarks during the third voyage, navigator and cartographer Juan de la Cosa (c. 1450–1510) either prepared the *pintura* (painting or picture) that Columbus claimed to have sent to the kings or later responded to this need on his own accord. His 1500 portolan chart depicts the lands that Columbus claimed to have discovered, including Cuba and the nearby islands, and two continental landmasses that extend along the left-most margin of the chart.[29] The map may be the earliest visualization of contested European claims to the Americas. It positions along the northern-most American landmass five British flags, and the description "Mar descubierta ynglesie" (Sea discovered by the English), in reference to the expedition of John Cabot (c. 1450–c. 1499) in 1497–1498, which contrast against the Spanish dominion below. The lands represented are otherwise vacant of any geographical features. These five flags likely reflect the five ships authorized by the British sovereign, who in his letter patent granted Cabot the authority to explore this area of the world at his own expense.[30] Henry VII (1457–1509) allowed Cabot, also Italian, and his male heirs to discover, claim, and possess "towns, castles, cities and islands" not already claimed by other Christians.[31]

Like the Spanish monarchs, the British king also anticipated that places, which themselves would have names, infrastructure, inhabitants, and governments, already existed in the territories that Cabot and his collaborators believed were located in eastern Asia.[32] Unlike Columbus, however, Cabot and his contemporaries did not assume that the inhabitants encountered in present-day North America were Indians, noting in one account of the inhabitants of "prima terra vista" (the land first seen [by Europeans]) that they marked their faces "in modo Indianichi" (in the Indian style), but otherwise referred to them as the land's *inhabitants* (also phrased *la gente*).[33] In subsequent editions of this text, however, the denominator for these people changes to become natives[34] and savages,[35] this last term being particularly popular in British and French accounts by the mid-sixteenth century. The increasing use of savage points to the European desire, particularly among the British and French, to justify claims to territory by relieving the land's original inhabitants of their capability and absenting them from the land altogether.[36] This practice continues within the realm of scholarship as well. Most scholarship on prima terra vista ignores altogether Indigenous peoples in order to ponder where Cabot made landfall—Cape Breton or Newfoundland—and muses over imagined conspiracy theories and supposed secrets preventing scholars from knowing more about Cabot's itinerary, as unlike Columbus, Cartier, and Champlain, Cabot left no written record.[37] Importantly, no scholarship pauses to consider the identities of the people who saw Cabot for the first time, whether Mi'kmaq or Beothuk, nor the likelihood that they expected to see people such as Cabot and his ships.

For centuries prior to Columbus and Cabot's voyages, the peoples of the Americas had established sophisticated trade and communication networks that stretched from coast to coast. During the Woodland Period (800 BC to 1500 AD) in the eastern United States, gardens and similar settlements for growing food became a primary source of nutrition, and the hunting trail networks expanded during and after that time to become trading networks. In areas such as the Mississippi region, large and permanent settlements emerged about 1200 years ago.[38] Excavations of the mound-building culture at Cahokia (near present-day St. Louis, Missouri), a city of as many as 50,000 residents, demonstrate that bead-producing workshops made use of shells collected from the northeast Atlantic and Gulf of Mexico coasts located 1340 and 1070 km away, respectively.[39] Wampum created in the Long Island region by the Lenape (Delaware) made their way across the Wabanaki Confederacy (comprised, from east to west, of the Mi'kmaq, Wolostoq, Passamaquoddy, Abenaki, and Penobscot peoples whose territories covered Newfoundland, Maritime Canada, and the northeastern United States, including Vermont and Quebec south of the Saint Laurence River) and traded as well with the Haudenosaunee (Five Nations or Iroquois Confederacy, comprised, from east to west, of the Mohawk, Oneida, Onondaga, Cayuga, and Seneca nations located traditionally along the border of present-day Canada and the United States between New York, Ontario, and Quebec), and Ojibwe (Anishinaabe, a group of nations traditionally located from present-day Quebec to eastern British Columbia, and sometimes along the border with the United States), among other peoples across this region of the world.[40]

These networks also penetrated physical barriers such as mountains and extended southward. The Great Warrior Path allowed travelers to pass through the Appalachian Mountains and to access areas such as present-day Tennessee and Alabama.[41] The Old North Trail (which connected Canada's far north to Mexico along the eastern side of the Rocky Mountains) and other trails (traces) facilitated these networks, along which communication challenges had been overcome, as demonstrated by the far-reaching presence of the Uto-Aztecan family of languages spoken along this corridor, from southern Alberta to Guatemala. Other ways emerged that allowed linguistically distinct peoples to trade. Indigenous groups in this region of the continent had long developed a sign language that allowed the Blackfeet, Blood, Cheyenne, Crow, Flathead, Gros Ventres, Mandans, Kutenai, Nez Perce, Pend d'Oreille, Piegan, Sioux, Snake, and Arapahoe to communicate despite their linguistic distinctiveness from one another.[42] Gesture-based languages can also be found in Central and South America, for example among the Tupí-Guaraní in Maranhão, Brazil, where there are also varieties of pidgin developed by African slaves who possessed different backgrounds and required means of communicating with one another.[43] Chinook jargon, or Wawa, performed a similar purpose in northwestern North America.[44] In Mexico, a visually expressed, ideographic language functioned as a lingua franca.[45]

With the circulation of people and goods came the circulation of knowledge. Indigenous place-naming practices along the eastern coast of the United States suggest the presence of Taíno or their linguistic influence in the region of present-day South Carolina, where Algonquian names are also present, which demonstrates contact between these language communities facilitated through trade and hunting corridors.[46] The transmission of information from the Caribbean to an area inhabited by the Mi'kmaq, whose language belongs to the Algonquian family of languages, is within the realm of possibility. Time was not a limiting factor, as David Ingram (fl. 1567–1583) demonstrates in his claim to have walked from the Gulf of Mexico to Cape Breton between 1568 and 1569.[47] Like the Cahokians and the members of the Wabanaki Confederacy, the Taíno participated in a complex trading environment and exported goods, particularly cotton for textiles such as capes, that were not products used in their culture; they, like other peoples of the Americas, nonetheless esteemed value in the resources at their disposal and mobilized them to regions where they were in demand.[48] It took only three days for Spanish goods given to a Taíno man, which included Spanish coins, to become part of the region's Indigenous interisland trade network.[49] Shells from Florida, obsidian mined in the Rocky Mountains, and mica originating from Tennessee turned up in the Algonquian northeast.[50] Beyond these material items and natural resources, some scholars argue that knowledge itself was commoditized and traded along the same networks that facilitated the exchange of goods. Thus, it seems likely that Indigenous knowledge about Europeans became commoditized and circulated broadly from one people to another, as were their goods.[51] Viewing the Mi'kmaw or Beothuk encounter with Cabot in this way converts the latter into an expected arrival and the former into informed and knowledgeable peoples.

The French expansion into the Americas also began in the same area visited by Cabot with the travels of Jacques Cartier (1491–1557) in 1534 and, after him, those of Jean-François de la Rocque de Roberval (c. 1500–1560). By this time Europeans had abandoned, for the most part, their belief that these lands formed part of Asia, but they persisted in the quest to nonetheless reach Asia by crossing or going around the Americas.[52] Following the successful circumnavigation of the southern-most continent by Fernão de Magalhães (1480–1521) fifteen years earlier, Cartier's task was, in addition to discovering lands for Francis I (1494–1547) of France, to find a northwest passage to Asia. Somewhere along the river that he had named the Saint Laurence, he relates how, upon coming to another river later named for Saguenay in 1535, "les sauuaiges que auions, nous a esté dicte que cestoit le commencement due Saguenay & terre habitable" (the savages that we have with us, they have told us that this was the start of Saguenay and habitable land).[53]

These so-called savages had the year before accompanied Cartier to France; Domagaya and Taignoagny were the sons of Donnacona (d. 1539), Haudenosaunee chief of Stadacona (later Quebec) who the Basques referred to as the Canadakoa (Fr. Canadaquois).[54] According to Cartier, Donnaconna's sons convinced him about the existence of a wealthy kingdom of hairy white people located northwest of the Saint Laurence River.[55] The explorer repeatedly refers to this wealthy kingdom of Saguenay, and his king had instructed him to locate it and its wealth, which was one of the purposes of Cartier and Roberval's journey in

1541–1543. We know from impressions of these first encounters related through Indigenous eyes unfolding across the Americas during this period that one of the notable characteristics deemed strange about the Europeans was their hirsuteness. It seems that Donnaconna and his sons' ridicule of the French explorers would also translate into a form of nativism on the part of European historians. The French mission to find Saguenay, locate a passage westward, and establish a settlement exemplifies the a priori coexistence of imagined places and features alongside established ones (in the case of Cathay or the empire of the Great Kahn) and future ones (in the case of French settlements and a northwest passage). In tandem, the possibility of finding individuals who resembled Europeans cultivated claims to the area through references to Cain and the creation of some form of shared heritage. Scholars since have pointed to the Norse as possibly influencing Cartier's Indigenous informants, a practice that results in the appearance of Indigenous knowledge becoming colonized by earlier Europeans.[56] Similar stances have been taken from within the Islamic world as well, particularly around the claim that dates and other foods traditionally found in the Middle East were encountered by Europeans along the Pacific coast of the Americas; some scholars have argued that the presence of this flora indicates that Muslims had come to the Americas before Europeans.[57]

Throughout the early-modern period, the Atlantic world remains in flux and scholars struggle at times to formulate adequate vocabularies and ways of looking at history that avoid supporting Euro-settler eminence. The purpose of Richard King's 2016 *Redskins: Insult and Brand* is to document how and why the racial slur contained in the book's title continues to live, particularly next to slurs for other racialized groups that have since been deemed offensive, and when Anglophones are aware that the term causes offense. The racial epithet furthermore has become thingified through its use as a mascot for a major American sports franchise, which objectifies and dehumanizes Indigenous bodies. In tandem, the franchise's name makes visible this racial objectification in ways that would never be accepted if the team was called the Blackskins or Whiteskins and represented with a black or white person as its mascot.[58] The use of color in this way also informs scholarly inquiries into the early-modern Atlantic world, with critical works of scholarship focused on the black and red Atlantics.[59] The white Atlantic thus becomes simply the Atlantic, which dangerously perpetuates the normativity of whiteness rather than challenge its hegemonic influence upon western epistemological frameworks and spaces. The name Oklahoma signals race in ways not evident where white Euro-settlers lived.[60] This cleavage in social and cultural values allows Redskins to exist as both a derogatory and familiar, cherished term. These values are furthermore apparent through the racialized nomenclature used for over five centuries to designate, characterize, and construct the original inhabitants of the Americas.

Context for Indian and its related forms (in Spanish *indio*, *india*; in French *indien*, *indienne*; and in Portuguese *índio*, *índia*) can be found in the etymology of India, which itself is a colonized word derived from the Greek (*indika*) and the Latin (*India*) names for the Indus River, known in Sanskrit as the Sindhu. Ancient Greek and Roman scholars named and conceived of Indians as the people of the Indus located in present-day India and Pakistan. The Americas' first European-derived name, *las Indias*, thus comprises a surrogate geography imposed upon it by Christopher Columbus and his contemporaries in Europe prior to his leaving Spain. The term disassociates the Indigenous inhabitants from their land and imposes upon them a surrogate place of origin. Using this name to designate Native-American peoples is thus problematic because it generically red-washes Indigenous peoples and effaces from them their cultural distinctiveness, as scholars have argued for decades, and the term is simply inaccurate.

A deliberate movement away from Indian in places such as Canada, where a significant population of people originating from India can also be found, began in the late twentieth century and today Indian in reference to Indigenous people is considered a dated, even racist name.[61] For various reasons (in Canada it was constitutional negotiations and the threat they posed to treaties; in Latin America it was resistance to multinational resource extraction), in the 1970s and 1980s, colonized peoples began to engage internationally through fora that had not existed for most of their histories with settler states, and which had implications for how they identified themselves and came to be identified. Indigenous peoples began to interact with one another at international bodies such as the United Nations and to realize the plurality of their collective subjecthood. This led to the elaboration of the international legal concept of the "Indigenous person," a concept that did not exist in international law before the 1980s. From this period of activity, a UN permanent forum on Indigenous peoples emerged, and it established the UN Declaration on the Rights of Indigenous Peoples (UNDRIP), which not only defends the right to self-definition and autonomy, but also specifies that Indigenous peoples should identify their own names rather than use those of the settler state. Canadian scholarship has taken up the term Indigenous, which has now percolated down to mainstream media and society, but this has not happened to the same degree elsewhere in the settler-colonial world nor in Canada's legal framework. Indigenous is not a legal political subject in Canada. Terms that appear in Canadian law, and thus that are recognized by the Canadian state, include Indian, First Nation, and Aboriginal. Each term has different legal connotations. And despite these evolving perspectives, in the United States and in scholarship executed in Spanish and Portuguese, Indian continues to be used without any contextualization.[62] The Library of Congress's subject matter terminology uses Indian today for both people from India and from the Americas.[63] Thus, new arrivals from India remain classified with the same adjective and noun used to describe the Indigenous peoples of the Americas, a practice that lays bare the discursive underpinnings of un-firsting.

The use of documentation arising from the early-modern period in legal contexts must also be considered in light of this terminology. Shortly before Cartier undertook his expedition westward and following the voyage of Amerigo Vespucci (1454–1512), another Italian explorer argued, the latter man that the lands encountered by Columbus were not of Asia but rather a region of the earth that had remained entirely unknown to Europeans. Following two accounts detailing his travels to South America published in 1503 and 1504, respectively, a German map maker published a Latin translation of these accounts and, in the same year, produced a map that named the Americas for the explorer.[64] Martin Waldseemüller's 1507 map depicts North America as an imagined terra incognita and features nonetheless the Caribbean region as it was known to Europeans at the time, as well as some of the recent voyages along the eastern coast of South America; upon this land he bestowed the name America.[65] The significance of this name, particularly within the United States, as the Library of Congress purchased the only known copy of the map for several million dollars, cannot be underestimated. Scholars have celebrated Vespucci as the namesake of America, which is colloquially used around the world as an abbreviation for the United States of America; they have implied, despite its posthumous attribution, that Vespucci generously or benignly bestowed his name upon this region of the world, appropriating the term to describe the country rather than the South-American region where it appears on Waldseemüller's map; and they have equated the map to being the modern-day nation's birth certificate, even though the nation itself does not emerge until later in the eighteenth century.[66] As with Indian, the implications of the United States' appropriation of America from this region of the world, and the view that the map offers some proto-certification of nationhood, model a firsting discourse that anachronistically elevates the objectives and values of the United States and converts Indigenous peoples into natives of either America or the Americas. Nowhere is this more apparent than in the proclivity to refer to the Americas using the singular form of the term because America also singularly designates the United States as a nation.[67] Even more clear is the fact that the Indigenous peoples of these continents do not descend from Vespucci.

One of the revised terms for Indian is Native American, and this name is increasingly being embraced by American scholars despite its problematic origins. Other terms include American Indian (Indian-American rather describing someone from India living in the United States, which points to an interesting pattern in how Indigenous peoples are seconded), Amerindian (Fr. amérindien, Sp. amerindio, Pt. ameríndio), First Nations (Indigenous people who are not Inuit nor Métis; this term arose in Canada and is now used elsewhere), and Aboriginal (Fr. Autochtone), all deployed with varying degrees of capitalization, and not all terms are used in all languages. Updating these terms, which may seem easy enough to do, nonetheless can have significant implications. This is particularly true in Canada where being legally recognized as Indian under the *Indian Act* by the settler-state stubbornly remains the narrow conduit through which Indigenous and treaty rights are exercised, and also through which the settler-state places limits on its own constitutional fiduciary obligations to Indigenous peoples. Indianness is defined in that act by the state and not by the peoples impacted by this form of categorization, which contradicts UNDRIP.[68] This categorization relies heavily on a blood purity politic used elsewhere in the Americas, particularly during Spanish colonial times, as Spain transposed its medieval *limpieza de sangre* (cleanliness of blood) protocols to the Americas.[69] Names that imply impure indigeneity are thus fraught and lend themselves well to un-firsting discourse: half breed, morisco, mestizo, mixed blood, metis and Métis, and so on. As a result of this contested vocabulary that is deeply rooted in individual and collective identities, there remains much conflict around the terminology used to describe Indigenous peoples, particularly on the part of settler governments, as demonstrated by recent controversies over who is entitled to refer to themselves as Métis (as opposed to metis), as Inuit (as opposed to Eskimo), and in the United States there are groups known as Métis Americans and Mestizo Americans.[70] In Latin America, where larger populations are Indigenous or mixed blood, these blood politics are even more contested.[71]

This book scratches the surface of the problems caused by centuries of firsting within scholarship and the primary sources upon which scholars of history and cultural studies rely to know people and their activities in the early-modern Atlantic world, from 1492 until approximately 1900. The subject is approached through three organizing themes that also correspond to the timeline for the European invasion of and settlement in the Americas. Each chapter is punctuated with a critical bibliography of sources, whether primary, published, or popular, that together comprise a significant resource for scholars wishing to build upon the research presented in this book. The first section examines the mechanics of firsting within the Americas, particularly on the part of the British, Portuguese, and Spanish in the sixteenth and early seventeenth centuries. The four chapters that comprise this section collectively lay out the foundations for firsting not only in primary sources, but also as a scholarly practice that has infected historiography and literature. Authors address the rhetorical procedures and practices through which Europeans articulated arguments that legitimated their authority to claim lands; they explore how the Spanish monarch found ways of delegitimizing the claims of conquistadors, essentially lasting and rendering them impotent within the colonial milieu; and they address the ways that Indigenous languages became shaped by textual culture in sixteenth- and seventeenth-century Brazil and Peru. The overall contribution of the first part of this book is its problematization of textual culture as a tool of conquest and colonization, one which becomes replicated throughout the historiography and literature produced during and after this period.

The second section explores the use of modernity and unfamiliarity as key elements of firsting discourse, particularly during and after the Enlightenment. Authors in this section explore colonial and modern-day projections of early-modern Euro-settler identity and the ways through which Indigenous peoples were made inanimate, bereft of agency, or were disappeared altogether from the landscape. They trace Indigenous and non-European responses to these developments during the formation of literary canons in the western world, the emergence of the field of anthropology, and the development of museum culture and local history. The posturing of Europeans and their knowledge as superior to American-borne and African-borne individuals and their knowledges is another subject explored in this section through the prism of scientific advancements. This section builds upon the last by proposing new critical readings of firsting that yield remedies, solutions, and rectifications to the problems created by firsting discourse that scholars, museum curators, and law makers can utilize today.

The last section of this book attempts to counter firsting in innovative ways. The first chapter outlines the Doctrine of Discovery, its origins and applications, and then pursues discovery from an Indigenous perspective that privileges the experiences of Native Americans from present-day North America. The next chapter problematizes textual culture and explores how the historical record can be transformed by relying upon visual and material sources of information through a series of case studies arising from Spanish-Indigenous contact in Mexico and Peru in the sixteenth century. The third chapter challenges the present and historical cartographical representation of the Canadian city of Vancouver by re-situating it as an Indigenous city. The fourth chapter in this section poignantly argues that many values and systems so esteemed in the western world, from democracy to environmentalism, have been exercised by and come from Indigenous peoples. These last two chapters both stake a claim to lands and resources through Indigenous knowledge while reflecting upon the twentieth and twenty-first century ramifications of late early-modern culture.

While this book at the outset tries to embrace the entirety of the early-modern Atlantic world, there are areas that still require attention, particularly French firsting practices in the Caribbean and North America, as well as non-European sources and works of scholarship that deliberately or inadvertently support the western architecture of firsting. Another area that is in urgent need of attention is the eastern Atlantic world. Much scholarship follows the western gaze to focus, as this book demonstrates, on the western Atlantic and the lands, cultures, and peoples that flourished across this body of water. Serious scholarly attention must be invested into better understanding firsting in Africa and Europe during this period, particularly with respect to the feedback loops that emerged following the independence of many European colonies in the Americas, their changing relationships with Europe and Africa, and in some cases, their attempts to re-patriate (thus un-firsting or firsting, depending on one's perspective) goods, people, and cultural practices eastward across the Atlantic. Finally, it remains to be seen how gender factors into firsting and whether, by dismantling firsting practices that range from the gendered segregation of sport to political and social infrastructure designed to support men and not women, gender equity might be better achieved in the west.

Notes

1. Harley and Woodward, "Preface," in Harley and Woodward, eds., *The History of Cartography*, vol. 1, pp. v–xxi: xix. Unless otherwise noted, all translations are my own.
2. Hakim, *The First Americans*, p. 60.
3. Miller, Ruru, Behrendt, and Lindberg, *Discovering Indigenous Lands*, esp. part 4, "The Doctrine of Discovery in Canada," pp. 89–125. Also see Scott, "Cultivating Christians in Colonial Canadian Missions," in Austin and Scott, eds., *Canadian Missionaries, Indigenous Peoples*, pp. 21–54.
4. In settler-colonial studies literature, the CANZUS settler states are viewed particularly culpable in this respect.
5. Binnema, *Common and Contested Ground*, pp. 9–10.
6. Byrd, *The Transit of Empire*, pp. xv–xxxix.
7. For an important discussion of the implications of deracinating Noah's family through the tripartite division of the world, see Feerick, *Strangers in Blood*, pp. 28–29. Also see Smith, *Race and Rhetoric in the Renaissance*, p. 141, and the chapters featured in Greer, Mignolo, and Quilligan, eds., *Rereading the Black Legend*.
8. Anne Baker explores this subject while tracing the expansion of nineteenth-century United States, in *Heartless Immensity*; for French thought on racialized geographies, see Staum, *Labeling People*; for a comparative perspective on race and geography from various national perspectives, see the essays in Dwyer and Bressey, eds., *New Geographies of Race and Racism*, and in Jackson, ed., *Race & Racism*.
9. For more context on the cultural difficulties in Spain during this period impacting religious identity, see Constable, *To Live Like a Moor*.
10. I have explored this elsewhere in *Transforming the Enemy in Spanish Culture*. Also see Harris, *Aztecs, Moors and Christians*.
11. For more on the ways language and cultural suppression have impacted Indigenous peoples, see the essays contained in Battiste, ed., *Reclaiming Indigenous Voice and Vision*; also see Harring, *White Man's Law*.
12. Campbell, *American Indian Languages*, p. 11.
13. Mazlish, *Civilization and Its Contents*, pp. 1–19. Also see Césaire, *Discourse on Colonialism*; Williams, Jr., *The American Indian in Western Legal Thought*, and by the same author, *Savage Anxieties*; and Cheyfitz, *The Poetics of Imperialism*.

14. Rabasa, *Inventing America*. Also see Matless, "The Uses of Cartographic Literacy: Mapping, Survey and Citizenship in Twentieth-Century Britain," in Cosgrove, ed., *Mappings*, pp. 193–212. For the use of cartography as a means of conquest and capitalist development, see Sutton, *Capitalism and Cartography in the Dutch Golden Age*.
15. See the essays in Akerman, ed., *The Imperial Map*. Also see Hiatt, "Blank Spaces on the Earth," pp. 223–250.
16. *Capitulaciones*, fol. 136r.
17. For examples of these grants, see Williamson, *The Cabot Voyages and Bristol Discovery under Henry VII*, pp. 183–186.
18. Falzetti, "Archival Absence," p. 138.
19. Columbus, *Epistola de insulis nuper inventis*.
20. See, for instance, Leandro de Cosco's edition titled *Epistola de insulis repertis de nouo* (Paris: Guyot Marchant, 1493) and Giuliano Dati's versified version titled *Lettera delle isole nuovamente trovate* (Florence: Lorenzo Morgiani and Johannes Petri, 1493).
21. A more complete study of these dictionaries cannot be undertaken here, however a representative list relating the Spanish language to other European ones includes Nebrija's Spanish-Latin dictionary (1495; 1516), a Spanish-Tuscan dictionary (1570), Percival's English-Latin-Spanish dictionary (1591), and Pallet's French-Spanish dictionary (1604).
22. Little research has been done on this topic. One work that comments on past research but otherwise contributes little to understanding how the meaning of discovery transformed in the early-modern period is Washburn's "The Meaning of 'Discovery' in the Fifteenth and Sixteenth Centuries," pp. 1–21. Another scholar argues that terminology such as Indian was employed deliberately as a means of covering up and overwriting the obvious uniqueness of the peoples and lands encountered by Europeans; see Dussel, *The Invention of the Americas*, esp. ch. 4.
23. *Capitulaciones*, fol. 135r.
24. Columbus, [*Letter from Columbus to Luis de Santángel, 15 February 1493*], n/p.
25. Miller, *Native America, Discovered and Conquered*, p. 21. Also see Richardson, *People of Terra Nullius*.
26. Borrows, *Recovering Canada*, p. 4.
27. Pagden, "Law, Colonization, Legitimation, and the European Background," in Grossberg and Tomlins, eds., *The Cambridge History of Law in America*, vol. 1, pp. 1–31: 18–23.
28. Beck, "La fundación de pueblos españoles e indígenas en el siglo XVI," in Palma, ed., *Del mundo al mapa y del mapa al mundo*, pp. 223–232.
29. Cosa, *Carta universal de Juan de la Cosa*.
30. Pope, *The Many Landfalls of John Cabot*, p. 14.
31. The patent granted in 1496 is reproduced in Biggar, *The Precursors of Jacques Cartier 1497–1534*, pp. 7–10.
32. See Williamson, *The Cabot Voyages*, pp. 209–210.
33. Montalboddo and Vespucci, *Paesi nouamente retrovati*, book 6, n/p. Also see Williamson, *The Cabot Voyages*, p. 230, and section 8 of Cabot, [*World Map*].
34. Markham, *Journal of Christopher Columbus*, p. 19.
35. Deane, "The Mappemonde of Sebastian Cabot," p. 63.
36. For a poignant examination of this problem, see Paul, *We Were Not the Savages*.
37. Cuthbertson, "John Cabot and His Historians," pp. 16–35.

38. Hemperley, *Historic Indian Trails of Georgia*, pp. 3–5; Peregrine, "Networks of Power: The Mississippian World-System," in Nassaney and Sassaman, eds., *Native American Interactions*, pp. 247–265.
39. Yerkes, "Specialization in Shell Artifact Production at Cahokia," in Stoltman, ed., *New Perspectives on Cahokia*, pp. 49–64: 55. Also see Nash and Strobel, *Daily Life of Native Americans*, p. 84.
40. Fenton, *The Great Law and the Longhouse*, p. 225.
41. Luther, *Our Restless Earth*, p. 54.
42. McClintock, *The Old North Trail*, pp. 404–405.
43. Campbell, *American Indian Languages*, pp. 10 and 22.
44. Lutz, *Makúk*.
45. For an introduction to this form of communication, see Brotherston, "The Mexican Codices and the Visual Language of Revolution," in Andermann and Rowe, eds., *Images of Power*, pp. 36–50. Nahuatl also remained an important language used in the region as a lingua franca.
46. Rudes, "Pre-Columbian Links to the Caribbean: Evidence Connecting Cusabo to Taíno," in Picone and Davies, eds., *New Perspectives on Language Variety in the South*, pp. 82–93. About Taino travels to Florida, Mexico, and South America, see Wilson, *Hispañola*, pp. 27–28.
47. See Probasco's chapter in this volume. Taking a coastal route to his destination would have resulted in a distance of 7,150 kilometers from the Tampico River in Mexico to Cape Breton, and require that he cover just under 20 kilometers per day on foot.
48. Wilson, *Hispañola*, p. 50. Also see Deagan and Cruxent, *Columbus's Outpost among the Taínos*, pp. 38–39; and Guzauskyte, *Christopher Columbus's Naming in the "Diarios" of the Four Voyages (1492–1504)*, pp. 71–73.
49. Wadsworth, *Columbus & His First Voyage*, p. 20.
50. Mann, *1491*, pp. 38–39.
51. Wesson, "America in 1492," in Hoxie, ed., *The Oxford Handbook of American Indian History*, pp. 17–39: 32–33.
52. The possibility that Asia might be found farther west of the Americas nonetheless remained alive; see, for instance, depictions of the Great Kahn on maps inspired by the voyages of Cartier and his contemporaries, such as the map of New France contained in the *Vallard Atlas*, chart 9.
53. Cartier, *Brief receipt*, fol. 9v.
54. Loewen, "Intertwined Enigmas: Basques and the Saint Lawrence Iroquoians in the Sixteenth Century," in Loewen and Chapdelaine, eds., *Contact in the 16th Century*, pp. 57–76: 62.
55. Cartier, *Brief receipt*, fol. 40v.
56. Gordon, *The Hero and the Historians*, pp. 18–21. Also see Boucher, "'The Land God Gave to Cain'," pp. 28–42.
57. Another argument in this vein centers on the Spanish use of translators knowledgeable of Arabic in the Americas. See Álvarez de Toledo, *África versus América*.
58. King, *Redskins*.
59. See, for example, the excellent work of Gilroy, *The Black Atlantic*; Gates, Jr., *Tradition and the Black Atlantic*; Weaver, *The Red Atlantic*; and Silverman, *Red Brethren*.
60. Bonnett, "Whiteness and the West," in Dwyer and Bressey, eds., *New Geographies of Race and Racism*, pp. 17–28.
61. Muehlebach, "What Self in Self Determination?," pp. 241–268.
62. Contextualization of this nature is often found at the beginning of a book as a means of informing the reader why she may encounter a certain range

of terminology. See an excellent one prepared by Moore, *That Dream Shall Have a Name*, p. xiv.
63. Kam, "Subject Headings for Aboriginals," pp. 18–22.
64. Vespucci's works were translated into Latin by Waldseemüller, *Cosmographiae introductio.*
65. Waldseemüller, *Universalis cosmographia secundum Ptholomaei traditionem et Americi Vespucci alioruque lustraciones.*
66. See O'Mahony and Broome, *The 1507 Waldseemüller World Map*; and Fernández-Armesto, *Amerigo.*
67. Morison, *The European Discovery of America.*
68. Patrick, "Inuitness and Territoriality in Canada," in Forte, ed., *Who Is an Indian?* pp. 52–70: 57; Coulthard, *Red Skin, White Masks*; and Simpson, *Mohawk Interruptus.*
69. For a broader discussion of this problem, see Palmater, *Beyond Blood.*
70. For Canada's Supreme Court ruling and recognition of Métis peoples as Indigenous, see the Daniels Decision: Daniels v. Canada (Indian Affairs and Northern Development), 2016 Supreme Court of Canada 12, [2016] 1 S.C.R. 99. For more on the Métis, see Anderson, *Metis*; and Giroux, "New Directions and Revisionist Histories in Métis Studies," pp. 142–150.
71. Lucero, "Encountering Indigeneity: The International Funding of Indigeneity in Peru," in Forte, ed., *Who Is an Indian?*, pp. 194–217.

Bibliography

Akerman, James R., ed., *The Imperial Map: Cartography and the Mastery of Empire* (Chicago: University of Chicago Press, 2009).

Álvarez de Toledo, and Luisa Isabel, *África versus América: La fuerza del paradigma* (Cordoba: Junta Islámica, 2000).

Andermann, Jens, and William Rowe, eds., *Images of Power: Iconography, Culture and the State in Latin America* (New York: Berghahn Books, 2005).

Anderson, Chris, *Metis: Race, Recognition, and the Struggle for Indigenous Peoplehood* (Vancouver: UBC Press, 2014).

Austin, Alvyn, and Jamie S. Scott, eds., *Canadian Missionaries, Indigenous Peoples: Representing Religion at Home and Abroad* (Toronto: University of Toronto Press, 2005).

Baker, Anne, *Heartless Immensity: Literature, Culture, and Geography in Antebellum America* (Ann Arbor: University of Michigan Press, 2006).

Battiste, Marie, ed., *Reclaiming Indigenous Voice and Vision* (Vancouver: UBC Press, 2000).

Beck, Lauren, *Transforming the Enemy in Spanish Culture: The Conquest through the Lens of Textual and Visual Multiplicity* (Amherst, NY: Cambria Press, 2013).

Biggar, Henry P., *The Precursors of Jacques Cartier 1497–1534: A Collection of Documents Relating to the Early History of the Dominion of Canada* (Ottawa: Government Printing Bureau, 1911).

Binnema, Theodore, *Common and Contested Ground: A Human and Environmental History of the Northwestern Plains* (Norman: University of Oklahoma Press, 2001).

Borrows, John, *Recovering Canada: The Resurgence of Indigenous Law* (Toronto: University of Toronto Press, 2002).

Boucher, Christophe, "'The Land God Gave to Cain': Jacques Cartier Encounters the Mythological Wild Man in Labrador," *Terrae Incognitae* 35.1 (2003), pp. 28–42.

Byrd, Jodi A., *The Transit of Empire: Indigenous Critiques of Colonialism* (Minneapolis: University of Minnesota Press, 2011).

Cabot, Sebastian, [*World Map*], 1544. Bibliothèque nationale de France, département Cartes et plans, GE AA-582 (RES).

Campbell, Lyle, *American Indian Languages: The Historical Linguistics of Native America* (New York: Oxford University Press, 1997).

Capitulaciones de Santa Fe, 1492. Archivo de la Corona de Aragón, Cancillería, Registros, núm. 3569, fols. 135v-136v.

Cartier, Jacques, *Brief receipt, & succincte narration, de la navigation faicte es ysles de Canada, Hochelage & Saguenay & autres, avec particulieres meurs, langaige, & cerimonies des habitans d'icelles* (Paris: P. Roffet & A. Le Clerc, 1545).

Césaire, Aimé, *Discourse on Colonialism*, trans. Joan Pinkham (New York: Monthly Review Press, 1972).

Cheyfitz, Eric, *The Poetics of Imperialism: Translation and Colonization from the Tempest to Tarzan* (Philadelphia: University of Pennsylvania Press, 1997).

Columbus, Christopher, *Epistola de insulis nuper inventis* (Rome: Stephan Plannck, 1493).

———, [*Letter from Columbus to Luis de Santángel, 15 February 1493*] (Barcelona: Pero de Posa, 1493).

Constable, Olivia Remie, *To Live Like a Moor: Christian Perceptions of Muslim Identity in Medieval and Early Modern Spain*, ed. Robin de Vose (Philadelphia: University of Pennsylvania Press, 2018).

Cosa, Juan de la, *Carta universal de Juan de la Cosa, 1500*. Museo Naval, Madrid, inv. 2603.

Cosgrove, Denis, ed., *Mappings* (London: Reaktion Books, 1999).

Coulthard, Glen, *Red Skin, White Masks: Rejecting the Colonial Politics of Recognition* (Vancouver: UBC Press, 2014).

Cuthbertson, Brian, "John Cabot and His Historians: Five Hundred Years of Controversy," *Journal of the Royal Nova Scotia Historical Society* 1 (1998), pp. 16–35.

Deagan, Kathleen, and José María Cruxent, *Columbus's Outpost among the Taínos: Spain and America at La Isabela, 1493–1498* (New Haven, CT: Yale University Press, 2002).

Deane, Charles, "The Mappemonde of Sebastian Cabot," *Science* 1.3 (1883), pp. 62–65.

Dussel, Enrique, *The Invention of the Americas: Eclipse of 'The Other' and the Myth of Modernity* (New York: Continuum, 1995).

Dwyer, Claire, and Caroline Bressey, eds., *New Geographies of Race and Racism* (Burlington, VT: Ashgate, 2008).

Falzetti, Ashley Glassburn, "Archival Absence: The Burden of History," *Settler Colonial Studies* 5.2 (2015), pp. 128–144.

Feerick, Jean, *Strangers in Blood: Relocating Race in the Renaissance* (Toronto: University of Toronto Press, 2010).

Fenton, William N., *The Great Law and the Longhouse: A Political History of the Iroquois Confederacy* (Norman: University of Oklahoma Press, 1998).

Fernández-Armesto, Felipe, *Amerigo: The Man Who Gave his Name to America* (New York: Random House, 2007).

Forte, Maximilian C., ed., *Who Is an Indian? Race, Place, and the Politics of Indigeneity in the Americas* (Toronto: University of Toronto Press, 2013).

Gates Jr., Henry Louis, *Tradition and the Black Atlantic: Critical Theory in the African Diaspora* (New York: BasicCivitas, 2010).

Gilroy, Paul, *The Black Atlantic: Modernity and Double Consciousness* (Cambridge, MA: Harvard University Press, 1993).

Giroux, Monique, "New Directions and Revisionist Histories in Métis Studies," *Acadiensis* 47.2 (2018), pp. 142–150.

Gordon, Alan, *The Hero and the Historians: Historiography and the Uses of Jacques Cartier* (Vancouver: UBC Press, 2010).

Greer, Margaret R., Walter D. Mignolo, and Maureen Quilligan, eds., *Rereading the Black Legend: The Discourses of Religious and Racial Difference in the Renaissance Empires* (Chicago: University of Chicago Press, 2007).

Grossberg, Michael, and Christopher Tomlins, eds., *The Cambridge History of Law in America*, vol. 1: *Early America (1580–1815)* (New York: Cambridge University Press, 2008).

Guzauskyte, Evelina, *Christopher Columbus's Naming in the 'Diarios' of the Four Voyages (1492–1504): A Discourse of Negotiation* (Toronto: University of Toronto Press, 2014).

Hakim, Joy, *The First Americans: Prehistory—1600* (New York: Oxford University Press, 2003).

Harley, J. B., and David Woodward, eds., *The History of Cartography*, vol. 1: *Cartography in Prehistoric, Ancient, and Medieval Europe and the Mediterranean* (Chicago: University of Chicago Press, 1987).

Harring, Sidney L., *White Man's Law: Native People in Nineteenth-Century Canadian Jurisprudence* (Toronto: University of Toronto Press for Osgoode Society for Canadian Legal History, 1998).

Harris, Max, *Aztecs, Moors and Christians: Festivals of Reconquest in Mexico and Spain* (Austin: University of Texas Press, 2000).

Hemperley, Mario R., *Historic Indian Trails of Georgia* (Athens: The Garden Club of Georgia, 1989).

Hiatt, Alfred, "Blank Spaces on the Earth," *The Yale Journal of Criticism* 15.2 (2002), pp. 223–250.

Hoxie, Frederick E., ed., *The Oxford Handbook of American Indian History* (New York: Oxford University Press, 2016).

Jackson, Peter, ed., *Race & Racism: Essays in Social Geography* (London: Allen & Unwin, 1987).

Kam, D. Vanessa, "Subject Headings for Aboriginals: The Power of Naming," *Art Documentation: Journal of the Art Libraries Society of North America* 26.2 (2007), pp. 18–22.

King, C. Richard, *Redskins: Insult and Brand* (Lincoln: University of Nebraska Press, 2016).

Loewen, Brad, and Claude Chapdelaine, eds., *Contact in the 16th Century: Networks among Fishers, Foragers and Farmers* (Ottawa: Canadian Museum of History and University of Ottawa Press, 2016).

Luther, Edward T., *Our Restless Earth: The Geologic Regions of Tennessee* (Knoxville: University of Tennessee Press, 2003).

Lutz, John Sutton, *Makúk: A New History of Aboriginal-White Relations* (Vancouver: UBC Press, 2008).

Mann, Charles C., *1491: New Revelations of the Americas before Columbus* (New York: Alfred A. Knopf, 2005).

Markham, Clements R., *Journal of Christopher Columbus (During His First Voyage, 1492–93) and Documents Relating to the Voyages of John Cabot and Gaspar Corte Real* (Burlington, VT: Ashgate, 2010).

Mazlish, Bruce, *Civilization and Its Contents* (Stanford, CA: Stanford University Press, 2004).

McClintock, Walter, *The Old North Trail: Life, Legends & Religion of the Blackfeet Indians* (Lincoln: University of Nebraska Press, 1992).

Miller, Robert J., *Native America, Discovered and Conquered: Thomas Jefferson, Lewis & Clark, and Manifest Destiny* (Westport, CT: Praeger, 2006).

Miller, Robert J., Jacinta Ruru, Larissas Behrendt, and Tracey Lindberg, *Discovering Indigenous Lands: The Doctrine of Discovery in the English Colonies* (Oxford: Oxford University Press, 2010).

Montalboddo, Fracanzino da, and Amerigo Vespucci, *Paesi nouamente retrovati* (Venice: Henrico Vicentino, 1507).

Moore, David L., *That Dream Shall Have a Name: Native Americans Rewriting America* (Lincoln: University of Nebraska Press, 2013).

Morison, Samuel Eliot, *The European Discovery of America*, 2 vols. (New York: Oxford University Press, 1971–1974).

Muehlebach, Andrea, "What Self in Self Determination? Notes from the Frontiers of Transnational Indigenous Activism," *Identities: Global Studies in Culture and Power* 10.2 (2003), pp. 241–268.

Nash, Alice, and Christoph Strobel, *Daily Life of Native Americans: From Post-Columbian through Nineteenth-Century America* (Westport, CT: Greenwood Press, 2006).

Nassaney, Michael S., and Kenneth E. Sassaman, eds., *Native American Interactions: Multiscalar Analyses and Interpretations in the Eastern Woodlands* (Knoxville: University of Tennessee Press, 1995).

O'Mahony, Kieran, and Rodney Broome, *The 1507 Waldseemüller World Map: America's Birth Certificate* (Seattle, WA: Educare Press, 2002).

Palma, Alejandra Vega, ed., *Del mundo al mapa y del mapa al mundo: Objetos, escalas e imaginarios del territorio* (Santiago: Pontificia Universidad Católica de Chile, 2017).

Palmater, Pamela, *Beyond Blood: Rethinking Indigenous Identity* (Vancouver: UBC Press, 2011).

Paul, Daniel N., *We Were Not the Savages: A Micmac Perspective on the Collision of European and Aboriginal Civilizations* (Halifax, NS: Nimbus, 1994).

Picone, Michael D., and Catherine Evans Davies, eds., *New Perspectives on Language Variety in the South: Historical and Contemporary Approaches* (Tuscaloosa: University of Alabama Press, 2015).

Pope, Peter E., *The Many Landfalls of John Cabot* (Toronto: University of Toronto Press, 1997).

Rabasa, José, *Inventing America: Spanish Historiography and the Formation of Eurocentrism* (Norman: University of Oklahoma Press, 1993).

Richardson, Boyce, *People of Terra Nullius: Betrayal and Rebirth in Aboriginal Canada* (Vancouver: Douglas and McIntyre, 1993).

Silverman, David J., *Red Brethren: The Brothertown and Stockbridge Indians and the Problem of Race in Early America* (Ithaca, NY: Cornell University Press, 2015).
Simpson, Audra, *Mohawk Interruptus: Political Life across the Borders of Settler States* (Durham, NC: Duke University Press, 2014).
Smith, Ian, *Race and Rhetoric in the Renaissance: Barbarian Errors* (New York: Palgrave Macmillan, 2009).
Staum, Martin S., *Labeling People: French Scholars on Society, Race and Empire, 1815–1848* (Montreal: McGill-Queens University Press, 2003).
Stoltman, James B., ed., *New Perspectives on Cahokia* (Madison, WI: Prehistory Press, 1991).
Sutton, Elizabeth, *Capitalism and Cartography in the Dutch Golden Age* (Chicago: University of Chicago Press, 2015).
Vallard Atlas, 1547. Huntington Library, San Marino, California, HM 29.
Wadsworth, James E., *Columbus & His First Voyage: A History in Documents* (London: Bloomsbury, 2016).
Waldseemüller, Martin, *Cosmographiae introductio: cum quibusdam geometriae ac astronomiae principiis ad eam rem necessariis Insuper quattuor Americi Vespucii navigationes* (St. Die: Gaultherus & Nikolaus Lud., 1507).
———, *Universalis cosmographia secundum Ptholomaei traditionem et Americi Vespucci alioruque lustraciones* (Strasbourg: n/p, 1507). Library of Congress, Washington, DC, Geography and Map Division G3200 1507.W3.
Washburn, Wilcomb E., "The Meaning of 'Discovery' in the Fifteenth and Sixteenth Centuries," *The American Historical Review* 68.1 (1962), pp. 1–21.
Weaver, Jace, *The Red Atlantic: American Indigenes and the Making of the Modern World, 1000–1927* (Chapel Hill: University of North Carolina Press, 2014).
Williams Jr., Robert A., *The American Indian in Western Legal Thought: Discourses of Conquest* (New York: Oxford University Press, 1993).
———, *Savage Anxieties: The Invention of Western Civilization* (New York: St. Martin's Press, 2014).
Williamson, James Alexander, *The Cabot Voyages and Bristol Discovery under Henry VII* (Burlington, VT: Ashgate, 2010).
Wilson, Samuel M., *Hispañola: Caribbean Chiefdoms in the Age of Columbus* (Tuscaloosa: University of Alabama Press, 1990).

Part I

The Foundations for Firsting in Historiography and Literature

1 John Dee, Humphrey Gilbert, and Richard Hakluyt's Erasure of Native Americans

Nate Probasco

John Dee (1527–1609), Richard Hakluyt (1552–1616), and Sir Humphrey Gilbert (c. 1539–1583) were among the first people to conceptualize the British Empire: Dee, who coined the term; Hakluyt, who promoted it widely in print; and Gilbert, who organized the earliest English expedition seeking to colonize lands beyond the British Isles. The trio's efforts culminated in the 1583 voyage captained by Gilbert to colonize Narragansett Bay in present-day Rhode Island, a region then known to them as Norumbega, having already been explored in 1524 by Giovanni da Verrazzano (1485–1528), an Italian sailing for France.[1] Unlike their predecessors, who intended to sail around the Americas or who hoped to extract commodities and quickly return home, they needed to establish their legal right as Englishmen to possess American territory. Failing to evince their entitlement to the land would make it difficult to entice investors to bankroll the expedition and to convince sailors, soldiers, and specialists such as masons, miners, and surveyors to sail across the Atlantic. They had to demonstrate that the law of nations permitted them to settle in the Americas and that they need not fear reprisals from other European powers.[2]

Considering the scholarly attention given to Gilbert's colonial successors at Roanoke and Jamestown, his venture seems comparatively understudied.[3] Cross-cultural interactions taking place in those colonies garner more attention than failed plans, and yet Gilbert's colonial blueprint provides a wealth of information and highlights aspects of colonization often forgotten once European ships dropped anchor in American ports. The depth of Gilbert's inquiry regarding English, Spanish, and Native-American land rights comes across as strikingly modern. He and his associates referenced a variety of sources ranging from rare manuscript poems and hard-to-come-by papal bulls to recently printed chronicles about the Americas, the bible, and personal interviews. Just as Jean O'Brien has shown that nineteenth-century New Englanders wrote Native Americans out of existence to contest their land rights, Gilbert's circle used print and manuscripts to help potential colonists forget indigeneity in Norumbega.[4] For England's first attempt at overseas colonization, Dee, Gilbert, and Hakluyt began the practice of excluding Native Americans in ways that would endure for centuries. Examining their attempts to discredit Spanish and Native-American claims to land provides much-needed insight into England's colonial history from its beginning and into practices that continue in North America today.

The spectrum of evidence that English expansionists used to declare their right to colonize North America has become a prominent topic in recent historical scholarship.[5] During the late sixteenth century, when Europeans' comprehension of North America's geographic composition remained fragmentary, English, French, and Spanish monarchs all staked claims to portions of the continent. Some of their putative domains overlapped, and Gilbert's preparations coincided with an uptick in these rival claims, as Anglo-Spanish disputes over the region intensified throughout the 1580s. French and English explorers challenged the validity of the Papal Bulls of Donation as well as the basis of claims resulting from so-called discoveries in determining the matter of possessing American territories.[6] Most European polemicists acknowledged that Columbus had "discovered" the Americas in 1492, but as Peter Fitzpatrick has noted, Spanish monarchs including Philip II (1527–1598) needed to "secure continuing recognition among the community of nations" that their claims were sound and that they were beyond refutation.[7] In post-reformation England and France, papal decrees got short shrift from Protestants such as Dee, Gilbert, and Hakluyt, nor did they simply countenance that discovery constituted possession; even if they had, the research conducted by the group suggested to them that their British ancestors had made landfall at North America prior to Columbus. They were among the most outspoken members of the emerging anti-Spanish faction at court who strove to impede the progress of the Spanish empire to further their own expansionist agenda.

While contesting the American claims made by a scattered group of recently arrived Spaniards required considerable research, challenging the land rights of the more populous Native-American tribes demanded a different rationale. Native-American hegemony in North America was not in question during the lifetimes of Dee, Gilbert, and Hakluyt; yet, the trio questioned the native entitlement to the land primarily by criticizing their non-European farming techniques and religious practices. Like other ethnocentric Europeans, they felt that non-Christians utilizing lands in a fashion unfamiliar to Europeans rendered the lands vacant.[8] Unlike most English colonists to follow, however, they respected Native-American power, hoped to learn from them, and intended to trade with them even as they planned to impose European cultures and values upon them. From the beginning of this encounter between the British and Native Americans, the latter were significant actors in the Englishmen's plan, but eventually they disappeared from their scheme. Would-be colonists mentally wiped from existence the Indigenous population before ever setting foot on American soil.

The soldier-turned-explorer Gilbert began his decades-long quest to colonize North America during the 1560s, but his research and writings did not bear fruit until 1578, when at last he received letters patent to colonize the continent from Elizabeth I (1533–1603).[9] Letters patent were a public means of expressing the patentee's rights in England and abroad as bestowed by the imperial crown, and Gilbert's would serve as the blueprint for future English colonization ventures.[10] The patent defined his prerogatives in North America, endowing him and his heirs "to have hould occupie and enjoye [. . .] sea and land" not possessed by other Christians. He could expel anyone who lived within two hundred leagues of his colony, or who sought "to annoye [him] eyther by Sea or lande."[11] Gilbert's sweeping powers were matched by his immense (as yet unclaimed) territory: a great circle centered at his expectant colony with a diameter of nearly 1400 miles that encompassed some 1.5 million square miles and nearly one billion acres. Had he established his settlement on Narragansett Bay, his reputed lands would have stretched from South Carolina to central Quebec, and from Ohio to a point more than 600 miles east of Cape Cod in the Atlantic.[12] On the basis of contiguity, Gilbert believed that he had rights to these vast lands contiguous to his settlements, as well as rights to nearby islands and the entire drainage system of the Norumbega River (likely the modern-day Blackstone), which he planned to fortify.[13]

Gilbert's territory as per his patent would not have reached Spanish Florida nor the Newfoundland fishery, the few North American lands inhabited for at least part of the year by Spaniards and other Europeans. He still needed to prove that the English people had the right to settle in the Americas, a landmass generally considered to be Spanish territory. According to Philip and to the papacy, Columbus's seminal voyage and the ensuing papal bulls entitled Iberians to the entire western hemisphere. Gilbert contested this claim. Even after Philip annexed Portugal in 1580, Gilbert maintained that the 1494 Treaty of Tordesillas partitioning the Americas between Castile and Portugal exceeded papal authority. At the very least, the edict only bound those two realms to remain within their limits. Non-Iberians, he reasoned, could go where they pleased in the western hemisphere. Gilbert argued that trading and colonizing should be considered lawful for Europeans in places that the Iberians had "not alredie added to their possession"[14] or settled with colonists. He cited the example of his own cousin, Thomas Stukeley (c. 1525–1578), for whom Elizabeth had provisioned a ship to colonize Spanish Florida in 1563.[15] French colonists in Florida and Brazil, who owed allegiance to papal authority, cited the natural rights of trade and temporal dominion to traffic in the Americas; English merchants, wrote Gilbert, deserved the same privileges.[16]

To prove England's claim to North America, Gilbert turned to John Dee, an old friend regarded as the preeminent English authority on international law.[17] Dee served as Gilbert's legal expert during his preparations for the voyage, and Gilbert's investors visited Dee's Mortlake home to discuss matters relating to the voyage. Dee noted in his diary that the topics of discussion with investor Sir George Peckham (d. 1608) included "the tytle for Norombega in respect of Spayn and Portugall parting the whol world's distilleryes."[18] Dee met twice with Peckham, "Clement the seamaster," and David Ingram (fl. 1567–1583), an Essex sailor interviewed by Gilbert who had walked from the Gulf of Mexico to Cape Breton. Dee must have provided them with satisfactory reassurance of England's right to colonize Norumbega, as Peckham granted Dee 50,000 acres of Norumbegan lands purchased from Gilbert in June 1582.[19]

More significantly, Dee created a chart to guide Gilbert to Norumbega and used the space on the verso to present a case for Britain's claim to the region. Dee alternatively titled his work "the Queenes Majesties Title Royal to these foreyn Regions, and Ilands," and "A brief Remembraunce of Sondrye foreyne Regions, discovered, inhabited, and partlie Conquered by the Subjects of this Brytish Monarchie."[20] Taking ideas from his copy of antiquarian William Lambarde's (1536–1601) *Archaionomia, sive de priscis anglorum legibus libri* (1568), Dee argued (without providing much proof) that Britain's claim could be upheld by civil law, divine law, and the law of nations. His research indicated that much of the continent had been discovered, briefly inhabited, and "partly conquered" by English, Irish, Scottish, and Welsh explorers.[21]

The dozen British voyages to North America cited by Dee range from historically substantiated expeditions to mythical journeys. John Cabot (c. 1450–c. 1499) undoubtedly led an expedition to Labrador in 1497, arriving on the North American continent before the Spaniards, and although Dee instead named his son Sebastian (c. 1484–1557) in the manuscript, the teen may have accompanied his father on the voyage. By 1580, primary sources on Cabot were rare. Nevertheless, several of Dee's contemporaries included details of his voyage in their books, so information must have been available.[22] His expedition, the voyage of Stephen Borough (1525–1584) to Russia in 1556, and the three voyages of Martin Frobisher (c. 1539–1594) eight decades later are heavily documented.[23] Dee personally knew Borough from at least 1557 and acted as a consultant for Frobisher's expeditions, making details of their voyages easy to come by.[24]

Less verifiable is Dee's reference to the voyage of Bristol merchants Robert Thorne the elder (d. 1519) and Hugh Eliot (fl. 1480–1510) to Newfoundland c. 1494, and yet the famed polymath had ample documentation at his disposal. He borrowed the personal papers of Thorne's son from London author Cyprian Lucar (1544–c.1611), whose father Emanuel (1494–1574) had been a merchant's apprentice.[25] In his manuscripts, Thorne referred to his father and to Elliot as "the discoverers of the Newfownd Landes," of which, he claimed, "there is no dowt." The younger Thorne's confidence moved Dee, who drew a manicule (hand-with-pointing-finger symbol) on the manuscript to emphasize Thorne's statement. He underlined other passages and included another manicule next to Thorne's comment regarding "the land we fownd, which is called Terra De Labarador." Throughout the manuscript, Thorne referred to Newfoundland as an English territory discovered by Englishmen, and he claimed that the Americas had been unjustly divided among the Iberians.[26]

Dee also referenced Edward III (1312–1377), who may have spearheaded a northern expedition in 1360, and the voyages to Iceland directed by King Arthur and King Malgo, both of whom may never have existed.[27] The reputed American colony established by the Welsh Prince Madoc ab Owain Gwynedd in 1170 borders on myth, as does the expedition of Irishman Saint Brendan of Clonfert (c. 484–578) to his namesake island in 560. Although these examples will seem dubious to modern readers, Dee's evidence validated most of his claims. A few medieval European universities and libraries owned manuscript accounts of Saint Brendan's explorations, such as *Vita Sancti Brendani* and *Navigatio Sancti Brendani Abbatis*. "Saint Brendan's Isle" was a fixture of early-modern maps and remained common into the eighteenth century.[28] Dee likewise owned manuscripts that he related to Madoc's voyage, including one containing verses on the explorer by the Welsh poet Maredudd ap Rhys (f. 1450–1485).[29] His copy of Giovanni Battista Ramusio's (1485–1557) *Della Navigationi et Viaggi* contains copious marginalia and other annotations about Madoc and the Americas.[30] Dee heavily marked his copy of *Historia del mondo nuovo di Fernando Colombo*, a biography of Columbus written by his second son Ferdinand (1488–1539). Dee believed that the "white men" (fol. 114v) encountered by Columbus in the Americas descended from Madoc's colonists and that the supposed "Brytishe custom of names" (fol. 125r) in some places had the same origin.[31] Dee initiated the project to compile the first printed history of Wales, which was finished in 1584 by the Welsh antiquarian David Powel (c. 1522–1596) and included a lengthy account of Madoc's voyage. Powel's sources featured Gilbert's interview with Ingram and his 1576 *A discourse of a discouerie for a new passage to Cataia*, both of which indicated that Madoc led three voyages and left male and female colonists in Mexico, where they formed the Aztec Empire and continued using English and Welsh words such as Penguin and Briton.[32] As fanciful as these accounts may sound, Dee's research offered Gilbert proof of Britain's long history in the western hemisphere.

The unsigned manuscript instructions for Gilbert's voyage corresponded with Dee's research and included a similar list: "How the crowne of England hath most right to all the mayne land and Islands alongest the coste of America from the cape of Florida to .58. degrees northward."[33] Ken MacMillan has verified that the document's author or authors had access to the 1493 bull *Inter Cætera* by pope Alexander VI (1431–1503), as they asserted that the bull's verbosity, a staple of papal decrees, did not bestow territorial rights or allow the pope to partition the Americas between Spain and Portugal.[34] Although Gilbert's patent employed similar linguistic conventions, English explorers had no qualms about challenging the edict of a long-dead Spanish pope, especially after Elizabeth's 1570 excommunication by Pius V (1504–1572). The bulls precluded non-Iberians from claiming North America, but Gilbert took umbrage with the papal supposition of jurisdiction in the spiritual as well as the temporal worlds.

Moreover, the authors rightfully suggested that the Spanish exploration of North America proper postdated England's exploration of the continent. They wrote that Sebastian Cabot had discovered the region from the Cape of Florida to 58 degrees north latitude in 1495, citing the "Story of the West Indies" by Estevão Gomes (c. 1483–1538) (fol. 125).[35] The reference alludes to *History of Trauayle in the VVest and East Indies* (1577) by Pietro Martire d'Anghiera (1457–1526), in which he recalls that Cabot, whom he had interviewed in Spain sometime between 1512 and 1516, traveled west from England until encountering mountains of ice at 58 degrees north and then turning southwest toward Cuba.[36] The authors also cited the same text to prove that Juan Ponce de León (1460–1521), the first Spaniard to reach North America, landed on the continent after Cabot. Even if Ponce de León explored Florida in 1513 rather than in 1512 as suggested by Martire, Ponce de León nonetheless sailed more than fifteen years after Cabot's trailblazing voyage.[37]

Not only did Dee and Gilbert dispute Spain's claim of prior discovery, but they also argued that its poor treatment of Native Americans ceded the nation's territorial claims. They criticized the Spaniards' surreptitious objectives in their brutal colonizing of North America, placing Spain's depredations in a religious context. Alluding to Numbers 13, the authors compared Native Americans to Canaanites, whom the Israelites (Spaniards) feared, which led God to condemn them to death in the wilderness. They referenced Spanish avarice in quoting Exodus 11, a description of the final plague in Egypt that began with inquiries over gold and silver, the very metals that enriched Spain to the detriment of the Aztecs, Incas, and others. The authors insinuated that the Spanish would incur God's wrath as the Egyptians had. In citing Luke 12:2, they recalled Jesus's prophesy that "[t]here is nothing concealed that will not be disclosed." Gilbert and his supporters implied that the Spanish colonists' poor treatment of Native Americans contradicted biblical teachings and therefore voided their claim to North America. As a consequence, they deemed it lawful "for all christyans to invade and conquere any suche countryes kingdomes and domynions" held by the Spaniards.[38]

In addition to establishing England's right to colonize North America, Gilbert's circle needed to determine where they could settle. Discrepancies concerning the quintessence of possession complicated this process by creating confusion regarding the boundaries of Spain's American empire.[39] For instance, following the circumnavigation of Sir Francis Drake (c. 1540–1596) in 1577, Spain's ambassador residing in London, Bernardino de Mendoza (1540–1604), launched a formal protest to Elizabeth about Drake's depredations of the Spanish empire. For Mendoza, his nation's initial discovery of the Americas and its continued presence there made it entitled to the entire continent. The queen retorted that Spain did not actually possess many of the lands and seas within its empire. By her reasoning, Spaniards merely had "touched here and there upon the Coasts" and had ascribed place names to rivers, towns, and regions. She concluded that the Spaniards' activities did not "entitle them to ownership," declaring that "[p]rescription without possession is worth little."[40] Elizabeth and her sea dogs maintained that the Spanish needed to erect and inhabit settlements in all parts of the Americas to claim the entirety of what was then treated as a single landmass (though separate from nearby archipelagos).[41] The queen agreed with England's legal experts that settlers had to improve the land by establishing towns, building homes, peopling those homes, and fencing off territory to denote possession.[42] Because there were no Spaniards permanently occupying American lands north of the present-day Carolinas during the late sixteenth century, Gilbert felt that he could stake his claim to the region.[43]

The incipient grasp of American geography among the English and Spanish colonialists made it even more difficult to pinpoint where Spanish sovereignty existed in North America. Prior to the seventeenth century, terms like "the Indies," "the West Indies," "America," and "Norumbega" were nebulous and used indiscriminately when discussing North America.[44] That the northern limit of Spain's American empire was relatively ambiguous and that its hold on that empire was rather tenuous further complicated matters. Philip occasionally repelled encroachments on his North American territories with violence, such as the attack on the French Huguenot Fort Caroline in 1565 that compelled prospective English and French colonists to be certain of their respective claims to North America. During his third slaving voyage in the late 1560s, John Hawkins (1532–1595) also lost several ships to Spanish attacks in the Gulf of Mexico. In many cases, however, English and French corsairs and traders engaged in secretive or open trade in the Americas on an ad-hoc basis.[45] Between 1568 and 1585, for example, English pirates and privateers conducted fourteen raids on the Spanish West Indies, and there were probably at least as many assaults that went undocumented.[46]

Even if Elizabeth turned a blind eye to her subjects' indiscretions in the Spanish Caribbean, she remained ambivalent about the founding of English colonies in the Americas.[47] As with much of her foreign policy, Elizabeth preferred to be reactive rather than proactive when it came to colonization. When she finally acquiesced to Gilbert's pleas for letters patent, the document specified that he not settle any lands possessed by other Europeans. Elizabeth underscored in her patent to Gilbert that settling Spanish lands would void his license and would in consequence eliminate any support that he might expect to receive from the English crown. Therefore, his specialists needed to determine at what point Spanish dominion ceased in North America, which would give them an idea of where they could legally settle.

Gilbert had no intention of settling an area that would arouse Spanish ire or that might elicit an attack. Yet he also wanted to be within reach of Spain's Caribbean settlements and the *Flota de Indias* that transported American bullion back to Spain, because he had used the potential of pirating the fleet to convince Elizabeth to grant his patent in the first place. If he failed to acquire trade goods from Native Americans that were coveted in Europe, his colony could still profit by serving as a base for raids on Spain's American empire.[48] Based upon the English definition of possession, one might expect Dee, Gilbert, and Hakluyt to propose Saint Augustine or some other Spanish fortification as the boundary, but they agreed that the May River (present-day St. John's River, Florida) constituted the border between Spanish lands and settleable lands. Rivers are among the most easily identifiable borders and have served as demarcation lines between states and nations for centuries. The Wye and the Tweed formed England's borders with Scotland and Wales, respectively; the May River was a natural choice.[49]

When Gilbert began amassing evidence on where to plant his colony, he exclusively focused on the region north of the May River. He stated that Philip could not claim dominion over lands not under "manual occupation" by his subjects. Up to that point, Spanish colonists had only settled lands "within the River of May or a very little thereabouts," so territory to the north remained open for colonization.[50] When Gilbert and his associates, including secretary of state Sir Francis Walsingham (c. 1532–1590), interviewed Ingram, they specifically questioned him about his travels north of the river, being a *tabula rasa* upon which to establish his colony.[51]

Richard Hakluyt the younger, who became the unrivaled promoter of English colonization, authored his first publication, *Divers Voyages touching the Discoverie of America*, as an advertisement for Gilbert's colony. He posited that England legally possessed North American lands between 30 and 67 degrees north, the area from the May River to the Arctic Circle.[52] Fellow colonization promotor Michael Lok (c. 1532–1620) reinforced Hakluyt's beliefs with a map included in the pamphlet (Figure 1.1). It prominently displayed the May River at the north end of Florida, complete with a Spanish settlement on an island near its mouth. To the north is "Apalchen," which abuts Norumbega farther north.[53] Hakluyt and Lok had good reason to select this river, one of the first North American rivers explored and named by Europeans, as the de facto boundary.[54] Rumors that the river and its tributaries led to the wealth of Cathay (China) intrigued potential colonists hoping to match Spanish

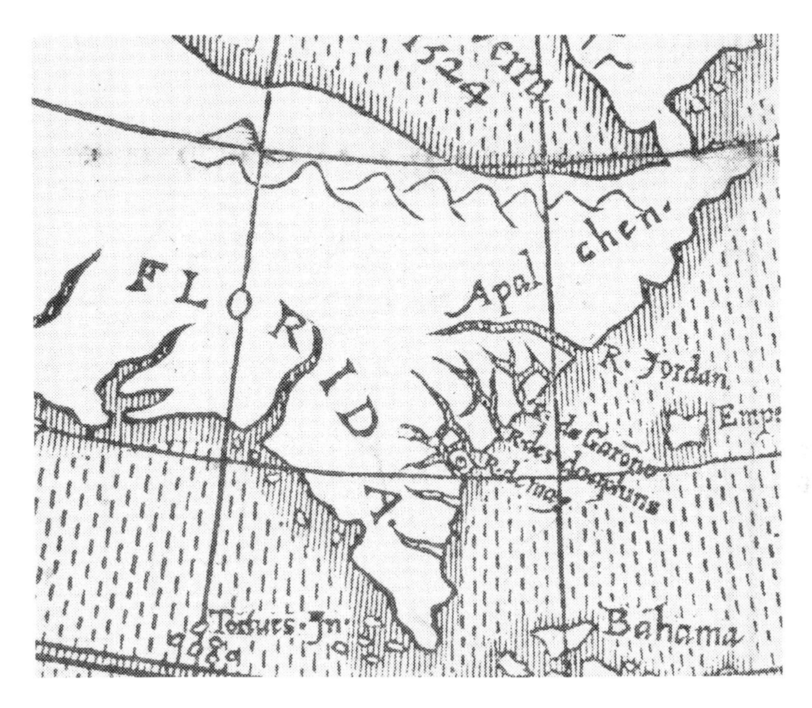

Figure 1.1 Detail of Florida and the location of the May River from Lok's map of the Americas. Michael Lok, *Illvstri Viro, Domino Philippo Sidnæo Michael Lok Civis Londinensis hanc Chartam Dedicabat: 1582* (London: Thomas Woodcocke, 1582).

successes.[55] Many cartographers included the May River on their maps, and Hakluyt likely surmised that the 1560s Franco-Spanish disputes over the river stemmed from the riches that it contained. In his 1584 "Discourse on Western Planting," Hakluyt specified that the river, despite having few tributaries, flowed toward the Pacific and that one of its branches reached Mexico City. The river is, in fact, quite wide (up to 3 miles across) for several miles into the Florida interior, and explorers may have confused it for an inland sea because of its unusually slow flow rate of one third of a mile per hour.[56]

Dee probably consulted similar sources as Hakluyt had for his guide chart, which depicts the May River as Florida's northern border. It serves as the demarcation line for Spain's sphere of influence in North America and flows to the coast of Florida from an inland sea that has tributaries to both the Gulf of Mexico and to Mexico City itself. Dee outlined Florida in yellow, the area adjoining the river to the north "Apalachia" in red, and Gilbert's Norumbega beyond this location.[57] Dee's chart, Hakluyt's pamphlet, Lok's map, and Gilbert's manuscripts created the sense that

Norumbega, well to the north of the May River and Spain's American forts, beckoned English colonists to settle there.

At the time that Gilbert was preparing for his voyage, no Europeans lived permanently north of the May River, and yet hundreds of thousands of Native Americans did.[58] The Narragansett Bay was home to several tribes including the Narragansetts and Wampanoags, Algonquian-speaking eastern woodland peoples whose ancestors had inhabited the region for tens of thousands of years. During the late sixteenth century, each group numbered more than 10,000 that lived in dozens of villages. Few European explorers had ventured into North America by this point, and fewer expeditions had encountered the many peoples in this bay. Yet Gilbert and his supporters found a surprising amount of data on the tribes inhabiting the region that they would attempt to colonize. Gilbert's most significant source was the document that convinced him to settle Norumbega in the first place: Verrazzano's descriptions of Narragansetts and Wampanoags living on the west and east coasts of the bay. When the Italian explorer arrived in 1524, he found individuals who were noticeably taller and healthier than Europeans, calling them "the most beautiful" and "the most civil" of all the peoples with whom he met on his voyage. For Verrazzano, the region seemed like an earthly paradise because Narragansetts and Wampanoags lived long lives and rarely became ill. Like many explorers who came before and after Verrazzano, however, he complicated his narrative by proclaiming that the Indigenous population wore little clothing and traded "all they have" for what were considered mere trifles in Europe.[59]

Gilbert and his coterie also personally interviewed three Englishmen who had traveled up the Norumbega River, a remarkable feat considering few Europeans knew of its existence. The group questioned Ingram about his 1560s travels in the region, focusing attention on Native-American clothing. The 1576 sack of Antwerp by Spanish soldiers had eliminated England's primary outlet for English cloth, the nation's most valuable export, and Gilbert sought out new markets. Ingram responded favorably in Gilbert's eyes, recalling that the people he encountered used only leaves and furs as covering. The otherwise unknown sailor John Walker voyaged to the river in 1580, perhaps at the behest of Gilbert. Seven miles from its banks he happened upon a village, whose inhabitants possessed large tanned animal hides, likely elk or bison.[60] Gilbert even dispatched his own navigator, the Portuguese-born Simon Fernandes (c. 1538–1590), who made a remarkably swift reconnaissance voyage to the river in 1580. The three voyagers made it clear to Gilbert that healthy people in need of English cloth inhabited the region near the Norumbega River.

Richard Hakluyt the elder (c. 1530–1591), a London-based lawyer whose interest in geography and colonization inspired his nephew of the same name, offered Gilbert numerous recommendations on how to maximize the potential for British-Native-American commerce, many of which were reissued as instructions for the voyage. Of the utmost importance, wrote Hakluyt, was to use "all humanitie and curtesie and much forbearing of revenge" to acquire American commodities and secure reliable allies who would serve English interests in conflicts against other Europeans. Discerning which commodities each group possessed and needed, as well as their strengths, weaknesses, and alliances, could benefit the English colonizers, too. Unlike earlier European colonizers, Hakluyt presumed that Native Americans would dictate interactions with the English, suggesting that the colonists "might not be suffered by the savages to enjoy an whole countrey or any more then the scope of a Citie."[61] To prevent casualties from potential surprise attacks while trading upriver, he told Gilbert to construct barges and boats with a canopy of linen as protection from arrows. Even if Gilbert failed to secure an alliance with his nearest neighbors, by controlling a safe-haven near the sea he could engage in trade along the coast and gain access to fish for sustenance and barter. Hakluyt optimistically believed that Native Americans would provide Gilbert with supplies and trade a variety of American commodities that would eliminate England's dependance upon European realms such as Spain and France. Rather than enriching their "doubtfull friendes" and wasting England's precious commodities through intra-European commerce, Hakluyt advised Gilbert to establish a lucrative trade network in North America.

Based upon Hakluyt's advice and their own research, Gilbert's leadership devised instructions for the ship captains to take note of Native-American garb and to record "the thinges that they in every particuler place shall most esteme either of their owne contryes commodyties or of ours." They also instructed artists among the crew to draw "the figures and shapes of men and women in their apparel."[62] Not only would these drawings offer a sense of the inhabitants' appearances to Gilbert's associates in England, but they also would indicate what clothing Norumbega's Native Americans needed most. They intended to discern what trade goods Native Americans desired, ever hopeful that clothing was among them. Gilbert even designated one of his crewmembers to carry an English dictionary to record Native-American words next to their English equivalents. The colonists could use this knowledge to make amicable relations and establish trade.

Members of Gilbert's circle made clear their intentions to trade with natives whom they encountered, but commerce was a secondary goal behind land acquisition. Gilbert devised intricate plans for the layout of his colony, divvying up millions of acres of territory prior to setting sail. He knew from Verrazzano's writings that numerous towns existed in the region, and he asked aristocrats to bring arms for their defense. Yet, there is no indication that Gilbert was leading a conquering army into one of the most densely settled regions of North America. Like later English colonists, he hoped to live alongside Native Americans to ensure the survival of his colony. To claim Indigenous lands while simultaneously benefitting from the population, Gilbert and his supporters would write them out of existence in England while maintaining their goal of trading with Native Americans. The colonists needed to find a different rationale with which to challenge Native American rather than European land rights, because obvious signs of possession such as homes meant that the "unsettled" argument would not suffice. Fortunately for Gilbert's purposes, English law discounted all territorial claims made by non-Christians, and legal writers argued that nonbelievers could occupy but not truly possess land.[63] Essentially, they were considered caretakers, which is why Gilbert's patent specified that he not settle lands claimed by Christians. For the English, non-Christian lands were up for grabs.

English legal theory specified that any land not under cultivation was virgin land suitable to be claimed. Such a means of seizing territory had its basis in the Roman concept of *res nullius* (things without owners), which stated that untilled or unoccupied lands remained available for the common good until an individual or group took them into possession through cultivation or some other labor. In the minds of sixteenth-century Europeans, unplanted so-called wastelands squandered God's benevolence and needed to be improved through cultivation to make them productive. Thus, not only did English experts assert that colonists like Gilbert had a legal right to North America, but they also suggested that leaving the land fallow was a disservice to humanity. It was the duty of good Christians to settle and improve lands being un- or under-utilized.[64]

Gilbert's supporters used these ideas as justification to discount Native-American land rights, which they publicized in the promotional tracts written for the voyage. In his 1583 *True Reporte*, Peckham said little about Native Americans but contended that they ceded their territorial rights by only harvesting crops that occurred naturally. They needed to plant their own produce, wrote Peckham, to improve the land and thus possess it.[65] Unbeknownst to Peckham, Narragansetts, Wampanoags, and other Indigenous peoples in the region planted a variety of crops after felling trees and depositing ash through controlled burns. Some Native Americans left fallow surplus grounds for a few years to increase fertility, but Europe's first explorers misjudged their agricultural practices, assuming these were otherwise wasted lands primed for settlement. Semi-sedentary Wampanoags traveled throughout their lands on a seasonal basis. Men on fishing expeditions might leave their families for months, and entire populations migrated to the coast to find food and plant crops at the onset of summer. In many cases, Europeans did not even recognize these agricultural fields in plain sight. Wampanoag utilized companion plantings of the "three sisters"—climbing beans, maize, and winter squash—in a single field without rows. The beans climbed the maize stalks and provided nitrogen for the other plants. The prickly squash vines irritated pests, and its large leaves shaded the ground, both inhibiting weed growth and preserving soil moisture. Multiple plant species growing together seemed out of place to Europeans accustomed to monocrop fields arranged in neat rows, but the Indigenous practice generated crop yields that outpaced English ones.[66]

Many Native-American groups also wore little clothing because of the coast's hot and humid summers, the season when European ships arrived. Though functional, European explorers misjudged this lack of clothing and the different technologies in the Americas as forms of incivility that forfeited native land rights.[67] Moreover, northeastern Native Americans such as the Narragansetts viewed possession much differently than Europeans. Their conception of private land ownership meant that certain groups or families had the right to use (often communally) land rather than own it:[68] "The woods, the streams, everything on it belongs to everybody and is for the use of all," declared the seventeenth-century Wampanoag sachem Massasoit, "How can one man say it belongs only to him?"[69] Gilbert expected to encounter Native Americans when he landed in Norumbega, but any lands used in a way not recognized by England's legal system were considered vacant. In fact, Gilbert believed that he did not need to offer Native Americans a written acknowledgment of his taking possession of their land when he arrived. Engaging in commerce or simply working the soil sufficed as a declaration of intent according to English law. The English did not give ownership privileges to Native Americans or to other Europeans who tilled American soil because English rights did not extend to citizens of other nations.[70]

Gilbert finally set sail from England in June 1583, less than one year before his patent was to expire. Aside from encountering storms and once resorting to piracy, the crossing was uneventful, and the fleet reconvened on 3 August at the agreed upon re-provisioning station: St. John's Bay, Newfoundland, the busiest fishing port in the Americas. Although not yet at his destination, Gilbert nonetheless saw the opportunity to claim the first overseas territory for England. He ordered his tent pitched near the bay and summoned his ship captains and masters, as well as the masters and owners of fishing vessels at port. His letters patent were read aloud in English and were interpreted for other Europeans, which granted him possession of all lands and waters within 200 leagues. Invoking English common law, Gilbert performed the so-called "turf and twig" or more formally the "livery of seisin" ceremony, wherein he removed some soil and stuck it on a branch to represent land transfer.[71] Gilbert established three English-based laws for his new territory: only the Church of England would be tolerated; Elizabeth was to be defended against any traitors; and anyone blaspheming the queen would lose their ears, ships, and goods. He ordered the laws and his claim written down, and all present consented to abide by the new laws. Gilbert's crew erected the arms of England engraved in lead on a wooden pillar, and he allotted drying grounds for any fishermen who agreed to pay rent to he and his heirs.

The cartographers drew maps of the region and its surrounding waters, and Gilbert also made passports for foreign fishermen present in the bay, allowing them to troll his waters for their catch.[72] Although Gilbert never reached the Narragansett Bay and drowned on the return voyage to England, in taking formal possession of Newfoundland he gave rise to the nascent British empire.

Despite Gilbert's elaborate ceremony, and like so many European declarations of possession, his did not hold. His kinsman Bernard Drake (c. 1537–1586) all but eliminated the Iberian presence at the Grand Banks fishery by attacking several of its vessels at Newfoundland in 1585, but France continued to utilize the fishery for centuries. England simply lacked the will and resources to enforce its claim.[73] Yet, farther south at Jamestown, nearer to Gilbert's intended colony site, his vision began to take shape in the early seventeenth century. Virginia colonist William Strachey (1572–1621), whose writings inspired Shakespeare's *The Tempest*, echoed Gilbert in citing the Madoc and Cabot voyages to prove that Florida to Cape Breton rightfully belonged to the English crown. Strachey declared that Spain's failure to maintain an army in the region and its lone settlement at St. Augustine hardly entitled it to the entire landmass.[74] At the time of his writing, Spain's presence on the continent remained confined to present-day Florida, just as it had been during Gilbert's lifetime. Spain's inability to colonize North America after several tries, wrote Gilbert's voyage chronicler Edward Hayes (c. 1550–1613), could be explained by divine intervention. It was as if God had granted the Spaniards lands to the south but prevented them from settling northern areas destined to become English territory.[75]

Noticeably absent from Haye's report and from Gilbert's ceremony at St. John's Bay were the people from whom they were taking possession of the land, the Beothuk and Mi'kmaq populations of the island. In the lone surviving account of the voyage, Hayes barely mentioned Indigenous peoples or what the colonists expected to do when they met them. He only noted that the crew brought English cloth to trade as well as musicians and toys "to delight the savage people, whom we intended to win by all fair means possible."[76] Regardless of their altruistic goals, the Englishmen set a precedent in pigeonholing Native Americans as easily amused and manipulated, and thus hardly a threat to the technologically advanced English. Even though the earliest English colonists in the Americas suffered far more deaths at the hands of Native Americans than other Europeans, their forts, like the one Gilbert envisioned, faced the sea rather than the interior. The colonists' fears of a Spanish attack were intense but unwarranted, and instead they faced fierce resistance culminating in the Pequot War (1636–1638), which was the Pequot's response to epidemics and unchecked English incursions into their lands. Native Americans had served as crucial allies and even saviors of the English; the Plymouth colony certainly would have failed without Wampanoag assistance. Once the colonists gained a foothold, however, the English people flooding the region gave little attention to incorporating Native Americans into Anglo-American society. Two worlds existed in New England: one English, one native.

Notes

1. Verrazzano called the bay "Refugio" or "Bay of Refuge." Unless otherwise noted, all translations are my own.
2. Lacking papal support, Elizabethan expansionists resorted to claims of prior discovery to gain national and/or international recognition for their colonies.
3. See, for instance, Horn, *A Kingdom Strange*; Oberg, *The Head in Edward Nugent's Hand*; Kelso, *Jamestown*; Ordahl Kupperman, *The Jamestown Project*, and by the same author, *Roanoke*; and Horn, *A Land as God Made It*.
4. O'Brien, *Firsting and Lasting*.
5. Discussions of this topic include Benton, "Atlantic Law: Transformations of a Regional Legal Regime," in Canny and Morgan, eds., *The Oxford Handbook of Atlantic World, 1450–1850*, pp. 400–416; Miller, Ruru, Behrendt, and Lindberg, *Discovering Indigenous Lands*; Benton, *A Search for Sovereignty*; Tomlins, *Freedom Bound*; Benjamin, *The Atlantic World*, pp. 214–215; Ogborn, *Global Lives*, pp. 18, 47–48, 52–53; MacMillan, *Sovereignty and Possession in the English New World*; Mancke, "Chartered Enterprises," in Mancke and Shammas, eds., *The Creation of the British Atlantic World*, pp. 237–262: 240; Tomlins, "Law's Empire: Chartering English Colonies on the American Mainland in the Seventeenth Century," in Kirkby and Coleborne, eds., *Law, History, Colonialism*, pp. 26–45.
6. Eccles, *The French in North America, 1500–1783*, pp. 3 and 8.
7. Fitzpatrick, "Terminal Legality: Imperialism and the (De)Composition of Law," in Kirkby and Coleborne, eds., *Law, History, Colonialism*, pp. 9–25: 18.
8. European colonizers often cited the Roman legal term *res nullius* (nobody's thing) to justify their acquisition of territory. See Elliott, *Empires of the Atlantic World*, pp. 12 and 30–32. On later English colonists' use of the Lokean *res nullius*, see Pagden, "The Struggle for Legitimacy and the Image of Empire in the Atlantic to c.1700," in Louis, ed., *The Oxford History of the British Empire*, vol. 1, pp. 34–54: 42–50.
9. Gilbert first circulated his research in manuscript form in 1566, and a decade later it was printed in support of Martin Frobisher's first voyage to North America. See Gilbert, *A Discourse of a Discouerie for a New Passage to Cataia*; and Quinn, *Voyages of Gilbert*, vol. 2, pp. 6–11 and 29–31.
10. MacMillan, *Sovereignty and Possession*, pp. 79–80; similar patents were issued to Walter Raleigh in 1584 and to the Virginia Company in 1606. They are transcribed in Quinn, ed., *The Roanoke Voyages 1584–1590*, vol. 1, pp. 82–89. Also see Barbour, ed., *The Jamestown Voyages Under the First Charter, 1606–1609*, vol. 1, pp. 24–33. For a brief comparison of the liberties assurance of each, see Bilder, "Charter Constitutionalism," pp. 1577–1584.
11. Gilbert's patent is transcribed in Quinn, *Voyages of Gilbert*, vol. 2, pp. 188–190.
12. A league was comprised of approximately three nautical miles. A single nautical mile equals about 1.15 miles, so three nautical miles equal roughly 3.45 miles. Therefore, 200 leagues equal 690 miles. This number is the radius of Gilbert's great circle of land, and by doubling it one gets the diameter of his circular territory (roughly 1,381 miles). By multiplying the circle's radius (690) by itself, and then multiplying that number by pi (3.14) one gets the

square miles of the territory. Ergo, Gilbert's dominion extended over almost exactly 1.5 million square miles, or roughly 958,553,073 acres—about half of which was land and the other half sea.

13. Miller, *Discovering Indigenous Lands*, pp. 258–259; Gilbert's circle alternatively called the river the Canada, Norumbega, or Dee River, which marks one of the earliest instances of a Briton ascribing a place name to an American landmark, sight-unseen, as a means of denoting possession.
14. The National Archives of the United Kingdom (hereafter TNA), State Papers (hereafter SP) 12/95, fol. 139v. This manuscript dates from 1574 and was authored by Gilbert, Sir George Peckham, Richard Grenville, and Christopher Carleill.
15. See Hatfield House Archives (hereafter HHA), Cecil Papers (hereafter CP) 153/147, fol. 1r; in 1570, at a banquet at the home of Robert Dudley, earl of Leicester, Gilbert quarreled with Francis Russell, second earl of Bedford, over Stukeley's reputation. Gilbert insisted that Stukeley had fled to Spain to assist the Spanish against the Moroccans, but others called him a traitor. Gilbert had to be restrained by his friends. See Ordahl Kupperman, *Jamestown Project*, pp. 45–49; and Tazón, *The Life and Times of Thomas Stukeley (c. 1525–78)*, pp. 64–75 and 90–92.
16. TNA, SP 12/95, fol. 139v. Gilbert and his supporters were not the only ones in England who were discussing this topic. In a late sixteenth-century English manuscript, an unidentified writer asked whether English subjects could "lawfully trade into the Indies [the Americas]." The author claimed that Alexander VI's 1493 papal bull *Inter Cætera* (among other texts), which gave the crowns of Castile and Aragon the ability to colonize in the Americas, did not pertain to Native Americans, because the pope "had no awthoritie to subiect temprallie the infidells or to take away their land without cawse." The pope could not simply eschew the law of nations and the right of navigation that permitted English merchants to trade by sea and on land. Spanish traders engaged in commerce in England, and English ones in Spain, so "by the Lawe of Nature and Nations," the pope and his Spanish coreligionists could not prevent trade "in their gulff in the Adlatick Sea" or elsewhere in the Americas. HHA, CP 10/80, fol. 1r. Also see Hakluyt, *A Particuler Discourse*, pp. 96–113.
17. Dee knew Gilbert from at least 1567. See British Library (hereafter BL), Additional MS 36674, fols. 58r–62v. Dee served as an informal advisor to Elizabeth and had presented her with various tables based upon ancient and contemporary sources to prove England's title to various territories. According to civil lawyer Charles Merbury, Dee made it apparent to the queen and to her subjects that they had as much of a right to colonize North America as any other Europeans. Dee was so highly regarded that in 1577 Elizabeth took the remarkable step of visiting his home where he declared to her England's title to Greenland and other North Atlantic islands. See Dee, *The Limits of the British Empire*, p. 29; Merbury, *A Briefe Discovrse of Royall Monarchie*, sig. A2v. The most complete assessment of Dee's life is by Parry in *The Arch-Conjuror of England*.
18. Dee, *The Private Diary of Dr. John Dee*, p. 4.
19. Fitzmaurice, *Humanism and America*, p. 44; Clulee, *John Dee's Natural Philosophy*, p. 187; Peckham promised an equal amount of land from Gilbert's gift to fellow Catholic Thomas Gerrard.
20. BL, Cotton MS Augustus I.i, fol. 1v. Much of Dee's argument was a reiteration of his unpublished "famous and Ryche Discoveries" from 1577; see BL, Cotton MS Vitellius C. VII, fols. 26r–269v.

21. Roberts and Watson, eds., *John Dee's Library Catalogue*, entry 681, n.p.; Lambarde, *Archaionomia*. Also see MacMillan, *Sovereignty and Possession*, p. 62. MacMillan has argued convincingly that Dee never presented the map and its corresponding text to Elizabeth. See MacMillan, "John Dee's 'Brytanici imperii limites'," p. 155.
22. Best, *A True Discovrse of the late voyages of discouerie*, book 1, p. 16. Dee owned this book. See Roberts and Watson, eds., *Dee's Library Catalogue*, entry 1319, n.p. Also see Martire d'Anghiera, *The Decades of the newe worlde*, book 3, fols. 118v–119r.
23. Hakluyt included an account of Borough's voyage in his 1589 *Principall Navigations*. See "The voyage of Steuen Burrough towarde the riuer Ob intending the discouerie of the northeast passage, An.1556," in Hakluyt, *The principall navigations*, pp. 311–321.
24. On Dee and Borough, see BL, Cotton MS Vitellius C. VII, fol. 60v.
25. See Lucar's note "To Mr. John Dee, 1577," at BL, Cotton MS Vitellius C. VII, fol. 344r. Lucar's papers on Thorne include BL, Lansdowne MS 100, fols. 65r–80v, and BL Cotton MS Vitellius C. VII, fols. 329r–341v. See also HHA, CP 245/5.
26. BL Cotton MS Vitellius C. VII, fols. 331r, 333r, 334r, 338v, 339r, 340r. See Roberts and Watson, eds., *Dee's Library Catalogue*, entry DM34, n.p. On Dee's manicule, see Sherman, *Used Books*, pp. 25–52. A newly-discovered butlerage account record of Eliot's putative voyage to "the new found isle" gives additional credence to Thorne's story. See Jones, "Henry VII and the Bristol Expeditions to North America," pp. 452–454. The document in question dates from 1502 rather than 1494, but it reveals Eliot's involvement in Newfoundland at an early date.
27. BL, Cotton MS Augustus I.i, fol. 1v. Contemporary English chroniclers substantiated the earliest voyages mentioned by Dee. Robert Fabyan, in his 1533 *chronicle*, recorded that King Malgo began his reign in 552 and conquered Norway, Iceland, Orkney, and other realms. See Fabyan, *Fabyans cronycle*, fol. 47. In his more famous 1577 *Chronicles*, Raphael Holinshed asserted that King Arthur had conquered Iceland, Götaland in southern Sweden, and other territories during his early sixth-century reign. See Holinshed, *The Firste Volume of the Chronicles of England*, p. 133. Dee also owned this book. See Roberts and Watson, eds., *Dee's Library Catalogue*, entry 1681, n.p. Hakluyt included accounts of Arthur and Malgo's conquests in his *Principall Navigations* (1589), pp. 243–245; Dee used Arthur's discoveries to prove to Elizabeth and to Hakluyt the elder, among others, that several North Atlantic islands belonged to England. He owned many of the so-called "Brut Histories" that trace their origins to Geoffrey of Monmouth in the twelfth century and that detail the legendary exploits of the Trojan soldier Brutus, who, it was said, founded Britain, united the British Isles, and descended from Arthur. See Dee, *Diary*, pp. 4 and 6; Roberts and Watson, eds., *Dee's Library Catalogue*, entries 274, 548, 601, 669, 1200, 1681, 1686, 1687, 1699–1703, 1747, and 1968, n.p.; and MacMillan, *Sovereignty and Possession*, pp. 59–60. Dee was somewhat obsessed with Arthur, even giving the name to his first-born son.
28. Allen, "From Cabot to Cartier," pp. 502–503.
29. Roberts and Watson, eds., *Dee's Library Catalogue*, entry DM35, n.p.; also see p. 40. The manuscript remained in Dee's library until at least 1583.
30. Dee's copy is located at Trinity College in Dublin.
31. Roberts and Watson, "*John Dee's Library Catalogue*: Additions and Corrections," pp. 8 and 11; Sherman, "John Dee's Columbian Encounter," in Clucas, ed., *John Dee*, pp. 131–140: 133–136. Dee's copy is now at the British Library.

32. Caradoc of Llancarfan, *The Historie of Cambria, Now Called Wales*, pp. 227–229. Hakluyt included some of Powel's Madoc material in his compilations, and he cited his voyage as proof of Britain's discovery of North America. See "The voyage of Madoc the sonne of Owen Gwinned prince of Northwales to the West Indies. Anno. 1170," in Hakluyt, *Principall Navigations* (1589), pp. 506–507; and Hakluyt, *Western Planting*, pp. 88–89. A modern analysis of Madoc can be found in Williams, *Madoc*. Also see Gilbert, *Discourse of discouerie*.
33. MacMillan, *Sovereignty and Possession*, p. 77.
34. Ibid., p. 107.
35. BL, Additional MS 38823, fols. 5v–6r; Sebastian's father John led two voyages for England during the late fifteenth century. However, beginning in the early sixteenth century, authors began attributing them to Sebastian, hence the confusion in the Gilbert manuscript. 1495 is the year in which Cabot probably arrived in England, as he did not embark on his first voyage for Henry VII until 1496. Hakluyt gave this as the date of his voyage in *Divers Voyages* as well, so Hakluyt may be responsible for this misdating. Authors who have confused Sebastian with John Cabot include Camden, *Annales the True and Royall History of the Famous Empresse Elizabeth Queene of England France and Ireland*, book 3, p. 44.
36. Martire, *The History of Trauayle in the West and East Indies*, fols. 125r, 228. See Jones, "Alwyn Ruddock," pp. 244–245. Sebastian Cabot was about fourteen years old in 1495, and Martire never mentions the date of his exploration. Henry VII only granted letters patent to Cabot's father John in March 1496, but it is possible that the younger Cabot sailed on his father's initial transatlantic voyage. In his *Divers Voyages*, Hakluyt reprinted Cabot's letters patent in both English and in the original Latin, and he dated them 5 March 1495 (1496 new calendar; Hakluyt, *Divers Voyages*, sigs. A1v–A2v. Cabot did not depart until 1496, so Gilbert may have been referring to the patent as his source. In either case, it served Gilbert's purposes to mention Sebastian rather than his father because John was born in Venice. By his own account, Sebastian was born in Bristol, so attributing the 1496 voyage to him strengthened England's claim to North America.
37. BL, Additional MS 38823, fol. 6r; Martire, *History of Trauayle*, fol. 228v.
38. BL, Additional MS 38823, fols. 6v–7r.
39. On the differing notions of possession among Europe's early-modern colonial powers (the Dutch, English, French, Spanish, and Portuguese), see Seed, *Ceremonies of Possession*, pp. 8–40, and among the British, French, and Spanish, see Pagden, *Lords of All the World*, pp. 44–62, 76–102.
40. Seed, *Ceremonies of Possession*, p. 10.
41. Miller, *Discovering Indigenous Lands*, pp. 18–19; and Seed, *Ceremonies of Possession*, pp. 8–10. For the Portuguese, controlling the trade of a territory denoted possession, as did the technological advances (maps, navigational expertise, and knowledge of winds) that allowed them to reach these places.
42. See Miller, *Discovering Indigenous Lands*, pp. 251–252; and Pagden, *Lords of All the World*, pp. 81–102.
43. The time-worn thesis that early-modern Iberian monarchs sought to control people and that English colonists primarily concerned themselves with controlling and possessing land is oversimplified. The former primarily based their claim to North America on their prior discovery and the latter on their control and mastery over land. See Seed, *American Pentimento*, pp. 3 and 12–14. This view is complicated by Elliott, *Empires of the Atlantic World*, pp. 16–28; and MacMillan, *Sovereignty and Possession*, p. 11.
44. Contemporaries described Raleigh's destination as Norumbega until he dubbed it Virginia in 1585. Although Frobisher landed in present-day

Canada, his destination was called the West Indies. After Raleigh's reconnaissance of Roanoke in 1584, Spaniard Pedro Cubiaur wrote that "Las naos deRalý qui ý ban a noronbega han luculos" (The ships of Raleigh which were going to Norumbega have returned). See TNA, SP 94/2, fol. 77. Hakluyt similarly deemed Raleigh's destination Norumbega. See Hakluyt, *Western Planting*, pp. 120–121. Yet William Cecil, in a discussion of Martin Frobisher's second voyage to present-day Canada, referred to his "viage to the West Indies." HHA, CP 8/93, fol. 1r. In another document, Frobisher's destination was identified as "the Northwest Indias." See HHA, CP 8/88, fol. 1r. The Latin title of Dee's 1580 map for Gilbert indicated that the Americas were "named the West Indies in the ordinary way," but Dee preferred the term Atlantis to describe the newly-discovered continents. See BL, Cotton MS Vitellius C. VII, fol. 8v, where Dee lists his map as "Atlantidis, (Vulgariter Indiae Occidentalis nominatae), emendatior descriptio quàm adhuc est divulgata—A° 1580." On the fluidity of terms describing American and Norumbega in particular, see Seaver, "Norumbega and 'Harmonia Mundi' in Sixteenth-Century Cartography," pp. 34–58; and Pope, *Fish into Wine*, p. 15.

45. Lane, *Pillaging the Empire*, pp. 17–49; Wright, Jr., *Anglo-Spanish Rivalry in North America*, pp. 5–6 and 17–31.
46. Benjamin, *Atlantic World*, p. 232.
47. Seed, *Ceremonies of Possession*, pp. 9–10.
48. See Probasco, "Elizabeth I, Sir Humphrey Gilbert, and the Anglo-Spanish Conflict," pp. 119–135.
49. On the importance of rivers in European claims to the Americas during the sixteenth century, see Benton, *Search for Sovereignty*, pp. 40–59.
50. BL, Additional MS 38823, fols. 5v–6r.
51. Ingram claims to have traveled north of the River May for seven months; see BL, Sloane MS 1447, fol. 1r. The copy of his report at the Bodleian Library, Tanner MS 79, fol. 172r gives the same time span. Yet the report at TNA, SP 12/175, fol. 163r says that he spent just three months north of the river. According to Maurice Browne, Gilbert claimed that Ingram had traveled in the region for "above Three monethes," too. Browne's letter to John Thynne, dated 20 August 1582, is reprinted in Quinn, Quinn, and Hillier, eds., *New American World*, vol. 3, pp. 247–248.
52. Hakluyt, *Divers Voyages*, sig. ¶3v. Gilbert's 1582 instructions put the northern extent of the claim at 58 degrees north because his source, Francisco López de Gómera, indicated that Cabot had reached that latitude. See BL Additional MS 38823, fol. 5v. The most complete assessment of Hakluyt's life is Mancall, *Hakluyt's Promise*.
53. Lok, *Illvstri Viro, Domino Philippo Sidnæo Michael Lok Civis Londinensis Hanc Chartam Dedicabat: 1582*; Hakluyt, *Divers Voyages*, n.p.
54. Spanish colonists technically inhabited land north of the river at Santa Elena in present-day South Carolina, but they abandoned the small fort after Drake exposed it in 1586. Hakluyt knew that the fort was still occupied as of 1584. See his *Western Planting*, pp. 50–51. On Santa Elena, see Weber, *The Spanish Frontier in North America*, pp. 66–75.
55. BL, Cotton MS Otho E. VIII, fols. 57r–58v.
56. By 1575, Spanish colonizers recognized that the May River originated from a lake in central Florida. See John Carter Brown Library (hereafter JCB), MS Codex Sp 7-1 SIZE, map insert between fols. 7v–8r.
57. BL, Cotton MS Augustus I. i, fol. 1.
58. Krech III, *The Ecological Indian*, p. 94.
59. Wroth, *The Voyages of Giovanni da Verrazzano, 1524–1528*, pp. 87 and 134–140.

60. TNA, CO 1/1, fols. 9v–10r. How Walker determined that the river he encountered on his exploration was the Norumbega is unknown.
61. Hakluyt, *Divers Voyages*, sigs. K1r–K3v. Although written in 1578, Hakluyt the elder's notes were not printed until 1582, when his namesake included them in his *Divers Voyages* to promote Gilbert's forthcoming voyage. The younger Hakluyt titled them "Notes framed by a Gentleman heretofore to bee given to one that prepared for a discoverie. and went not: And not unfitt to be committed to print, considering the same may stirre up considerations of these and of such other thinges, not unmeete in such new voyages as may be attempted hereafter." Gilbert had slightly different intentions in 1578 than he did for his final voyage, but his initial colonization experience no doubt impacted his later endeavors. On Hakluyt's notes, see Tomlins, "Law's Empire," p. 31; and Quinn, Quinn, and Hillier, eds., *New American World*, vol. 3, pp. 2 and 23.
62. BL, Additional MS 38823, fols. 1r–v, 5r. Mathematician Thomas Hariot wrote such a lexicon of Algonquian words at Raleigh's Roanoke colony, while artist John White drew the common clothing of the region.
63. Ordahl Kupperman, *The Atlantic in World History*, p. 15.
64. Linklater, *Owning the Earth*, pp. 27–29.
65. Peckham, *A Trve Reporte*, sigs. C1r–C3v.
66. Ordahl Kupperman, *Indians and English*, pp. 157–160; Krech III, *Ecological Indian*, pp. 76 and 107; and Dolittle, "Agriculture in North America on the Eve of Contact," pp. 386–401.
67. Probasco, "Virgin America for Barren England," pp. 406–419; Miller, *Discovering Indigenous Lands*, pp. 260–261; MacMillan, *Sovereignty and Possession*, pp. 8–9; Seed, *American Pentimento*, pp. 29–44.
68. Linklater, *Owning the Earth*, pp. 103–104; O'Brien, *Firsting and Lasting*, p. 3.
69. Linklater, *Owning the Earth*, p. 26.
70. Seed, *American Pentimento*, pp. 13–26.
71. Traditionally, the landholder would hand the turf or twig to the new owner as a symbol of transferring ownership. "Livery of seisin" translates to "delivery of possession." The practice began during the High Middle Ages.
72. Hayes, "A Report of the Voyage and Successe Thereof, Attempted in the Yeere of Our Lord, 1583. by Sir Humfrey Gilbert Knight," in Hakluyt, *Principall Navigations*, pp. 686–688. An example of Gilbert's passport is in *Transcripts of Selected Documents from Various Archives in Spain*, fols. 1r–2v.
73. See Probasco, "Elizabeth, Gilbert, and Conflict," pp. 119–135. Seventeenth-century English colonizers of Newfoundland recalled that Gilbert's voyage had guaranteed English domination of the island. See JCB, MS Codex Eng 4-2 SIZE, pp. 1–2.
74. JCB, MS Codex Eng 105-1 SIZE, pp. 8–14.
75. Hayes, "A Report of the Voyage," p. 680. Spanish failures included Ponce de Léon's expedition to Florida in 1521 and the Spanish Jesuit mission at Ajacán in Virginia in 1570.
76. Hayes, "A Report of the Voyage," pp. 684–685.

Bibliography

Allen, John L., "From Cabot to Cartier: The Early Exploration of Eastern North America, 1497–1543," *Annals of the Association of American Geographers* 82.3 (1992), pp. 500–521.

Barbour, Philip L., ed., *The Jamestown Voyages Under the First Charter, 1606–1609* (London: Cambridge University Press, 1969).

Benjamin, Thomas, *The Atlantic World: Europeans, Africans, Indians, and Their Shared History, 1400–1900* (Cambridge: Cambridge University Press, 2009).

Benton, Lauren, *A Search for Sovereignty: Law and Geography in European Empires, 1400–1900* (Cambridge: Cambridge University Press, 2010).

Best, George, *A True Discovrse of the Late Voyages of Discouerie, for the Finding of a Passage to Cathaya, by the Northvveast, Vnder the Conduct of Martin Frobisher Generall: Deuided into Three Bookes. In the first wherof is shewed, his first voyage. Wherein also by the way is sette out a Geographicall description of the Worlde, and what partes thereof haue bin discouered by the Nauigations of the Englishmen. Also, there are annexed certayne reasons, to proue all partes of the Worlde habitable, with a generall mappe adioyned. In the second, is set out his second voyage, with the aduentures and accidents thereof. In the thirde, is declared the strange fortunes which hapned in the third voyage, with a seuerall description of the Countrey and the people there inhabiting. VVith a particular Card thervnto adioyned of Meta Incognita, so farre forth as the secretes of the voyage may permit* (London: Henry Bynnyman, 1578).

Bilder, Mary Sarah, "Charter Constitutionalism: The Myth of Edward Coke and the Virginia Charter," *North Carolina Law Review* 94.5 (2016), pp. 1545–1598.

Bodleian Library, Oxford, Tanner MS 79.

British Library, London: Additional MS 36674; Additional MS 38823; Cotton MS Augustus I.i; Cotton MS Otho E. VIII; Cotton MS Vitellius C. VII; Lansdowne MS 100; and Sloane MS 1447.

Camden, William, *Annales the True and Royall History of the Famous Empresse Elizabeth Queene of England France and Ireland &c. True Faith's Defendresse of Diuine Renowne and Happy Memory. Wherein all such memorable things as happened during hir blessed raigne, with such acts and Tratises as past betwixt hir Matie and Scotland, France, Spaine, Italy, Germany, Poland, Sweden, Denmark, Russia, and the Netherlands, are exactly described* (London: George Purslowe, Humphrey Lownes, and Miles Flesher, 1625).

Canny, Nicholas, and Philip Morgan, eds., *The Oxford Handbook of Atlantic World, 1450–1850* (New York: Oxford University Press, 2011).

Clucas, Stephen, ed., *John Dee: Interdisciplinary Studies in English Renaissance Thought* (Dordrecht: Springer, 2006).

Clulee, Nicholas H., *John Dee's Natural Philosophy: Between Science and Religion* (New York: Routledge, 1988).

Dee, John, *The Private Diary of Dr. John Dee, and the Catalogue of His Library Manuscripts*, ed. James O. Halliwell (London: Camden Society, 1842).

———, *The Limits of the British Empire*, eds. Ken MacMillan and Jennifer Abeles (Westport, CT: Praeger, 2004).

Dolittle, William E., "Agriculture in North America on the Eve of Contact: A Reassessment," *Annals of the Association of American Geographers* 82.3 (1992), pp. 386–401.

Eccles, William J., *The French in North America, 1500–1783*, rev. ed. (East Lansing: Michigan State University Press, 1998).

Elliott, John H., *Empires of the Atlantic World: Britain and Spain in America, 1492–1830* (New Haven, CT: Yale University Press, 2006).

Fabyan, Robert, *Fabyans Cronycle Newly Prynted Wyth the Cronycle, Actes, and Dedes Done in the Tyme of the Reygne of the Moste Excellent Prynce Kynge*

Henry the Vii: Father Vnto Our Most Drad Souerayne Lord Kynge Henry the Viii. To whom be all honour, reuerēce, and ioyfull contynaunce of his prosperous reygne, to the pleasure of god and weale of this his realme amen (London: Wyllyam Rastell, 1533).

Fitzmaurice, Andrew, *Humanism and America: An Intellectual History of English Colonisation* (Cambridge: Cambridge University Press, 2003).

Gilbert, Humphrey, *A Discourse of a Discouerie for a New Passage to Cataia* (London: Henry Middleton, 1576).

Hakluyt, Richard, *Divers Voyages Touching the Discoverie of America and the Ilands Adjacent unto the Same, Made First of All by Our Englishmen and Afterwards by the Frenchmen and Britons: With Two Mappes Annexed Hereunto* (London: Thomas Dawson, 1582).

———, *The Principall Navigations, Voiages and Discoveries of the English Nation, Made by Sea or Ouer Land, to the Most Remote and Farthest Distant Quarters of the Earth at Any Time within the Compasse of These 1500. Yeeres: deuided into three seuerall parts, according to the positions of the Regions wherunto they were directed* (London: George Bishop and Ralph Newberie, 1589).

———, *A Particuler Discourse Concerninge the Greate Necessitie and Manifolde Commodyties That Are Like to Growe to This Realme of Englande by the Westerne Discoueries Lately Attempted, Written in the Yere 1584: Known as Discourse of Western Planting*, eds. David B. Quinn and Alison M. Quinn (London: Hakluyt Society, 1993).

Hatfield House Archives, Hatfield, Cecil Papers, 8/88; 8/93; 10/80; 153/147; and 245/5.

Holinshed, Raphael, *The Firste Volume of the Chronicles of England, Scotlande, and Irelande Conteyning the Description and Chronicles of England, from the First Inhabiting Vnto the Conquest: The Description and Chronicles of Scotland, from the First Original of the Scottes Nation Till the Yeare of Our Lorde 1571: The Description and Chronicles of Yrelande, Likewise from the First Originall of That Nation Untill the Yeare 1571 Faithfully Gathered and Set Forth by Raphaell Holinshed* (London: Iohn Hunne, 1577).

Horn, James, *A Land as God Made It: Jamestown and the Birth of America* (New York: Basic Books, 2005).

———, *A Kingdom Strange: The Brief and Tragic History of the Lost Colony of Roanoke* (New York: Basic Books, 2010).

John Carter Brown Library, Providence, RI: MS Codex Eng 4–2 SIZE; MS Codex Eng 105–1 SIZE; and MS Codex Sp 7–1 SIZE.

Jones, Evan T., "Alwyn Ruddock: 'John Cabot and the Discovery of America'," *Historical Research* 81 (2008), pp. 224–254.

———, "Henry VII and the Bristol Expeditions to North America: The Condon Documents," *Historical Research* 83 (2010), pp. 444–454.

Kelso, William M., *Jamestown: The Buried Truth* (Charlottesville: University of Virginia Press, 2008).

Kirkby, Diane, and Catherine Coleborne, eds., *Law, History, Colonialism: The Reach of Empire* (Manchester: Manchester University Press, 2001).

Krech III, Shepard, *The Ecological Indian: Myth and History* (New York: Norton, 1999).

Lambarde, William, *Archaionomia, siue de priscis anglorum legibus libri sermone Anglico, vetustate antiquissimo, aliquot abhinc seculis conscripti, atq[ue] nunc demum, magno iurisperitorum, & amantium antiquitatis omnium commodo, è tenebris in lucem vocati. Gulielmo Lambardo interprete. Regum qui has leges scripserunt nomenclationem, & quid praeterea accesserit, altera monstrabit pagina* (London: John Day, 1568).

Lane, Kris E., *Pillaging the Empire: Piracy in the Americas, 1500–1750* (Armonk, NY: M.E. Sharpe, 1998).

Linklater, Andro, *Owning the Earth: The Transforming History of Land Ownership* (New York: Bloomsbury Press, 2015).

Llancarfan, Caradoc of, *The Historie of Cambria, Now Called Wales: A Part of the Most Famous Yland of Brytaine, Written in the Brytish Language Aboue Two Hundreth Yeares Past*, ed. David Powel, trans. Humphrey Llwyd (London: Rafe Newberie and Henrie Denham, 1584).

Louis, William Roger, ed., *The Oxford History of the British Empire* (Oxford: Oxford University Press, 1998).

MacMillan, Ken, "John Dee's 'Brytanici Imperii Limites'," *Huntington Library Quarterly* 64 (2001), pp. 151–159.

———, *Sovereignty and Possession in the English New World: The Legal Foundationsof Empire, 1576–1640* (Cambridge: Cambridge University Press, 2006).

Mancall, Peter C., *Hakluyt's Promise: An Elizabethan's Obsession for an English America* (New Haven, CT: Yale University Press, 2007).

Mancke, Elizabeth, and Carole Shammas, eds., *The Creation of the British Atlantic World* (Baltimore, MD: Johns Hopkins University Press, 2005).

Martire d'Anghiera, Pietro, *The Decades of the Newe Worlde or West India, Conteynyng The nauigations and Conquestes of the Spanyardes, with the Particular Description of the Moste Ryche and Large Landes and Ilandes Lately Founde in the West Ocean Perteynyng to the Inheritaunce of the Kinges of Spayne. In the which the diligent reader may not only consyder what commoditie may hereby chaunce to the hole christian world in tyme to come, but also learne many secreates touchynge the lande, the sea, and the starres, very necessarie to be knowẽ to al such as shal attempte any nauigations, or otherwise haue delite to beholde the strange and woonderfull woorkes of God and nature*, trans. Rycharde Eden (London: Guilhelmi Powell, 1555).

———, *The History of Trauayle in the West and East Indies, and Other Countreys Lying Eyther Way, towardes the Fruitfull and Ryche Moluccaes. As Moscouia, Persia, Arabia, Syria, Ægypte, Ethiopia, Guinea, China in Cathayo, and Giapan: With a discourse of the Northwest passage*, ed. Richarde Willes, trans. Richarde Eden (London: Richard Iugge, 1577).

Merbury, Charles, *A Briefe Discovrse of Royall Monarchie, as of the Best Common Weale: Wherin the Subiect May Beholde the Sacred Maiestie of the Princes Most Royall Estate* (London: Thomas Vautrollier, 1581).

Miller, Robert J., Jacinta Ruru, Larissa Behrendt, and Tracey Lindberg, *Discovering Indigenous Lands: The Doctrine of Discovery in the English Colonies* (Oxford: Oxford University Press, 2010).

The National Archives of the United Kingdom, Kew: CO 1/1; State Papers, 12/95; State Papers, 12/175; and State Papers, 94/2.

Transcripts of Selected Documents from Various Archives in Spain. Newberry Library, Chicago, Ayer MS 1236.

Oberg, Michael Leroy, *The Head in Edward Nugent's Hand: Roanoke's Forgotten Indians* (Philadelphia: University of Pennsylvania Press, 2008).

O'Brien, Jean M., *Firsting and Lasting: Writing Indians out of Existence in New England* (Minneapolis: University of Minnesota Press, 2010).
Ogborn, Miles, *Global Lives: Britain and the World, 1550–1800* (New York: Cambridge University Press, 2008).
Ordahl Kupperman, Karen, *Indians and English: Facing Off in Early America* (Ithaca, NY: Cornell University Press, 2000).
———, *The Jamestown Project* (Cambridge, MA: Harvard University Press, 2007).
———, *Roanoke: The Abandoned Colony*, 2nd ed. (Lanham, MD: Rowman & Littlefield, 2007).
———, *The Atlantic in World History* (New York: Oxford University Press, 2012).
Pagden, Anthony, *Lords of All the World: Ideologies of Empire in Spain, Britain and France c. 1500–c. 1800* (New Haven, CT: Yale University Press, 1998).
Parry, Glyn, *The Arch-Conjuror of England: John Dee* (New Haven, CT: Yale University Press, 2011).
Peckham, George, *A Trve Reporte, of the Late Discoueries, and Possession, Taken in the Right of the Crowne of Englande, of the Newfound Landes: By That Valiaunt and Worthye Gentleman, Sir Humfrey Gilbert Knight. Wherein is also breefely sette downe, her highnesse lawfull Tytle therevnto, and the great and manifolde Commodities, that is likely to grow thereby, to the whole Realme in generall, and to the Aduenturers in particular. Together with the easines and shortnes of the Voyage. Seene and allowed* (London: John Charlewood, 1583).
Pope, Peter E., *Fish into Wine: The Newfoundland Plantation in the Seventeenth Century* (Chapel Hill: University of North Carolina Press, 2004).
Probasco, Nate, "Elizabeth I, Sir Humphrey Gilbert, and the Anglo-Spanish Conflict," *Explorations in Renaissance Culture* 37 (2011), pp. 119–135.
———, "Virgin America for Barren England: English Colonial History and Literature, 1575–1635," *Literature Compass* 9.6 (2012), pp. 406–419.
Quinn, David B., *The Voyages and Colonising Enterprises of Sir Humphrey Gilbert* (London: Hakluyt Society, 1940).
———, ed., *The Roanoke Voyages 1584–1590* (London: Hakluyt Society, 1955).
Quinn, David B., Alison M. Quinn, and Susan Hillier, eds., *New American World: A Documentary History of North America to 1612* (New York: Arno Press, 1979).
Roberts, Julian, and Andrew W. Watson, eds., *John Dee's Library Catalogue* (London: Bibliographical Society, 1990).
———, "*John Dee's Library Catalogue*: Additions and Corrections, November 2009," www.bibsoc.org.uk/sites/www.bibsoc.org.uk/files/John%20Dee%27s%20Library%20Catalogue%204.pdf
Seaver, Kirsten A., "Norumbega and 'Harmonia Mundi' in Sixteenth-Century Cartography," *Imago Mundi* 50 (1998), pp. 34–58.
Seed, Patricia, *Ceremonies of Possession in Europe's Conquest of the New World, 1492–1640* (Cambridge: Cambridge University Press, 1995).
———, *American Pentimento: The Invention of Indians and the Pursuit of Riches* (Minneapolis: University of Minnesota Press, 2001).
Sherman, William H., *Used Books: Marking Readers in Renaissance England* (Philadelphia: University of Pennsylvania Press, 2008).

Tazón, Juan E., *The Life and Times of Thomas Stukeley (c. 1525–78)* (Aldershot, UK: Ashgate, 2003).

Tomlins, Christopher, *Freedom Bound: Law, Labor, and Civic Identity in Colonizing English America, 1580–1865* (New York: Cambridge University Press, 2010).

Weber, David J., *The Spanish Frontier in North America* (New Haven, CT: Yale University Press, 1992).

Williams, Gwyn, *Madoc: The Making of a Myth* (London: Eyre Methuen, 1979).

Wright, Jr., J. Leitch, *Anglo-Spanish Rivalry in North America* (Athens: University of Georgia Press, 1971).

Wroth, Lawrence C., *The Voyages of Giovanni da Verrazzano, 1524–1528* (New Haven, CT: Yale University Press for Pierpont Morgan Library, 1970).

2 The Last of the First? Madness and the Jungle in the Chronicles of the Indies

Lope de Aguirre and His Writing

Manuel Lucena Giraldo

Madness and the jungle in the Spanish-American imaginary are one and the same. Even today, there is an expression commonly used in the tropical countries, namely that "he was swallowed up by the forest" (se lo tragó la selva). The expression conveys the sensation experienced by people in their minds and in their bodies when they visit the tropical forest. Someone's disappearance in the jungle arouses a shared sense of inevitability, as if a fatal destiny proscribed by the act of entering the jungle has been fulfilled. In this sense, literary and historical tradition make madness and disappearance essential elements of a single experience that is mapped onto a concrete geography. People enter the forest, become mad, and disappear.

Is there a cultural and historical explanation for such attitudes and popular traditions? The literature arising from the first European arrivals and their so-called discovery and conquest of the Americas contains some important clues to help us answer this question. The equation of madness and the experience of the forest no doubt came from the classical tradition and was later grafted by Europeans onto the New World, providing the necessary ingredients for this mythical geography of disappearance. This characterization of the New World can be detected in the early chronicles of the Indies: from Columbus's widely read and cited writings about his voyages and explorations, Hernan Cortés's five "Letters of Relation" about the conquest of Mexico explaining and asking for compensation, and Pietro Martire d'Anghiera's *De orbe novo* (1530), to Pedro Cieza de León's narration of the conquest of Peru and the origins of the Incas (1553).[1]

During the first period of contact, after 1492 and before the conquest of Mexico, the idea abounded that the European discoveries of so-called new lands and kingdoms were providential. Between 1519 and 1521, however, some narratives (no doubt promoted by Cortés) began to move away from the writing modes adopted by Columbus and which were deeply rooted in medieval maritime discursive models. After the fall of Tenochtitlan, a new renaissance-style of narrative emerged, one based on the ideas of colonization, the foundation of cities, the segregation of Indians into their so-called "republics" away from the cities and towns inhabited by their Spanish overlords, and where conquistadors expressed their belief that they deserved a reward for gaining such wealthy, fruitful, and enormous kingdoms in the name of their Catholic emperor. This second period was over by 1550 following years of civil war in Peru between conquistadors. Consequently, further colonization incentivized by the promise of benefits for the would-be conquistador was ruled out. The result was that the restless and turbulent conquistadors, particularly in Peru and Chile, had little else to do but complain about the behavior of royal officers and authorities, as well as "the ingratitude of the emperor of Spain."[2] It was in this atmosphere of despair and anachronism that Lope de Aguirre's history of the Americas suddenly appeared. Basque-born Aguirre (c. 1511–1561), characterized as "the pilgrim" and "the mad," took part in a bloody expedition to conquer El Dorado from 1560 to 1561. Historical facts relating to this period also became obscured by a moral and menacing *post factum* fiction. The narrative of Aguirre's madness, killings, and subsequent punishment constituted a remarkable example of the misfortunes that awaited late and mutinous conquistadors, especially given the geographical context for the place where he lost his mind. At the same time, his death signaled a new era. He was the last of the first: a conquistador out of time and place.

At about 50 years of age when he initiated his expedition in 1560, Aguirre had spent a lot of his life in Peru, New Granada, and Central America. He participated in several expeditions or "entradas" as a soldier of fortune; he made his living by killing, looting, and plotting against the masters of different "huestes" or groups of conquistadors that he encountered along his path.[3] After such a long career of violence, it seems clear from sources about his life that Aguirre could not be considered sane when he was readying himself for what would become his last expedition, when he left Peru to pursue El Dorado's mythical wealth in the region of the Amazon River. He was no doubt seeking revenge after years of humiliation and perceived ingratitude, and he realized too well that he was aging and growing infirm yet remained without the compensation that he felt he deserved from the king and his appointed officials in the New World. Aguirre complained that individuals such as himself undertook great risk and experienced misfortune in the pursuits of discovery and conquest without recompense, and he felt victimized. Complicating matters was a policy created by the crown that limited the inheritance structure whereby lands as well as natives who lived in labor camps or settlements (*encomiendas*) could no longer pass from a Spanish father to his son nor from a conquistador to his family.[4]

The chronicles' documentation of Aguirre's mutinous character almost foretold what would befall him later in life, and while the events he experienced as a rebel occurred in the region of the Amazon River, they began in Lima. Counting himself among the landed nobility, Pedro de Ursúa (1526–1561), according to his version of events, was a good and honest captain from Navarre who was betrayed and killed by Aguirre at the start of the latter man's rise to power. It was from Lima that Ursúa began the last journey of his life. As Aguirre explains to us, Ursúa lost touch with reality after leaving Lima and during this final expedition into the jungle; he blamed this madness on the supposed witchcraft wielded by Ursúa's manipulative, mixed-race lover, Doña Inés de Atienza.[5] This narrative posturing is essential for understanding how the chronicles contrasted urban spaces against those that lay outside of urbanity, including the forest, which become idealized settings for both crime and insanity. During the transition from conquest to colonization in the sixteenth century, Spaniards struggled with the need to stabilize cities and urban life, which became core components of colonization, and what lay outside of Spanish settlements, for instance the Amazonian region, was viewed as dangerous and harmful. By the seventeenth century, narratives commonly inscribed madness along the frontiers of Spanish colonial geographies in ways that echo the central plot of Aguirre's search for El Dorado. Another consideration is the appearance of the *Ordenanzas de descubrimiento, nueva población y pacificación de las Indias dadas por Felipe II* in 1573.[6] This series of new laws impacted the ways in which Spanish-American cities were viewed, regulated, and managed. The rule of law and royal permission would be the only means through which settlements could be founded. Foundational cities metamorphosed into providential metropoles upheld as republics of civic virtue that promised wealth and health for Spanish-American creoles (people of Spanish origin, but born and raised in the Americas, as opposed to the *peninsulares*, the people born and raised in Spain who later immigrated to the New World).

Spanish colonial society would always retain its urban, as opposed to natural, character.[7] Outside of these cities stretched the vast frontier of the New World, and the tropical forest was undoubtedly the most extreme human and natural frontier that could be imagined in that context. Many of the frontier narratives emanating from Spanish America were indebted to and inspired by the expedition by Pedro de Ursúa and Lope de Aguirre to El Dorado. Importantly, after 1600, these expeditions could no longer be conceived of as episodes of conquest, but rather as tales of Spanish captivity (some of them related by or about women) in the hands of so-called savage peoples. That was how the tropical forest, madness, and disappearance became inextricably unified through a style of chronicling that emerged in the original stages of conquest; yet, and as we will see, these qualities later came to redefine the mental landscape of an entire continent.[8]

At the beginning of 1493, Columbus prepared a letter to the Catholic kings explaining his arrival in the Indies:

> And, generally, in whatever lands I travelled, they believed and believe that I, together with these ships and people, came from heaven, and they greeted me with such veneration [. . .] upon arriving at whatever settlement, the men, women and children go from house to house calling out, "come, come and see the people from heaven."[9]

The meaning of his account was clear to European eyes. At the moment of his arrival, Columbus claimed to have secured the spontaneous obedience of the Indians. His account is a good example of the early-modern use of rhetorical language; it was and remains a powerful tool for the recognition and activation of the experience of conquest. At the same time, his rhetoric served the new imperial order in that this form of expression was also a means "to demonstrate that their presence had brought a new and final authority" in the form of Europeans.[10]

The implementation of a narrative of discovery vindicated European preeminence, but it also embodied a classification of men and nature that was ethnocentric and selective, and that favored Europeans. The purpose of this framing has been established by scholars in recent decades: to delineate and fabricate a whole new world.[11] After the people of this New World and their nature were conceived, narrated, named, and possessed, they became encompassed by a territory belonging forever to the western world.[12] Importantly, the existence of extraordinary elements in both men and nature (especially in the tropics) has been characterized by Stephen Greenblatt as a register comprised of European claims about the real and wonderful, which went on to become a *tropo* or trope. Thus, we see the etymological link underlining the characterization of the tropics as a place of wonder, and of trope as a discursive mode.[13] Much scholarship has been produced about the effects of the discovery of the Americas on what then passed for some form of received wisdom, as well as the increasing value within the western world of first-hand experience. But, we must also remember that discovery narratives emanate above all from a moment of confusion occasioned by a lack of knowledge about the place, people, or thing encountered. This reality made room for madness fueled by a lack of awareness and knowledge during the moment in which discovery occurred, and as the example of Ursúa's death by his mixed-blood sorceress-lover demonstrates, the condition of madness could involve an evil presence, perhaps even a gap in the memory, a hypnotic experience, and the incapacity to express that which was being witnessed.

There are other sources for this view that discovery could occasion both madness and wonder, and western readers were familiar with how authors, narrators, and characters reached out to readers for their understanding and sympathy when they struggled to relate what they had witnessed and experienced. *Captatio benevolentiae* is a classic rhetorical strategy designed to obtain kindness from the reader, and it could also be heard throughout European cities in publicly shared chronicles and tales of discovery and exploration. As the wonders of the New World manifested themselves before European eyes, silence protected the human mind from insanity and prevented it from losing the language and the meaning of words. Amerigo Vespucci (1454–1512) pointed out in one of his most famous letters written to Lorenzo di Pierfrancesco de Medici (1463–1503), and after proclaiming that during his exploration of the New World he believed that he was so near to the terrestrial paradise, that "I did not want to go on at this point for longer, because I doubt you will believe me."[14] As a result, if silence protected against madness and also one's response to wonder, which characterizes a world without the order and meaning of words, silence also served as a proclamation of the language of conquest as well as foretold the transition from contact to permanent presence.

Early in 1504, a young Hernán Cortés (1485–1547) departed for the Indies. He spent the ensuing years in Santo Domingo and Cuba, turning himself into a *baquiano*, somebody who survived the *baquía* or tropical fever, which was a rite of passage experienced by Europeans during their adaptation to life in the tropics. By 1519, when he initiated the invasion of Mexico, the European colonization of the Americas was at a turning point. After two decades of discoveries, the foundation of trading posts, and the occupation of the Antilles—all completed somewhat in the tradition of the Portuguese maritime expansion into Africa—rumors about the existence of wealthy and powerful empires on the American continent were rife. But, as providentialism was the official explanation for Spanish imperial expansion, individual initiatives by the likes of Cortés did not marry well with the measure of legality imposed by the monarchy or the will of God or the pope's rulings expressed through papal bulls—these three sources of authority being important allies in the justification and execution of Spanish expansion into the Americas. Cortés managed to find a way to use these models of authority despite his ignoring the instructions given to him by Diego Velázquez (1465–1524), governor of Cuba. Cortés made himself into a supreme local authority by founding the coastal city of Veracruz in 1519 (following his own instructions, of course), and the *cabildo* or town hall, which he quickly created for the town, then elected him its ruler.[15] Beyond describing this important moment in the conquest of the Aztecs, Cortés's first letter, which was widely published and translated in Europe, also marked a new stage in the development of the conquest narrative. Cortés's letters establish his self-portrait as a hero.[16] Nonetheless, as Cortés was a man of letters, and known as a *letrado*, he was deeply rooted in the classical and humanist traditions. From this perspective, the beauty and teachings to be learned from history came by loving the truth. Cortés was not only a writer, but also a witness of first-sighting. He possessed the typical education of an Extremaduran *hidalgo*, was trained in law, and possessed knowledge of the medieval romances, histories, and the lives of saints; he was also a man of the renaissance who tried to control his fate by being clever and talented, which is what Machiavelli meant by *virtu*.[17] The tradition established by Cortés, and which enabled him to be successful and well-compensated despite authorities' appetite for the contrary, became the same means through which Lope de Aguirre justified his own rebellious behavior in a letter to Philip II in 1561.

In accordance with his position as a conquistador and a letrado, which ensured that he commanded both arms and words, Cortés positioned his actions as necessary and fair. Even if he was acting temporarily against the laws of the crown and the orders he received from the governor of Cuba, Cortés presented his decisions at that time as being of urgent necessity in the service of the emperor. Each of his five letters mixed together the arts of letter writing and of formulating a legally valid declaration following Castilian judicial custom. They not only explained events but also provided a model of formulating the truth that eschewed the device of silence found in earlier works, such as those of Vespucci. Cortés knew too well that veracity was an impression based upon textual authority and direct observation. But this change in the narrative model undermined the possibility of using or even imagining that silence could rescue the conquistador's mind from fear and unrest. Unlike Vespucci, there was no silence in Cortés's written accounts, and of course there was no danger or hint of madness in his behavior, at least not according to his own narratives. Instead, he described a blunt reality using appropriate language for the period, plausible analogics, and descriptions of heroism, while claiming to be fulfilling a destiny. His narrative tone was about colonization, not discovery. Cortés's writing provided contemporaries with a narrative that characterized the model conqueror, somebody who never under any circumstance could confess that he was losing his command: that is, his command of words and his ability to share his exploits in textual form.

As Columbus's accounts of his discoveries became anachronistic by the 1520s, Cortés's conquistador model in turn became obsolete by 1550, and Lope de Aguirre's vindication of his services and heroism condemned to marginality. At that time, the myth of El Dorado itself was in crisis. The earliest references to El Dorado appear in 1534, but the complete mythology emerges from its chrysalis after three veteran conquistadors go in search of another Peru. The expedition was commanded by Nicolás de Federmann (c. 1505–1542), Sebastián de Belalcázar (1480–1551), and Gonzalo Jiménez de Quesada (1509–1579), and they explored the surroundings of what is now Bogota. In fact, the city's founding in 1538 was justified by the need to search the lake where a native ceremony was performed. According to stories shared with these European explorers by

Indigenous informants, an Indian chief or *cacique* covered his naked body from head to toe with fine gold powder and proceeded to make offerings and sacrifices in the middle of the lake by throwing gold pieces and emeralds into the water. In 1539, Belalcázar used the name El Dorado for the first time to refer to a province "with great tales of gold and stones," possibly a reference to the Golden Quersonesus from Antiquity, but evidently without reference to the cacique and the ceremony.[18]

Following the subsequent expeditions conducted by Hernán Pérez de Quesada (c. 1500–1544), Gonzalo Pizarro (c. 1510–1548), and Felipe de Hutten (1505–1546), some elements of the El Dorado myth transferred from the Andes to the Orinoco and Amazon regions, impacting the imaginary representation of the continent for centuries. Moreover, the arrival of Pedro de la Gasca (1493–1567) in Peru and the victory of the loyalists over the rebels in their contest for the viceroyalty, established the king of Spain and his designate viceroy as the sole authority of the region. Active dissatisfaction nonetheless stemmed from the frustration felt by several generations of conquistadors and was mounting as they gradually lost any hope of seeing their expected remuneration materialize.[19] Because generations of conquistadors had been required to follow royal, legal, and papal orders to colonize—and certainly this entailed leaving behind the vestiges of Spanish control—any rebellion met with harsh punishment by royal authorities. After 1548, Pizarro was beheaded in Peru; Francisco de Carvajal (1464–1548) was drawn and quartered; and some of their companions were hanged. In Panama, a land that Aguirre knew well, the rebel Hernando de Contreras (d. 1550) had defied royal rule and proclaimed himself "Captain General of Liberty" in 1550.[20] After capturing the colony's capitol and killing the bishop, Antonio de Valdivieso (1495–1550), Contreras escaped with his brother Pedro to the forest, where an alligator supposedly devoured him. Another infamous rebel, Francisco Hernández Girón (c. 1510–1554), was executed in Lima in 1554.

Sending these frustrated, old, and angry conquistadors on missions of discovery and exploration along the frontiers of Peru could resemble at first glance a solution to the violence and the instability of royal authority: the removal of men who were violent and opposed royal rule from the colonial realm. By the mid-sixteenth century, conquests of the sort undertaken by Cortés and pure violence were no longer acceptable in the view of readers as well as officials in the Americas and in Europe.[21] The timing for Aguirre's tale to unfold ensured that his crimes and unnatural behavior engender the typology of the mad conquistador who was pathetically backward in his ways and thus anachronistic. For some scholars, Aguirre's life and deeds nonetheless became a precedent for Simón Bolívar (1783–1830) and the Spanish-American independence movement, as well as Basque nationalism; they all rejected royal authority and, as we will see, sought denaturalization as the solution for their dissatisfaction. For others, however, Aguirre remained an archaic and medieval figure, a tyrant, madman, and criminal, and non-Spanish perceptions of conquistadors reinforce these associations.[22] But what can be said about Aguirre's own vocalization of his rebellion spurred by his perception of the king's ingratitude, and of his pilgrimage away from colonized space, in addition to his attempts to justify his actions as retribution for a series of injustices, the disappearance of his dreams, and decades of bodily pain and harsh living conditions?

Several narrative accounts provide insight into Ursúa's expedition and Aguirre's rebellion, including the latter man's death, which occurred after Aguirre killed his own mixed-race daughter, Elvira, in the Venezuelan city of Barquisimeto 27 October 1561. Again, associating mixed-bloodedness with the devil and believing himself in part the carrier of devil's spawn, the reason Aguirre gives for killing his daughter is "to avoid her turning into the whore of all of them."[23] Some accounts come from witnesses such as the soldiers and companions of Aguirre, who served Ursúa and then Aguirre either freely of their own accord or out of fear. These individuals include Gonzálo de Zúñiga, Pedro de Munguía, Francisco Vásquez (1510–1554), Pedrarias de Almesto (c. 1540–?), Custodio Hernández, and Juan Vargas Zapata. There is another account by an unknown author as well as some second-hand accounts written sometime after the events by historians Diego de Aguilar y Córdoba (c. 1546–1631; produced in 1578) and Toribio de Ortiguera (produced in 1585–1586), in addition to romances, letters, and judiciary reports.[24]

Even if the more famous material evidence from Aguirre's time in the Americas is a much-debated flag preserved in Barquisimeto and emblazoned with the Spanish word "sigo" (I follow), the most important textual evidence is the letter he wrote to Philip II on 23 March 1561. In it, Aguirre forwards many arguments in favor of his rebellion and through which some hints of his madness can be detected.[25] The letter shows how, like Cortés, Aguirre was deeply concerned about his image and no doubt he felt he was caught up in a war of propaganda. His narrative model followed that of the *memorial de agravios* (memoir of grievances) in the form of an epistle. Importantly, Aguirre declares, in addition to his rebellion against the Spanish king, his intention to denaturalize from the Spanish empire and to seek personal sovereignty in Peru:

> I and my companions (whose names I will give later), unable to suffer further the cruelties of your judges, viceroy, and governors, have resolved to obey you no longer. Denaturalizing ourselves from our land, Spain, we make the most cruel war against you that our power can sustain and endure.[26]

In some ways, this goal to denaturalize could be considered a symptom of his madness. In other ways, Aguirre's rejection of the entire project of American discovery and colonization paved pathways for a radically new way of viewing the Spanish Americas. He broke with the traditional complaint narrative that had become paired with the negotiation of loyalty in exchange for mercy and wealth. According to Aguirre, the king's priests and royal officers had stolen the hard-won New World from the conquistadors; their friends and relatives benefited from the unpaid loyalty of good vassals such as Aguirre; without people like him, Aguirre blatantly states, the king would have nothing: "King of Spain, your government is just air and wind."[27]

Aguirre's vision of the Americas was not the utopia that religious minds had fondly imagined at first, but quite the opposite. Aguirre's belief that he was living in a dystopia not only shows the state of mind belonging to this generation of defeated Spanish (and creole, sometimes African) conquistadors, it also marks a reorientation of the narrative trajectory expressed in the chronicles of the Indies. This view paved the way for the invention of the New World and particularly the Amazon and the frontiers in general as a landscape without hope:

> We went along our route down the Marañón river while all these killings and bad events were taking place. It took us ten and a half months to reach the mouth of the river, where it enters the sea. We travelled a good hundred days and travelled 1,500 leagues. It is a large and fearsome river, with 80 leagues of fresh water at the mouth. It is very deep, and for 800 leagues along its banks it is deserted, with no towns, as your majesty will see from the true report we have made. Along the route we took there are more than 6,000 islands. God only knows how we escaped from such a fearsome lake! I advise you, King and lord, not to attempt nor allow a fleet to be sent to this ill-fated river, because in Christian faith I swear, King and lord, that if a hundred thousand men come none will escape, because the stories are false and in this river there is nothing but despair, especially for those newly arrived from Spain.[28]

Aguirre's words hint at his mind's loosening on reality in some ways, but it is also important to read the letter in the context of the textual tradition in which it is embedded. The chronicle of Francisco Vázquez, for example, focuses on Aguirre's behavior during the expedition, the killing of Ursúa, the proclamation of Fernando de Guzmán as a "prince of Tierra Firme and Peru," and his subsequent murder.[29] The letter in this light appears self-incriminating and proof of Aguirre's insanity and betrayal. Of course, the judiciary and accusatory accounts systematically denounce and demonize Aguirre forever as far as the condemnation of his memory and fame were concerned. According to a judgement given and read in public in Tocuyo at the end of 1561, "his legitimate or bastard sons [would be] ashamed forever as sons of a tyrant and traitor father."[30]

This last act of dehumanization was matched by Aguirre's admission that he had killed several of his companions, including "the new king:"

> They appointed me their field commander, and because I did not consent to their insults and evil deeds they tried to kill me, and I killed the new king, the captain of his guard, the lieutenant-general, his majordomo, his chaplain, a woman in league against me, a knight of Rhodes, an admiral, two ensigns, and six other of his allies. It was my intention to carry this war through and die in it, for the cruelties your ministers practice on us, and I again appointed captains and a sergeant major. They tried to kill me, and I hung them all.[31]

This account could be considered ultimate proof of Aguirre's madness, and the last episode of Aguirre's life became much-publicized as such. Contradictory versions of what happened circulated during the time, not the least which can be found in Walter Raleigh's influential *The discoverie of the Large, Rich and Bewtiful Empyre of Guiana* (1596), and much later in Robert Southey's *The Expedition of Orsua: and the Crimes of Aguirre* (1821).[32] If a rebellion against the king of Spain, the killing of priests, and doubts about the existence of God were inconceivable, the murder of his own daughter by stabbing shortly before being killed himself by soldiers offered a perennial image of Aguirre's insanity. Even more important, it was that image and the abandonment of his soldiers or *marañones* while being possessed in the jungle by some evil force that later inspired José Oviedo y Baños (1671–1738), the author of the foundational creole narrative of the province of Venezuela in 1721.[33]

The tale of Lope de Aguirre's mad behavior and his judicial punishment through decapitation, quartering, and being thrown to the dogs were incorporated into the overarching discovery and conquest narrative. In tandem, a new political impulse emerged shortly after his death that gave rise to the reorganization of the Council of the Indies in 1571, the foundation of more cities, and the militarization of colonial frontiers. Aguirre's premonition that nothing but danger could be expected from the Amazon was widely publicized up to, during, and after the wars of independence. A literary trope of the period infected primary sources about the Spanish Americas so that an association between the jungle, madness, and disappearance contrasted with the ideal of being in a city, of good mental and physical health, and the assertion of claims to possession that both invented and took up space.

Despite the man's madness and Aguirre's contravention of the laws of his time, moreover, the seventeenth-century Spanish-American frontier experience made room for narratives of a different sort. The experience of captivity in the jungle dovetailed with the experience of utopia. This trope overcame the negative feelings associated with captivity and envisioned a return to the western world through some transition from another culture (either Indian or even African) to rejoin (whether sane or insane) the western world. Fray Juan Falcón de los Ángeles, himself a captive in Chile, wrote about the captivity of Spanish women. If they were to have children with Indians, he believed they certainly would secretly teach them to be Christians. And Francisco Núñez de Pineda (1607–1682) detailed in his *Cautiverio feliz* (1683) the happiness that he experienced when he lived with the Indigenous peoples from Arauco, though he suffered the effects of war and human sacrifice as well.[34] The tale of Lope de Aguirre's madness was rooted in the myth and tragedy of first encounters and grew to become an official narrative as well as an example of moral awareness.

As a creole tradition, nevertheless, the proclamation by first arrivals about rewards and compensation for service rendered were never forgotten. As was seen elsewhere in the Americas, for instance in the United States in 1776, the justification to launch a rebellion against the European colonizer grew and, in due course, these colonies declared independence. Read another way, this model for independence rests upon the same demand to restore liberty expressed by conquistadores such as Aguirre, making them the founding fathers of still-unborn creole nations. The disappearance of conquistadors is another consideration, as by the mid-sixteenth century that typology of soldiering was no longer tolerated, nor were the benefits that in the past had motivated individuals to enter this profession. These changes to social and economic policies and values ultimately resulted in unseating individuals who had previously claimed to be the first to have discovered areas of the Americas.

Notes

1. Amodio, "El oro de los caníbales," p. 96. Unless otherwise noted, all translations are my own.
2. By then, "the number of lazy and unemployed people numbered several thousand;" see Lastres and Seguín, *Lope de Aguirre, el rebelde*, p. 25.
3. Nevertheless, Aguirre remained loyal to the crown in the most dangerous rebellions in Peru, those of Gonzalo Pizarro and Hernández Girón. See Ramos, "Lope de Aguirre en Cartagena y su primera rebelión," p. 514.
4. For more on how these policies impacted *encomenderos*, see Himmerich y Valencia, *The* Encomenderos *of New Spain*.
5. "Doña Inés, his friend, had him bewitched and had changed his carácter;" see Toribio de Ortiguera, "Jornada del Río Marañón, con todo lo acaecido en ella, y otras cosas notables dignas de ser sabidas, acaecidas en las islas occidentales," in Maspell González and Escandell Tour, eds., *Lope de Aguirre*, pp. 31–174: 68; and Pastor and Callau, eds., *Lope de Aguirre y la rebelión de los marañones*, p. 460. This last work includes an updated edition and a brilliant interpretation based on three narrative moments: discovery, misfortune, and disintegration. Also see Galster, *Aguirre o la posteridad arbitraria*, p. 8.
6. For an English language translation of these laws, see Tyler, *Spanish Laws Concerning Discoveries*.
7. Elliott, *Empires of the Atlantic World*, p. 43.

8. "The discovery and its discourse continued for decades, even centuries, after Columbus, as Las Casas' treatment of the Columbian texts illustrates;" see Zamora, *Reading Columbus*, p. 7.
9. Sanz, ed., *La carta de Colón*, p. 18.
10. Bitterli, *Cultures in Conflict*, p. 23.
11. See, for example, O'Gorman, *The Invention of America.*
12. Pagden, *European Encounters with the New World*, p. 35.
13. Greenblatt, *Marvelous Possessions*, p. 17.
14. Sara Castro-Klarén, "Mímesis en los trópicos: el cuerpo en Vespucci y Léry," in García Castañeda, ed., *Literatura de viajes*, pp. 31–38: 34.
15. Restall, *Seven Myths of the Spanish Conquest*, p. 49.
16. Pastor, *The Armature of Conquest*, p. 81.
17. Elliott, *España y su mundo*, p. 59.
18. Gil, *Mitos y utopías: El Dorado*, p. 66.
19. Pastor, *The Armature of Conquest*, p. 172.
20. For more on this period, see Contreras y López de Ayala Lozoya, *Vida del segoviano Rodrigo de Contreras.*
21. Iwasaki Cauti, "Conquistadores o grupos marginales," p. 234.
22. For such extreme classical positions, see Ispízua, *Historia de los vascos en el descubrimiento*, p. 428; and Jos, *La expedición de Ursúa al Dorado*, p. 296.
23. Armas, "Lope de Aguirre," p. 144.
24. Barba, *Historiografía indiana*, pp. 409–416. For Zúñiga, Ortiguera, Munguía, Hernández, Vázquez, and Almesto, the anonymous account, and other related material, see Maspell González and Escandell Tour, eds., *Lope de Aguirre.* Also see Lohmann Villena, "'El Marañón' de Diego de Aguilar y Córdoba," p. 275.
25. Two other notable letters include "Carta al padre Montesinos por Lope de Aguirre," and "Carta de Aguirre a Pablo Collado, gobernador de Venezuela," in Maspell González and Escandell Tour, eds., *Lope de Aguirre*, pp. 285–287.
26. "Carta de Lope de Aguirre a Felipe II" (23 February 1561), in Rosa Arciniega, *Dos rebeldes españoles en el Perú*, pp. 386–392: 387.
27. "Carta de Lope de Aguirre a Felipe II," p. 390.
28. Ibid., p. 391.
29. Maspell González and Escandell Tour, eds., *Lope de Aguirre*, pp. 201–271.
30. "Sentencia de Bernáldez contra la memoria y fama de Aguirre," Tocuyo, 16 December 1561, in Maspell González and Escandell Tour, eds., *Lope de Aguirre*, pp. 285–287.
31. "Carta de Lope de Aguirre a Felipe II," p. 391.
32. "This Pedro de Osua had among his troupes a Byscain called Agiri [. . .] this Agiri raised a muteny [. . .] in a fight in the said Nuevo reygno he was overthrowne, & finding no way to escape;" see Raleigh, *The discoverie of the Large, Rich and Bewtiful Empyre of Guiana*, pp. 142–143. A recent edition in Spanish of Southey's work contains a prologue by Pere Gimferrer and features a translation by Soledad Martínez de Pinillos; see *La expedición de Ursúa y los crímenes de Aguirre* (Madrid: Reino de Redonda, 2010), p. 200.
33. Oviedo y Baños, *Los Belzares*, p. 298. His *Historia de la conquista y población de Venezuela* was first published in 1721. For other literary works inspired by Lope de Aguirre, see especially Ramón J. Sender, *La aventura equinoccial de Lope de Aguirre* (1964); Arturo Uslar Pietri, *El camino de El Dorado* (1947); and Miguel Otero Silva, *Lope de Aguirre, príncipe de la libertad* (1979). Also see Gnutzmann, "Un ejemplo de recepción literaria," pp. 111–128; Barrientos, "Aguirre y la rebelión de los marañones," pp. 98–115; and Zandanel, *Los procesos de ficcionalización*, p. 394.
34. Operé, *Historias de la frontera*, pp. 71–79.

Bibliography

Amodio, Emanuele, "El oro de los caníbales: geografía y habitantes míticos del Nuevo Mundoen los textos de Cristóbal Colón," *Antropológica* 75/76 (1991), pp. 93–125.

Arciniega, Rosa, *Dos rebeldes españoles en el Perú: Gonzalo Pizarro ("el gran rebelde") y Lope de Aguirre ("el cruel tirano")* (Buenos Aires: Editorial Suramericana, 1946).

Armas, Ingrid de, "Lope de Aguirre. El doble mito: tirano o príncipe de la libertad," *Cahiers du CRICCAL* 3.1 (1988), pp. 141–169.

Barba, Francisco Esteve, *Historiografía indiana* (Madrid: Editorial Gredos, 1992).

Barrientos, Juan José, "Aguirre y la rebelión de los marañones," *Cuadernos americanos* 11.2 (1988), pp. 98–115.

Bitterli, Urs, *Cultures in Conflict: Encounters between European and Non-European Cultures, 1492–1800* (Stanford, CA: Stanford University Press, 1989).

Contreras y López de Ayala Lozoya, Juan de, *Vida del segoviano Rodrigo de Contreras: Gobernador de Nicaragua (1534–1544)* (Toledo: Editorial Católica Toledana, 1920).

Elliott, John H., *España y su mundo, 1500–1700* (Madrid: Alianza Editorial, 1991).

———, *Empires of the Atlantic World: Britain and Spain in America, 1492–1830* (New Haven, CT: Yale University Press, 2006).

Galster, Ingrid, *Aguirre o la posteridad arbitraria* (Bogota: Editorial Universidad del Rosario and Editorial Pontificia Universidad Javeriana, 2011).

García Castañeda, Salvador, ed., *Literatura de viajes. El Viejo Mundo y el Nuevo* (Madrid: Editorial Castalia and Ohio State University, 1999).

Gil, Juan, *Mitos y utopías del descubrimiento*, vol. 3: *El Dorado* (Madrid: Alianza Editorial, 1989).

Gnutzmann, Rita, "Un ejemplo de recepción literaria: Lope de Aguirre recreado por Ramón J. Sender y M. Otero Silva," *Revista de Literatura* 50.99 (1988), pp. 111–128.

Greenblatt, Stephen, *Marvelous Possessions: The Wonder of the New World* (Chicago: University of Chicago Press, 1991).

Himmerich y Valencia, Robert, *The Encomenderos of New Spain, 1521–1555* (Austin: University of Texas Press, 1991).

Ispízua, Segundo de, *Historia de los vascos en el descubrimiento, conquista y civilización de América*, vol. 4: *Venezuela*, vol. 5: *Lope de Aguirre* (Madrid: Gráficas Mateu, 1918).

Iwasaki Cauti, Fernando, "Conquistadores o grupos marginales. Dinámica social del proceso de conquista," *Anuario de Estudios Americanos* 42 (1985), pp. 217–242.

Jos, Emiliano, *La expedición de Ursúa al Dorado, la rebelión de Lope de Aguirre y el itinerario de los marañones* (Huesca: Talleres Gráficos Editorial V. Campo, 1927).

Lastres, Juan B., and Carlos Alberto Seguín, *Lope de Aguirre, el rebelde. Estudio histórico-psicológico* (Buenos Aires: El Ateneo, 1942).

Lohmann Villena, Guillermo, "'El Marañón' de Diego de Aguilar y Córdoba," *Revista de Indias* 7.24 (1946), pp. 271–302.

Maspell González, Elena, and Neus Escandell Tour, eds., *Lope de Aguirre. Crónicas, 1559–1561* (Barcelona: Universitat de Barcelona, 1981).
O'Gorman, Edmundo, *The Invention of America* (Westport, CT: Greenwood Press, 1977).
Operé, Fernando, *Historias de la frontera. El cautiverio en la América hispánica* (Mexico City: FCE, 2001).
Oviedo y Baños, José de, *Los Belzares. El tirano Aguirre. Diego de Losada* (Caracas: Monte Ávila, 1972).
Pagden, Anthony, *European Encounters with the New World: From Renaissance to Romanticism* (New Haven, CT: Yale University Press, 1993).
Pastor, Beatriz Bodmer, *The Armature of Conquest: Spanish Accounts of the Discovery of America, 1492–1589*, trans. Lydia Longstreth Hunt (Stanford, CA: Stanford University Press, 1992).
Pastor, Beatriz Bodmer, and Sergio Callau, eds., *Lope de Aguirre y la rebelión de los marañones* (Madrid: Castalia, 2011).
Raleigh, Walter, *The Discoverie of the Large, Rich and Bewtiful Empyre of Guiana*, ed. Neil L. Whitehead (Norman: University of Oklahoma Press, 1997).
Ramos, Demetrio, "Lope de Aguirre en Cartagena y su primera rebelión," *Revista de Indias* 18 (1958), pp. 511–540.
Restall, Matthew, *Seven Myths of the Spanish Conquest* (Oxford: Oxford University Press, 2004).
Sanz, Carlos, ed., *La carta de Colón anunciando el descubrimiento del Nuevo Mundo, 15 febrero-14 marzo 1493* (Madrid: Hauser y Menet, 1956).
Tyler, S. Lyman, *Spanish Laws Concerning Discoveries, Pacifications, and Settlements among the Indians* (Salt Lake City: American West Center and University of Utah, 1980).
Zamora, Margarita, *Reading Columbus* (Berkeley: University of California Press, 1993).
Zandanel, María Antonia, *Los procesos de ficcionalización del discurso histórico en la leyenda de El Dorado* (Mendoza: Universidad Nacional de Cuyo, 2004).

3 Dying in Their Own Minds

Firsting and Lasting in the Early Jesuit Work With the Tupi Language in Brazil

Vivien Kogut Lessa de Sá

> they pleaded with us not to cast death upon them, because they thought we brought death. In some houses in the villages, to prevent us from coming, they would set fires [. . .] but we would come through, singing praises to Our Lord.[1]

From their arrival in Brazil in 1500, the Portuguese showed little interest in Indigenous languages except for how they could fulfill their immediate needs. Accordingly, as elsewhere in the New World throughout the sixteenth century, existing Indigenous place names were replaced with the names of Christian saints, and the newly-discovered land itself received the name "Land of the True Cross" (Terra da Vera Cruz).[2] The first consistent attempt by Europeans to learn and systematize the Indigenous languages of Brazil came only with the arrival of the Jesuits in 1549. Perceiving that effective evangelization must be carried out in the native language—following the rules established by their founder, Ignatius of Loyola, in 1540—the Jesuits soon began an intense campaign of learning Tupi and translating the catechism.[3] This linguistic work, remarkable for its pioneering nature, also meant long-lasting and intense attempts at using language as a tool for cultural, political, and religious conquest.

This chapter examines how Indigenous languages were alternately neglected, used, or misused by the Portuguese during the early colonization of Brazil. It focuses on the linguistic work carried out by the first Jesuit missionaries and the creation of what became known as the "Língua Geral" (general language), which comprised an amalgam of a myriad of interrelated, spoken Tupi dialects that became recorded and standardized in a singular written form. Organized into grammars, vocabularies, and translated doctrines, the written Tupi established by the Jesuits for the purposes of converting the Indigenous populations had the paradoxical result of recording Indigenous dialects just as their speakers were disappearing, while also enabling their suppression. Seen as both a firsting and a lasting of Tupi, this linguistic project elicits complex cultural encounters and barriers that grow particularly evident in the presence of untranslatable concepts. This chapter also meditates upon the broader missionary strategy of subjecting the perceived changeability of Indigenous language, beliefs, and habits to the strict confines of mission life.

In 1554, Luis da Grã (1523–1609), a Jesuit who had recently arrived in Brazil, wrote to Ignatius of Loyola about the progress of the missionary work among the local Indigenous people since their first arrival five years earlier.[4] Grã himself worked in the Colégio da Bahia, the first Jesuit school set up in Salvador to instruct the Catholic faith, but most of the missionary work involved traveling to Indigenous villages to indoctrinate their populations with the use of interpreters. A small group of preachers had been striving to bring Christianity to far-flung tribes living in several provinces in Brazil where the missionaries would preach the gospel in the evenings or early hours of the morning, because this was "when they are all gathered and at peace," and persuaded the Indians to embrace Christian principles by relinquishing their own.[5] Gradually, the Jesuits began to organize mission villages where mass catechesis was possible. However, one of the pivotal strategies adopted to further the project of conversion was the translation of prayers and the doctrine into the Tupi language, a pioneering project which would influence the fate of native dialects spoken mostly along the coast. Grã, however, seemed skeptical about converting a people that, he claimed, were "so darkened by their brutal ways, that the light of reason in them seems to have been completely extinguished."[6] He was particularly exasperated by how the natives often fled at the arrival of the missionaries, hiding their children in the woods, and purposely singing over the litanies, to prevent them from being heard. Some Tupi had come to believe that becoming Christian would kill them, given that so many died soon after contact with the missionaries—an accurate perception, given the missionaries' unwitting and devastating spread of pathogens.[7] Other Tupi were persuaded by the Jesuits that the devastating spread of disease and high mortality were signs of "God wanting to people His glorious kingdom and warning those who want to go there to observe His commandments."[8] Still, the missionaries themselves seemed perplexed, as is clear from a letter prepared in 1549 by one missionary: "We are bewildered with only one thing, which is that almost all of those we baptize fall ill [. . .] which has led their sorcerers to say that the water we use to baptize them brings them sickness and the doctrine death."[9] The association drawn by the Pagés (Indigenous shamans) between the Christian doctrine and death points to the symbolic dimension and to the destructivity of the encounter between the Jesuits and the natives: for the wary Tupi, part of the missionaries' deadly power lay in the very words they used to convert them. As Grã himself remarked, "They detest hearing about death because they believe that in this way it is cast upon them, and the mere thought of it is all it takes for them to die by imagination."[10] Indeed, the use of Tupi language as an instrument of conversion would impact the survival of the Indigenous cultures subjected to catechesis in two significant ways.

The linguistic work embedded in the Jesuits' evangelizing project in Brazil examples the simultaneous firsting and lasting of Tupi dialects, to borrow from Jean O'Brien's apt terminology.[11] Firsting was done on two levels: from without, because composing a fixed, written form of interrelated oral dialects meant creating a new, unified lingua franca; and from within, because the texts produced by the Jesuits in Tupi aimed at replacing that lingua franca with a seemingly corrected version of itself, one which would work to rectify a perceived lack of Europeanness using Christian perceptions of society, time, and spirituality. Paradoxically, this led to a lasting because the newly forged language of conversion only succeeded by obfuscating preexisting methods of communication and by inflicting "death by imagination" while inevitably pushing classical Tupi dialects closer to extinction.[12]

The presence of the Jesuits in Brazil was inextricably bound with the Portuguese expansionist movement initiated in the fifteenth century. Though material gain and commercial hegemony were primary incentives for the Portuguese imperial project, the crown also saw its maritime ventures as a means of spreading the Christian faith to the heathen lands where a Portuguese foothold had been established. This project was substantially helped by the creation of the Society of Jesus in 1540 and its early association with Portugal, its first European province.[13] The Jesuits' central proselytizing mission provided an effective complement to Portugal's colonial ambitions: conquering lands became inextricably linked to conquering souls.

Unlike Spain, however, which began the large-scale exploitation of its new territories in the Americas from the early decades of the sixteenth century, Portugal was initially more interested in its rich trading posts located in Africa and India. As a result, until the mid-sixteenth-century, the Portuguese settlement of Brazil was sparse and patchy. The first systematic attempt at colonization began in 1534 with the establishment of the donatory system under which the immense territory was divided into fifteen hereditary captaincies, strips of land which were then granted to donatories who were all trusted men of king João III. Fifteen years later, however, the donatory system had proved to be a failure: several captaincies had been left vacant while others had been abandoned by their captains due to Indigenous resistance.[14] As a result, in 1549 the Portuguese crown decided to establish a central government by repurchasing one of the failed captaincies, Bahia, and sending there a newly appointed governor-general with the task of establishing a central government and building a capital city, Salvador. As a crucial part of this colonizing project, the fleet also carried the first Jesuit mission to Brazil.

Brazil would soon become the first Jesuit province in the New World, which reflected the territory's perceived potential for large-scale catechesis.

It was not long before hostility between the missionaries and the existing settlers and rulers erupted over who would have control over the Indigenous population. Landowners in the captaincies relied heavily on Indigenous slave labor, which fed an ever-growing slave trade. Many settlers and slavers also used Indigenous women as concubines. The Jesuits, for their part, engaged in a fierce and moralizing campaign since their first arrival, imposing baptism and marriage on illicit relationships. More importantly, they disputed the settlers' enslavement campaigns and denounced their ill treatment of people who they believed were ripe for conversion. Some administrators took the Jesuit's side. The Ouvidor (auditor) of Porto Seguro wrote in 1550 that he had set free all the unlawfully enslaved Indians at the behest of the Jesuits, because "this [unlawful enslavement of Indians by white men] had been the main reason why these heathens wage war against the Christians."[15] The Jesuits accused settlers of instigating warfare between tribes or prompting the Tupi to sell their own relatives into slavery. In 1559, the Jesuit Brás Lourenço (1525–1605) intervened into this practice within the captaincy of Espírito Santo, finally leading the captain to prohibit slavery, much to the settlers' discontent.[16] In light of this violence and conflict, the Jesuits, who promised protection in exchange for conversion, often served as the Tupi's only recourse from forced labor and captivity. Yet, evangelization was to become one of the main instruments of colonial domination, as a Jesuit wrote in 1554: "no fruit, even the slightest, can be had lest the secular arm, with its strength, tames and forces them [the Indians] into obeying."[17] Indeed, systematic efforts to convert the Indigenous population at times also involved their forced relocation and abduction, a topic to which we will return. Importantly, the concept and practice of conversion soon became bound up with those of translation, a connection implied by these terms' entwined etymology.[18]

By the early 1550s, the Jesuits had concluded that their evangelizing project in Brazil would bear more fruit if indoctrination was carried out in the Indigenous language, a strategy that would be pursued elsewhere in Jesuit provinces around the world.[19] Thus, the missionaries began learning the language most widely used along the coast in a variety of interrelated dialects that were variously referred to by the Portuguese as Tupi, Tupinambá, or Língua Brasílica; they set about translating doctrinal materials into that language.[20] In 1560, Grã himself, in his capacity as the head of the Jesuit province of Brazil, made the learning of Tupi mandatory for any Jesuit involved in educating and Christianizing the Indigenous populations.[21]

Given the rapid decimation of Tupi speakers over the following centuries, it is undeniable that this enterprise undertaken by the missionaries was instrumental for preserving in written form elements of Tupi that would have otherwise disappeared along with its speakers.[22] The process of mastering Tupi was, however, inextricably linked to the project of subjecting Indigenous tribes to a Christian way of life, of forcing them to abandon what one missionary termed "the vomit of their old habits."[23] In other words, while Tupi as a spoken language was subjected to a written form primarily informed by Latin grammar and infused with neologisms expressing Christian concepts, Tupi-speaking peoples were being forced to abandon their traditional ways of life (ritual festivities, anthropophagy, nomadism, and polygamy) in favor of accepted Christian norms for behavior. This religious and linguistic conversion brought indelible changes not only to the language of Tupi-speaking tribes, but also to their cultural fabric.

One byproduct of the Jesuits' use of Tupi for indoctrination was the production of a written lingua franca (Língua Geral), which amalgamated several dialects into one standardized written form; this common language had been evolving in oral form between settlers and natives in the mid-sixteenth century.[24] As a contact language, it spread to inland areas still largely unexplored by settlers via slave-raiding expeditions and missionary activity long into the seventeenth century. The written materials produced by the Jesuits for catechesis were "the greatest expression of the idealized existence of a homogeneous language, common to all."[25] Eventually, this contact language would outlive the Jesuits in Brazil and become the most spoken language in parts of the colony in the eighteenth century, before being prohibited in 1758 and virtually disappearing from the southern provinces.[26] It is safe to conclude that until the nineteenth-century Indigenous languages in Brazil were either neglected or used only for instrumental purposes by European settlers.

There was no significant interest in the native language when the Portuguese and Tupi met for the first time, as can be seen in Pero Vaz de Caminha's letter to Manuel describing the Portuguese travelers' chance arrival in Brazil in April 1500. Variously referred to as "Brazil's birth certificate" and "the first page in the history of Brazil,"[27] the letter is an example of firsting in its own right. The landfall has since been inscribed in Brazilian history as "the discovery of Brazil." The letter, believed lost for the best part of three hundred years, was only found in the late eighteenth century and first published in 1817, shortly before Brazil gained its independence from Portugal in 1822 and Brazilian historiography began in earnest. The numerous editions that followed comprised a timely addition to the larger project of asserting a distinctive national identity for the fledgling country.[28] Most importantly, the letter, when read in a post-Enlightenment and post-independence context, ideally legitimized the notion that Brazil began with the arrival of the Portuguese and their civilizational project. In its detailed descriptions of the first encounter between the Portuguese and the people living on the coast of Bahia, however, there is hardly any mention of language.

Still, the letter offers a fascinating glimpse of the dynamics of this intercultural encounter and anticipates the creation of the Indigenous other that would become apparent in and guide much of the Jesuits' work fifty years later. Caminha's usually transfixed impressions of the natives were focused on the exposed nature of their bodies: "they were dark, and naked, without anything to cover their shame," he wrote, after seeing a group walking along the beach for the first time.[29] Very little or no verbal communication followed, for Caminha often reported on gestures and signs as modes of communication. By the time the Portuguese left nine days later, they had met with hundreds of native Brazilians, now known to have been a tribe of Tupinikim living on the shores of the present-day state of Bahia, with whom they bartered, danced, and interacted. When the Portuguese and Tupinikim parted ways, not a single native word for the variety of plants, animals, objects, and landmarks that the Portuguese saw had been recorded or retained. Yet, the Portuguese had taken possession of the land for the king of Portugal, renaming it Terra da Vera Cruz, proving at once their religious zeal and utter disregard for any preexisting culture.[30] They sailed off in the belief that, being empty of culture, religion, and civility, the Tupinikim were ripe for colonization.

It is interesting to note that Caminha's failure to recognize any cultural presence starkly contrasted with his insistence in noting the Indians' physical presence. Nowhere is this more evident than in the letter's extensive descriptions of the naked body. Though Caminha details body paint, lip plugs, and headdresses, at no point does he perceive these items and their associated practices as cultural elements invested with meaning, which confirms David Treece's assertion that "in Western culture it is still the absence of any covering of sexual parts that defines nakedness."[31] In fact, for most European travelers to the Americas, Indigenous nakedness would become directly associated with the absence of culture, mirrored in what they saw as a lack of religion, of hierarchy, and of meaningful language. When the Tupinikim happily mimicked the Portuguese before a wooden cross erected on the beach, Caminha interpreted their response to the cross as coming from a lack of any religion: "it appeared to all that they have no idolatry and no worship."[32] Conversion, therefore, would be not only easily attainable but, as Caminha assured the king, "the best profit which can be derived from [this land is] [. . .] an opportunity to fulfil and do that which Your Highness so much desires, namely, the increase of our Holy Faith."[33]

It would take another fifty-odd years for any systematic evangelization to be attempted. And although efforts to translate devotional materials into Tupi began early in the 1550s, it was with the arrival of José de Anchieta (1534–1597) in 1553 that the mastering and use of Tupi took on a new dimension. Anchieta was still a young novice when he arrived in Bahia with the third Jesuit mission, but he soon emerged as a talented linguist, being placed in charge of teaching Latin in the Jesuit college in Salvador. By 1555, he was drafting a grammar of Tupi, which was later published in Coimbra and used to assist missionaries desiring to work in

Brazil.[34] A Christian doctrine in Tupi also came out in print in 1618,[35] although versions of it had been circulating in manuscript form from as early as 1553,[36] greatly due to the efforts of father João de Azpicuelta Navarro (d. 1557), who in that year mentioned the translation of extensive passages from the catechism.[37] Anchieta is considered the first European to systematically learn and record the Indigenous languages spoken along the coast of Brazil. The corpus of written work he produced or co-produced in Tupi, which included plays, songs, and poems, remains one of the most important sources of knowledge for the "most used language on the coast of Brazil," to borrow from the title of his grammar.

Anchieta's sole purpose in mastering Tupi was the conversion and subjection of a people he viewed as stubbornly barbaric: "often, just as it seems we have won them over, they reoffend, because there is no one to force them to obey."[38] At the core of this perceived barbarity lay an aspect of Indigenous behavior that the Jesuits termed inconstancy, a characteristic that seemed to Jesuit eyes to pervade native existence and behavior. The initial impression that the Brazilian Indians would be easily converted, first proposed by Caminha and later reiterated by the first Jesuits, gradually began to fade. Not only would most tribes continue to lead a nomadic lifestyle, migrating continuously and thus preventing effective catechesis, but also individuals could easily be persuaded to embrace Christianity only to soon fall back on their traditional habits abhorred by the priests, namely polygamy, the reliance on shamans, and cannibalism. As Eduardo Viveiros de Castro has pointed out, it was not the Indians' rejection of Christianity, but rather their "perplexing relationship to belief itself" that exasperated the missionaries; the Tupi showed "an enthusiastic but highly selective acceptance of a totalizing but exclusive discourse, and the refusal to follow this discourse to the end."[39]

Most letters written by the missionaries during the sixteenth century allude to the constant risk that catechumens (individuals receiving the missionaries' education about Christianity) would return to the traditional habits that missionaries found so unacceptable, as well as their many attempts to counter this outcome. As one Jesuit wrote in 1551:

> I do not dare baptize the heathen here so readily even when they ask me to because I fear their inconstancy and lack of determination, except when they are about to die. We have very little trust in them here because they are very changeable, and it seems impossible for them to become true Christians, because we have baptized some who later escaped back to the heathens and there they become worse than before, and go back to their previous sins and to eating human flesh.[40]

This changeability was seen to be facilitated by the Tupi nomadic way of life, as they relocated their villages every few years. One strategy used to prevent this geographical inconstancy was to forcibly gather individuals from a myriad of ethnic groups into what the Jesuits called *aldeias* (villages) or *reduções* (reductions) where they would live by the Christian principles of regularity, obedience, restraint, and order.[41] The priests would impose a fixed routine of work and prayer, and they also restructured tribal family groups by forcing the converts to adopt monogamous marriages. But reducing the Tupi to aldeias was not always an easy task. By the 1560s, Anchieta was convinced that conversion could only be successful by force, an opinion increasingly shared by other Jesuits involved in catechesis. "There is no better preaching to this people," he wrote in a letter dated March 1563, "than with using the sword and iron rod, with which, more than with any other, it is necessary to fulfil the 'compelle eos intrare'."[42]

Because compelling adult Indians to enter the world of Christian values was often a frustrating task, the missionaries soon focused their actions on youngsters and children, who seemed more pliable than their resistant parents and could be indoctrinated from a young age. Moreover, children would be instrumental also as interpreters acting on behalf of the missionaries.[43] In 1554, Luis da Grã claimed to have brought many youngsters from the coast, where they used to go fishing and swimming with their parents, by luring some with "promises and tenderness" and dragging others against their will; the parents were reassured they could come and visit their children whenever they wanted.[44] The indoctrination of Indigenous children had always been at the core of the Jesuit project, which sustained the belief that the children would convince their elders of the truth of Christianity. According to the letters, it was not uncommon for children to visit their parents only to berate them for their heathen ways, or at least to "instruct the parents in their own language, and the parents follow their children with their hands together."[45]

The process of "reducing" Indigenous cultural traits to the rules of Christian life was replicated in the linguistic work that formed an essential part of this regulating process. Anchieta and other Jesuits with a linguistic inclination strove to reduce the various Tupi dialects spoken along the coast to one uniform language that was also refashioned to serve as a religious instrument. Thus, Tupi was converted formally into a written language compliant with Latin grammatical rules and metrics, and conceptually to accommodate a Christian ethos entirely foreign to the language. As Andrea Daher has pointed out, "writing would have, along with the sword and iron rod, an essentially colonizing role."[46] Colonizing and converting the native populations with the Tupi language, or reducing it to one standard language, were in turn directly linked to the idea that Indian existence was pervaded by a sense of insufficiency, as we have already seen in Caminha's description of his experiences earlier in the century. The Tupi lack of clothing, religion, king and, very importantly, shame, meant that their language was also viewed as incomplete. This notion was famously phrased by Portuguese chronicler Pero de Magalhães de Gândavo (c. 1540–c. 1580) in 1578 and became endlessly repeated for much of the colonial period: "The language they use along all the coast is but one [. . .] it lacks three letters, namely, F, L, or R, which is very amazing because likewise they do not have Faith, nor Law nor King [Rei], and thus live in disorder."[47]

It is in this context that conversion was adopted as a far-reaching solution for the perceived lack of crucial Europeanizing principles in Brazil. As an important tool for conversion, translation and writing addressed the absence of the very words that expressed such concepts, supplying the Indigenous language with that which it lacked in European eyes. Importantly, turning the various oral Tupi dialects into a single comprehensible written medium meant imposing coherence, stability, and homogeneity upon an otherwise disordered culture, to borrow from Gândavo's phrasing. Like the aldeias and reduções, the Christian doctrines, sermons, and plays translated or written in Tupi by the Jesuits decontextualized elements of Indigenous culture, re-casting them in a Christian light. As João Adolfo Hansen has observed, in transforming and rewording the Tupi language from within by infusing it with new concepts and re-signifying others, the priest would manage to light up the "inner verb" in its speakers' hearts, thereby reminding them of some long-forgotten goodness.[48]

However, the processes of translation and conversion were not without their problems. Several terms remained untranslated despite the efforts of the priests. Tellingly, the terms sin, Sunday, Paradise, kingdom, and Holy Spirit, for example, were left in Portuguese in the translated doctrinal materials.[49] Other translations were only achieved through appropriating existing Tupi words and replacing their original meaning with the intended Christian concepts, themselves alien to Indigenous culture. Notable examples are *Tupã* (thunder), used to signify God and *anhanga* (a fearful forest spirit), used to signify the devil. Here, the Christian rewording of Tupi transforms two co-existing entities into opposing forces, inscribing these two terms within the binary of good and evil understood from a Christian perspective, yet nonetheless completely removed from the circularity of the Tupi's understanding of the cycles of nature.[50] Sometimes these lexical appropriations led to a new term forged out of existing ones, such as *Tupãsy* (thunder + mother), used as a translation for Our Lady, which describes a phenomenon defined by Alfredo Bosi as the "invention of a syncretic imaginary."[51] The neologism *caraíbebé* (flying holy man), created by the Jesuits to signify angel, is a particularly interesting case of linguistic conversion. "Caraí" or "caraíba" was a term used by Tupi peoples to denote the wandering prophets who were believed to hold supernatural powers of divination and curing. These "holy men" became the target of fierce persecution by the Jesuits because they posed a threat to catechesis and instigated messianic mass migrations toward a seeming "Land without Evil."[52] Eventually, however, all white men, with their new technology, their mysterious medicine, and their unknown diseases, through an ironic semantic twist, came to be termed caraíbas.[53] Hence, the word epitomizes what Carlos Fausto calls "a slippage of signifieds," by slowly incorporating new meanings that, in their turn, carried conflicting connotations.[54] In a similar way, the word for cross was first translated through the paraphrase *ioaçaba*, which literally meant crossing one thing with another.[55] The full expression would be *santa ioaçaba* (holy cross), as it appears in one of the earliest known manuscript versions of the doctrine in Tupi.[56] However, by 1557 there were reports that the catechumens resisted using the phrase "because to them it resembled ridiculous gestures."[57] Eventually the expression would be used only in Portuguese (santa cruz).[58]

Suppression, adaptation, and compounding: these were a few of the strategies employed by Jesuits in their attempts to reduce Indigenous linguistic diversity, along with their perceived instability and variety, to "the totalizing aim of religious conversion" and its imperative of unicity (one God, one religion).[59] This tentative process of transforming Tupi into an instrument of religious indoctrination speaks to the relative lack of communication between the Jesuits and their intended converts. The resulting language found in Anchieta's grammar and the translated Christian doctrine seems deceptively hybrid, suggesting a seamless transition. In fact, it reflects the inexorable process that began in early 1500 in which "almost all the populations that happened to meet in Brazil [. . .] had lost, or were in the process of losing, contact with the certainties of their past."[60] Textual culture in this way should be viewed as a technology for containing and lasting Indigenous cultures and languages.

Notes

1. "[N]os rogavam lhes não deitássemos a morte, com medo de nós, porque a eles parecia-lhes que lançávamos a morte. Nalgumas casas das aldeias, para que não fôssemos lá, faziam fogo [. . .] e nós, entrando, íamos com cantares de Nosso Senhor," in "Carta dos Meninos do Colégio de Jesus," Bahia, 5 August 1552, ascribed to the boys from the seminary in Bahia, in Leite, ed., *Novas cartas*, p. 144. All translations are mine unless otherwise stated.
2. The name first appears in Pero Vaz de Caminha's letter to king Manuel reporting on the arrival of the Portuguese in Brazil on 22 April 1500. The name Brasil was first used to refer to the newly-discovered land in Afonso Albuquerque's 1512 letter to the king, pointing to an early association between the area and the abundant red dye wood known as "Pau Brasil" (*Cesalpinia Echinata*) with which it would become indelibly associated. See de Gândavo, *A primeira história do Brasil*, pp. 45, n. 8–46, n. 9.
3. Almeida Navarro, "A tradução de textos," pp. 215–234.
4. Leite, ed., *Monumenta*, vol. 2, p. 132.
5. "[P]orque es tiempo en que están juntos y sosegados." From a letter written by Manuel da Nóbrega from Bahia, 10 August 1549, in Leite, ed., *Monumenta*, vol. 1, pp. 140–141.
6. "[T]an entenebrecidos están em suas brutalidades, que quasi de todo parecen tener absorto el lume de la rezón," in Leite, ed., *Monumenta*, vol. 2, p. 132.

7. For more on the spread of disease in early Brazil, see Metcalf, *Go-Betweens and the Colonization of Brazil*, pp. 119–156; and Hemming, *Red Gold*, pp. 139–160.
8. "[Q]ueriendo el Señor poblar la gloria y avisar los que quisiesen allá ir, de manera que guarden sus mandamientos." Letter written by Vicente Rodrigues, 17 May 1552, in Leite, ed., *Monumenta*, vol. 1, p. 303.
9. "Solamente de una cosa estamos espantados, que casí quantos bautizamos adolecieron [. . .] y tuvieron ocasión sus hechizeros de dezir que nosotros con el agua, con que los bautizamos, les damos la dolencia y con la doctrina la muerte," in Leite, ed., *Monumenta*, vol. 1, p. 143.
10. "El hablar de la muerte es acerca dellos mui odioso, porque tienen para sí que se la echan, y este pensamiento basta para morriren de imaginación," in Leite, ed., *Monumenta*, vol. 2, p. 137.
11. O'Brien, *Firsting and Lasting*.
12. As noted by Hildo Honório do Couto, "Some of the Tupi-Guarani Language Varieties Are Now Lost Forever;" see Hildo Honório do Couto, "Amerindian Language Islands in Brazil," in Mufwene, ed., *Iberian Imperialism*, pp. 76–107: 77.
13. Serna, "Procurators and the Making of the Jesuits' Atlantic Network," in Bailyn and Denault, eds., *Soundings in Atlantic History*, pp. 181–209: 190; and Alden, *The Making of an Enterprise*, p. 38.
14. Johnson, "Portuguese Settlement, 1550–1580," in Bethell, ed., *Colonial Brazil*, pp. 1–38: 13–20.
15. "A causa que principalmente ffazia a estes gentios ffazer guerra aos christãos." Letter written by Dr. Pero Borges 7 February 1550, in Leite, ed., *Monumenta*, vol. 1, p. 175. In the same letter, Borges points to the distinction between the natives who had been "salteados" (snatched) and those "tomados em guerra" (seized in battle). This difference determined that enslavement was lawful when enacted during battles for conquest or in self-defense, or under the condition of so-called "guerras justas" (just wars). The concept of just war enabled unscrupulous settlers to interpret at will the justness of a war and to engage in systematic slaving for much of the colonial period, despite a law passed by king Sebastião in 1570 that forbade the enslavement of Indians, but it notably included a number of exceptions. See also Hemming, *Red Gold*, pp. 150–152.
16. Leite, ed., *Monumenta*, vol. 3, p. 41.
17. "[N]enhum fruto, ou ao menos pequeníssimo, se pode colher dele, se não se juntar a força do braço secular, que os dome e sujeite ao jugo da obediência," in Leite, ed., *Monumenta*, vol. 2, p. 114.
18. As Cesar Braga-Pinto noted, "the word conversion comes from the Latin 'convertere,' which means 'to translate into another language,' as well as 'to turn something into something else,' 'to alter,' 'to convert';" see Braga-Pinto, "Translating, Meaning and the Community of Languages," p. 36.
19. Leite, ed., *História*, tomo II, p. 545.
20. Most tribes living along the coast of Brazil in the sixteenth century spoke dialectal varieties of the Tupi-Guaraní linguistic branch, generally referred to as Tupi or Tupinambá, after one of the largest groups encountered by the Portuguese. It will be henceforth referred to as Tupi.
21. Leite, ed., *História*, tomo II, p. 561.
22. For the demographics of Tupi tribes along parts of the Brazilian coast in the sixteenth century and their decline, see Dean, "Indigenous Populations of the São Paulo—Rio de Janeiro Coast," pp. 3–26.
23. "[O]vómito dos antigos costumes." Letter written by José de Anchieta (1534–1597) in March 1555, in Leite, ed., *Monumenta*, vol. 2, p. 194.

24. The term Língua Geral has variously been used by ethnolinguists to describe lingua francas evolving from Tupi due to contact with Europeans at different times during settlement; see Rodrigues, "As línguas gerais sur-americanas," pp. 6–18. I use the term here to indicate the Tupi recorded in writing by the Jesuits in the sixteenth century and used orally for the purpose of catechesis.
25. Candida Barros, Borges, and Meira, "A Língua Geral como identidade construída," p. 194.
26. Buarque de Hollanda, *Raízes do Brasil*, p. 129; and Moore, "Historical Development of Nheengatu (Lingua Geral Amazônica)," in Mufwene, ed. *Iberian Imperialism*, pp. 108–142: 108. The variety known as LGA (Amazonian General Language) is still spoken in some areas of the state of Amazonas.
27. Greenlee, ed., *The Voyage of Pedro Alvarez Cabral*, p. 3. For the Portuguese original, see Cortesão, ed., *A carta de Pêro Vaz de Caminha*.
28. According to Pedro Serra, there were nine editions and reeditions in the nineteenth century alone: Rio de Janeiro (1818, reedited in 1845), Lisbon (1826), São Luís do Maranhão (1853), Lisbon (1892), Belém (1896, reedited in Lisbon in 1900), Lisbon (1900), Recife (1900). Twenty more editions came out in the twentieth century. Serra, "As notícias do descobrimento do Brasil," in Aparecida Ribeiro, ed., *A carta de Caminha e seus ecos*, pp. 198–245.
29. Greenlee, *Voyage of Pedro Alvarez Cabral*, p. 8.
30. Ibid., p. 7. See note 2.
31. Treece, *Exiles, Allies, Rebels*, p. 23.
32. Greenlee, *Voyage of Pedro Alvarez Cabral*, p. 31.
33. Ibid., p. 33.
34. Anchieta, *Arte de grammatica da lingoa mais usada na costa do Brasil*.
35. Araújo, ed., *Catecismo na lingoa brasílica*.
36. Only a handful of such manuscripts is extant, most of which are kept in the Archive of the Society of Jesus (ARSI) in the Vatican. One of them, believed to be in Anchieta's own hand, is reproduced in facsimile in a recent edition of his work. See Anchieta, *Doutrina cristã*. More recently, a manuscript discovered in England has shed new light on the collective production of doctrines in Tupi. See note 52.
37. In Leite, ed., *Novas cartas*, p. 159.
38. "[F]requentemente, quando os julgamos ganhos, recalcitram, porque não há quem os obrigue pela força a obedecer;" see Anchieta's letter of 1 September 1554, in Leite, ed., *Monumenta*, vol. 2, p. 114.
39. Viveiros de Castro, *The Inconstancy of the Indian Soul*, pp. 10–11.
40. "Não ouso aqui bauptizar estes Gentios tão facilmente, ainda que o pedem muitas vezes, porque me temo de sua inconstancia e pouca firmeza, sinão quando estão em o artigo da morte. Tem-se cá mui pouca confiança nelles porque são mui mudaveis, e parece aos homens impossível poder estes vir a ser bons christãos, porque aconteceu já bautizar os Christãos alguns, e tornarem a fugir para os Gentios, e andam depois lá peiores que d'antes, e tornam-se a metter em seus vicios e em comer carne humana," in Leite, ed., *Cartas avulsas*, p. 88.
41. The first mission village was founded in 1552 in Bahia and typically bundled together individuals from different villages and tribes. Whereas originally aldeias were temporary structures, the mission villages imposed a sedentary existence, with hunting and gathering being replaced by farming and grazing, often for the benefit of the Jesuits themselves. As John Hemming describes, "Mission Indians had to accept Jesuit tutelage in every aspect of their lives. The Fathers imposed a new discipline that occupied every hour of the day and controlled the life-cycle from cradle to grave." Hemming, *Red Gold*, pp. 104–105.

42. "[P]ara este género de gente, no ay mejor predicatión que espada y vara de hierro, en la qual más que en ninguna otra, es necessario que se cumpla el 'compelle eos intrare'." The Latin phrase refers to Luke 14:12–24 "to compel them to come in." See Leite, ed., *Monumenta*, vol. 3, p. 554.
43. For Indigenous interpreters working with the Jesuits in Brazil, see Metcalf, *Go-Betweens*, pp. 92–98.
44. "[D]ella truxe yo muchs moços per diversas vezes a unos con los atraer con alagos y promessas, y otros con mui poca muestra de voluntad suia [. . .] Se tenían padres o hermanos mandávales dizir que [. . .] lo fuesse ver quando pudiesse," in Leite, ed., *Monumenta*, vol. 2, p. 135. The head of the Jesuit mission, Manuel da Nóbrega (1517–1570), frequently referred to the gathering of Indigenous boys for the Jesuit colleges and seminaries as "acquiring" them; see Leite, ed., *Novas cartas*, pp. 102–112.
45. "[N]a sua língua ensinam os pais e os pais com as mãos postas vão atrás dos filhos." Letter by Nóbrega, cited in Leite, ed., *História*, tomo I, p. 38.
46. Daher, "Escrita e conversão," p. 33.
47. "A língua de que usam, por toda a costa, é uma [. . .] Carece de três letras, convém a saber, não se acha nela F, nem L, nem R, coisa digna de espanto, porque assim não tem Fé, nem Lei, nem Rei, e dessa maneira vivem desordenadamente," in Gândavo, *Primeira história*, p. 135.
48. The process replicated the neo-platonic ideals embraced by the Jesuits and very much part of humanist mentality at the time. Hansen, "A escrita da conversão," in Costigan, ed., *Diálogos da conversão*, pp. 15–43: 19.
49. Alves Filho and Milton, "Inculturation and Acculturation," pp. 275–296.
50. Cesar Braga-Pinto develops an interesting analysis of the Jesuit use of the word Tupã for the purpose of conversion; see Braga-Pinto, "Translating," pp. 38–39.
51. Bosi, *Dialética da colonização*, pp. 31 and 66.
52. For Tupi migrations, see Clastres, *The Land-Without-Evil*; and Metraux, "Migrations historiques," pp. 1–45.
53. Almeida Navarro, *Dicionário tupi*, pp. 219–220.
54. Carlos Fausto, "Fragmentos de História Tupinambá: da etnologia como instrumento crítico de conhecimento etno-histórico," in Carneiro da Cunha, ed., *História dos índios no Brasil*, pp. 381–396: 386.
55. Navarro, *Dicionário tupi*, p. 188.
56. This manuscript was stolen from the Santos Jesuit College in 1592 by English corsairs and preserved at the Bodleian library under the title "Doutrina Christã na Linguoa Brasilica." See Vivien Kogut Lessa de Sá and Caroline Egan, "Translation and Prolepsis: Jesuit Origins of a Tupi Christian Doctrine," in Newson, ed., *The Cultural Legacy of the Jesuits*, in press.
57. "[P]or lhes parecer aquilo gatimanhos," in a letter written by Antonio Blásquez in January 1557, in Leite, ed., *Monumenta*, vol. 2, p. 348.
58. See Cardoso, ed., *Obras completas*, vol. 1, p. 29.
59. Daher, "Escrita e conversão," p. 41.
60. Laborie, "From Orality to Writing," p. 57.

Bibliography

Alden, Dauril, *The Making of an Enterprise: The Society of Jesus in Portugal, Its Empire, and Beyond, 1540–1750* (Stanford, CA: Stanford University Press, 1996).

Almeida Navarro, Eduardo de, "A tradução de textos para línguas exóticas nos séculos XVI e XVII—Natureza e características," *Língua e Literatura* 26 (2000), pp. 215–234.

———, *Dicionário tupi antigo: a língua indígena clássica do Brasil* (San Paulo: Global, 2013).

Alves Filho, P. E., and John Milton, "Inculturation and Acculturation in the Translation of Religious Texts: The Translations of Jesuit Priest José de Anchieta into Tupi in 16th Century Brazil," *Target* 17.2 (2005), pp. 275–296.

Anchieta, José de, *Arte de grammatica da lingoa mais usada na costa do Brasil* (Coimbra: Antonio de Mariz, 1595).

———, *Doutrina cristã*, ed. Armando Cardoso (San Paulo: Loyola, 1992).

Aparecida Ribeiro, Maria, ed., *A carta de Caminha e seus ecos: estudio e antologia* (Coimbra: Angelus Novus, 2003).

Araújo, Antonio de, ed., *Catecismo na lingoa brasílica, no qual se contêm a summa da doctrina christã* (Lisbon: Pedro Crasbeeck, 1618).

Bailyn, Bernard, and Patricia L. Denault, eds., *Soundings in Atlantic History: Latent Structures and Intellectual Currents, 1500–1830* (London: Harvard University Press, 2009).

Bethell, Leslie, ed., *Colonial Brazil* (Cambridge: Cambridge University Press, 1991).

Bosi, Alfredo, *Dialética da colonização* (San Paulo: Companhia das Letras, 1994).

Braga-Pinto, Cesar, "Translating, Meaning and the Community of Languages," *Studies in the Humanities* 22.1 (1996), pp. 33–49.

Buarque de Hollanda, Sérgio, *Raízes do Brasil* (San Paulo: Cia. Das Letras, 2003).

Candida Barros, Maria, Luiz C. Borges, and Márcio Meira, "A Língua Geral como identidade construída," *Revista de Antropologia* 39.1 (1996), pp. 191–219.

Cardoso, Armando, ed., *Obras completas do Pe. José de Anchieta* (San Paulo: Loyola, 1992).

Carneiro da Cunha, Manuela, ed., *História dos índios no Brasil* (San Paulo: Cia. Das Letras, 1992).

Clastres, Helène, *The Land-Without-Evil: Tupi-Guarani Prophetism* (Chicago: University of Illinois, 1995).

Cortesão, Jaime, ed., *A carta de Pêro Vaz de Caminha* (Rio de Janeiro: Livros de Portugal Ltda., 1943).

Costigan, Lucia Helena, ed., *Diálogos da conversão* (Campinas: Unicamp, 2005).

Daher, Andrea, "Escrita e conversão: a gramática tupi e os catecismos bilíngues no Brasil do século XVI," *Revista Brasileira de Educação* 8 (1998), pp. 31–43.

Dean, Warren, "Indigenous Populations of the São Paulo—Rio de Janeiro Coast: Trade, Aldeamento, Slavery and Extinction," *Revista de História* 117 (1984), pp. 3–26.

Gândavo, Pero de Magalhães de, *A primeira história do Brasil: História da provincia de Santa Cruz a que vulgarmente chamamos Brasil* [1578], eds. Sheila Moura Hue and Ronaldo Menegaz (Rio de Janeiro: Jorge Zahar, 2004).

Greenlee, William, ed., *The Voyage of Pedro Alvarez Cabral to Brazil and India* (London: Hakluyt Society, 1938).

Hemming, John, *Red Gold: The Conquest of the Brazilian Indians* (London: Papermac, 1987).

Laborie, Jean-Claude, "From Orality to Writing: The Reality of a Conversion through the Work of the Jesuit Father José de Anchieta (1534–1597)," *Diogenes* 48.3 (2000), pp. 56–71.

Leite, Serafim, ed., *Cartas avulsas: 1550–1568* (Rio de Janeiro: Officina Industrial Graphica, 1931).

———, ed., *História da Companhia de Jesus no Brasil* (Rio de Janeiro: Civilização Brasileira, 1938).
———, ed., *Novas cartas jesuíticas: de Nóbrega a Vieira* (San Paulo: Cia. Ed. Nacional, 1940).
———, ed., *Monumenta Brasiliae*, 3 vols. (Rome: Monumenta Historica Societatis Iesu, 1956–1958).
Metcalf, Alida, *Go-Betweens and the Colonization of Brazil: 1500–1600* (Austin: University of Texas Press, 2005).
Metraux, Alfred, "Migrations historiques des Tupi-Guarani," *Journal de la Société des Americanistes* 19 (1927), pp. 1–45.
Mufwene, Salikoko S., ed., *Iberian Imperialism and Language Evolution in Latin America* (Chicago: University of Chicago Press, 2014).
Newson, Linda, ed., *The Cultural Legacy of the Jesuits* (London: Routledge, 2019).
O'Brien, Jean M., *Firsting and Lasting: Writing Indians out of Existence in New England* (Minneapolis: University of Minnesota Press, 2010).
Rodrigues, Aryon, "As línguas gerais sul-americanas," *Papia* 4.2 (1996), pp. 6–18.
Treece, David, *Exiles, Allies, Rebels: Brazil's Indianist Movement, Indigenist Politics, and the Imperial Nation-State* (London: Greenwood Press, 2000).
Viveiros de Castro, Eduardo, *The Inconstancy of the Indian Soul: The Encounter of Catholics and Cannibals in 16th-Century Brazil* (Chicago: University of Chicago Press, 2011).

4 Literacy and Colonial Beginnings

Inca Garcilaso's Story of the Letter in Context

Julián Díez Torres

In his essay published in 1958, *La invención de América*, the Mexican scholar Edmundo O'Gorman proposed that Columbus's discovery of America was not just a fact or event, but rather a retrospective invention that possessed a history of its own.[1] In another influential essay composed in 1982, the Bulgarian intellectual Tzvetan Todorov discussed some of the most famous Spanish accounts about the conquest of the New World, exposing the communicative clash between the invaders and the natives.[2] Although O'Gorman and Todorov contributed to shifting scholarly attention about early colonial texts from their documentary value to their argumentative problems, both scholars grounded their analyses in modern intellectual concepts and debates. O'Gorman did not consider that the term invention in the sixteenth century referred not only to the creation of something new, as in the catalogs of inventors found in renaissance encyclopedias, but also to the act of finding (as in the Latin term *inventio*). It also referred to the first canon of rhetoric, *inventio*, which consisted of cultivating and refining support for an argument. Furthermore, the view that Columbus's discovery was an epoch-changing event only became hegemonic during the Enlightenment when scholars and historians combined moral and providential conceptions of history in ways that ultimately grew to embrace viewing history in progressive, global, and secular ways. This cleavage between the rhetorical and the progressive conceptions of history was addressed by Todorov in his essay regarding narratives of Spanish discovery and conquest. He furthermore proposes that his book be read as an example within the moral debate of how to deal with the so-called other. Todorov simultaneously reveals the problematic assumption underlying his assertion: text, in the case his book, and in this chapter in the form of anecdotes intended to serve as lessons and provide insight about Indigenous peoples, powerfully structures time and space; it permits the author to accumulate knowledges and discard others. Rolena Adorno characterizes early colonial works in a similar light; she asserts that

> Taken, even recently, as proof of the rigidity of autochthonous American cultural tradition (Todorov, *The Conquest of America*), these post-Conquest testimonies, apart from their emphasis and exaggeration by

> Europeans, may be interpreted as an indication of the ability to incorporate and integrate that which was new and foreign. Early colonial writings—from Mayan códices to Peruvian chronicles—evidence this accumulative, improvisational, and adaptive quality.[3]

Exampling this problem again, Todorov also stresses the epistemological disadvantage of the Indians when they met with European culture, which textual culture had furthermore entrenched as an invented condition of indigeneity. This way of viewing Native Americans has infected scholarship of our own time, ensuring that they are always steps behind sophisticated, more advanced Euro-settlers.[4]

This problem is apparent when we consider how primary sources, and later scholars and historians, have represented the natives' ability to write and understand text, as well as the authority that the text has over them. While some first-hand accounts in the form of letters written by Spanish colonizers did claim that the Indians confused the invaders with gods and struggled with the superiority of alphabetical writing, other accounts point to the use of writing without highlighting any incapability on the part of Indigenous people.[5] And despite evidence to the contrary—that Native Americans had their own graphic languages and certainly acquired European systems of writing—an anecdote emerged in these sources that constructs Indigenous peoples, usually represented by an Indian messenger, as easily fooled by the written word of his Spanish master, ostensibly because Indians were unable to understand what writing was. Referred to as the story of the letter, this anecdote provides a rich point of entry into the cultural complexities of colonial Peru. Instead of dealing with examples of this story in chronological order, we will start with what is probably the most known of all the versions, the one appearing in the first part of the *Comentarios reales de los Incas* (1609) by Inca Garcilaso de la Vega (1539–1616). This history of Peru betrays the author's double ancestry as the son of an Incan mother and a Spanish conquistador, and stresses Garcilaso's value as an informant for early-modern culture.[6] After exploring his rendering of the anecdote, I will situate it within the first part of his *Comentarios* before dealing with the earlier and parallel versions, in order to demonstrate the issues pervading the written word and how it has lasted Indigenous people from the beginning of their contact with Europeans.

Garcilaso *el Inca* was the pen name of Gómez Suárez de Figueroa. After his Spanish father, Sebastián Garcilaso de la Vega, achieved a prominent position in Cuzco, he married a young Spanish woman, which resulted in his father's abandonment of Garcilaso's mother (who was the *ñusta*, a regal title, Isabel Chimpu Ocllo, and descended from the last Incan leader). While she raised and thus exposed Garcilaso to a traditional Incan education, he also studied alongside other mestizo boys from privileged backgrounds. Scholars have not uncommonly characterized his mother as the last of her people, and Garcilaso as the first mixed-blood author to be represented in the literary canon. In his will, his noble father provided support for Garcilaso to travel to Spain, to which he arrived in 1561, and subsequently took up the profession of soldiering; he later became a student with the Jesuits and served as an associate at Cordoba's cathedral. The genealogical dimension of the name Inca Garcilaso was represented visually in Garcilaso's coat of arms and remains visible today at the chapel where he was buried in Cordoba's cathedral. Both parts of the *Comentarios reales* expanded upon Garcilaso's double ancestry to create a seemingly balanced history of Peru that was styled after other renaissance chronicles about cities, nations, and empires. Published in Lisbon in 1609, the first part of the *Comentarios* narrates the political and imperial expansion of the Incas, and it also describes Incan customs and institutions; in this way, the chronicle celebrated the author's Indigenous heritage much as a European chronicle would praise Roman expansion practices. In 1617, a posthumous edition of the second part of the *Comentarios* dealing with the Spanish era of Peru was published in Cordoba. The title of this edition (chosen by the posthumous editors) was *Historia general del Perú*. The different titles associated with both volumes have created a cleavage in terms of the reception of the work's two parts, resulting in scholars knowing about one but perhaps not the other. Several chapters toward the end of the first part of the *Comentarios* concentrate on the author's celebration of Peruvian goods, including animals, plants, and minerals, for their quality, abundance, and sometimes extraordinariness, noting how he interacted with and experienced them.[7] These chapters combine the description of goods with personal and sometimes nostalgic memories about Garcilaso's childhood in Cuzco during the 1540s and 1550s. Garcilaso also inserts a certain degree of criticism about the loss of Incan culture, customs, institutions, monuments, and lineages. In some cases, the memories refer to matters that directly impacted Garcilaso's own development.[8]

The anecdote that interests us does not play a significant role in the construction of Garcilaso's authority or identity, yet he does describe his own processes of writing in ways that make him a witness to aspects of the anecdote. The passages concerned link to material items mentioned elsewhere in the book and whose inclusion were probably intended by him to entertain his Spanish reader with curious information about some of the vegetables being cultivated in colonial Peru while praising Peru's fertility.[9] Garcilaso relates how, while he was writing the chapter containing the anecdote between 1600 and 1602 in Cordoba, he talked to someone who had witnessed the growth of a large mint plant with impressive buds in Peru. He also mentions another conversation he had in Cordoba in 1595 with a Nicaraguan who assured him that he had eaten in Peru part of an enormous radish. This witness also declared that he had seen a melon so big that its owner called a notary to authorize an official record of its greatness. Garcilaso then quotes *Historia natural y moral* (1590) by José de Acosta (1540–1600), in which the Jesuit missionary and scholar mentioned the size of the melons from the Ica Valley in Peru, and to which Garcilaso adds: "none of those melons turned out to be bad."[10] To this mix of memories, descriptions, quotations, and personal commentary typical of the *Comentarios*, the chapter concludes with a "cuento gracioso" (funny tale). Garcilaso has woven throughout this chapter several references to melons as a Peruvian good and connected them to the fertility of Peru. But the anecdote itself is presented as an illustration of "the simplicity that the Indians had in their antiquity."[11] The word simplicity seems to refer here to both innocence and a lack of development.

Like other anecdotes in the *Comentarios* presented as derived from oral sources (from Garcilaso's Incan relatives as well as from soldiers, merchants, and friends), this one is also introduced by an assertion of its credibility. The informant cited by the author is someone called Antonio Solar, a "vecino" (a member of the town's ruling class) and a nobleman from Lima. Garcilaso mentions someone with that name in the second part of the *Comentarios*.[12] Instead of trying to distinguish between the fictional and the factual, we can assume that the story probably combined both elements to some degree. According to the story, Solar owned an estate near Lima. One day the estate's overseer decided to send Solar a present of ten melons along with a letter. The overseer asked two Indian servants to deliver the message and told them not to eat any melon or the letter would tell on them.[13] The two Indians ate one of the fruits while hiding the letter behind a wall so that the letter could not see their crime. Later, while still on their way, they ate a second fruit, hiding the letter once again. Upon their arrival, Solar read the letter, discovered the theft, and punished them. Confused, the two Indians declared that they then understood why their ancestors had mistaken the Spanish invaders as *Viracochas*, that is, relatives or embodiments of an Andean god.

Garcilaso comments on a similar case that had occurred in Cuba "in the beginning" (of the Spanish domination of the area), as reported by Francisco López de Gómara (1511–1566) in his *Historia general de las Indias* (1553). Both Garcilaso's story and the chapter end with the following remark: it is not surprising to find similar examples in different territories because "the simplicity of the New World Indians regarding what they had not achieved was one and the same with ignorance."[14] Garcilaso also highlights evidence of Spanish advancement, which for him included riding horses, plowing with bulls, building mills and arch bridges, and shooting harquebuses, that Indigenous people did not practice before the Spanish arrived to Peru. While it is possible that Garcilaso heard the story in Peru, he also acknowledged knowing Gómara's similar account, and it is well-known that he had read Gómara carefully.[15] Viewed in this way, Garcilaso as a mestizo may be replicating the colonizer's construction of indigeneity. This would mean that Garcilaso deliberately misled his readers when presenting his story as an oral account and then referencing Gómara to corroborate his view that Indigenous ignorance and forms of behavior pervaded the Spanish Americas. As in the case of Solar's testimony, we cannot easily delineate Garcilaso's literary development of the anecdote and his use of a specific source, whether oral or textual.

Many short stories appear in Garcilaso's historiographical narratives; he refers to them as "cuentos" and "casos."[16] He calls other stories recollections or simply defines them as things that were said or had happened. What constitutes a story raises issues about whether sources are oral or written, which as we will see implies ethnocentric and colonial ways of disempowering Indigenous peoples. Garcilaso proposes at the beginning of his work to tell not only the history of the Incan dynasty but also everything about the Inca "republic" (state, political entity) "from the lowest to the highest" altitude.[17] It is also important to consider Garcilaso's use of the terms "historia" and "historial." In Spanish, *historia* means both history and story. Garcilaso employs this term mostly in the sense of a historiographic narrative. With his use of the less common adjective *historial* in the chapter titled "Regarding the historical fables [fábulas historiales] about the origin of the Incas," he categorizes Andean accounts about the beginning of the Inca dynasty as dreams or fables and not *sucesos historiales* (historical events), thus differentiating between history and fable.[18] The apparently contradictory expression "fábulas historiales" probably refers to the truth hidden within fiction or to the exegetical distinction between the literal meaning of a text, also known as its historical meaning, and the subsequent two higher meanings: the moral and the theological.[19] Garcilaso relied upon the philosophical interpretation of Andean oral fables to show the prestige of Incan antiquity as the origin of Peru's national history. And as a renaissance scholar, he himself may have decided to add his own fables, passing them off as anecdotes in order to raise consciousness about important issues of his time.

A useful approach to studying short stories in the *Comentarios* is to explore the stories' function and their external influences.[20] Two cases (*casos*) concerning the last Incan leader, Atahualpa (c. 1500–1533), reveal how an Indigenous character responds to writing. The first one is the famous encounter at Cajamarca between Atahualpa and Francisco Pizarro (1478–1541).[21] Present in most of the Peruvian chronicles, letters, and *relaciones* (reports), Garcilaso departs from tradition when he relates this historically significant moment. Rather than following the traditional Spanish account according to which Atahualpa threw away the bible given to him by the Spanish friar Vicente Valverde (1498–1541) and following instead the Latin manuscript (now lost) by the mestizo Jesuit Blas Valera (1545–1597), Garcilaso claims that the Incan leader dropped the bible unintentionally. Garcilaso also underlines the accumulation of interpretative errors over time; his effort to provide a more complete understanding of the actors involved in this tragic event epitomizes the project of the *Comentarios*. The second passage appears some chapters later. While in prison, Atahualpa discovers the mechanics of writing and he realizes that some Spaniards, including the governor Francisco Pizarro, could not read and write properly. The anecdote fits well with the image of Pizarro as an uneducated but charismatic caudillo and condemns illiteracy as a dishonorable dismissal of the benefits of formal education.[22] Casos such as these ones usually engage with a well-known historical figure or event, whereas our anecdote rather describes in a humorous manner the temptations provoked by Peruvian goods. In this sense, the story about Atahualpa reflects other passages in which Garcilaso puts traditional jokes and sayings in the mouths of historical actors. Some of those actors are identifiable individuals within Peru's history and others reflect generic social samples or types (Indians, Spanish soldiers).[23] Historical figures and social samples complemented each other, just as the political expansion of the Incan empire intertwined with the description of Incan and colonial customs.

Garcilaso's story about the melons was re-written and popularized by the nineteenth-century costumbrist author Ricardo Palma with the title "Carta canta" (the singing letter) in the third section of his *Tradiciones peruanas*.[24] In the 1970s and 1980s, the story was analyzed by Juan José Arrom and Enrique Pupo-Walker.[25] Both critics emphasize Garcilaso's talent as evidenced in the use of dialog, hyperbole, and symmetries typical of the oral tradition. They also connect the passage to the emergence of a new type of identity that later gives rise to modern Latin American identity, basing this claim on the attention paid to the messengers' attitudes, on the mixing of tragic and comic elements, and on its autobiographical framing. More recently, Elena Romiti has examined the same passage, using the story of the letter to reflect upon the different types of epistemological and intercultural codes in the *Comentarios*.[26] She also documents how Garcilaso's story of the letter can be enriched by considering it and the *Comentarios* as a response to José de Acosta's classification of the world's nations according to literacy (with Europe and China at the top of the scale, and the Indians from Mexico and Peru in an intermediary position between literate and illiterate peoples).[27] This proposal fits well with the observation that Garcilaso championed his homeland no differently than a European would exert the importance of his own by emphasizing the quality of its goods and land. Finally, Gonzalo Lamana has re-interpreted the passage in terms of W. E. B. Du Bois's theory of "double consciousness," arguing that while the passage can be read literally as celebrating colonialist claims, it may also have a veiled meaning that both accommodates and resists European expectations.[28] This uniqueness can be better appreciated when considered in relation to earlier and parallel versions of the story of the letter.

Let us now consider the anecdote's rendering by López de Gómara. Much shorter than Garcilaso's passage, Gómara's appears at the end of the section devoted to the island of Hispaniola in his *Historia general*. The chapter, "De los milagros de la conversión" (Of the miracles of conversion), comes just after a chapter devoted to native prophecies regarding the arrival of the Spaniards; it contains several casos. These chapters are situated after the initial part of the work, dealing with the Caribbean during Columbus's time, and followed by a geographical description of North to South America. Before the anecdote, Gómara lists several providential events associated with the expansion of Christianity on Hispaniola (not Cuba, as Garcilaso misquoted), beginning with the admiration the Indians expressed for a cross left by Columbus and the names of the early evangelizers of the island. Then comes the anecdote of interest to this study. In Gómara's rendering, a Spaniard once sent a friend a dozen *hutias* (a rodent from the Caribbean islands) prepared as cold cuts. The Indian messenger tasked with delivering this gift ate three hutias and the friend who received the remaining hutias sent a letter back to the Spaniard thanking him for the nine hutias. When the gift's sender read the letter, he reacted angrily, and the Indian confessed his theft because he assumed that the letter had spoken. Then, the Indian told his people to be careful with letters because they "talked."[29] After the anecdote, and just before the end of the chapter, Gómara added that letters were sometimes written with needles on the leaves of Caribbean trees such as guiabara and copey. Gómara states the importance of sending and receiving letters for the goal of conversion because the Indians believed either that letters contained the spirit of prophecy or that paper talked. Gómara presented the story as a fact and not, as Garcilaso had, as someone's testimony, but both Gómara and Garcilaso situated the anecdote in the unprecise and turbulent beginning of colonial rule.

The 1553 Antwerp edition of Gómara's *Historia* is authorized by a list of the "historians of the Indies," including Pietro Martire d'Anghiera (1457–1526), Hernán Cortés (1485–1547), Gonzalo Fernández de Oviedo (1478–1557), and Gómara himself. These sources are useful for helping us understand from which source Gómara's version of the anecdote developed. While Oviedo mentions the use of leaves from the guiabara tree for writing letters, he does not include the anecdote.[30] Martire, a Lombard humanist, a teacher, and a *letrado* ("man of letters," the term often reserved for high-level functionaries) in the service of the Catholic kings, appears to be the source in his *Decadas de orbe novo* (1516).[31] Written in Latin, Martire's work consisted of a compilation of letters addressed to political and religious leaders settled in Italy, including several popes.[32] The work was composed in chapter-like form between the fourteen nineties and the fifteen twenties, and it appeared in several editions. Its success was greatly due to the skillful combination of first-hand information and classical themes. One of the main consequences of its popularity was the divulgation of the very term Martire used in his work's title: the New World.[33]

The passage from Martire that interests us appears at the end of the third decade. He describes the nature of Hispaniola, its valleys, lakes, fish, mountain chains, as well as its people. He praises the expansion of Christianity, laments the mistreatment of the Indians, and draws comparisons between Hispaniola and Egypt (Martire had previously served as ambassador to Egypt). Toward the end, he mentions an uncontacted community believed to "live in the golden age."[34] Finally, a description of the copey tree (*clusia major*) opens the way for the story of the Indian and the letter. The anecdote starts by presenting the copey leaf as the same leaf used by the inventors of letters, "the Chaldeans," in order to communicate "with those who were not present before the invention of paper."[35] Martire's rendering otherwise includes the same moments later recorded by Gómara; however, Martire seems to have placed more emphasis on the simplicity of the Indians and on the comical dimension of the episode. As a whole, the chapter follows Martire's entertaining mix of recent travel accounts with classical themes. This admixture also appears in his letters about late fifteenth-century and early sixteenth-century European affairs, but his writing about the New World enjoyed greater popularity.[36] Martire shared with Columbus and their contemporaries a belief in geographical myths that included both traditional and empirical knowledge.[37] In the *Decadas*, the populations of the New World are characterized as a remote and alternative humanity, an equivalent to the Hyperboreans that had inhabited the borders of the ancient world.[38] Another feature in Martire's representation of the New World is the description of illiterate peoples as barbarians. He referred to his fellow humanist, Antonio de Nebrija, who created the first dictionary and grammar of the Spanish language, as the eraser of barbarism in Spain.[39] The anecdote seems to reflect the humanist practice of hierarchically classifying nations according to their level of education, which evidently had become applied to the New World's peoples, and the letter resided emblematically at the top of that hierarchy.

Both Ciceronian rhetoric and humanist culture linked the transition from barbarism to civility with the discovery of institutions, technologies, and arts, including oration and writing. Echoes of those traditions can be found in Martire's reference to the Chaldeans in his story of the letter, and in Garcilaso's representation of the first Inca, Manco Capac, as a man who feigned to be a god in order to enlighten the so-called simple people of what would be the city of Cuzco.[40] Both of these examples make use of the device of reaching to the past in order to give meaning to the present. Furthermore, the story of the letter can be connected to the maxim, perhaps of judiciary origin, "verba volant, scripta manent" and its similar variants. This saying alluded to by classical authors such as Horace and Ovid also reflects the phrase "winged words," which implied words that move.[41] The maxim as such was recorded in written form only during the Middle Ages.[42] For medievals, this transition resulted in the movement away from oral culture and the embrace of textual culture. Less than a century after Martire, Sebastián de Covarrubias's *Tesoro de la lengua castellana o española* expresses the same idea with the saying "hablen cartas y callen barbas" (let letters talk and beards be silent, suggesting that documents are more credible than oral testimonies).[43] And the Italian saying "carta canta" existed as well in Spanish, as Ricardo Palma would later use it in the title of his remaking of Garcilaso's version of the story in the nineteenth century. A comic tradition centered on illiteracy was developing elsewhere in Europe and it cannot be surprising to see it cross the Atlantic.[44]

Martire, Gómara, and Garcilaso's versions of the story of the letter fit within the classification offered in Hans-Jörg Uther's global study of folktales, and in particular, in Uther's 1296B type, called "Doves in the letter." In this type, an illiterate messenger is fooled by a letter that reveals his thievery.[45] The first subtype within the 1296B group includes a dialog and the second subtype features the hiding of the letter, both being components that appeared in Garcilaso's version of the anecdote. Although Uther's compilation mentions versions from parallel and later periods, including sixteenth-century Spanish anthologies of sayings and tales containing funny stories about a fooled messenger or a fooled master, even if the letter does not seem to feature prominently in those stories.[46] A recent study about Spanish folktales similar to the "doves in the letter" category proposes that the precedent for a more modern version entitled "Os ollos de papel" ("the paper's eyes" in Galician) is in a passage from one of Lope de Vega's (1562–1635) historical plays.[47] And this reference to the famous playwright, poet, and novelist Lope de Vega brings us to the last rendering of this anecdote.

In Lope de Vega's play *El Nuevo Mundo descubierto por Colón* (1614), the Indian messenger hides the letter, just as Garcilaso did and according to the "dove in the letter" type. While the geography of the Caribbean and the anchoring of the play to Columbus's temporal context resemble Martire and Gómara's settings, Lope invests agency into Indigenous peoples by narrativizing their first encounter with Europeans from their perspective. Because Lope seems to have used information provided by Oviedo and Gómara, it makes sense to suppose that the rendering in *El Nuevo Mundo* was inspired by Gómara's version of the anecdote.[48] And yet, it is also possible that Lope was equally familiar with Martire and with oral traditions.[49] Indeed, for an author of fiction, it was normal to draw inspiration from common places, themes, and surprising elements that historiographical works would only state briefly. The play commences with Columbus certain about his future greatness and his efforts to secure funding, which then becomes providentially intertwined with the Christian conquest of Granada, which reached its conclusion in 1492.[50] The Indians appear only in the second act (giving them a secondary role in the event of the discovery), and they do so while celebrating the civil and religious rituals in which their sun god features prominently. Contrary to Martire's letters, Lope's version situates Indians viewing Spaniards as novel interjections into their landscape, and they remark on an eclipse, refer to harquebuses as rays and to the Spaniards as children of the sun, as well as to an Indian who states that the Spaniards are not gods.[51] One of the Indian characters is Auté, a humorous man who first spots the Spanish ships at sea.[52] In the third act, he becomes a messenger for one of the Pinzón brothers, and during his travels from island to island, Auté serves as the protagonist of our anecdote twice. On the first occasion, he delivers a package of oranges, and on the second, the present consists of olives.[53] At first, Auté hides his crime and makes funny excuses for having eaten some of the fruit, but he later realizes that the letter cannot be deceived, and he acknowledges his thievery.

All versions of the story of the letter share a comical component that appeals to the moral function of the narrative. The story includes both the image of the Indian as innocent and naïve, and the retrospective explanation of the Spanish domination of the New World. These two discursive elements appear in broader colonial discourse intended to defend the Indians. As far as our anecdote is concerned, Martire seems to have constituted the starting point, and his invention may have derived from his practice of mixing testimonies about the New World with humanist common places about antiquity, education, and wit. Gómara located the story retrospectively in the imprecise time of the "beginning" and related it to the providential signs of conquest within his imperialist discourse. Garcilaso provided an extended version with more details, and his story contrasted pre-invasion Indian "antiquity" against colonial Peru, and therefore broke away from Gómara's use of Europeans' first encounter with his people. Finally, writing in the same chronological context as Garcilaso, Lope de Vega inserted the anecdote into a play about then-famous Columbus. Both Garcilaso and Lope extended the anecdote and provided it with literary consistency, but each of them approached the history of the New World from different perspectives. For Garcilaso, the story represented a serious and longstanding commitment to the colonial project, while Lope was more interested in re-creating an increasingly durable image of European discovery, one that matures in the Enlightenment, while brandishing an alternative version of events told through a fictional informant. Lope also chooses fruit of Spanish origin, instead of the Caribbean rodents described by Gómara; in the *Comentarios*, however, the fruit is of Peruvian extraction. Both the folkloric components dealing with messengers and fools, and the maxim about the power of the written word, offer parallel and earlier cultural elements related to the anecdote's features.

Among other considerations, the renderings of our anecdote reflect the combination of three ways of approaching the past: exemplary and entertaining anecdotes, the development of civil customs, and providential history. Typical of literature (including historiography), exemplarity relied upon shared values and helped to create a sense of community.

Civil development became especially significant to humanists writing about the New World, such as Martire and also Juan Ginés de Sepúlveda (1494–1573). Martire applied the humanist theme of distinguishing educated nations from uneducated ones to the New World, but the theme only became the object of extensive reflection at a global scale in the second half of the sixteenth century, when the humanist movement was transforming into a myriad of specialized disciplines under the influence of new forms of national and transnational power. The linking of literacy and text to the power relations of the world rendered the Americas well behind western nations such as Spain, and we must remember that text and literacy are valued in the west, which projects western values onto the world in a way that defines the modern era. Furthermore, while Columbus had been interested in interpreting his life according to his own reading of the bible, Martire did not emphasize the role of Christian providence neither in his rendering of the anecdote nor more generally in his work. But soon after, at least since Bartolomé de las Casas (1484–1566), the discussion about the Indians' innocence and idolatry continued to shape narratives in which the New World became discussed within the scope of universal history; this dovetails well with the increasing consequence of text.[54] Las Casas, Gómara, and other chroniclers mixed civil institutions and providential theses to justify either missionary or imperialist agendas (or both). The combination of the civil and the providential was especially important for authors writing about Indigenous pasts, including Garcilaso, and the role of geography within these universalist approaches became increasingly more significant.[55]

Regarding the story of the letter, it is worth observing that, while Gómara included the story within a series of anecdotes about providence and Lope placed it in Columbus's age, Garcilaso situated it within a section praising Peruvian goods. Thus, rather than using the anecdote to reinforce the event of the discovery of the New World, Garcilaso focused instead on the beginnings of colonial society in ways that honors his people's past, not unlike comparisons to Egypt and the Chaldeans seen in some Spanish sources. It is only at the end of his rendering that Garcilaso adds the corollary that Indians confused the Spaniards for gods. Instead, he isolated the discussion of providence to other sections of his chronicle in which he expressed his tragic understanding of Peru's history (including the Incan prophecies, the Cuzco miracles, and the uprising of the Spanish *encomenderos*). The contextualization of his passage shows therefore that Garcilaso was neither an isolated figure nor a mere imitator of Spanish chroniclers. Rather, he should be considered key transformer of the literary traditions of the early-modern colonial period.

Notes

1. O'Gorman, *La invención de América*. Unless otherwise noted, all translations are my own.

2. Todorov, *La Conquête de l'Amérique.*
3. Rolena Adorno, "Cultures in Contact: Mesoamerica, the Andes, and the European Written Tradition," in Gonzalez Echeverría and Pupo-Walker, eds., *The Cambridge History of Latin American Literature*, vol. 1, pp. 33–57: 43.
4. For Todorov's moral interest, see Todorov, *La Conquête de l'Amérique*, p. 12.
5. Fernández de Oviedo writes about the Caribbean cacique Enriquillo in his *Historia general y natural de las Indias*, book 5, ch. 7, p. 259; Díaz del Castillo on Hernán Cortés's use of native messengers in his *Historia verdadera de la conquista de la Nueva España*, p. 129; Fernández el Palentino with regard to an expedition to the Río de la Plata in his *Historia del Perú*, book 2, ch. 4, p. 102; and both the Inca Garcilaso and the anonymous Fidalgo de Elvas about Hernando de Soto's expedition to Florida (North America), in the former's *Comentarios reales*, book 2, ch. 1, p. 795, book 5, ch. 2, pp. 1151–1152, and the latter's *Relaçao verdadeira*, ch. 35, p. 190.
6. For two recent collective surveys on Garcilaso, see López, Ortiz, and Firbas, eds., *La biblioteca del Inca Garcilaso de la Vega*; and Castro-Klarén and Fernández, eds., *Inca Garcilaso*. A recent contextual approach that goes beyond the study of Garcilaso in isolation has been recently developed by Cárdens Bunsen, *La aparición de los libros plúmbeos*.
7. Judith Pollmann explains that early-modern autobiographical writing tended to focus on the narrator's family and body, on exemplary tales, and on cultural scripts or patterns; see Pollmann, *Memory in Early Modern Europe*, pp. 18–46.
8. Garcilaso, *Comentarios*, book 9, ch. 31, p. 708.
9. The structure of books 8 and 9 of the first part of the *Comentarios* is based on the alternation between sections devoted to the narration of the final expansion of the Incas (book 8), the war between Huascar and Atahualpa (book 9), and the description of Peruvian goods (book 8, ch. 9–25: goods existing before the arrival of the Spaniards; book 9, ch. 16–21: goods brought by the colonizers). The chapter that contains the anecdote is the 29th of book 9, entitled "De la hortaliza y yerbas, de la grandeza de ellas;" see Garcilaso, *Comentarios*, pp. 701–705.
10. "[S]e puede añadir que los melones tuvieron otra excelencia entonces, que ninguno salía malo, como lo dejasen madurar; en lo cual también mostraba la tierra su fertilidad." Garcilaso, *Comentarios*, book 9, ch. 29, p. 704.
11. "Y porque los primeros melones que en la comarca de Los Reyes se dieron causaron un cuento gracioso, será bien lo pongamos aquí, donde se verá la simplicidad que los indios en su antigüedad tenían." Garcilaso, *Comentarios*, p. 704.
12. Supposedly born in Medina del Campo, Solar appears in this chapter and in the following ones as an enemy of the viceroy. There also exists documentary evidence of a "regidor" (councilor) in Lima in 1549 named Antonio Solar. Archivo General de las Indias, Seville, Lima, 177, núm. 10; and Garcilaso, *Historia general del Perú*. I quote from the 2009 edition, book 6, ch. 4, p. 308.
13. "A la partida les dijo el capataz: 'no comáis ningún melón de estos porque si lo coméis lo ha de decir la carta'." Garcilaso, *Comentarios*, p. 704.
14. "Otro cuento refiere Gómara que pasó en la isla de Cuba a los principios, cuando ella se ganó. Y no es maravilla que una misma ignorancia pasase la simplicidad de los indios del Nuevo Mundo en lo que ellos no alcanzaron toda fue una." Garcilaso, *Comentarios*, p. 705.
15. Garcilaso's attentive and critical reading of Gómara's, *Historia* is attested by an existing copy of the *Historia* with annotations by Garcilaso. When reading

Gómara, Garcilaso paid attention to both key themes such as Inca religion and minor issues including the word "hutías," which is related to Gómara's rendering of the anecdote. Rivarola, "Para la génesis de los *Comentarios reales*," pp. 59–139: 69 and 71.

16. A study of the literary features of these short stories can be found in Pupo-Walker, *Historia, creación y profecía*, pp. 149–193. For a survey of the cuentos, see Iniesta, *El valor literario en la obra del Inca Garcilaso*, ch. 3 "Narrativa," section four: "Cuento," pp. 777–778.
17. Garcilaso, *Comentarios*, p. 8.
18. Ibid., book 1, ch. 18, p. 58.
19. Garcilaso's use of the adjective "historial" may have derived from his interest in the philosophical interpretation of gentile fables, as in Leone Ebreo's (1465–1523) *Dialoghi d'amore*, a neo-platonic treatise that Garcilaso had translated into Spanish (his translation was published in 1590). In Leone Ebreo's *Dialoghi d'amore* the term "cuento historial" refers both to history and to narrative: "encerrar en un cuento historial, verdadero o fingido, tantas y tan diversas y altas sentencias;" see Hebreo, *La traducción del Indio*, p. 75.
20. For the precedents of the story of the two caciques' toast in the first part of *Comentarios*, see Rodríguez Mansilla, "A vueltas con el brindis de los curacas," pp. 53–61. About Pedro Serrano's shipwreck, Carmen Bernand stressed the importance of the story's position between the first and the second age of Peruvian history, and Domingo Ledezma discussed a possible historical precedent. See Bernand, *Un Inca platonicien*, p. 260; and Domingo Ledezma, "Los infortunios de Pedro Serrano: huellas historiográficas de un relato de naufragio," in Mazzotti, ed., *Renacimiento mestizo*, pp. 31–50.
21. Garcilaso, *Historia general*, book 1, ch. 20–25, pp. 67–82.
22. Ibid., book 1, ch. 38; it is entitled "Una agudeza del ingenio de Atahuallpa, y la cantidad de su rescate," p. 103.
23. For the anecdotes associated with the rebel soldier, Francisco de Carvajal, see Rodríguez Mansilla, "Francisco de Carvajal," pp. 61–76.
24. Palma, *Tradiciones peruanas*, pp. 146–148.
25. Arrom, *Certidumbre de América*, pp. 27–35; and Pupo-Walker, *Historia, creación y profecía*, pp. 174–178.
26. Romiti, *Los hilos de la tierra*, p. 49. Romiti expands the post-colonial approach proposed by Juan Antonio Mazzotti in his *Incan Insights*.
27. Acosta, *Historia natural y moral de las Indias*, book 6, ch. 6, pp. 205–206.
28. Gonzalo Lamana, "Signifyin(g) Double Consciousness, and Coloniality: The *Royal Commentaries* as Theory of Practice and Political Project," in Castro-Klarén and Fernández, eds., *Inca Garcilaso*, pp. 297–315: 305.
29. The passage of the anecdote reads as follows: "Hicieron también mucho efecto las letras y las cartas que unos españoles a otros se escribían; ca pensaban los indios que tenían espíritu de profecía, pues sin verse ni hablarse se entendían, o que hablaba el papel, y estuvieron con esto embobados y corridos. Aconteció una vez a los comienzos que un español envió a otro una docena de hutías fiambres, para que no se corrompiesen con el calor. El indio que los llevaba se durmió o se cansó por el camino, y tardó mucho en llegar a donde iba; y entonces tuvo hambre o golosina de los hutías, y por no quedar con dentera ni deseo, se comió tres. La carta que trajo en respuesta decía cuánto le agradecía los nueve hutías y la hora del día en que le llegaron. El amo riñó al indio: él negaba, como dicen, a pies juntillas, mas como comprendió que lo decía la carta, confesó la verdad. Quedó corrido y escarmentado, y publicó entre los suyos que las cartas hablaban para que se guardasen de ellas;" see López de Gómara, *Hispania Victrix*, ch. 34, fol. 19.

30. Fernández de Oviedo, *Historia general y natural de las Indias*, part I, book 8, ch. 13, p. 301.
31. Todorov, *La Conquête de l'Amérique*, p. 104.
32. The term decades reflects his plan of dividing his work into ten books, but the first complete edition of Martire's *Decadas* included only eight sections and was published in 1530, four years after his death. The first *Decade* had appeared in 1511 and the next three decades in 1516. See Brigitte Gauvin, "Introduction," in Martire, *De orbe novo decadas*, pp. 85–86.
33. The term Nuevo Mundo or Mundus Novus was probably coined by Columbus himself, but it became popular thanks to Amerigo Vespucci, Martire, and other authors from the early 1500s. See Gil, *Mitos y utopías*, vol. 1, p. 205.
34. I quote from the first complete edition by Martire, *De orbe nouo*, fol. 51. Also see his *The decades of the newe worlde*, pp. 134–135. An Italian version appeared in Ramusio's widely read *Delle nauigationi et viaggi*, fol. 34.
35. We can compare this against the etymological explanation in Pedro Mexía's humanist encylopedia: "todos los antiguos afirman que, al principio, los hombres no tenían papel ni pergamino, y escribían en hojas de palma, y esto dura hasta hoy llamar hojas las de los libros;" see Castro, ed., *Silva de varia lección*, vol. 2, part 1, p. 17. Also see Mexía, *Silva de varia lección.*
36. For example, Martire who, writing to Giovanni Borromeo in 1487, referred to the Catholic kings as two deities descending from the sky: "iustiticiae tenacissimos et summa pollentes prudentia principes, virum et uxorem, qui eam unanimes veluti collapsa coelo duo numino;" see Mártir, *Opus epistolarum*, fol. 1. For the contribution of this letter to political propaganda, see Cátedra, *La historiografía en verso*, p. 80.
37. For example, for Ptolemy's geographical texts, Marco Polo's travels, legends about semi-human nations, and the term "alter orbis," see Juan Gil, *Mitos y utopías*.
38. Ibid., vol. 1, p. 93, with references to Pliny and Solinus.
39. See Mario Damonte, "Pietro Martire d'Anghiera e l'umanesimo spagnolo," in *Pietro Martire d'Anghiera*, pp. 175–185: 177. Damonte also mentions other humanists who impacted barbarism in Spain at that time. For Martire's poem with Nebrija's commentary, see Nebrija, *Comentario al poema*. Regarding earlier authors, see Gómez Moreno, *España y la Italia de los humanistas*, p. 125.
40. Garcilaso, *Comentarios*, book 1, ch. 21, p. 68. For the importance of such an analogy in the representation of the first Inca (Manco Capac) and in Garcilaso's self-interest as a "pure blood," see Cárdenas Bunsen, *La aparición de los libros plúmbeos*, p. 378.
41. "[N]ec retinent patulae commissa fideliter aures, semel emissum volat irrevocabile verbum," in Horace, *Satires*, vol. 1, p. 375. Also see Horace, *Satires and Epistles*, p. 89. For Ovid, see Tissol, *The Face of Nature*, p. 48.
42. Defined as "littera scripta manet" and "vox audita perit, litera scripta manet," in Riley, ed., *Dictionary of Latin Quotations*, p. 206 and 506, respectively. According to the editor, the saying was "probably a portion of a medieval pentameter" (p. 206). For a discussion of Ovid in relation to the verba volant maxim, see Tissol, *The Face of Nature*, pp. 47–48.
43. Covarrubias Horozco, *Tesoro de la lengua castellana*, p. 467.
44. There existed, however, jokes regarding people who were unable to read, who misread letters or lacked the sufficient familiarity with lettered culture. For example, in a section of *Il corteggiano* dealing with the rivalry among cities, there is an anecdote about a man from Siena who, after having heard a letter that had been read aloud at a council meeting, asked "who is the aforementioned?" (wrongly thinking that "aforementioned" was someone's name). Castiglione, *El cortesano*, p. 281.

45. Uther, *The Types of International Folktales*, p. 111. Uther documented the existence of versions of this type of folktale in modern times in Finland, Lithuania, Denmark, Frisia, Flanders, Germany, Italy, Rumania, Iran, Japan, and Cuba. For the Cuban version, see Hansen, *The Types of the Folktale in Cuba*, p. 154.
46. These tales appear in the collections published by Santa Cruz, Luis de Pinedo and Juan de Timoneda, as well as in a popular saying known as "habla Beltrán y habla por su mal," in earlier medieval tales from Arabic Spain, and in tales from later periods. For example, the story titled "Tres brevas" (three figs): "El obispo don Pedro del Campo envió a fray Bernaldino Palomo seis capones. El mozo que los llevaba tomó uno de ellos. Como [Palomo] los contó, dijo: decid a su señoría que le beso la mano por los cinco y besádselas vos por el uno;" see Santa Cruz, *Floresta española*, p. 18. In a note, the editors explain that Bernardino Palomo or Bernardino de Flores was a popular preacher. Also see Granja, "Tres cuentos españoles," pp. 123–141.
47. Beltran Llavador, "Dos cuentecillos de Timoneda," pp. 26, 36–37.
48. Regarding the reading of Gómara, see Madera Allan, "Shouting Distance: Local History and the Global Empire in Lope de Vega's *Famosa comedia del Nuevo mundo descubierto por Cristóbal Colón*," in Kavey and Kethner, eds., *Imagining Early Modern Histories*, pp. 12–26: 22.
49. For examples of folkloric tales in Lope de Vega, see Fradejas Lebrero, "Media docena de cuentos," pp. 121–144.
50. Lope de Vega, *El Nuevo Mundo*, Act I, v. 21–22: "Una secreta deidad / a que lo intente me impele." In the same act, v. 715–820, a dialog takes place between Columbus, Imagination, Christianity, and Idolatry, and v. 930–949 portrays Columbus telling Isabel that after the conquest of Granada it was time to win the entire world.
51. With regard to claiming that the Spaniards are not gods, see Lope de Vega, *El Nuevo Mundo*, Act III, v. 2191: "Basta que aqueste español / no es dios, pues que no conoce / el pensamiento que traigo."
52. For Auté's discovery of what he thinks are three houses in the sea, see Lope de Vega, *El Nuevo Mundo*, Act II, v. 1480.
53. See Lope de Vega, *El Nuevo Mundo*, Act II, v. 2250–2288 for the "papel" (letter) and the oranges, and v. 2375–2405 for the olives.
54. For a comparison between las Casas's prophetic approach, Motolonía's millenarian basis, and Quiroga's utopianism in relation to the evangelization of the New World, see Orique, "Journey to the Headwaters," pp. 1–24. For Garcilaso and the tradition of universal history, see Guillermo Serés, "Los *Comentarios reales* y la historia universal," in Mora, Serés, and Serna, eds., *Humanismo, mestizaje y escritura*, pp. 319–347.
55. Subrahmanyam, "On World Historians," pp. 26–57; and Rubiés, "The Concept of a Gentile Civilization in Missionary Discourse and Its European Reception: Mexico, Peru and China in the *Repúblicas del Mundo* by Jerónimo Román," in Castelnau, Copete, Maldavski, and Zupanov, eds., *Missions d'évangélisation et circulation des savoirs*, pp. 311–350.

Bibliography

Acosta, José de, *Historia natural y moral de las Indias*, ed. Fermín del Pino (Madrid: Consejo Superior de Investigaciones Científicas, 2008).
Archivo General de las Indias, Seville, Lima, 177, núm. 10.
Arrom, Juan José, *Certidumbre de América* (Madrid: Gredos, 1971).

Beltran Llavador, Rafael, "Dos cuentecillos de Timoneda ('Dos reales de lo que hay' y 'Así los rompí') en la tradición oral moderna," *Estudios de Literatura Oral Popular* 2 (2013), pp. 23–43.
Bernand, Carmen, *Un Inca platonicien. Garcilaso de la Vega, 1539–1616* (Paris: Fayard, 2006).
Cárdens Bunsen, José Alejandro, *La aparición de los libros plúmbeos y los modos de escribir la historia: de Pedro de Castro al Inca Garcilaso de la Vega* (Madrid: Iberoamericana, 2018).
Castelnau, Charlotte de, Marie-Lucie Copete, Aliocha Maldavski, and Ines Zupanov, eds., *Missions d'évangélisation et circulation des savoirs XVIe-XVIIIe siècles* (Madrid: Casa de Velázquez, 2011).
Castiglione, Baldassare, *El cortesano*, trans. Juan Boscán, ed. Mario Pozzi (Madrid: Cátedra, 2011).
Castro, Antonio, ed., *Silva de varia lección* (Madrid: Cátedra, 1990).
Castro-Klarén, Sara, and Christian Fernández, eds., *Inca Garcilaso & Contemporary World-Making* (Pittsburgh: University of Pittsburgh Press, 2016).
Cátedra, Pedro, *La historiografía en verso en la época de los Reyes Católicos* (Salamanca: Universidad de Salamanca, 1989).
Convegno internazionale di studi americanistici, *Pietro Martire d'Anghiera nella Storia e nella Cultura* (Genoa: Associazione Italiana Studi Americanistici, 1980).
Covarrubias Horozco, Sebastián de, *Tesoro de la lengua castellana o española*, ed. Ignacio Arellano and Rafael Zafra (Madrid: Iberoamericana, 2006).
Díaz del Castillo, Bernal, *Historia verdadera de la conquista de la Nueva España*, eds. Ángel Delado and Luis A. Arocena (Madrid: Homo Legens, 2008).
Elvas, Fidalgo de, *Relaçao verdadeira dos trabalhos que o governador D. Fernando de Souto e certo fidalgos portugueses passaram no descobrimento da província da Florida*, ed. Maria da Graça A. Mateus Ventura (Lisbon: Comissão Nacional para as Comemoraçoes, 1998).
Fernández de Oviedo, Gonzalo, *Historia general y natural de las Indias* (Madrid: Real Academia de la Historia, 1851).
Fernández el Palentino, Diego, *Historia del Perú*, ed. Juan Pérez de Tudela (Madrid: Atlas, 1963).
Fradejas Lebrero, José, "Media docena de cuentos de Lope de Vega," *Anales de Literatura Española* 5 (1986–1987), pp. 121–144.
Garcilaso de la Vega, el Inca, *Historia general del Perú* (Cordoba: viuda de A. de Barrera, 1617).
———, *Comentarios reales; La Florida del Inca*, ed. Mercedes López-Baralt (Madrid: Espasa, 2003).
———, *Historia general* (Lima: SCG, 2009).
Gil, Juan, *Mitos y utopías del descubrimiento*, vol. 1: *Colón y su tiempo* (Madrid: Alianza, 1989).
Gómez Moreno, Ángel, *España y la Italia de los humanistas: primeros ecos* (Madrid: Gredos, 1992).
Gonzalez Echeverría, Roberto, and Enrique Pupo-Walker, eds., *The Cambridge History of Latin American Literature* (Cambridge: Cambridge University Press, 1996).
Granja, Fernando de la, "Tres cuentos españoles de origen árabe," *Al-Andalus* 33.1 (1968), pp. 123–141.

Hansen, Terrence Leslie, *The Types of the Folktale in Cuba, Puerto Rico, the Dominican Republic, and Spanish South America* (Berkeley: University of California Press, 1957).
Hebreo, León, *La traducción del Indio de los tres diálogos de amor de León Hebreo* (Madrid: Pedro Madrigal, 1590).
Horace, *Satires, Epistles and Ars Poetica*, ed. H. Rushton Fairclough (Cambridge, MA: William Heinemann Ltd., 1929).
———, *Satires and Epistles* (New York: Oxford University Press, 2011).
Iniesta, Amalia, *El valor literario en la obra del Inca Garcilaso de la Vega* (PhD dissertation) (Madrid: Editorial Complutense, 1982).
Kavey, Allison, and Elizabeth Kethner, eds., *Imagining Early Modern Histories* (Farnham, UK: Ashgate Publishing, 2016).
Lope de Vega, Félix, *El Nuevo Mundo descubierto por Cristóbal Colón*, ed. Rosa Durá Celma (Artelope, 2018). http://artelope.uv.es/biblioteca/textosAL/AL0779_ElNuevoMundoDescubiertoPorCristobalColon
López, Esperanza, Marta Ortiz, and Paul Firbas, eds., *La biblioteca del Inca Garcilaso de la Vega* (Madrid: Biblioteca Nacional/AECID, 2016).
López de Gómara, Francisco, *Hispania Victrix. Primera y segunda parte de la Historia general de las Indias* (Medina del Campo: Guillermo de Millis, 1553).
Martire, Pietro d'Anghiera, *De orbe nouo* (Compluti: apud Michaelem d'Eguia, 1530).
———, *Opus epistolarum Paetri Martyris Anglerii* (Alcalá de Henares: Miguel de Eguía, 1530).
———, *The Decades of the Newe Worlde or West India*, trans. Richard Eden (London: In aedibus Guilhelmi Powell, 1555).
———, *De orbe novo decadas: oceana decas—Décades du nouveau monde: La decade océane* (Paris: Les Belles Lettres, 2003).
Mazzotti, José Antonio, ed., *Incan Insights: El Inca Garcilaso's Hints to Andean Readers* (Madrid: Iberoamericana Editorial, 2008).
———, *Renacimiento mestizo: Los 400 años de los Comentarios reales* (Madrid: Iberamericana, 2010).
Mexía, Pedro, *Silva de varia lección* (Seville: Juan Cromberger, 1540).
Mora, Carmen de, Guillermo Serés, and Mercedes Serna, eds., *Humanismo, mestizaje y escritura en los Comentarios Reales* (Madrid: Vervuert, 2010).
Nebrija, Elio Antonio de, *Comentario al poema In Ianum de Pedro Mártir de Anglería*, ed. Carmen Codoñer (Salamanca: Universidad de Salamanca, 1992).
O'Gorman, Edmundo, *La invención de América. Investigación acerca de la estructura histórica del Nuevo Mundo y el sentido de su devenir* (Mexico City: FCE, 1958).
Orique, David T., "Journey to the Headwaters: Bartolomé de las Casas in a Comparative Context," *The Catholic Historical Review* 95.1 (2009), pp. 1–24.
Palma, Ricardo, *Tradiciones peruanas* (Madrid: Aguilar, 1957).
Pollmann, Judith, *Memory in Early Modern Europe, 1500–1800* (Oxford: Oxford University Press, 2017).
Pupo-Walker, Enrique, *Historia, creación y profecía en los textos del Inca Garcilaso de la Vega* (Madrid: Porrúa, 1982).
Ramusio, Giovanni Battista, *Delle nauigationi et viaggi* (Venice: I Giunti, 1606).
Riley, Henry Thomas, ed., *Dictionary of Latin Quotations, Proverbs, Maxims, and Mottos, Classical and Medieval* (London: Henry G. Bohn, 1856).

Rivarola, José Luis, "Para la génesis de los *Comentarios reales*: edición y comentario de las apostillas del Inca Garcilaso (y otros) a la *Historia general de las Indias* de F. López de Gómara," *Nueva Revista de Filología Hispánica* 50.1 (2002), pp. 59–139.

Rodríguez Mansilla, Fernando, "Francisco de Carvajal, *Vir facetus* en el libro V de la *Historia general del Perú*," *Boletín de la Academia Peruana de la Lengua* 44 (2007), pp. 61–76.

———, "A vueltas con el brindis de los curacas: un cuentecillo tradicional en la narrativa peruana," *Boletín de Literatura Oral* 4 (2014), pp. 53–61.

Romiti, Elena, *Los hilos de la tierra: relaciones interculturales y escritura: el Inca Garcilaso de la Vega* (Montevideo: Biblioteca Nacional, 2009).

Santa Cruz, Melchor de, *Floresta española*, eds. M. Pilar Cuartero and Maxime Chevalier (Barcelona: Crítica, 1997).

Subrahmanyam, Sanjay, "On World Historians in the Sixteenth Century," *Representations* 91 (2005), pp. 26–57.

Tissol, Garth, *The Face of Nature: Wit, Narrative, and Cosmic Origins in Ovid's Metamorphoses* (Princeton, NJ: Princeton University Press, 1997).

Todorov, Tzvetan, *La Conquête de l'Amérique. La question de l'autre* (Paris: Le Seuil, 2013).

Uther, Hans-Jörg, *The Types of International Folktales: A Classification and Bibliography Based on the System of Antti Aarne and Stith Thompson* (Helsinki: Suomalainen Tiedeakatemia, Academia Scientiarun Fennica, 2004).

Part II

Modernity and Unfamiliarity as Firsting Principles

5 The Grammar of Inanimacy

Frances Brooke and the Production of North American Settler States

Rachel Bryant

In the fifth letter of the 1769 epistolary novel *The History of Emily Montague* by Frances Brooke (1724–1789), the British officer Ed Rivers admits to feeling "tir'd of the lovely landscape" of Canada, having now "enjoy'd from it all the pleasure meer inanimate objects can give." He complains to his sister in London that although "the scenery" of Canada "is to be sure divine,"

> one grows weary of meer scenery; the most enchanting prospect soon loses its power of pleasing, when the eye is accustom'd to it: we gaze at first transported on the charms of nature, and fancy they will please for ever; but alas! it will not do; we sigh for society, the conversation of those dear to us; the more animated pleasures of the heart.[1]

At this early point in the novel, Rivers fears that his personal vitality may be dwindling due to his physical removal from the precise kind of social stimulation that he had grown accustomed to at home in England. Thus, longing for the "animated pleasures" of British society, he frets to his sister about the "state of vegetation" into which he fears himself "falling" in Canada.[2]

The essential distinction that Rivers draws in this letter between culture and nature is a central theme from Brooke's well-trod text, one that surfaces and resurfaces across the letters of each of her characters, fundamentally informing and even circumscribing their reflections and actions. The social world of this novel rests upon a series of almost constantly drawn distinctions between characters' perceptions of a preferred and *animate* cultural world and an inferior, *inanimate* natural world; the adjective "vegetative," for example, is routinely deployed by characters seeking an insulting way to describe those poor souls who are incapable or unworthy of happiness or of true love.[3] To date, critics of *Emily Montague* have underemphasized the importance of this theme to the functions of Brooke's novel, preoccupying themselves instead with her Euro-western feminism, her views on British colonial policies, and the question of where (or even if) her novel fits within the nationalist literary traditions of Britain, Canada, and the United States. The novel has been greatly "neglected in Britain," where it was originally published, but where Brooke's other works are comparatively well-known;[4] it has been variously embraced and rejected as the first Canadian novel in English;[5] and it has been almost entirely ignored in the United States, where "the logic that the creation of the republic in 1789 coincides with the invention of the American novel" continues to maintain "a deep hold" on literary history.[6]

Arguably far more important are the ways in which Brooke's novel belongs to each of these national formulations—British, American, and Canadian—in equal measure. Across the corpus of Anglophone Atlantic-world literature, distinctions between culture and nature helped normalize and canonize what the Potawatomi botanist Robin Wall Kimmerer might call a "profound error in grammar," referring to the essential limitations in vision that continue to undergird English thought and verbalization, sustaining and furthering assaults on Indigenous land, peoples, and worldviews at the level of language. In *Braiding Sweetgrass*, Wall Kimmerer characterizes English as an imported "language of objects," one that systematically severs networks of relations and reduces complex beings to things, refusing the existence of what Anishinaabe peoples have traditionally understood as "a world of being, full of unseen energies that animate everything."[7] Recounting her own early struggles when first learning to speak Potawatomi, or Bodewasmimwin, Wall Kimmerer explains that today, Indigenous peoples whose languages were stolen from them in previous generations cannot re-acquire those languages through vocabulary lessons or through rote memorization exercises that simply substitute one noun for another—exercises that ultimately preserve the scaffolding of an English cultural grammar in which the world is steadfastly perceived and portrayed as a collection of objects. Like other Indigenous languages, Potawatomi extends what Wall Kimmerer calls "the grammar of animacy" to not only "plants and animals" but also to rocks, water, fire, place, and more. "Beings that are imbued with spirit," she explains,

> our sacred medicines, our songs, drums, and even stories, are all animate. The list of inanimate seems to be smaller, filled with objects that are made by people. Of an inanimate being, like a table, we say, "*What* is it?" And we answer *Dopwen yewe*. Table it is. But of apple, we must say, "*Who* is that being?" And reply *Mshimin Yawe*. Apple that being is.[8]

All languages enshrine and perpetuate culturally specific values and worldviews; Potawatomi is simultaneously a language and a perspective that reflects and engages with the agency of a diverse world of beings worthy of respectful interaction, and with an autonomous physical sphere imbued with spirit, one that is by no means subservient to human beings but rather "full of thought, desire, contemplation, and will."[9] Through a grammar of animacy, human Potawatomi speakers forge and uphold the relational framework of a vast and mysterious living world; in turn, those relationships manifest and shape the ways in which Potawatomi speakers perceive and engage with their surroundings.[10]

Using Wall Kimmerer's writing on the grammar of animacy as a point of departure, this chapter foregrounds and explores Brooke's grammar of inanimacy—her candid reliance on an English system of classification and perception through which colonial (and, later, settler-colonial) writers and readers actively if often unthinkingly stripped beings "of selfhood and kinship," severing existing relationships and functionally reducing distinct and autonomous worlds to collections of mindless, exploitable objects.[11] Today, to borrow words from the Mi'kmaw poet Shalan Joudry, the grammar of inanimacy is an essential component of the "machine" that Anglophone settlers are taught to "work automatic" from birth, perpetuating not only the poverty and dispossession of Indigenous peoples across Turtle Island (North America), but also the denial of their cultures and worldviews.[12] In *Emily Montague*, the grammar of inanimacy both anchors to and facilitates what the Ojibwe historian Jean O'Brien calls firsting narratives, which are the conventional stories that Euro-Americans use to seize Indigenous homelands for themselves. The reductive and controlling functions of English as a language of objects emerge from this novel as an essential ideology that produces and naturalizes a culturally specific social world, establishing clear rules for human thought patterns and for the ways in which people locate and imagine themselves in relation to other (always inferior) beings. And while the English language denies the agency of plants, land, and animals automatically, bolstering and protecting the heightened place of the human species within a deeply and strategically stratified universe, Brooke employs the mechanisms of this system hungrily, widely, and explicitly, inadvertently emphasizing the ways in which its logics produce and order the dominant social contexts in which the descendants of British colonists continue to live their lives.

The History of Emily Montague is, as its title suggests, the story of a woman's prior life. More specifically, it is the story of the life that Emily Montague lives before starting her new life with Captain Ed Rivers, a presumably happy life that plays out in England, beyond the final pages of Brooke's text. The site of Emily's relevant history is 1766–1767 Quebec following the British conquest of Canada. These years roughly correspond with Brooke's own sojourn in Quebec, where she recorded her impressions of colonial life, material which became the basis of her novel, while her husband worked as a military chaplain.[13]

When the story of *Emily Montague* begins, its title character is engaged to be married to Sir George Clayton, who is away in New York when Rivers arrives on the scene, and the novel's primary plot thus hinges on the question of whether or not Emily will escape from her prior engagement—a gradual process that allegorically mirrors a conventionally perceived conflict between culture and nature. According to Brooke, the most significant danger that Emily faces as a young British person in Canada is the threat to her animacy. This threat is plainly embodied by Sir George, who is variously described as a "dull clod of uninformed earth," a "piece of still life," a man who exists in a "natural vegetative state," and one who "resembles the form" of "Prometheus's man of clay, before he stole the celestial fire to animate him."[14] The "proper wife" for Sir George, Rivers reasons, would be "a rich, sober, sedate, presbyterian citizen's daughter, educated by her grandmother in the country, who would roll about with him in unwieldy splendor, and dream away a lazy existence."[15] In other words, Sir George is a "lifeless composition of earth and water" and a poor match for a modern woman like Emily, who is composed of comparably "active elements."[16] Even Emily understands that her feelings for her fiancé are unsatisfying, and she wishes her "tenderness for him" was "more lively."[17] To maintain her animacy and her place within what is portrayed as an elite "society of friends," she must resist slipping into a "vegetative state" with Sir George in Canada and instead nurture ties with those "people of sensibility and sentiment" who comprise the novel's preferred community.[18] In the final section of the novel, once Emily has escaped the snare of the dull, vegetative Sir George, Brooke repeats this basic plot once more. Rivers encounters a French-Canadian woman named Madame Des Roches, who briefly "seems to rival" Emily for his love, and he must, at this juncture, resist sacrificing his own place within animate society—a consequence that would surely follow were he to settle down with Des Roches for a life spent within a rival culture in rural Quebec.[19]

With the development of this central metaphor and the resolutions of each of these supporting conflicts, Brooke actively mythologizes the existence of an elite class of British subjects who can successfully exist for a time in the so-called New World without being changed by the experience and without forging transformative bonds with the beings who exist outside of their closed society. Their struggles against the forces of a collectively perceived inanimacy mirror the conflict that previous generations of colonists had imagined to exist between themselves and the natural world.[20] The very fact that Brooke's characters are able to leave Canada at the end of this novel and slip so easily back into British society functions as a further testament to their collective spine of fortitude and abstention, qualities long deemed necessary for the successful consolidation of imported and supposedly superior European values against the existing structures and environments of Turtle Island. To date, critics have read the conclusion of this novel, in which the central characters all return to England, as a scathing critique of the viability of Canada as a British colony; on the contrary, it is perhaps the primary key to Britain's success as an elite colonizing culture.[21]

Thus, to understand what animates beings in the closed and contained society portrayed in Brooke's novel, the work must first be situated as a relatively conventional work of Anglo-American colonial abstention. Rivers sentimentally if vaguely describes his society's animating forces as "the lively sweet affections, the only sources of true pleasure" that are "the portion only of a chosen few."[22] Of course, Rivers is not the only character in this novel who adopts an explicit grammar of inanimacy to divide and order the world around him—in his own words, to make "order and beauty gradually rise from chaos"[23]—or to draw fundamental distinctions between what Stephen Carl Arch calls "the elite few and the vulgar many."[24] In one letter, Arabella ("Bell") Fermor submits to her dear friend Emily that

> Half of the world [. . .] have no souls; at least none but of the vegetable and animal kinds: to this species of beings, love and sentiment are entirely unnecessary; they were made to travel through life in a state of mind neither quite awake nor asleep; and it is perfectly equal to them in what company they take the journey. You any I, my dear, are something awakened; [. . .] our souls, being of the active kind, can never be totally at rest.[25]

Extending Arch's reading of *Emily Montague*, one could reasonably argue that Brooke's relentless development of this divisive metaphor represents not only the concept of an elite society but also a secularization of the Puritan doctrine of *the elect*—the belief, so influentially advanced by the French theologian John Calvin (1509–1564) in sixteenth-century Europe, that the Judeo-Christian god bestowed grace and salvation upon only a few chosen people whose collective responsibility it was to light and lead the world.[26]

As I have argued elsewhere, this core and self-aggrandizing belief remains fundamental to both settler-Canadian and -American origin myths and to ideologies of exceptionalism.[27] In 1630, John Winthrop (1588–1649) preached a famous message of social and cultural abstention to his followers, who were instructed—before their arrival on the shores of Turtle Island—to "resist" the "enemies" and temptations that would inevitably exist outside the walls of their closed society by remaining "knit [. . .] together in the bonds of brotherly affection."[28] From the perspective of Winthrop and the Puritans, "Christ and his church" comprised "the most perfect and best proportioned body in the world"—a single body held together by the "bonds" or "ligaments" of "love" and consisting of "parts" that "mutually participate with each other, both in strength and infirmary, in pleasure and pain."[29] Importantly, this perfect human body was closed to nature, to perceived outsiders, and to transformation—closed, in other words, to anything or anyone who might undermine its divine structure and most beloved mythologies.[30] And because Christ was the spirit that animated the Puritans' self-protecting body, individual compromise was cast as the most significant threat to the collective's sacred mission and to their eternal destiny.

Within the context of Turtle Island, the Massachusetts Bay social model is an archetypal example of the way in which "settler colonial spaces displace and replace Indigenous spaces. Spaces in this sense are social—they are the animate geographies of our everyday lives. Spaces are not predetermined but empowered by collective agreement that they exist."[31] While comparably secular, a fundamentally similar model is invoked, explained, and empowered in *Emily Montague*: implicitly, through the novel's central conflicts and constructed cultural world, and explicitly, when, for example, Bell separates humans from vegetables and animals, or when Captain Fermor writes of the "mutual confidence" that is "so necessary to keep the bands of society from loosening, and without which man is the most ferocious of all beasts of prey."[32] In the most general sense, the elite characters who comprise Brooke's empowered collective are animated simply through their willing participation in a society that exists through its members' mutual insistence or agreement. Emily at one point has her "inexpressible melting languor" transformed into "a joy which [animates] her whole form" simply by spending a few minutes standing idly with Rivers by a window.[33] In this scene, lonesome characters are mutually energized by and through brief moments of fateful fellowship because they belong together, because, in Bell's terms, they have awakened souls, and because their essential ideas about how society should function align.

Much like Winthrop's Puritans, then, the members of Brooke's empowered collective are tasked with the responsibility of helping each other to resist transgressing the established boundaries of their social world and thereby slipping into the vegetative world—the domain of the majority, those inferior beings who lack sufficient standing in human, cultural, and universal spheres. By developing and openly trafficking in this ideology, Brooke inadvertently highlights some of the ways in which English colonists traditionally extended or withheld ideas of worth or animacy to include or exclude beings (both human and non-human) from a closed society. Her characters work in concert to maintain and protect that ideal or idealized social body, and as Captain Fermor eventually argues, again invoking Winthrop, "nothing is a stronger tie of brotherhood and affection, a greater cement of union, than speaking one common language."[34] To reiterate, a primary common language that binds Brooke's elite collective together is their English grammar of inanimacy—their shared and consistent invocations of an imported language of objects that denies the agency of beings deemed extraneous or contrary to the furtherance of their own sense of mission. On a fundamental level, this grammar is regulated by what the Kanien'keha (Mohawk) and Anishinaabe scholar Vanessa Watts calls "the epistemological-ontological divide," which is the system of thought, based in seventeenth-century European philosophy, that "separates" the "constituents of the world from how the world is understood," effectively "[limiting] agency to humans" and ensuring an "exclusionary relationship with nature."[35] This Cartesian separation elevates "humankind [. . .] outside or above the natural world," stripping that world of its innate capacities for thought and reason; thus, non-human beings, such as rivers, "may act (i.e. flow)," but as brute entities incapable of thought or will, they cannot "perceive or contemplate" those actions.[36]

Although systematized through the English "language of objects," the epistemological-ontological divide is not natural or neutral but is rather the culturally specific ideological construction that produces and polices the disruptive governing perspectives that were, across centuries, furthered and increasingly normalized by and through the corpus of Anglophone Atlantic-world literature.[37] In this specific case, the divide is not only an essential basis for understanding Brooke's plot trajectory and social metaphors but also the cultural logic behind her characters' objectifications of their surroundings. Rivers, for example, at one point laments that the "numerous rivers" of Canada "roll their waters in vain" simply because those waters have not yet been harnessed for human purposes.[38] Because he assumes that humankind exists above and apart from the physical world, or that nature is soulless—extraneous and wholly subservient to human society—the only value he can perceive in a river lies in its ability to contribute to his own relatively narrow mission, which involves the extraction and accumulation of personal property and wealth.[39] Here, as elsewhere, Rivers's grammar of inanimacy functions as an intellectual barrier, not only circumscribing the way in which he personally experiences and understands the non-human world, but also protecting him and his audience from the unsettling and potentially transformative knowledge that there might be other purposes, other perspectives, and other well-established ways of existing as a human being in relation to this land and its diverse inhabitants. It does not or cannot occur to Rivers that the land might be alive or animate because he learned, through his own childhood process of language acquisition, to understand and identify beings such as rivers not as neighbors but as objects.

Yet, the fictional characters of this novel, like Brooke herself, or like the Massachusetts Bay settlers, would have been surrounded by evidence of those other ways of being and of understanding while moving about on the land. They would have been surrounded, for example, by Indigenous peoples for whom "habitats and ecosystems" were and are "understood as societies" with distinct "ethical structures and inter-species treaties and agreements."[40] As Watts's affirms, beings such as rivers are not only "active members" of Indigenous social worlds but "they also directly" and thoughtfully "influence how humans organize themselves" within those worlds; "the very existence of clan systems evidences these many historical agreements between humans and non-humans. Clan systems vary from community to community and are largely dependent on the surrounding landscape."[41] As Wall Kimmerer reminds us, the respect that many Indigenous peoples traditionally extended to their non-human neighbors is preserved in the structures of their languages. Rivers's adverse view of those same beings is circumscribed by his own language; the idea that a river, a valley, a boulder, or an animal population might thoughtfully influence or deliberately organize human society is both beyond and contrary to his established imaginary, in which non-human beings are resources that exist for human use or consumption, and human beings are steadfastly the agents and never the subjects of transformation.

Throughout this novel, the grammar of inanimacy manifests in subtle and explicit ways as a common language and as a powerful shared ideology for English characters seeking to shape and control relational frameworks: the rules by which human beings live in relation to one other, to the land, and to the land's diverse inhabitants. Importantly, however, Brooke's characters periodically if backhandedly acknowledge the grammar of animacy that is employed by the Wendat (Huron) people, and the few Wendat figures who feature in *Emily Montague* maintain this grammar even when conversing in European languages. "Their style even in speaking French is bold and metaphorical," Rivers at one point muses, and

> even in common conversation they speak in figures, of which I have this moment an instance. A savage woman was wounded lately in defending an English family from the drunken rage of one of her nation. I asked her after her wound; "It is well," said she; "my sisters at Quebec (meaning the English ladies) have been kind to me."[42]

Notably, this woman uses an imported language not to objectify or undermine a perceived rival but to instead forge an inclusive relationship with beings who are different from herself. By generously extending kinship to the English interlopers, she is attempting to share her territory and to usher the newcomers into long-established ways of living together. For Rivers, her kinship metaphor is pleasing, quaint, and highly amusing, but that is all. It is in no way taken seriously or thoughtfully reciprocated, and Rivers's dismissive inclusion of this information in his letter thus reflects nothing of a greater degree of sophistication, legitimacy, or generosity that might exist among the people he so disparagingly describes—the people whose own language, he stubbornly concludes, is "[irreducible] to rules," chaotic and capable of conveying "much fewer ideas" than English.[43]

In another letter, Bell reveals to her friend in London that her Wendat neighbors routinely converse and exchange information with beavers. "The savages assure us," she writes, "on the information of the beavers, that we shall have a very mild winter; it seems, these creatures have laid less in a winter stock than usual. I take it very ill, Lucy, that the beavers have better intelligence than we have."[44] By sharing information from the beavers with the English colonists, the Wendat instructively demonstrate their perspective of land as a space that is held in common by and among many nations, human and non-human alike.[45] This, again, is a valuable and generous teaching, but in a subsequent letter to the same friend, Bell denounces beavers as a reliable source of intelligence, writing, "I will never take a beaver's word again as long as I live: there is no supporting this cold; the Canadians say it is seventeen years since there has been so severe a season. I thought beavers had been people of more honor."[46] By ultimately modeling information about beaver intelligence and peoplehood as a kind of joke, Bell asserts a conventional Euro-western hierarchy of beings, presenting any possibility that animals might be recognized or counted as members of society as a source of provincial amusement.

These two brief anecdotes are notable for the ways in which they openly acknowledge and then hastily dismiss an Indigenous grammar of animacy, and arguably, they are essential to the functions of Brooke's novel as a whole. In her work on New English mythologies and their legacies, the Ojibwe historian Jean O'Brien explains why such specific information about Indigenous peoples was so often included in early Anglophone-American writings, such as letters, travel journals, and settlement narratives. First, as is evident in both Bell and Rivers's letters, colonial authors needed to Americanize their texts for the benefit of European-based audiences who were curious about life in the colonies. They also needed to establish an intelligible sense of what O'Brien calls "prefatory history" in their texts—a sufficiently specific construction against which arguments "for the sole legitimacy of New English ways" could then be tested or developed.[47] Within the confines of an Anglophone Atlantic-world tradition, information about beaver intelligence, or about an "Indian world" that was "rooted in nature, tradition-bound, and confounded by superstition," could serve as a convenient backdrop for larger story arcs starring an always heroic contingent of English colonists, courageously engaged "in a valiant struggle to make the wilderness 'blossom as the rose,' a phrase that is repeatedly invoked as the metaphor for subduing the land in English ways."[48] In such narratives, O'Brien explains, Indigenous ways of being and of understanding the world are relegated to bygone days and denied present and future relevance in their home territories.[49]

Rivers and Bell's mocking and dismissive anecdotes are designed to cast the Wendat (and their cultural grammar) as not simply ridiculous but as irrelevant to the present and future of the contested territory—or as part of the backdrop against which a cohort of elite English speakers might forge their own superior and supposedly uncontested stories. These are stories of what O'Brien calls firsting, which are the conventional narratives that Anglophone Americans have always used to claim Indigenous places as their own personal and intellectual properties while simultaneously asserting what it is that supposedly makes them so elite and deserving: their modernity. But when the stories about the wounded Wendat woman and the untrustworthy beavers are read within the context of Indigenous cultural grammars, they become an uneasy foundation for firsting. They suggest that during the British colonization of what some now call Quebec, Indigenous peoples were fighting for the future of their shared home, using a grammar of animacy to extend and maintain traditional connections among and across an increasingly diverse community of beings. At the same time, the stories show English colonists engaged in processes meant to deny or conceal those same connections. Instead of seriously contemplating the meaning or value of the evidence before them, Brooke's characters stubbornly proceed as though "non-Indians were the first people to erect the proper institutions of a social order worthy of notice" on Turtle Island.[50]

As O'Brien notes, a key way in which Anglophone-American writers mythologized and reinforced their own supposed modernity was through narrative themes of environmental exploitation and industrialization. In *Emily Montague*, as previously discussed, these themes frequently emerge from characters' understandings and portrayals of the non-human world as inanimate and as subordinate to the human world. But it is additionally important to note that at almost every turn in this novel, the objectification of non-human worlds is echoed by the objectification of human bodies. The purpose of this human objectification is almost entirely dependent on ethnicity. The efforts of characters to metaphorically collapse European colonists, like Sir George or Madame Des Roches, into the realm of vegetation signal the low standing of those individuals within an elite English cultural realm, but they do not render those characters subhuman. At other points in the text, people are targeted as part of a separate process that is indeed meant to render those persons subhuman, and in such moments, characters' reductive portrayals of the non-human world and their obsessive condemnations of French and Indigenous "indolence" function as mutually reinforcing processes.[51]

For instance, in what is surely among the most oblivious moments from this text, Bell criticizes her non-English neighbors for being "too indolent to take pains for any thing more than is absolutely necessary to their existence."[52] The essential principle observed by many Indigenous peoples that humans should take only what they need to survive from the communities around them is fundamental to numerous seventeenth- and eighteenth-century treaty agreements, and it remains a key component of how networks of nations across the continent and indeed the world share space.[53] But, because Bell can see only a failure of New English ways and logics in the behavior of her neighbors, she is led to dismiss those people as lazy. Similarly, Rivers describes the "Indians" he encounters as "idle beyond anything we can conceive" simply because they are not out razing the land, harnessing the rivers, harvesting objectified resources to exhaustion, and accumulating vast stores of personal wealth.[54] And in a letter detailing the perceived similarities between French-Canadian and Indigenous populations, Captain Fermor identifies a "resemblance" that "has been brought about, not by the French having won the savages to receive European manners, but by the contrary: the peasants having acquired the savage indolence in peace, their activity and ferocity in war, their fondness for field sports, and their hatred of labor."[55] Here, the French are criticized as a weak colonizing culture because the integrity of their social body has not been adequately protected—proof, Captain Fermor concludes, of the inferiority of the French language.[56] French habits of indolence are thus primarily attributed to the influence of the Wendat, who are portrayed as "children of the sun," brutish beings who pass their days fighting or running "thro' woods as wild as themselves."[57] These descriptions of Wendat habits and bodies are fundamentally similar to Rivers's complaints about the waters of Canada, which roll in vain because they have not yet been exploited for profit. Through such portrayals, Brooks develops an insidious sense of unexploited labor within the bodies of Wendat people, arguably appealing to the same exploitative ideology that, by the mid eighteenth century, was justifying the enslavement of Indigenous peoples across and beyond Turtle Island.[58]

At the end of this novel, it remains Britain's job to import modern society into a place where it otherwise does not exist and to establish a system that, while not requiring the physical presence of Britain's most culturally elite, will operate in accordance with those peoples' most beloved logics and values.[59] Through the voice of Captain Fermor, Brooke imagines Canada as a melting pot where people from various western-European nations will gather, "adopt [. . .] our manners," learn "our language" of objects, respect "the mild genius of our religion and laws," and ultimately acquire "the spirit of industry, enterprize, and commerce, to which we owe all our greatness."[60] In many ways, *Emily Montague* is a story about what that society will look like, what it will value, and how it will systematically reproduce itself in perpetuity without the physical presence of its architects. In this novel, the English language provides the framework for the perpetuation and proliferation of English society around the world. The supposed superiority of this language is offered as evidence of the superiority of English culture. Yet, in *Braiding Sweetgrass*, Robin Wall Kimmerer powerfully laments what continues to be forgotten and may be lost through the Anglophone world's ongoing attack on Indigenous cultural grammars. She observes that

> toddlers speak of plants and animals as if they were people, extending to them self and intention and compassion—until we teach them not to. We quickly retrain them and make them forget. When we tell them that the tree is not a who, but an it, we make that maple an object; we put a barrier between us, absolving ourselves of moral responsibility and opening the door to exploitation.[61]

Wall Kimmerer speaks of a colonizing society that, like the cultural world of Brooke's novel, reproduces itself automatically at the level of language acquisition. She provides context for a people who, like Brooke's characters, cannot easily respect, understand, or empathize with beings who are different from themselves because the very language through which they perceive and describe the world prevents it. And she gestures, like the mocking anecdotes of Bell and Rivers, to the enduring existence of a generous, animate world that is functioning just beyond the dominant contexts in which Anglophone settlers continue to live their lives.

Notes

1. Brooke, *The History of Emily Montague*, p. 10.
2. Ibid.
3. See Ibid., pp. 33, 98, 350.
4. Howells, "Dialogism in Canada's First Novel," p. 438. While the novel has been mostly neglected by British and Irish literary scholars in the twentieth and twenty-first centuries, it was well received upon its initial publication, and it was at one time "required reading for early British travelers to Canada." See McMullen, "Reception," in Brooke, *The History of Emily Montague*, pp. 375–380: 379.
5. See, for example, Pacey, "The First Canadian Novel," pp. 143–150; McMullen, "All's Right at Last," pp. 95–104; McMaster, "Young Jane Austen and the First Canadian Novel," pp. 339–346; and Hammill, *Literary Culture and Female Authorship*.
6. Arch, "Frances Brooke's 'Circle of Friends'," p. 465.
7. Wall Kimmerer, *Braiding Sweetgrass*, p. 49.
8. Ibid., pp. 55–56.
9. Vanessa Watts, "Indigenous Place-Thought and Agency," p. 23.
10. For a discussion of how and why Indigenous languages are destroyed, see Bear Nicholas, "Linguicide." Lisa Brooks has discussed how the Indigenous human communities of the northeast think through their relations with non-human communities; see Brooks, "Alnôbawôgan, Wlôgan, Awikhigan: Entering Native Space," in *The Common Pot*, pp. 1–50.
11. Wall Kimmerer, *Braiding Sweetgrass*, p. 55. For a discussion of how the Anishinaabe (for example) negotiate and maintain treaty relations with non-human nations, see Simpson, "Looking after Gdoo-naaganinaa," pp. 29–42.
12. Joudry, "Another Poverty," in Joudry, *Generations Re-Emerging*, pp. 38–39: 39. The term settler is shorthand for "settler colonist," which describes a non-Indigenous person who benefits from, and is complicit in, the functions and effects of settler colonialism, which is "a system defined by unequal relationships (like colonialism) where an exogenous collective aims to locally and permanently replace indigenous ones (unlike colonialism);" see Lorenzo Veracini, "Settler Colonialism as a Distinct Mode of Domination," in Cavanagh and Veracini, eds., *The Routledge Handbook of the History of Settler Colonialism*, pp. 1–8: 4. The idea of "Turtle Island" comes from the creation stories of numerous Indigenous nations. In Chippewa creation teachings, for example, the land upon which the people live is carried on the back of a female turtle; see Champagne, *Notes from the Center of Turtle Island*, p. viii. In academia and elsewhere, it has become fashionable in recent years to use this noun in place of the far more common "North America." Of course,

the term does not and cannot speak to the diverse creation teachings of all Indigenous nations. In this sense, it is an imperfect replacement; however, I have chosen to use the term Turtle Island in this chapter to avoid using North America uncritically.

13. For a much more complete biographical sketch of Brooke, see McMullen, *An Odd Attempt in a Woman*.
14. Brooke, *The History of Emily Montague*, pp. 43, 33, 33, 32.
15. Ibid., p. 42.
16. Ibid.
17. Ibid., p. 34.
18. Ibid., pp. 230 and 162.
19. McCarthy, "Sisters under the Mink," pp. 340–357.
20. See Nash, *Wilderness and the American Mind*, pp. 23–43.
21. Arch, for example, notes that "the plot" of this novel "is resolved in defiance of" Brooke's apparent optimism "about Canada's future;" see "Frances Brooke's 'Circle of Friends'," p. 469. Katherine Binhammer ties characters' return to England to her thesis that "Brooke's novel tries to narrate a plot of infinite wealth accumulation, but Canada's particular political and economic problems will not abide; and the novel ends up laying bare the contradictions at the heart of this emerging liberal economic theory;" see her "The Failure of Trade's Empire," p. 298.
22. Brooke, *The History of Emily Montague*, p. 117. As Arch explains, "the novel of sensibility insists that the knowledge of the passions can only be felt, not known intellectually or described in mere words. [. . .] In separating out the 'mass of mankind' from those who have truly known the sensation of love, Brooke imagines [. . .] a new elite;" see "Frances Brooke's 'Circle of Friends'," p. 472.
23. Brooke, *The History of Emily Montague*, p. 1.
24. Arch, "Frances Brooke's 'Circle of Friends'," p. 472.
25. Brooke, *The History of Emily Montague*, p. 204.
26. See Morgan, *Visible Saints*; see also Bercovich, *The Puritan Origins of the American Self*, pp. 72–108.
27. See Bryant, *The Homing Place*, pp. 63–89.
28. Winthrop, "A Model of Christian Charity," in Heimert and Delbanco, eds., *The Puritans in America*, pp. 81–92: 83 and 91.
29. Ibid., p. 86.
30. For useful overviews of how the Euro-western world has mythologized its own shifting relationship with nature across centuries, see early chapters in Sale, *Dwellers in the Land*. See also Pogue Harrison, *Forests*.
31. Battell Lowman and Barker, *Settler*, p. 31.
32. Brooke, *The History of Emily Montague*, p. 153. In an early letter to his sister, Rivers articulates his belief that the members of his society should be shaped not by nature but by the influence of one another; he condemns all those who choose to "[cut] themselves off from that state of society in which [God] has placed them, and for which they were form'd;" ibid., p. 12.
33. Ibid., p. 146.
34. Ibid., p. 214.
35. Watts, "Indigenous Place-Thought," p. 23.
36. Ibid., p. 24. Some Indigenous scholars, such as the Métis anthropologist Zoe Todd, have objected to the use of "non-human" for its hierarchical connotations, even though these connotations are culturally conditioned. She has supported "more-than-human" as a viable replacement. While I maintain the usage of non-human in this chapter as a means of referring to beings who are

not of the human species, this term is not synonymous with "subhuman," nor is it intended to denote the legitimacy of a Euro-western hierarchy of beings.
37. Wall Kimmerer, *Braiding Sweetgrass*, p. 49.
38. Brooke, *The History of Emily Montague*, p. 3. In another letter, Bell refers to the Montmorency River today in the province of Quebec as "the most lovely of all inanimate objects;" ibid., p. 23.
39. Rivers elsewhere describes Canada as "a rich mine yet unopen'd"; Captain Fermor identifies British colonies as a whole as "our greatest and surest sources of wealth;" ibid., pp. 20 and 187.
40. Watts, "Indigenous Place-Thought," p. 23.
41. Ibid.
42. Brooke, *The History of Emily Montague*, p. 28.
43. Ibid. The question of how or whether Indigenous languages could be "reduced to rules" was a preoccupation of English and French colonial authors for centuries. The Jesuit missionary Paul le Jeune, for example, who proselytized to the Innu of Tadoussac in 1633 and 1634, and who was apparently tired of living by the Innu's seasonal movement patterns, believed that "if we could understand their language, and reduce it to rules, there would be no more need of following these Barbarians;" see "Relation de ce qui s'est passé en La Nouvelle France, en l'année 1634 Paul le Jeune; Maison de N. Dame des Anges, en Nouvelle France, August 7, 1634," in Thwaites, ed., *The Jesuit Relations*, vol. 7, pp. 5–236: 62.
44. Brooke, *The History of Emily Montague*, pp. 76–77.
45. When it comes to the idea of lands held in common, Brooke's characters predictably riff on Locke's *Second Treatise*. See Captain Fermor's discussion of the "equal distribution of property," which is tied to English notions of labor and is "not to be understood to mean such an equality as never existed, not can exist but in idea;" see Brooke, *The History of Emily Montague*, p. 200.
46. Ibid., p. 85.
47. O'Brien, *Firsting and Lasting*, pp. 6 and 52.
48. Ibid., p. 26.
49. Rivers articulates his perspective of the increasing irrelevance of Indigenous peoples when he describes "the Indians of both sexes" as "the happiest people on earth; free from all care, they enjoy the present moment, forget the past, and are without solicitude for the future;" see Brooke, *The History of Emily Montague*, p. 8.
50. O'Brien, *Firsting and Lasting*, p. xii.
51. See Brooke, *The History of Emily Montague*, p. 232. For a historical discussion of the seventeenth-century Wendat, their alliances with the French, their eastern dispersal at the hands of the Haudenosaunee, and their eventual establishment in Quebec City, see Labelle, *Dispersed but Not Destroyed*. Adam Barker has explored why Indigenous peoples are imagined as features of the landscape in settler-colonial contexts in several venues. See Battell Lowman and Barker, *Settler*; see also Barker and Pickerill, "Radicalizing Relationships to and through Shared Geographies," pp. 1705–1725.
52. Brooke, *The History of Emily Montague*, p. 51.
53. One famous example of this is the Dish with One Spoon agreement. See early chapters in Hill, *The Clay We Are Made of*.
54. Brooke, *The History of Emily Montague*, p. 7.
55. Ibid., p. 232.
56. Ibid., pp. 189 and 214–215.
57. Ibid., pp. 5 and 41.

58. On the enslavement of Indigenous peoples by colonists and settlers, see Chaplin, "Enslavement of Indians in Early America: Captivity without the Narrative," in Mancke and Shammas, eds., *The Creation of the British Atlantic World*, pp. 45–70; Newell, *Brethren by Nature*; Warren, *New England Bound*; and Gallay, ed., *Indian Slavery in Colonial America*.
59. Captain Fermor argues that the colonies must be supported with "as little expense to our own inhabitants as possible;" see Brooke, *The History of Emily Montague*, p. 187.
60. Ibid., p. 189.
61. Wall Kimmerer, *Braiding Sweetgrass*, p. 57.

Bibliography

Arch, Stephen Carl, "Frances Brooke's 'Circle of Friends': The Limits of Epistolarity in the *History of Emily Montague*," *Early American Literature* 3 (2004), pp. 465–485.

Barker, Adam J., and Jenny Pickerill, "Radicalizing Relationships to and through Shared Geographies: Why Anarchists Need to Understand Indigenous Connections to Land and Place," *Antipode* 44.5 (2012), pp. 1705–1725.

Battell Lowman, Emma, and Adam J. Barker, *Settler: Identity and Colonialism in 21st Century Canada* (Halifax, NS: Fernwood Publishing, 2015).

Bear Nicholas, Andrea, "Linguicide: Submersion Education and the Killing of Languages in Canada," *Briarpatch Magazine*, 1 March 2011. https://briarpatchmagazine.com/articles/view/linguicide

Bercovich, Sacvan, *The Puritan Origins of the American Self* (New Haven, CT: Yale University Press, 1975).

Binhammer, Katherine, "The Failure of Trade's Empire in *The History of Emily Montague*," *Eighteenth Century Fiction* 23.2 (2010–2011), pp. 295–319.

Brooke, Frances, *The History of Emily Montague*, ed. Laura Moss (Ottawa: Tecumseh Press, 2001).

Brooks, Lisa Tanya, *The Common Pot: The Recovery of Native Space in the Northeast* (Minneapolis: University of Minnesota Press, 2008).

Bryant, Rachel, *The Homing Place: Indigenous and Settler Literary Legacies of the Atlantic* (Waterloo: Wilfrid Laurier University Press, 2017).

Cavanagh, Edward, and Lorenzo Veracini, eds., *The Routledge Handbook of the History of Settler Colonialism* (New York: Routledge, 2016).

Champagne, Duane, *Notes from the Center of Turtle Island* (Lanham, MD: AltaMira Press, 2010).

Gallay, Alan, ed., *Indian Slavery in Colonial America* (Lincoln: University of Nebraska Press, 2009).

Hammill, Faye, *Literary Culture and Female Authorship in Canada, 1760–2000* (New York: Rodopi, 2003).

Heimert, Alan, and Andrew Delbanco, eds., *The Puritans in America: A Narrative Anthology* (Cambridge, MA: Harvard University Press, 1985).

Hill, Susan M., *The Clay We Are Made of: Haudenosaunee Land Tenure on the Grand River* (Winnipeg: University of Manitoba Press, 2017).

Howells, Robin, "Dialogism in Canada's First Novel: *The History of Emily Montague*," *Canadian Review of Comparative Literature* 20 (1993), pp. 437–439.

Joudry, Shalan, *Generations Re-Emerging* (Kentville: Gaspereau Press, 2014).

Labelle, Kathryn Magee, *Dispersed But Not Destroyed: A History of the Seventeenth-Century Wendat People* (Vancouver: UBC Press, 2013).
Mancke, Elizabeth, and Carole Shammas, *The Creation of the British Atlantic World* (Baltimore, MD: Johns Hopkins University Press, 2005).
McCarthy, Dermot, "Sisters under the Mink: The Correspondent Fear in *the History of Emily Montague*," *Essays on Canadian Writing* 51/52 (1993/1994), pp. 340–357.
McMaster, Juliet, "Young Jane Austen and the First Canadian Novel: From *Emily Montague* to 'Amelia Webster' and *Love and Friendship*," *Eighteenth Century Fiction* 11 (1999), pp. 339–346.
McMullen, Lorraine, "All's Right at Last: An Eighteenth-Century Canadian Novel," *Journal of Canadian Fiction* 21 (1978), pp. 95–104.
———, *An Odd Attempt in a Woman: The Literary Life of Frances Brooke* (Vancouver: UBC Press, 1983).
Morgan, Edmund S., *Visible Saints: The History of a Puritan Idea* (Ithaca, NY: Cornell University Press, 1963).
Nash, Roderick, *Wilderness and the American Mind* (New Haven, CT: Yale University Press, 2001).
Newell, Margaret Ellen, *Brethren by Nature: New England Indians, Colonists, and the Origins of American Slavery* (Ithaca, NY: Cornell University Press, 2015).
O'Brien, Jean, *Firsting and Lasting: Writing Indians out of Existence in New England* (Minneapolis: University of Minnesota Press, 2010).
Pacey, Desmond, "The First Canadian Novel," *Dalhousie Review* 26 (1946), pp. 143–150.
Pogue Harrison, Robert, *Forests: The Shadow of Civilization* (Chicago: University of Chicago Press, 1993).
Sale, Kirkpatrick, *Dwellers in the Land: The Bioregional Vision* (Philadelphia, PA: New Society Publishers, 1991).
Simpson, Leanne, "Looking after Gdoo-Naaganinaa: Precolonial Nishnaabeg Diplomatic and Treaty Relationships," *Wicazo Sa Review* 23.2 (2018), pp. 29–42.
Thwaites, Reuben Gold, ed., *The Jesuit Relations and Allied Documents: Travels and Explorations of the Jesuit Missionaries in New France, 1610–1791*. Vol. 7 (Cleveland, OH: Burrows Brothers Company, 1897).
Wall Kimmerer, Robin, *Braiding Sweetgrass: Indigenous Wisdom, Scientific Knowledge, and the Teachings of Plants* (Minneapolis, MN: Milkweed Editions, 2013).
Warren, Wendy, *New England Bound: Slavery and Colonization in Early America* (New York: Norton, 2016).
Watts, Vanessa, "Indigenous Place-Thought and Agency amongst Humans and Non Humans (First Woman and Sky Woman Go on a European World Tour!)," *Decolonization: Indigeneity, Education & Society* 2.1 (2013), pp. 20–34.

6 Firsting and Lasting in the History of Science

Francisco José de Caldas and the Priority Dispute Over Hypsometry

Jorge M. Escobar

This chapter examines a scientific controversy that took place in the early-modern transatlantic world, one that typifies the ways that scientific developments of the Enlightenment crossed paths with perceptions about one's place of origin and place of study in the Americas. The main character in this controversy was Francisco José de Caldas (1768–1816), a key figure in the Royal Botanical Expedition to New Granada (1783–1808) and a leader in the Spanish-American wars of independence until his execution during the Reconquista led by the so-called pacifier Pablo Morillo (1775–1837).[1] Caldas saw himself as a criollo, that is, as a Spaniard who simply happened to be born in the Americas. Specifically, he was a criollo in the viceroyalty of New Granada, in the territory of present-day Colombia, whose scientific work touched upon topics as diverse as mathematics, astronomy, botany, geography, cartography, and engineering, among others. He also devoted part of his time to the invention and building of scientific instruments and was the editor of his own weekly scientific journal, the *Semanario del Nuevo Reyno de Granada*, between 1808 and 1810. Due to this wide range of interests, Caldas received the nickname of *el Sabio* (the Wise), and he remains broadly regarded both as the first Colombian scientist and as the first Colombian to have studied a good number of scientific fields, even though Colombia did not yet exist as a national state when he died.

This emphasis on associating these firsts with Caldas, particularly in light of the firsting ideology explored elsewhere in this book, will be problematized in this chapter. My purpose is to determine how the framework of firsting and lasting developed by Jean O'Brien to study western accounts of the history of the Indians in New England could also be helpful for understanding the history of early-modern transatlantic science.[2] This framework can contribute to a better understanding of the history of science and the way it privileges certain types of, and sources for, knowledge.

One important aspect of O'Brien's framework involves the anthropological approach to science proposed by Bruno Latour in his 1991 book originally published in French, *We Have Never Been Modern.*[3] Latour identifies the tendency to conflate two distinct and conflicting practices in modern scholarly inquiry: on the one hand, the practice of purification, which creates a dichotomy between culture (humans) and nature (non-humans), and on the other, the practice of translation, which resolves this dichotomy by creating hybrids of culture and nature that let us see each concept in terms of the other. In the early-modern period and beyond, these concepts had become grafted onto Euro-settlers (culture) and Indigenous peoples (nature). For moderns, these practices generated a series of paradoxes in which nature and society could appear at the same time both as transcendent things and as artificial constructions, depending on the epistemological and political agendas at play. According to Latour, a modern could claim, without feeling any sense of contradiction, that nature and society are transcendent because the laws of nature and society do not arise from human will; a modern could simultaneously argue that nature corresponds exactly to what she produces in her laboratory and that society is simply the outcome of our freely taken decisions and actions. For Latour, the versatility of these paradoxes is what has made the modern project so powerful and difficult to undermine. O'Brien draws on this anthropological approach to scientific inquiry to argue that embracing Indians was precisely a way for New Englanders to establish their own modernity through a set of practices that accentuated purification and translation. She brings these practices together under the general framework of firsting and lasting.

Firsting is a practice that allowed European settlers to differentiate culture from nature by representing Indians and all things related to them as nature, and settlers and all things related to them as culture. This practice can be identified in the case of New Englanders, as O'Brien shows in her study,[4] but can also be extended to other places in the Americas such as New Granada, where whiteness and purity of blood worked as a mechanism for settlers (*colonos*) and later for criollos to distinguish themselves from other social groups in that territory.[5] Firsting legitimized the view that European settlers were breaking with the past and re-founding their origins in an old, and in their view uninhabited, land. Whether in New England or in New Granada, they were the first among their Old-World nation to come to this area of the Americas and to institutionalize their culture. In this sense, they were the present and the future because they were the first moderns in a territory hitherto populated by purely natural things, having purified their world of Indigenous peoples by defining them as belonging to the natural world and thus bereft of culture.[6]

Lasting is a practice that allowed European settlers to explain the existence of hybrids comprised of both nature and culture within the land that they claimed as their territory—that is, the persistence of Indians among the settler population. Both in New England and in New Granada, Indians were seen as something not from the past, but in the past; settlers viewed them as a race whose last pure specimens—those who displayed the authentic features of Indianness that a true Indian should display—could be individualized in a specific place and at a particular time, but who did not actually exist anymore. Instead, the present was populated with admixtures. In New England, some Indians were no longer considered Indian because they did not meet the blood purity standards crafted by Euro-settlers, who looked to the genealogical makeup of their ancestors, and therefore, were regarded by western eyes as a degenerated version of authentic past Indians.[7] In New Granada, white colonos first and criollos later relied upon the *casta* (caste) system developed within the Spanish empire both to reinforce their own standards of blood purity, which no caste besides their own could really satisfy, and to justify their social and epistemic superiority over the other castes. In that way, Indian mixed-bloodedness could never be taken as modern because they could at no point reach the status of contemporary whites, who were the idealized moderns. Yet, whites could possess some degree of mixed blood because they could be esteemed as some improved version of past Indians, as an improvement of the Indian race. O'Brien concludes that the practices of firsting and lasting functioned as devices that let European settlers decide who could be included among *us*, the moderns, and who belonged among *them*, the non-moderns. In this chapter, we will take O'Brien's general framework of firsting and lasting and allow it to inform the study of early-modern transatlantic science, particularly scholars' insistence on viewing Caldas as the first scientist to develop certain scientific discoveries. What does this tendency reveal about the mechanisms employed by criollo scientists and historians of science to establish modernity within the viceroyalty of New Granada?

To answer this question, I also rely upon the work of Colombian scholars Olga Restrepo Forero, Renán Silva, Santiago Castro Gómez, and Mauricio Nieto Olarte.[8] Among the different elements of New-Granadian science that they highlight, I want to call attention to the view that there existed an intrinsic asymmetrical relationship between criollo knowledge and European science. This view, widespread among criollo scientists and later historians of science, relates to the means through which criollo knowledge could gain epistemic, social, political, and historical value. Elevating criollo knowledge thus depended entirely upon its relationship to the universalism of European science, which provided the standards used to validate any kind of knowledge about nature and society in the scientific world. Criollo knowledge was either simply discarded or positively valued if some connection could be identified with European science. Almost by definition, Indigenous knowledge could never reach the place of universal science, even though it was at times used, but criollo knowledge, which also was viewed by Europeans as inferior, could sometimes obtain some degree of recognition through its validation by European scientists. Science became in that way a form of politics—a means for New-Granadian thinkers to exercise control over their territory and its inhabitants and to establish clear distinctions between them and other groups belonging to New-Granadian society. This politics of knowledge as expressed through this accepted asymmetry was a basic assumption held by criollo scientists and later historians of science who collectively established a western sense of modernity with respect to the different types of natural and social knowledges produced in the viceroyalty of New Granada. To see how this applies to Caldas, I begin with a story told many times—the story of how Francisco José de Caldas, the first Colombian scientist, became interested in the study of hypsometry.[9]

In the first months of 1801, Caldas organized a trip with a couple of friends to examine different aspects of a volcano near the city of Popayán in the south of the viceroyalty of New Granada. Fortunately for him, or so he tells us, while he was making his observations of the volcano, he accidentally broke the tube of his thermometer. The immediate consequence of this accident was that he could not continue with his observations. But, this limitation, he says, gave rise to ideas that would not have occurred to him otherwise.[10] As expressed in the chapter-length studies included in the volume edited by Pamela H. Smith, Amy R. W. Meyers, and Harold J. Cook, material culture is a key factor in the study of the history of science, and particularly the history of early-modern science, because this discipline helps us to observe how the development of science has depended not only upon the mind, but also upon the hand.[11] Put differently, the development of science indeed relies more easily on the more familiar forms of academic and textual knowledge to which we are accustomed, but it also depends upon other forms of knowledge about material things such as instruments, books, specimens, cabinets, and museums, as well as with artisanal practices and technologies. Material culture becomes in that way a crucial means of understanding how science has evolved throughout its history. Caldas's case is a good example of this type of knowledge.[12]

Due to the general lack of scientific instruments in the viceroyalty of New Granada, Caldas could not simply replace his broken thermometer with a new one. Before that could happen, he first had to try to fix it or build a new one, either from scratch or from other instruments employed for other purposes, as he had done before and did afterward for telescopes, chronometers, and quadrants, among others. According to Lino de Pombo, Caldas's nineteenth-century biographer, Caldas built these instruments with the help of artisans, including carpenters, blacksmiths, and silversmiths, and with the random materials available to him at any given moment.[13] With these instruments and their related processes, Caldas started searching for ways to fix his thermometer so to continue with his observations. Although he could find the lower point of the thermometer's temperature scale relatively easily with the help of snow, the same was not possible to determine the thermometer's highest temperature reading. When he attempted to fix his instrument, he realized that the new scale did not correspond exactly with the original one, and this was particularly clear when he tried to establish the boiling point of water, which appeared to vary on his new instrument. In fact, the different results obtained up to that moment with the original thermometer had suggested that there existed a correlation between the temperature of water's ebullition and a place's altitude, a correlation that he could not know otherwise.

According to Caldas, and thanks to the fact that his thermometer was still broken, he was forced to think about these same issues repeatedly until a solution could be found, one that he had not read before in any of the few books available to him. He understood at that moment that when one knew the boiling point of water, one could know the atmospheric pressure, and knowing the atmospheric pressure, one could know the altitude of a place. This principle, the basic principle of what will be known later as hypsometry, was the explanation for the correlation that popped up recurrently from his data while trying to fix the scale of his broken thermometer. It was also the foundation for the construction of a new instrument, one that, he tells us, was much less costly, less fragile, and easier to use in the Andes than the barometer, which was the standard instrument to measure altitude at that time.[14] That instrument would later be known as the hypsometer.

Caldas was proud of his little discovery, as he called it. He communicated news about it for the first time on 20 May 1801 in a letter to his friend, Santiago Pérez de Arroyo y Valencia, asking him to be discreet and silent about his discovery.[15] As the letters to his friend show, in the following months he continued working intensely on it, doing several expeditions to obtain more data in order to confirm his observations. On 5 June of that year, he expressed surprise upon learning that his discovery remained unknown in Europe, given that he could not find it in his books, and he claimed that, once confirmed, it would bring honor to his fellow countrymen and the Americas in general.[16] Finally, on 5 August, he stated that the discovery had been unequivocally confirmed after this two-month study.[17]

Yet, the more he studied the matter, the more intrigued he became by the uncertainty about his discovery being already known in Europe. The question that slowly started to arise in his mind was whether he had truly discovered a new physical principle that explained some relationship between altitude, atmospheric pressure, and the boiling point of water, or whether it was already a principle well-established in Europe that he had just happened upon but could not corroborate due to his lack of books. Was it possible, Caldas asked himself, that a New-Granadian from the small, remote town of Popayán could be the first one to have discovered a physical principle hitherto unknown in Europe?[18] Caldas's own answer was that he in fact had no way to determine the truth, since there was no information about it in his books, and for any people across the world, including those in the Americas, the only way to establish priority, defined in due course, in the study of nature was through European science.[19] Hence, his only option was to continue working on his discovery and to improve it as much as he could. The reason for this choice and the dilemma that immediately came to his mind was simple: either the principle was already known in Europe, and his work would be evidence that the same truth could always be found in different places at the same time, or the principle was unknown, and his work would be a way to confirm it and secure an important place for himself in the history of science as its first discoverer.[20] In both cases, the issue at play was clear to Caldas because he had to determine whether the priority over the discovery could be rightly attributed to him or whether it should be attributed to another person in Europe, a person still unidentified due to his inability to consult a library. This situation became the priority dispute created by Caldas at the beginning of the nineteenth century in New Granada. But why did Caldas care so much about being the first discoverer of the principle and the first inventor of the instrument, and what would he gain or lose through this recognition? To answer these questions, let us turn to the general topic of priority disputes in the history of science.

Priority in science can be understood as the acknowledgment that an individual first discovered or invented something—a fact, a law, a theory, an instrument, and so on.[21] However, this acknowledgment can come from two distinct sources, each with its own agenda: the historical figures themselves and the historians of science. In both cases, if no disagreement about the attribution of the discovery or the invention exists, the priority will be easily conceded to some specific individual, who will appear as the first discoverer or the first inventor, provided that he or she is publicly recognized as such. In this sense, there would be agreement among scientists and later among historians about who was first, and there would be no need to question the attribution. But the matter grows more complicated when disagreements over priority arise because in those cases the decision about who was first is influenced by many interrelated factors, depending on whether the historical figures or the historians of science acknowledge the discovery or the invention and to whom they attribute it. This is the origin of priority disputes in science, and scholars today may ponder how and why scientists become involved in such disputes.

As Robert K. Merton's work has demonstrated, priority disputes have become generally understood not in terms of the psychological characteristics of individual scientists, but rather as an institutional feature of science that expresses the norms regulating science's reward system.[22] According to this rationale, the main motivation for scientists to get involved in a priority dispute is the reward that they receive from being identified as the first to have discovered or invented some scientific principle. The nature of these rewards varies, as Merton explains; in his view, the primary reward incentivizing scientists to seek out priority was the acknowledgment of originality because this was the only reward that scientists could truly retain once their discoveries became public, and thus, made universally available according to the Mertonian norms of universalism, communalism, disinterestedness, and organized skepticism.[23] Hence, a dispute over priority could be seen as a dispute over a possible violation of the institutional norms of science in the sense that the recognition of originality could be misattributed to someone who did not deserve it. Pedro Ruiz-Castell and Michael Strevens agree with this general view, although they claim that scientists are more driven by prestige, which becomes associated with other rewards, such as one's contributions to society, resources for research, legitimacy, and power.[24] For Alan G. Gross, the situation is a bit different. Although he also accepts the institutional approach to priority disputes, he emphasizes two points. On the one hand, he argues that discovery is not an historical event, but rather a retrospective social judgment. On the other, he believes that discovery has a public, and not a private, nature.[25] From these two points, he concludes that a scientific discovery relies upon the public attribution of novelty to a claim regarded by a relevant scientific community as possible and as arising from appropriate scientific methods. Hence, because discovery is also an assertion of priority, differences over priority are more than differences in science; also, under dispute is what the appropriate set of institutional norms should be. The reward for the scientist in this respect is to be regarded as the individual who followed or proposed that set of methods for the first time in such a way that they can be considered to have inaugurated a new way of doing science.

Let us return to the question about why Caldas cared so much about being acknowledged and the reasons for which he started a priority dispute when his lack of access to books prohibited him from unequivocally identifying the existence of any possible adversary to his claim. Evidently, the pursuit of priority was incentivized by the reward he would receive for his discovery and his invention. And in the reward system of the viceroyalty of New Granada at the turn of the eighteenth to the nineteenth century, the main reward that a scientist received was nothing else but to be seen as on a par with his European counterparts. Caldas's main motivation was not so much the acknowledgment of his originality or the prestige that comes with the recognition, and certainly not the opportunity to create new ways of doing science. He just wanted to prove to himself and the scientific world that he, a New-Granadian studying nature in a remote place like Popayán, as he put it, could produce science with the same epistemic and practical values exampled by his European colleagues.[26] Caldas did not even consider the possibility that the same discovery could perhaps have been made before outside of Europe in some other place in the Americas, much less in Asia or Africa. The reward system of his place and time led Caldas to view the admission of his work to the ranks of

European science as the maximum reward that he could obtain from his involvement in a priority dispute, a dispute that he started by himself with no acknowledged adversary. In Caldas's mind, any adversary would have had to have been European.

In fact, an actual European adversary soon manifested himself in the figure of the naturalist Alexander von Humboldt (1769–1859), who at that time was visiting the New Granada as part of his Spanish-American expedition (1799–1804). Caldas's letters during this period, before and after their encounter, reveal both his great admiration for Humboldt and the deep uncertainty and uneasiness that Humboldt generated in Caldas regarding his discovery.[27] The reason for this mixed response was that Humboldt initially represented in Caldas's eyes precisely what his books could not give him—complete access to European science. Humboldt met Caldas just as the opportunity arose to determine whether Caldas was the first one to have made the discovery or whether he was the second or somewhere else down the list of people who had already discovered his principle and related invention. Yet when pressed on this subject by Caldas, the information supplied by Humboldt was not always consistent. In Caldas's view, Humboldt seemed to ignore the topic or at least claimed not to have enough knowledge about it, and at other times, Humboldt was not always transparent about his knowledge.[28] For Caldas, the question of priority remained undecided. Humboldt could not resolve the priority dispute for him, and Caldas nonetheless remained convinced that if the discovery was already made somewhere, it had to be in no other place but Europe.

While Caldas never resolved the priority dispute during his lifetime, his own approach to the dispute provides a good example of how firsting and lasting worked in the case of a historical figure such as Caldas in New Granada. In a way analogous to what happened with New Englanders concerning Indians, firsting and lasting allowed criollo scientists to establish their own modernity. Yet, they did so by referencing culture rather than nature in the sense that they saw themselves as already part of culture, that is, as Europeans that simply happened to be born in the Americas. They were modern by blood in this respect, and to prove it they relied, as Castro Gómez has argued, on the discourse of blood purity, which worked as a social mechanism that enabled criollos to see themselves as part of Europe's heritage while simultaneously differentiating themselves from other groups of people born in or brought to the Americas.[29] However, their blood did not immediately turn their knowledge of nature into an expression of modernity. To become modern, that knowledge had to be validated as such by European science. Being the first discoverer was important for Caldas because it demonstrated that criollos could also produce modern science even in a remote place like Popayán. But even so, the only way to determine the epistemic value of his work, and so decide whether he was the first modern discoverer of the principle and the first modern inventor of the instrument, was to appeal to European science as his only source of validation, either through his books or through a figure such as Humboldt. Hence, even when recognized as the first in these two ways, the knowledge produced by criollo scientists such as Caldas appeared as a hybrid entity existing in a sort of intermediate phase between Indigenous knowledge of nature and true universal science, a phase whose modernity could only be established through the verdict of western science.

Let us consider the second source of acknowledgment when it comes to priority in science—the historians of science and their involvement in the study of priority disputes. Priority disputes belong to a broader field encompassing the study of controversy within the history of science, which also involves the exploration of how science is made and conducted, and what we learn from it.[30] Once again, we can turn to Merton, who claimed that the study of priority disputes is a way for historians of science to identify firsts. In doing so, these scholars contribute to sustaining the prevailing institutional emphasis on the importance of priority and the set of norms regulating science's reward system.[31] Scientific knowledge in this respect can continue to be impersonal and to make claims whose truth needs to be assessed independently of its individual sources. The task of the historian of science is to ensure that the collective memory of science's origins is not lost: she functions as the keeper of science's firsts once scientific knowledge becomes objective and universal. We must also remember, and following Gross again, that discovery itself is not a historical event, but rather a retrospective social judgment made by scientific communities that read scientific articles written by their peers and also the history of the judgements about those articles.[32] Hence, going back to Merton, one can rather claim that historians of science get involved in the study of priority disputes because, in identifying firsts, they contribute not only to sustaining the prevailing institutional emphasis on a particular set of rewards, but also reinforce the institutional acceptance of certain retrospective social judgments made by the scientific communities about themselves, including those related to national pride arising from a discovery.[33]

In Caldas's case, historians of science have used at least two different approaches to the priority dispute over hypsometry. The first approach, which can be found in the work of Colombian historians such as Lino de Pombo, Luis María Murillo, Alfredo D. Bateman, Jorge Arias de Greiff, and Santiago Díaz Piedrahita, maintains that Caldas's discovery and invention was his alone and that he should be recognized accordingly.[34] These historians argue that there were indeed antecedents in Europe, but the differences are also important, and when studied carefully, one can notice that Caldas was thinking in terms of methods not previously known in Europe. Significantly, they claim that he was dealing with altitudes that did not exist in Europe, and the sort of empirical evidence obtained in New Granada was one of the key factors that allowed Caldas to arrive at his own conclusions about hypsometry. This first approach likewise maintains that Caldas's clash with Humboldt can be seen anew to understand why Humboldt offered a rather negative reaction to Caldas during their first meeting. According to these historians, Humboldt clearly hid information from Caldas at certain moments and even misguided him on purpose. They even claim that Humboldt was not able to be the source of European knowledge that Caldas and his contemporaries expected him to be; he simply did not know enough about hypsometry and in tandem disregarded Caldas as a valid scientist. In fact, for these historians, Caldas was in danger of having his work stolen, as apparently happened with Caldas's other ideas, such as those related to plant geography. In these scholars' view, before Humboldt was the opportunity to exclusively credit himself for Caldas's discovery, with just a few minor references to Caldas's work.

The second approach, which can be found in the work of American historian John Wilton Appel and in the work of Colombian historians such as Víctor Samuel Albis and Regino Martínez-Chavanz, Luis Carlos Arboleda, and Mauricio Nieto Olarte, maintains that Caldas's discovery and invention were perhaps his, but only in the context of the viceroyalty of New Granada, and due to that, he should not be recognized as the discoverer of hypsometry.[35] The rationale for this position rests upon the recognition that a discussion about hypsometry had commenced in Europe in the eighteenth century, which started at least with Fahrenheit and continued later with others after Caldas.[36] This fact of course does not diminish Caldas's genius as a scientist and as an inventor for this second group of historians, but it shows how isolated he was from European science precisely because this isolation prevented him from answering his own question about who could have made his discovery before he had, and how. This second approach also views the Humboldt affair differently. These historians claim that Humboldt positively and respectfully addressed Caldas and his work, and thus made himself available to Caldas as a source of European scientific knowledge so to enable Caldas to decide whether he really had made a discovery. Yet, they argue, maybe that access was insufficient because Humboldt was not completely aware of the state of research within this field and may not have been aware that the field already existed in Europe as such. But the fact of the matter is that Humboldt took his own height measurements and correlated them with the temperatures of his own thermometer during his expedition. For these historians, perhaps Humboldt did not understand Caldas's ideas completely, but he did not do anything inappropriate with them, as the first group of historians argue, and in any case, he would doubtless be able to find similar developments about hypsometry after his return to Europe, as he enjoyed the sort of connections with European science that Caldas lacked.

The attribution of firsts is a significant issue, and each of the two approaches outlined in this chapter reaches a different conclusion about whether Caldas can be considered a discoverer and in that sense *firster*—the former confirms it, the latter denies it. To reach these conclusions, both approaches follow the same basic line of argument employed by Caldas. To start with, these approaches frame the priority dispute in the same terms that we found before while attempting to answer Caldas's own question about the legitimacy of a criollo from a remote place discovering knowledge and inventing instruments. The aim of these historical approaches is not to understand the specific intellectual and material conditions under which Caldas's discovery took place, the developments that could be recognized in his later work, nor how his research on this subject could be connected to his research in other areas such as botany, geography, and cartography. Rather, both approaches attempt to do what Caldas was unable to do: to single out a specific European adversary and decide who was first based on that information. The two approaches thus try to identify firsts and, importantly, situate them in the viceroyalty of New Granada, as opposed to Europe; yet the validation of Caldas's criollo knowledge was undertaken nonetheless by European science. It is against the background of European science that Caldas's work is valued or dismissed, and by contrasting his work with European science, including the likes of Humboldt, Caldas's work has gained historical value, either as a first or as part of a larger narrative of discoverers. This is particularly explicit in the tendency to offer lists of discoverers to establish Caldas's place in the history of hypsometry, as Albis and Martínez-Chavanz and Appel do. For example, Appel provides the following list:

Hypsometer	*Year*
Fahrenheit	1724
DeLuc	1772
Caldas	1801
Belloni	1805
Wollaston	1817
Regnault	1845[37]

In conclusion, firsting and lasting has significantly informed the work of science historians. Due to the tacit acceptance of the intrinsic asymmetry between criollo knowledge and European science in this period, historians' attempts to identify firsts have become a means of accomplishing two objectives. First, the scholarly drive to identify firsts purifies culture from nature through the purification of science (that is, science conducted in Europe) from criollo knowledge. In that way, European science's criteria for value and methods could later be employed to validate criollo knowledge and identify any firsts that it may offer. Second, scholars have desired to explain the existence of hybrids formed between European science and criollo knowledge in New Granada. These hybrids demonstrate the ways through which criollo knowledge found its way into more typical narratives relied upon by science historians and exemplified by the recurrent updating of the list of European discoverers of hypsometry found in some science history, but with Caldas's name now included on the list. From this perspective, the attribution of historical value to Caldas's work depends entirely on finding a proper place for it in the narratives of European science. These historical and scholarly objectives have contributed to maintaining the same institutional system of rewards and reinforce the same retrospective social judgments that scholars implicate when they comment on Caldas's own claims. Based on the acceptance of the intrinsic asymmetry between criollo knowledge and European science, that system of rewards and those retrospective social judgments have helped to spread the view that the epistemic and historical value of criollo science should be verified and determined not on its own intellectual, material, and contextual terms, but rather exclusively against the background of European science. This is the problematic process through which the science historian relies upon firsting and lasting to re-situate criollo knowledge within modernity.

We therefore see that both criollo scientists and historians of science rely upon the same basic practices of firsting and lasting when dealing with the priority dispute over hypsometry. Both sources of information take European, and arguably western, science as a justification for certain forms of epistemic power, which in turn becomes social and political power, through the assumption of a two-fold epistemic asymmetry between criollo knowledge and Indigenous knowledge, on the one hand, and European science and criollo knowledge, on the other. Caldas's anxiety about being recognized as the discoverer, and the focus of science historians on deciding whether he could actually be characterized as such, are simply manifestations of the same phenomenon: the practices of firsting and lasting established modernity in the viceroyalty of New Granada, either through the work of historical scientists such as Caldas or that of science historians working on either the period or the history of hypsometry.

The study of a priority dispute over hypsometry suggests that the practices of firsting and lasting are mainly practices belonging to the politics of knowledge. Either in the case of New Englanders deciding firsts and lasts in their territory or in the case of New-Granadians deciding firsts and lasts in the history of science, we observe that both contexts share the same basic mechanisms designed to establish modernity in the early-modern transatlantic world. These mechanisms relied fundamentally on the uncritical acceptance of European science and related worldview as a touchstone required to attribute epistemic, social, political, and historical value to any form of life that could be encountered in that world. Science, or more generally, knowledge was not simply part of the politics of that time, but rather comprised all politics of the time.[38] The emergence of nature and society as forms of modern scientific knowledge let New Englanders and New-Granadians believe that there were social and cognitive hierarchies among different peoples, that some territories were deserted or populated, that some human groups had these or those physical, mental, and moral characteristics, and that some beliefs about nature and society were either reliable or superstitious, among many other factors. Firsting and lasting have always been concerned with knowledge. Yet, as usually comes to pass, matters of knowledge become a different way of expressing matters of power and politics. To decide who was the first discoverer in the history of science examples the sort of knowledge politics that helped to build the early-modern transatlantic world, and in it, the viceroyalty of New Granada.

Notes

1. For Caldas's biography, see Bateman, *Francisco José de Caldas*; and Díaz Piedrahita, *Nueva aproximación a Francisco José de Caldas*. For the intellectual and material context of Enlightenment thinkers in the viceroyalty of New Granada and Caldas's place among them, see Silva, *Los ilustrados de Nueva Granada*; and Nieto Olarte, *Orden natural y orden social*. Unless otherwise noted, all translations are my own.
2. O'Brien, *Firsting and Lasting*.
3. Latour, *We Have Never Been Modern*. The book first appeared in French as *Nous n'avons jamais été modernes: essai d'anthropologie symétrique* (Paris: La Découverte, 1991).
4. O'Brien, *Firsting and Lasting*, pp. 1–53.
5. Castro Gómez, *La hybris del punto cero*, pp. 66–139.
6. Modernity and, by consequence, moderns are understood here in the sense given to these terms by Latour, which O'Brien takes as a basis for her argument. The underlying assumption is that modernity would be a historical process that started in the sixteenth century and was definitively established in the seventeenth and eighteenth centuries, all in connection with the rise of modern natural science. For how this process took place in New Granada, see Silva, *Los ilustrados de Nueva Granada*; and Castro Gómez, *La hybris del punto cero*.
7. Castro Gómez, *La hybris del punto cero*, pp. 184–227; and O'Brien, *Firsting and Lasting*, pp. 105–143.
8. Restrepo Forero, "En busca del orden," pp. 33–75. Also see Silva, *Los ilustrados de Nueva Granada*; Castro Gómez, *La hybris del punto cero*; and Nieto Olarte, *Orden natural y orden social*.
9. The main sources for this story are found in "Ensayo de una memoria sobre un nuevo método de medir la altura de las montañas por medio del termómetro y el agua hirviendo, seguida de un apéndice" and "Memoria sobre el origen del sistema de medir las montañas y sobre el proyecto de una expedición científica," both included in Caldas, *Obras*, pp. 153–173 and 293–302, respectively.
10. Caldas, *Obras*, pp. 153–154.

11. See the essays in Smith, Meyers, and Cook, eds., *Ways of Making and Knowing*.
12. For the general topic of material culture in New Granada, and different references to Caldas in that context, see Silva, *Los ilustrados de Nueva Granada*, especially chapter 8.
13. Lino de Pombo, "Francisco José de Caldas, biografía del Sabio," in Pombo, Murillo, and Bateman, eds., *Francisco José de Caldas*, pp. 9–49: 12.
14. Caldas, *Obras*, p. 168.
15. Caldas, *Cartas*, letter 35, pp. 71–72.
16. Ibid., letter 36, p. 75.
17. Ibid., letter 40, p. 91.
18. Caldas, *Obras*, pp. 157–158 and 295–296.
19. Ibid., p. 158.
20. Ibid., pp. 158–159.
21. For the general topic of priority disputes in science, see Merton, "Priorities in Scientific Discovery," pp. 635–659; Ruiz-Castell, "Priority Claims and Public Disputes in Astronomy," pp. 509–531; Strevens, "The Role of the Priority Rule in Science," pp. 55–79; Gross, "Do Disputes over Priority Tell Us Anything about Science?," pp. 161–179; and Ambrose, "Immunology's First Priority Dispute," pp. 1–8.
22. See Merton, "Priorities in Scientific Discovery."
23. Merton, "The Normative Structure of Science," in Merton, ed., *The Sociology of Science*, pp. 267–278.
24. See Ruiz-Castell, "Priority Claims and Public Disputes in Astronomy;" and Strevens, "The Role of the Priority Rule."
25. Gross, "Do Disputes over Priority Tell Us Anything about Science?"
26. To reinforce this point, see Caldas, "Ensayo de una memoria," section 8, in *Obras*, pp. 157–158; and Caldas, *Cartas*, letters 36 (pp. 73–75), 44 (pp. 106–107), 45 (pp. 112–113), and 60 (pp. 159–160).
27. Caldas, *Cartas*, letters 35–68, pp. 71–185.
28. Ibid., letters 44 (pp. 106–107), 45 (pp. 112–113), 46 (pp. 114–115), 60 (pp. 159–160), and Caldas, *Obras*, pp. 166–168, 171–173, 297–299, 301–302.
29. See Castro Gómez, *La hybris del punto cero*.
30. See Gross, "Do Disputes over Priority Tell Us Anything about Science?;" and Ruiz-Castell, "Priority Claims and Public Disputes in Astronomy."
31. Merton, "Priorities in Scientific Discovery," pp. 645–646.
32. See Gross, "Do Disputes over Priority Tell Us Anything about Science?"
33. This nationalistic aspect of priority disputes is emphasized by Merton, "Priorities in Scientific Discovery," pp. 641–642. Also see Charles T. Ambrose, "Immunology's First Priority Dispute."
34. Pombo, "Francisco José de Caldas," in Pombo, Murillo, and Bateman, eds., *Francisco José de Caldas*, pp. 9–49: 14–20; Murillo, "El amor y la sabiduría de Francisco José de Caldas," in Pombo, Murillo, and Bateman, eds., *Francisco José de Caldas*, pp. 51–66; Bateman, "Caldas y la hipsometría," in Pombo, Murillo, and Bateman, eds., *Francisco José de Caldas*, pp. 67–93; Bateman, *Francisco José de Caldas*, pp. 101–132; Arias de Greiff, "El método de Caldas para medir la elevación de las montañas," pp. 63–69; and Díaz Piedrahita, *Nueva aproximación*, pp. 130–139.
35. Appel, *Francisco José de Caldas*, pp. 12–19; Albis and Martínez-Chavanz, "Las investigaciones meteorológicas de Caldas," pp. 413–432; Luis Carlos Arboleda, "Caldas y la matematización de la naturaleza: La querella con Humboldt sobre el hipsómetro," in Recio Blanco and Castrillón, eds., *Independencia, educación y cultura*, pp. 227–246; and Nieto Olarte, *Orden natural y orden social*, pp. 89–96.

36. Though somehow critical about it, even Nieto Olarte could also be included in this group; see *Orden natural y orden social*, pp. 89–96. He argues that discovery is a collective social practice and, following Appel, he likewise maintains that Caldas could never find a place for himself in the scientific networks of his time emanating from Europe. From these two premises, he concludes that it is hard to talk about discovery in Caldas's case. Had he been able to find a place for himself in those European networks, he would indeed be recognized as the discoverer, or at least, as one of the discoverers of hypsometry.
37. Appel, *Francisco José de Caldas*, p. 16; and Albis and Martínez-Chavanz, "Las investigaciones meteorológicas."
38. On the relationship between science and politics during this period, see Nieto Olarte, *Remedios para el imperio*.

Bibliography

Albis, Víctor Samuel, and Regino Martínez-Chavanz, "Las investigaciones meteorológicas de Caldas," *Quipu. Revista Latinoamericana de Historia de las Ciencias y la Tecnología* 4 (1987), pp. 413–432.

Ambrose, Charles T., "Immunology's First Priority Dispute: An Account of the 17th-Century Rudbeck-Bartholin Feud," *Cellular Immunology* 242 (2006), pp. 1–8.

Appel, John Wilton, *Francisco José de Caldas: A Scientist at Work in Nueva Granada* (Philadelphia, PA: The American Philosophical Society, 1994). pp. 12–19.

Arias de Greiff, Jorge, "El método de Caldas para medir la elevación de las montañas," *Academia Colombiana de Ciencias* 20.76 (1996), pp. 63–69.

Bateman, Alfredo D., *Francisco José de Caldas: El hombre, el sabio* (Cali: Banco Popular, 1978).

Caldas, Francisco José de, *Obras completas* (Bogota: Universidad Nacional de Colombia, 1966).

———, *Cartas* (Bogota: Academia Colombiana de Ciencias Exactas, Físicas y Naturales, 1978).

Castro Gómez, Santiago, *La hybris del punto cero: Ciencia, raza e ilustración en la Nueva Granada (1750–1816)* (Bogota: Pontificia Universidad Javeriana and Instituto Pensar, 2004).

Díaz Piedrahita, Santiago, *Nueva aproximación a Francisco José de Caldas: Episodios de su vida y de su actividad científica* (Bogota: Academia Colombiana de Historia, 1997).

Gross, Alan G., "Do Disputes over Priority Tell Us Anything about Science?" *Science in Context* 11.2 (1998), pp. 161–179.

Latour, Bruno, *We Have Never Been Modern*, trans. Catherine Porter (Cambridge, MA: Harvard University Press, 1993).

Merton, Robert K., "Priorities in Scientific Discovery: A Chapter in the Sociology of Science," *American Sociological Review* 22.6 (1957), pp. 635–659.

———, ed., *The Sociology of Science: Theoretical and Empirical Investigations* (Chicago: University of Chicago Press, 1973).

Nieto Olarte, Mauricio, *Remedios para el imperio: Historia natural y la apropiación del nuevo mundo*, rev. ed. (Bogota: Universidad de los Andes, 2006).

———, *Orden natural y orden social: Ciencia y política en el Semanario del Nuevo Reyno de Granada* (Bogota: Uniandes-Ceso, 2009).

O'Brien, Jean M., *Firsting and Lasting: Writing Indians out of Existence in New England* (Minneapolis: University of Minnesota Press, 2010).

Pombo, Lino de, Luis María Murillo, and Alfredo D. Bateman, eds., *Francisco José de Caldas: Su vida, su personalidad y su obra. El descubrimiento de la hipsometría* (Bogota: Academia Colombiana de Ciencias Exactas, Físicas y Naturales, 1958).

Recio Blanco, Carlos Mario, and Humberto Quiceno Castrillón, eds., *Independencia, educación y cultura: Memorias del simposio* (Cali: Alcaldía de Santiago de Cali and Universidad del Valle, 2010).

Restrepo Forero, Olga, "En busca del orden: Ciencia y poder en Colombia," *Asclepio* 50.2 (1998), pp. 33–75.

Ruiz-Castell, Pedro, "Priority Claims and Public Disputes in Astronomy: E. M. Antoniadi, J. Comas i Solà and the Search for Authority and Social Prestige in the Early Twentieth Century," *British Journal for the History of Science* 44.4 (2011), pp. 509–531.

Silva, Renán, *Los ilustrados de Nueva Granada 1760–1808: Genealogía de una comunidad de interpretación* (Medellin: Fondo Editorial Universidad EAFIT and Banco de la República, 2002).

Smith, Pamela H., Amy R. W. Meyers, and Harold J. Cook, eds., *Ways of Making and Knowing: The Material Culture of Empirical Knowledge* (New York: Bard Graduate Center, 2014).

Strevens, Michael, "The Role of the Priority Rule in Science," *Journal of Philosophy* 100.2 (2003), pp. 55–79.

7 History and Progress

Regional Identity and the Useable Past in Nova Scotia, 1857–1877

Nicolas Haisell

Jean O'Brien's *Firsting and Lasting: Writing Indians out of Existence in New England* offers scholars of Indigenous-settler relations a valuable framework for the study of nineteenth-century local histories. While these local histories should be considered more than simply biased, skewed, or historically valueless documents, O'Brien's work illustrates the very real and consequential cultural work that unfolded within the pages of such histories.[1] Although O'Brien focuses specifically on New England, the contents of this volume illustrate that similar literary processes of firsting and lasting took place throughout the early-modern Atlantic world.

This observation certainly holds true in the case of Nova Scotia where from 1857 to 1877 the region witnessed a notable increase in the publication of such local histories and selected archival documents.[2] Taken as a whole, this material clearly demonstrates O'Brien's concurrent processes of firsting and lasting; at the same time, this published and archival material starkly emphasized the colony's independence, progress, and historicity while simultaneously relegating potentially disruptive Indigenous and French-speaking Acadian inhabitants to a premodern realm that stood apart from an authentic, progressive history of the region.[3] Yet, unlike in New England where "antiquarians [. . .] were preoccupied with forging dense chronicles of the origins and historical happenings of mostly small towns and often with connecting these small places with the project of forging Anglo-Saxon nationalism," in Nova Scotia the useable past was mobilized and produced in order to resist Canadian confederation.[4] Even as calls for repealing the new union faded in the early- to mid-1870s, the project of asserting Nova Scotia's freestanding British modernity continued well into the early national era.

This chapter seeks to complicate the often-assumed relationship between the narrative construction of local colonial modernity and the establishment of, or desire for, a federally governed nation-state. As Jerry Bannister eloquently notes, "an often unspoken axiom plots imperial subjecthood as a backward social relationship to be overcome by more modern forms of national citizenship."[5] For anti-confederates, freestanding and local historical development as well as a strong imperial standing is what characterized a modern Nova Scotia, and a union likely to be dominated by Ontario and Quebec was a clear threat to this vision.

As confederation rhetoric gathered steam, the local useable past became a critical instrument of anti-confederation rhetoric in Nova Scotia.[67] Historians, antiquarians, and political officials used firsting narratives to depict Nova Scotia as independent, modern, and yet simultaneously wholly British in an attempt to resist confederation and the assumed attenuation of imperial ties that would ensue. At the crux of this political and cultural project was Thomas Beamish Akins (1809–1891) who, with the support of prominent anti-confederationists, including Joseph Howe (1804–1873) and Adams George Archibald (1814–1892), was installed as the first commissioner for public records in 1857. Scholarly, motivated, and politically connected, Akins served as an essential link between the intellectual, cultural, and political spheres of the anti-confederation project.[8] As Archibald later narrated to the Nova Scotia Historical Society, Akins convinced the "practical politicians of the day" of the value of local historical ownership.[9] Akins was "one of these enthusiasts who appear from time to time," wrote Archibald, "to preach or prophesy, as the necessities of the age require, who, by strong belief, and with the courage of their convictions, shape and mould the thoughts of their fellows."[10] As commissioner, Akins collected and organized local historical records, politicized selections of them within a single volume published in 1869 (the printing having been approved in 1865), titled *Selections from the Public Documents of the Province of Nova Scotia*. In addition, the commissioner established the Akins Historical Prize in 1864 to encourage the production of county histories that illustrated Nova Scotia's historical progress. Taken together, Akins's work "participated in the assertion" of a recognizable Nova Scotian modernity during a period of looming political change in Nova Scotia.[11]

As O'Brien notes, such articulations of modernity sharply contrasted with the premodernity of Indigenous (and in the case of Nova Scotia, Acadian) peoples. Several scholars have discussed the concept of premodernity as an exclusionary tool of otherization. In a colonial and imperial context, this designation was often employed to cleave undesirable subjects from having membership to a liberal body politic (both historically and contemporarily). Uday Singh Mehta has noted the tension between liberalism's "universality and politically inclusionary character" and historical reality, characterizing it as "a period [from the seventeenth century onward] defined by the systematic and sustained exclusion of various groups and types of people."[12] The universal character of liberalism is predicated on what Mehta terms an "anthropological minimum" consisting of natural freedom, moral equality, and rationality.[13] Yet not all peoples meet such requirements. The inscrutability of Indigenous (and to a lesser extent Acadian) peoples relegated them to a timeless premodernity that stood apart from the seemingly true, progressive history of the region.

Relatedly, in *On Liberty*, John Stewart Mill (1806–1873) emphasizes the foundational importance of individual liberty for political modernity. Tellingly, Mill notes that "Liberty, as a principal, has no application to any state of things anterior to the time when mankind have become capable of being improved by free and equal discussion. Until then, there is nothing for them but implicit obedience to an Akbar or a Charlemagne, if they are so fortunate to find one."[14] In the mid- to late nineteenth century, such concepts were further bolstered by novel anthropological understandings of race and unilinear cultural evolution.

Although confederation would not be confirmed until 1867, in 1857 (the year of Akins's appointment) the Nova Scotia Legislature first appointed delegates to examine the ramifications of an impending colonial union.[15] Rhetoric strengthened in subsequent years, and the formation of a union became an ever more conspicuous possibility by the early 1860s, dominating newspaper editorials and public debate in the colony. In 1861, Jonathan McCully, an anti-confederate politician, newspaper editor, and ally of Joseph Howe, sponsored "An Act Relating to Public Records," which was passed by the general assembly on 13 March 1861. The act stipulated that "the books, papers, and records, of all public offices, Provincial and County, are hereby vested in her Majesty the Queen, and her successors."[16] Clearly designed to support and strengthen Akins's authority as the "proper custodian" of public records, the act further stipulated that "if any person shall wrongfully take, withhold, or retain possession of any public document, book, record, writing, or other paper, he may be proceeded against for the recovery of the same."[17] Tellingly, Akins had pressed the Halifax Mechanic's Institute to establish a depository of colonial records in 1841; however, a lack of interest thwarted the venture. This change of perspective, from a clear indifference in 1841 to an act that essentially criminalized the withholding of historical documents twenty years later, was not a coincidence: for men such as Howe, McCully, and the nominally nonpartisan Akins, the seemingly proper use of Nova Scotia's historic documents became critically important in this politically turbulent period.

In the years following his appointment, Akins kept the assembly and relevant committees constantly abreast of his work, submitting a total of thirteen reports between 1858 and 1887 that were recorded in the appendices of *The Journal and Proceedings of the House of Assembly*. When examined in conjunction with supporting documents, Akins's reports demonstrate that the antiquarian was not simply interested in objectively collecting and preserving documents relating to the colony's history, as perhaps might be expected from a nominally nonpartisan civil servant. In his third report, for example, Akins assured the assembly that he had been diligently engaged in the project of "examining, preserving, and arranging ancient records and documents illustrative of the history and progress of society in this province either for reference or publication as the legislature may hereafter determine."[18] Understood within O'Brien's framework, Akins's hands-on work as commissioner focused primarily on the act of firsting through his collection and organization of evidence of British origin that Nova Scotian settlers had erected the first notable forms of "social order," being "the first houses, institutions, polities, and economies."[19] One can also argue that such an overwhelming focus on the collation of records relating to the British origin of development within Nova Scotia was itself an implicit process of lasting because it comprised a program of colonial erasure that was enacted at the archival level. This way of viewing history also privileges textual culture as containing the authoritative version of the historical record.

With this focus firmly in mind, Akins dedicated himself to the task, working full time to curate evidence of Nova Scotia's historic progress. James Farquhar, who was employed to work alongside Akins, kept a meticulous daily diary that documented the commissioner's hands-on role in "examining and making selections of material."[20] From the "several thousand" papers that passed under Akins's "personal inspection" during this period, the commissioner marked the "papers and memorabilia concerned with the erection of early townships" as particularly valuable.[21] Material documenting the construction of roads, critical in the development of a modern and interconnected colony, was also deemed worthy of preservation.

Alongside such rather monotonous daily entries, Farquhar's diary contains several transcripts of letters sent by Akins inquiring about potential sources of information. Tellingly, two such letters asked after a work titled *New York Minutes of the Proceedings of the Port Rosway Association of Loyalists 1783*. The arrival of the loyalists, commonly touted at this time as the best example of loyalty and Britishness in North America, fit comfortably into the notion that Nova Scotia's historical trajectory birthed a freestanding yet resolutely British citizenry. Furthermore, the successful acquisition of this material would illustrate a longstanding connection to the British metropole, a relationship that was simultaneously integral to Nova Scotia's modernity and implicitly under threat as confederation loomed.[22] It is notable that, while documents relating to Indigenous peoples were seen as unimportant and were often simply overlooked (itself a form of lasting), Akins was keen to include copies of treaties and oaths of fidelity because this material lent credence to the notion of longstanding British authority and control of the region.[23]

The commissioner worked steadily from 1857 to 1864, noting in his report presented on 24 February 1864 that his selections "occupy sixty-four volumes and have been bound up and their contents carefully catalogued."[24] Although progress was being made, clearly a lot of work remained. "A large quantity of papers," wrote Akins in the same report, "from which selections have been made, have been placed in boxes but not yet arranged or classified."[25] Despite the fact that this was quite obviously an ongoing project, the commissioner concluded his 1864 report by arguing that "I think it is right to revert to the idea suggested in the resolution of the Assembly in 1857, of printing and publishing selections from these archives, believing they would prove very interesting."[26] Read in isolation, Akins's proposal to publish selections at that time means little. Historian Brian C. Cuthbertson suggests that the commissioner simply "considered the work of the record commission complete: 211 volumes of documents had been bound and thirty-seven boxes of documents had been sorted and arranged in bundles."[27] Akins, however, does not explain his rationale for publishing these documents in this way and at that time; in fact, he continued to suggest that the work was an important, ongoing process in subsequent reports. If Akins had concluded that his work as the commissioner of public records was complete in 1864, then we struggle to understand why the post continued to be funded until his death in 1891.[28]

Arguably, Akins's desire to publish during this period was a response to the strengthening rhetoric in favor of a federal union in 1864. While a potential intercolonial union had been debated and discussed as early as 1857, 1864 is the year in which such debates took on a new sense of urgency, leaping to the forefront of public attention and emerging as the most pressing political question of the day. As historian J. Murray Beck points out, by early 1864 tangible steps toward an intercolonial (that is, federal) union had been taken.[29] On 4 February of that year, twenty days before Akins reported, the speaker of the Nova Scotia Provincial Assembly noted that

> the importance of consolidating the influence and advancing the common progress of the three Maritime Provinces [. . .] has for some time attracted a large share of public attention, and I propose [that] [. . .] a proposition in which the co-operation of the Governments of New Brunswick and Prince Edward Island will be invited, with a view to the union of the three Provinces.[30]

This debate, unfolding in both the assembly and the public sphere, led to the Charlottetown Conference, held from 1 to 7 September 1864. On hearing these developments, the Canadas sought permission to attend. Thus, following the Charlottetown and Quebec conferences, the union became a real possibility in the autumn of 1864. In a development that mirrored anti-confederate fears of powerful Canadian influence swamping local political autonomy, discussions of a regional maritime union were quickly engulfed by a push for a broader federal union.

Akins's *Selections from the Public Documents of the Province of Nova Scotia* was finally published in 1869, two years after the passage of the British North America Act. Yet, this was still a period of political flux. In the 1867 federal election, Nova Scotian voters elected 18 out of 19 anti-confederation candidates to the first dominion parliament. Historians have therefore characterized the months and years following the emergence of the union as a period defined by the "demand for repeal."[31] In the eyes of Nova Scotians, the future remained very much unwritten and the useable past project continued into the early to mid-1870s. In this political context, Akins had published "selected portions [of historical documents] which possess[ed] the greatest historical value."[32] As one might expect, a large segment of the 1869 volume is dedicated to dispatches and reports relating to the construction of Nova Scotia's British origin and its teleological march into modernity as signified by the settlement of Halifax in 1749, the first British colonies, and the establishment of responsible government in 1758. Much like the local histories studied by O'Brien, *Selections* recounts the unfolding of the seemingly social, military, economic, and political modern order in Nova Scotia. Crucial in light of the concepts of firsting and lasting, Akins contrasts this narrative of progress with material relating to the downfall of French power and, most importantly, the Acadian expulsion initiated in 1755. Akins was uncomfortable with the historical presence of Acadians because they comprised an unwanted complication within the narrative of peaceful progress in the colony, a narrative that evidently had also managed to eliminate Indigenous presence in that history as first peoples in Nova Scotia. Addressing the legislature in 1858, Akins tellingly noted that

> I mention in my report of last year my having caused many papers relating to the Acadian French population and their removal from this country to be transcribed in order to afford your excellency and the legislature the means of deciding on the course to be pursued whenever it shall be deemed desirable to publish portions of our manuscripts.[33]

As this passage suggests, Akins was not simply interested in collecting and preserving local historical documents. In addition, the commissioner sought to curate specific conceptions of sensitive events. While the legislature's response to this report is unknown, Akins's "pursued course of action" is clearly illustrated in the pages of *Selections from the Public Documents of the Province of Nova Scotia*. Here the commissioner desired to both disconnect the Acadian French-speaking population from the carefully curated history of Nova Scotian progress while also absolving Nova Scotian forbearers from charges of brutality relating to the expulsion. As a result, Acadians, who he portrayed as rustic, prehistoric peasants, are closely tied to Indigenous peoples in the pages of the *Selections*. Describing Nova Scotia in 1770, Paul Mascarine argues that Acadians are "very little industrious, their lands not improved as might be expected, they living in a manner from hand to mouth, and provided they have a good field of Cabbages and Bread enough for their families with what fodder is sufficient for their cattle they seldom look for much further improvement."[34] Furthermore, the governor of Nova Scotia prior to the expulsion, Richard Phillips (c. 1661–1750), complains that French inhabitants are "indeavoring at this time to disturb the peace of this Government, by practiseing with the Savages to [. . .] assert their native rights to this country."[35]

While both Indigenous and Acadian peoples were portrayed as being beholden by their shared faith to local Catholic priests (and France's geopolitical scheming by extension), it was ultimately the Acadians' status as proto-liberal individuals, who demonstrated meager environmental improvement and self-reliance, that sealed the expulsion as a tragic yet unavoidable event. Indigenous inhabitants, in contrast, were more easily characterized as premodern savages that, driven by new concepts of cultural evolution, would dissipate into the annals of deep history naturally. Akins's work therefore exhibits both firsting and lasting as strategies that addressed the challenge of constructing a peaceful liberal modernity in Nova Scotia. In Akins's mind, "although the [expulsion] has lately derived peculiar interest from the frequent reference made to it by modern writers [. . .] it has undergone little actual investigation, and in consequence the necessity for their removal has not been clearly perceived, and the motives which led to its enforcement have been often misunderstood."[36]

Several historians, including Martin Brook Taylor, Ian McKay, and Robin Bates, have noted a tangible re-engagement with the Acadian expulsion during the 1850s–1860s in Nova Scotia.[37] Most point to the publication of *Evangeline: A Tale of Acadie* in 1847 by Henry Wadsworth Longfellow (1807–1882) as a primary catalyst for renewed interest in the event. The poem follows the story of Evangeline, an Acadian teenager during what has been termed the Grand Dérangement (great upheaval) and her subsequent exile from Acadia as she searches for her betrothed in the United States, where she lived following her expulsion. Bleak and melancholic in tone, the work depicts the Acadians as a peaceful, rustic, and idealized rural community that had been uprooted and "scattered like flakes of snow" on the orders of a distant and calculating king, George II (1683–1760).[38]

There is no doubt that McKay and Bates are correct in noting that the poem "became a publishing sensation, selling out five editions of a thousand copies each."[39] Yet the poem was 22 years old by the time that Akins published his report in 1869. Taylor unconvincingly argues that "Akins quite simply used the Acadian controversy as a means to justify the creation of the archives as a whole," and this was "probably a decisive factor" in the government's decision to create the commission of public records.[40] Yet, there is no mention of the poem in the Commissioner of Public Records fonds held by Archives Nova Scotia, and the poem was far from new at this point.[41] In Nova Scotia, the looming union added a sense of urgency, so it is important to understand Akins and his contemporaries' re-engagement with *Evangeline* and the Acadian expulsion as a facet of this broader project to construct Nova Scotian modernity through its useable past. In Naomi Griffiths's words, the debate over the events of 1755 "was neither purely academic nor just the question of the historical reputation of Nova Scotia."[42]

Nova Scotians, like O'Brien's New Englanders, "symbolized the 'civilized' order of culture, science, and reason;" doing so allowed them to reckon with and explain away the violent expulsion of a seemingly peaceful Acadian population through the device of civilization.[43] In service of the usable past, Acadians and Indigenous peoples were similarly depicted as resistant and perpetually out of step with Nova Scotian progress. Such opposition worked to relegate non-British peoples to the status of premodern historical footnotes, disconnecting them from the constructed narrative that served as a crucial pillar of the anti-confederation project. On one occasion, Akins introduces a body of documentation, which he calls the "Papers relating to the Acadian French," that "throw[s] light on the history and conduct" of Acadians.[44] Taken together, the collection of primarily British-authored government reports and dispatches depict the Acadians' stubbornly refusing to take oaths of allegiance to the English crown and instead collaborating with their Indigenous neighbors and interrupting the natural progress of the colony. "Whilst the Indians were plundering the dry goods," complained Mascarine of one incident, the Acadians were "robbing the fish and transporting it away."[45] In this conception of events, the conduct of the Acadians was positioned as a clear and consistent threat to early British colonial efforts in Nova Scotia. The expulsion, according to Akins and his allies, was therefore harsh but necessary.

This type of argument groups together Indigenous and Acadian peoples as both less civil and perhaps less civilized than British colonial presence, which evinces one way through which British colonial authorities reordered the Acadians as no longer the first settlers of European descent. In a further attempt to group Indigenous and Acadian inhabitants together and to esteem Anglophone settlers and British colonial rule as having contributed to a seemingly valid progressive history of the region, Akins includes numerous documents that remind the reader of Acadian-Indigenous intermarriage and shared religion. In a letter from 24 November 1714 to the Lords of Trade, for example, colonel Samuel Vetch reports that "there [are] none but French and Indians [. . .] settled in those parts. And as they have intermarried, with the Indians, by which and their being of one Religion, they have a mighty influence upon them."[46] Similarly, Paul Mascarine (c. 1684–1760), who later served as lieutenant governor, informed the Lords of Trade in a 1720 letter that the inhabitants of the settlements located along the south side of the Bay of Fundy are "still all French and Indians," as well as missionaries "of the papish persuasion" who have "ascendance over that ignorant people." Missionaries are further described as "forever instigating the salvages to some mischief [. . .]

when any English settlement is proposed."[47] In the same paragraph, Mascarine continues to note that Acadians "are very little industrious, their lands are not improved as expected [. . .] [They live] in a manner from hand to mouth [. . .] they seldom look for much further improvement."[48] Mascarine concludes that British colonists, by contrast, are industrious, self-possessed individuals that would "better improve" the province as their "industry is far superior to the French."[49] Thus, rooted firmly in the notion of pursuing progress, the board of trade wrote to governor Phillips on 28 December 1720 that the Acadians should be expelled "for the protection and better settlement of Your Province."[50]

Although Akins continuously stressed the objectivity of his *Selections*, a number of historians later charged the commissioner with partiality and the selective inclusion of certain documents.[51] Perhaps the most vocal of these critics was Henri-Raymond Casgrain (1831–1904), a Catholic priest and historian who presented a paper titled *Eclaircissements sur la question Acadienne* before the Royal Society of Canada on 24 May 1888. Casgrain was clear in his criticism, arguing that

> The choice of documents published in Halifax was obviously made in order to justify the Nova Scotia government's deportation of the Acadians. For that we systematically eliminated and left behind the most compromising pieces, those that could best establish the rights of the Acadians.[52]

Casgrain dutifully included an appendix of documents, arguing that "I have found so many omissions so essential that they completely change the face of things."[53] As Martin Brooks Taylor argues, Casgrain demonstrated that local British officials has consistently blocked Acadians from moving to French territory, a freedom of movement that had been guaranteed by the Treaty of Utrecht (1713). As a result, Casgrain argued, British demands for an oath of allegiance were invalid.[54]

Understood as a project of historical constructionism, the *Selections* presents a familiar narrative of the British origin of historical progress and contrasts this progress with Indigenous and Acadian ahistoricity as well as their opposition to British progress. Linked by their shared devotion to the Catholic faith and the characterization of meddling priests, these non-British inhabitants become distant others and the expulsion in that light seems a necessary and prefatory act to the historical march toward modernity.

Akins's activities as the commissioner of Nova Scotian public records were only one component of the project to construct a usable past. Alongside his efforts to organize, catalog, and subsequently present politically relevant selections of the province's historical documents to the public, the commissioner established the Akins Historical Prize essay competition in 1864. Founded in an attempt to encourage the production of usable, progressive histories of Nova Scotia's counties, the prize urged the seemingly leading citizens of the colony to submit local county histories that illustrated a progressive history of the colony. As expected, the works selected to receive the yearly award (and thus the works that later were publicly circulated) were characterized by a teleological energy that imbued Nova Scotia with an unrelenting, internal sense of improvement and drive: winning essays were vivid examples of firsting and lasting in action. While O'Brien suggests that the authors of New England local histories were engaged in a more general version of the ideological project, at Akins's behest Nova Scotia bore witness to an accelerated, concentrated project of local historical production. Works selected to receive the prize emphasized British origins as well as social and economic development.

Isaiah Wilson's *A History and Geography of the County of Digby*, submitted for the prize in 1873, is one such example. Presented in twenty-four chapters, the work charts the arrival of English colonists in 1765 and the subsequent development of the county. Soon joined by loyalist settlers who recognized that the "climate was unquestionably superior to that of Canada," these British origin settlers were, according to Wilson, "animated by bright hopes, and cheered by unbroken successes." The future, according to Wilson, "was indeed most assuring."[55] The work charts the familiar tale of unfolding modernity in subsequent chapters: from the erection of churches in chapter eight, commercial progress in chapter 11, to improvements to highways in chapter 13, and culminating in the "Nova Scotia electric telegraph and its success."[56] The submission is imbued with an unrelenting sense of momentum, which Wilson addresses in his 1895 preface: "a fair and productive area is traced from the primeval wilderness, through the various stages of development [. . .] to our own time when we behold a rapidly growing and prosperous commonwealth which all happily share and enjoy."[57] Tellingly, Acadian inhabitants are discussed alongside "aborigines and their footprints" and "relics of ancient settlements" in an early chapter.[58] As O'Brien notes, such undesirable inhabitants serve as little more than premodern footnotes to the arrival of British forefathers and the spark of progress.

For Akins, Howe, and like-minded liberal Nova Scotian elites, violent and conflict-ridden histories had lasting impacts on the region's present and future viability; therefore, winning essays were those that consistently downplayed the violence and conflict that characterized Nova Scotia's past.[59] Akins received twenty-two papers in total between 1865 and 1891, however few met with Akins's "full hearted approval," and the commissioner later complained to Archibald MacMechan (1862–1933) before the former man's death in 1891 that "the poor quality of the material had defeated 'his main intention in founding [the Prize].'"[60] Nevertheless, sixteen awards were given. Each of these local histories selected for the prize devote themselves entirely to narrating the construction of public buildings, including churches, schools, and meeting halls.[61] Such public buildings were seen as proper institutions of social order, and therefore modernity was presented as within the exclusive purview of the British settlers who had erected them in their respective counties. Many of the amateur historians went so far as to present tables that illustrated an ever-increasing yield of fish, timber, and ore as further evidence of this objective to improve.[62] The lives of leading citizens garnered similar attention. The author of *The History of the County of Guysborough* (which won the 1877 prize), for example, mourned the untimely death of a Mr. Whitman because "there was every prospect he would materially advance the progress of Canso."[63] Such descriptions of local community leaders were common and served an important function. As O'Brien observes, the inclusion of detailed biographical and genealogical data serves to tangibly root communities to the geography and extended history of the region. In addition, it was important for authors of these texts to emphasize the local and independent origin of progressive development. The construction of churches, highways, electric telegraphs, and other indicators of modernity was not an external imposition of metropolitan benevolence. Rather, it was due to the diligence and toil of local people such as Mr. Whitman.

A clear narrative of progress was only one side of the story. In a colonial setting, both Indigenous and Acadian inhabitants fit uncomfortably into the narrative and were therefore simultaneously situated as opposing progress. Alongside extended discussions of the construction of public buildings and increasing economic prosperity stood the original Indigenous inhabitants of the region as ahistoric holdovers who, like the wilderness itself, were seemingly overcome by the toil of individual British settlers. Harriet Hart, the wife of a lawyer and the author of the winning *History of the County of Guysborough*, noted that British communities "were not allowed to flourish undisturbed" and were maliciously harassed by Indigenous peoples.[64] In each account, conflict between the colonizers and the colonized was never contextualized, and any violence perpetuated by British settlers was presented as "wholly defensive" in nature.[65] Works selected to receive the Akins Historical Prize are filled with passages describing Indigenous groups surprising villages at night, scalping settlers, and carrying off prisoners. Hart interrupted a rather dry discussion about the construction of a church and school with a tale of the Mi'kmaq creeping from the wilderness with the intention of, in her words, "exterminating pale faces and [to] carry off spoil as soon as reinforcements arrived;" luckily, a priest recently arrived from Cape Breton heard of these "murderous designs" and somehow "convinced them to abandon their project."[66] The author's abrupt shift in tone and style, from a monotonous, well-documented description of colonial development to an anecdotal narrative, serves as a vivid illustration of a broader effort to present a usable form of Guysborough's past.

Despite a clear desire to present a crafted image of progress, on the one hand, and of mindless opposition, on the other, narrative cracks appear in these works with some regularity. Termed "dialogic indices" by Carlo Ginsburg, these are passages, according to Gonzalo Lamana, in which "odd things emerge, and where one can recover 'an unresolved clash of conflicting voices.'"[67] In this instance, such unresolved clashes demonstrate explicit textual subjectivity and offer glimpses of a region characterized by a messy, contingent, and complex past. Akins himself contributes to this practice of inserting dialogic indices. Writing in his 1847 *Prize Essay on the History of the Settlement of Halifax* (which was later reprinted), Akins narrates that

> two men, named John Connor and James Grace, arrived at Halifax in a Indian canoe, bringing with them six Indian scalps. They informed the Council that they, and two others [. . .] were captured by the Indians and carried ten miles into the country, where their two companions were murdered; that they had surprised the Indians at night—killed several, whose scalps they secured—and having escaped to the sea side, seized a canoe and made their way to Halifax.[68]

The author is quick to place this action in what he sees as its proper context, noting that "along the coast both East and West from Halifax, Indian massacres had been frequent."[69] Although Akins endeavored to present Connor and Grace's actions as defensive and utilized language to downplay the inherent brutality of the event (Connor and Grace are described as having secured scalps, an unabrasive verb that is reserved for this specific episode), the passage nevertheless conveys more than the author intended. The men seemingly killed their captors in a bid to escape, yet took the time to remove their scalps. By perpetuating this additional act of otherwise unnecessary violence, the well-established association of scalping with settler-colonial conceptualizations of prehistoric Indigenous savagery is upended and Akins inadvertently offers a glimpse into a world that is less black and white than he sought to depict.[70]

This portrayal of wanton violence and barbarity served to demonstrate where Indigenous inhabitants were situated on the unilinear scale of human evolution. It was commonly understood that if Indigenous peoples were not rendered extinct, they would at best subsist as perpetual wards of merciful, paternalistic Nova Scotian settlers.[71] In addition, by constantly referring to the Mi'kmaq and other distinct groups as simply "Indians," local authors disconnected Indigenous peoples from any local particularities, and instead connected them to, in the words of O'Brien, the "vaguely claimed story of the end of the line that echoed resoundingly in the emergent national literature."[72] The blurring of the local and the general made Indigenous inhabitants instantly familiar yet simultaneously alien: these were the same so-called savage peoples described in American (and British North American) literature, poetry, and paintings. In either case, any claims that could challenge the legitimacy of a modern Nova

Scotian collective identity defined by independent, sober, and hardworking British settlers were preemptively contextualized and dismissed. Such an unrelenting dual narrative is perhaps best illustrated by the words of Mather B. DesBrisay (1828–1900), a key ally of Joseph Howe (1804–1873) and elected member of the Anti-Confederation Party in Nova Scotia. In *History of the Country of Lunenburg*, DesBrisay remarks

> [W]hat a strange contrast is presented to the mind, between the busy scene we witness at Bridgewater to-day, and the undisturbed domain of the Indian, as it then existed; the river ferried by the birch canoe, and human habitations represented by the equally frail wigwam. The village, and its adjacent districts, show a remarkable development of resources, and steady advancement in material prosperity.[73]

As this examination of Akins's work as commissioner of public records illustrates, a local Nova Scotian form of firsting and lasting grew from anti-confederate claims to become an expression of an exclusive, imperially settled British form of modernity. Playing out in the pages of the Akins Historical Prize-winning essays, in addition to the commissioner's hands-on work, Akins's project endeavored to illuminate a history of the British origins of progress while relegating Indigenous and Acadian inhabitants to the status of historical footnotes. And while anti-confederates ultimately failed to resist and later repeal confederation, an examination of Akins's work sheds light on a coherent project of firsting and lasting that was designed to illuminate Nova Scotia's freestanding, imperially situated modernity in the face of looming national reorganization.

Notes

1. For a discussion of amateur and local history, see Kammen, ed., *The Pursuit of Local History*; and Beckett, *Writing Local History*. In Canada specifically, see Wright, *The Professionalization of History in English Canada*, pp. 8–27; and Taylor, "Nova Scotia's Nineteenth-Century County Histories," pp. 159–167.
2. 1857 bore witness to Akins's installation as commissioner of public records (29 May). It was also the first year in which the provincial government appointed delegates to examine a potential union of the British North American colonies (16 June). See *Journal and Proceedings of the House of Assembly* [. . .] *1858*, appendix 3, pp. 48–50. While Akins continued in his role as commissioner and administrator of the Akins Historical Prize until his death 6 May 1891, by the mid-1870s a union was all but understood to be the new political reality. The politicized articulation of a local progressive past continued into the national era. Provincial elites sought to articulate a clear, freestanding Nova Scotian collective identity within the federal context.
3. For the authors of these texts, a history defined by Indigenous-settler interaction, be it cooperation or what could be construed as mutual or shared conflict, worked against the desired image of a singular British origin progress. Similarly, a parallel settlement and subsequent expulsion of French Acadian

settlers complicated the desired meta-narrative and thus had to be properly contextualized and explained away.

4. O'Brien, *Firsting and Lasting*, p. xvii.
5. Bannister and Riordan, "Loyalism and the British Atlantic, 1660–1840," in Bannister and Riordan, eds., *The Loyal Atlantic*, pp. 3–36: 4.
6. Van Wyck Brooks first discussed the useable past in his 1915 work *Americas Coming of Age*. For more recent engagements with the concept, see Kirkland, *Clio's Foot Soldiers*; and Taylor, *Promoters, Patriots, and Partisans*. In general terms, I understand a useable past to be one that is envisioned, constructed, and disseminated in a manner that facilitates the interaction between the past and the present (in contrast to history for its own sake). Often politicized, such works seek to foster understandings of past events that further the contemporary interests, goals, or movements of their authors.
7. Arguably, confederation is most fruitfully understood as a more broadly-defined set of processes that led to the formation of the Canadian nation-state, not simply the events of 1 July 1867.
8. Akins articled in the law offices of his first cousin, the politician and local historian Beamish Murdoch (1800–1876), in his early years. In addition, Akins assisted in the research for Haliburton's 1829 work *An Historical and Statistical Account of Nova Scotia* (published by Joseph Howe) and was also a founding member of The Club, "which gathered regularly in the late 1820s at the office of Joseph Howe's newspaper the *NovaScotian* for cakes, ale, and literary discussions;" see Cuthbertson, "Thomas Beamish Akins."
9. *Report and Collections of the Nova Scotia Historical Society*, vol. 1, p. 29.
10. Ibid. Archibald was serving as lieutenant governor of Nova Scotia at the time.
11. O'Brien, *Firsting and Lasting*, p. xiv.
12. Mehta, "Liberal Strategies of Inclusion," in Cooper and Stoler, eds., *Tensions of Empire*, pp. 59–86: 59.
13. Ibid., p. 63.
14. John Stewart Mill, *Three Essays* (Oxford: Oxford University Press, 1985), p. 16. As cited in Mehta, "Liberal Strategies of Inclusion," in Cooper and Stoler, eds., *Tensions of Empire*, p. 75.
15. Pryke, *Nova Scotia and Confederation*, p. 3.
16. *The Statutes of Nova Scotia*, p. 24.
17. Ibid.
18. Akins, *Third Report*.
19. O'Brien, *Firsting and Lasting*, p. 53.
20. See the diary of Farquhar, *Commissioner of Public Records Fonds*.
21. Akins, *Third Report*.
22. It is unknown if Akins acquired the loyalist documents.
23. Akins, *Third Report*.
24. Akins, "Record Commission, Report of Thomas Beamish Akins," in *Journal and Proceedings of the House of Assembly* [. . .] *1864*, appendix 25, pp. 1–7: 1.
25. Ibid., p. 1.
26. Ibid., p. 3.
27. Cuthbertson, "Thomas Beamish Akins: British North America's Pioneer Archivist," p. 91.
28. After Akins's death, the post of commissioner of public records was left vacant.
29. Beck, *Joseph Howe*, vol. 2, p. 181.
30. *Journal and Proceedings of the House of Assembly* [. . .] *1864*, p. 10.
31. Pryke, *Nova Scotia and Confederation*, p. 60.

32. Akins, ed., *Selections*, p. 11.
33. Ibid.
34. Mascarene, "Description of Nova Scotia," in Akins, ed., *Selections*, p. 42.
35. See "Gov. Phillips to M. St. Ovide Brouillan, Govr. of Cape Breton, May 14, 1720," in Akins, ed., *Selections*, p. 27.
36. Akins, ed., *Selections*, p. 11.
37. See Taylor, *Promoters, Patriots, and Partisans*; and McKay and Bates, *In the Province of History*.
38. Longfellow, *Evangeline*, p. 49.
39. McKay and Bates, *In the Provence of History*, p. 72.
40. Taylor, *Promoters Patriots and Partisans*, p. 192.
41. See *Commissioner of Public Records Fonds*.
42. Griffiths, "Longfellow's Evangeline," p. 35.
43. O'Brien, *Firsting and Lasting*, p. xxi.
44. Akins, *Selections*, p. 11.
45. Mascarene, "Description of Nova Scotia," in Akins, ed., *Selections*, p. 48.
46. "Colonel Samuel Vetch to the Right Honble: The Lords of Trade, November 24, 1714," in Akins, ed., *Selections*, p. 6.
47. Mascarene, "Description of Nova Scotia," in Akins, ed., *Selections*, p. 41.
48. Ibid., p. 42.
49. Ibid.
50. Westmoreland, Bladen, and Ashe, "Board of Trade to Governor Philipps," in Akins, ed., *Selections*, p. 58.
51. See, for example, Hector Fabre, "La fin de la domination française et l'historian Parkman," in *Proceedings and Transactions of the Royal Society of Canada*, vol. 6, pp. 3–12; and Smith, *Acadia*. American historian Francis Parkman, whose 1884 work *Montcalm and Wolfe* drew heavily from the *Sections*, and was also criticized.
52. "Le Choix des Documents publiés à Halifax a été évidemment fait en vue de justifier le gouvernement de la Nouvelle-Ecosse de la déportation des Acadiens. Pour cela on éliminé systématiquement et laissé dans l'ombre les pièces les plus compromettantes, celles qui pouvaient le mieux établir les droits des Acadiens;" see Henri-Raymond Casgrain, "*Eclaircissements sur la Question Acadienne*," in *Proceedings and Transactions of the Royal Society of Canada*, vol. 6, pp. 23–75: 24.
53. "J'ai constaté des omissions considérables et tellement essentielles qu'elles changent complétement la face des choses;" see ibid., p. 24.
54. Taylor, *Promoters, Patriots, and Partisans*, p. 200.
55. Wilson, *A History and Geography of the County of Digby*, pp. 39 and 46.
56. Ibid., p. 293.
57. Ibid., p. vi.
58. Ibid., pp. 21–33.
59. Reid, "Pax Britannica or Pax Indigena?," pp. 669–692. This article vividly dispels the notion that Nova Scotia's colonial history was defined solely by pleasant British development.
60. Thomas B. Akins, as cited in Taylor, "Nova Scotia's Nineteenth-Century County Histories," p. 161.
61. See, for example, Wilson, *A History and Geography of the County of Digby*.
62. See, for example, DesBrisay, *History of the County of Lunenburg*.
63. Hart, *History of the County of Guysborough*, p. 31. Hart's essay won the 1877 Akins Prize. Several of the winning essays, including Hart's, were reprinted by Mika Press in the 1970s.
64. Ibid., p. 12.

65. Ibid.
66. Hart, *History of the County of Guysborough*, p. 60.
67. Ginsburg, *Clues, Myths, and the Historical Method*, p. 164, as cited in Lamana, *Domination without Dominance*, p. 11.
68. Akins, *Prize Essay*, p. 29.
69. Ibid.
70. For a discussion of scalping and the association with concepts of savagery, see Axtell and Sturtevant, "The Unkindest Cut, or Who Invented Scalping?;" and Brantlinger, *Dark Vanishings*.
71. The mid-to late nineteenth century was characterized by the rapid development of public welfare institutions in British North America. Alongside schools, prisons, and asylums, the Indian Act of 1876 gave rise to the residential school system and other projects of cultural destruction. Ostensibly designed to civilize, these systems arguably entreated the secondary status of Indigenous peoples and their reliance upon the federal government. Although the construction of good liberal individuals was the stated goal, Indigenous peoples rarely transcended dependent status.
72. O'Brien, *Firsting and Lasting*, p. 142.
73. DesBrisay, *History of the County of Lunenburg*, p. 88.

Bibliography

Akins, Thomas B., *Prize Essay on the History of the Settlement of Halifax* (Halifax, NS: English and Blackadar, 1847).

———, *Third Report of Thomas B. Akins Appointed by Lt. Gov. on 20 May 1857 to Be Commissioner of Public Records. Commissioner of Public Records Fonds*. Nova Scotia Archives, Halifax, Accession 1999-000/001.

———, ed., *Selections from the Public Documents of the Province of Nova Scotia* (Halifax, NS: Charles Annand Publisher, 1869).

Axtell, James, and William C. Sturtevant, "The Unkindest Cut, or Who Invented Scalping?" *William & Mary Quarterly* 37.3 (1980), pp. 451–472.

Bannister, Jerry, and Liam Riordan, eds., *The Loyal Atlantic: Remaking the British Atlantic in the Revolutionary Era* (Toronto: University of Toronto Press, 2011).

Beck, James Murray, *Joseph Howe*, vol. 2: *The Briton Becomes Canadian, 1848–1873* (Kingston: McGill-Queen's University Press, 1982).

Beckett, John, *Writing Local History* (Manchester: Manchester University Press, 2007).

Brantlinger, Patrick, *Dark Vanishings: Discourse on the Extinction of Primitive Races, 1800–1930* (Ithaca, NY: Cornell University Press, 2003).

Commissioner of Public Records Fonds. Nova Scotia Archives, Halifax, Accession 1999-000/001.

Cooper, Frederick, and Ann Laura Stoler, eds., *Tensions of Empire: Colonial Cultures in a Bourgeois World* (Berkeley: University of California Press, 1997).

Cuthbertson, Brian C., "Thomas Beamish Akins: British North America's Pioneer Archivist," *Acadiensis* 7.1 (1977), pp. 86–103.

———, "Thomas Beamish Akins," in *The Dictionary of Canadian Biography*. Vol. 13 (University of Toronto/Université Laval, 2003). www.biographi.ca/en/bio/akins_thomas_beamish_12E.html

DesBrisay, Mather B., *History of the County of Lunenburg* (Halifax, NS: James Bowes & Sons, 1870).

Farquhar, James, *Commissioner of Public Records Fonds*. Nova Scotia Archives, Halifax, Accession 1999-000/001.
Ginsburg, Carlo, *Clues, Myths, and the Historical Method* (Baltimore, MD: Johns Hopkins University Press, 1989).
Griffiths, Naomi, "Longfellow's Evangeline: The Birth and Acceptance of a Legend," *Acadiensis* 11.2 (1982), pp. 28–41.
Hart, Harriet C., *History of the County of Guysborough* (Belleville, NS: Mika Press, 1975).
Journal and Proceedings of the House of Assembly of the Province of Nova Scotia, Session 1858 (Halifax, NS: W.A. Penney, Printer to the Assembly, 1858).
Journal and Proceedings of the House of Assembly of the Province of Nova Scotia, Session 1864 (Halifax, NS: Compton & Co., Printers to the Assembly, 1864).
Kammen, Carol, ed., *The Pursuit of Local History: Readings on Theory and Practice* (Walnut Creek, MD: Altamira Press, 1995).
Kirkland, Lara Leigh, *Clio's Foot Soldiers: Twentieth Century U.S. Social Movements and Collective Memory* (Amherst: University of Massachusetts Press, 2018).
Lamana, Gonzalo, *Domination without Dominance: Inca-Spanish Encounters in Early Colonial Peru* (Durham, NC: Duke University Press, 2008).
Longfellow, Henry Wadsworth, *Evangeline: A Tale of Acadie* (London: George Routledge and Sons, 1878).
McKay, Ian, and Robin Bates, *In the Province of History: The Making of the Public Past in Twentieth Century Nova Scotia* (Montreal: McGill-Queen's University Press, 2010).
Mill, John Stewart, *Three Essays* (Oxford: Oxford University Press, 1985).
O'Brien, Jean M., *Firsting and Lasting: Writing Indians out of Existence in New England* (Minneapolis: University of Minnesota Press, 2010).
Proceedings and Transactions of the Royal Society of Canada for the Year 1888. Vol. 6 (Montreal: Dawson Brothers Printers, 1889).
Pryke, Kenneth G., *Nova Scotia and Confederation 1864–74* (Toronto: University of Toronto Press, 1979).
Reid, John G., "Pax Britannica or Pax Indigena? Planter Nova Scotia (1760–1782) and Competing Strategies of Pacification," *Canadian Historical Review* 85.4 (2004), pp. 669–692.
Report and Collections of the Nova Scotia Historical Society for the Year 1879 (Halifax, NS: Morning Herald Office, 1879).
Smith, Philip H., *Acadia: A Lost Chapter in American History* (Pawling, NY: Published by the Author, 1884).
The Statutes of Nova Scotia Passed in the Second Session of the General Assembly of the Twenty-Fourth Year of the Reign of Her Majesty Queen Victoria, Held on the Thirty-First Day of January 1861 (Halifax, NS: E.M. McDonald, Queen's Printer, 1861).
Taylor, Martin Brook, "Nova Scotia's Nineteenth-Century County Histories," *Acadiensis* 10.2 (1981), pp. 159–167.
———, *Promoters, Patriots, and Partisans: Historiography in Nineteenth Century English Canada* (Toronto: University of Toronto Press, 1989).
Wilson, Isaiah, *A History and Geography of the County of Digby* (Halifax, NS: Holloway Bros. Printers, 1900).
Wright, Donald, *The Professionalization of History in English Canada* (Toronto: University of Toronto Press, 2005).

8 The Afterlife of Settler-Colonial Occupation

Archaeological Excavation as Militarization in the United States-Mexico Borderlands

Claire Urbanski

In 1866, while on duty at Camp Lincoln (later named Fort Verde) in what is now called the state of Arizona, United States army surgeon Edward Palmer (1831–1911) wrote in a diary entry he had titled "Burial of an Apache child I wanted as a specimen" that

> One of the little children was wounded and two days afterwards it died in camp. The females of the camp laid it out after their custom and covered it with wild flowers and carried it to a grave, chanting a Catholic hymn and at the grave initiated a regular Catholic burial. They hid it so completely that its body could not be found as I had a wish to have it for a specimen. These women had the forethought to hide it, and no persuasion could induce them to tell the secret. So, I did not get the specimen.[1]

Edward Palmer was seeking the body of the Apache child to dig up, study, and send to the Smithsonian Institute. In his journal entry, Palmer reveals that he could not find the body, which informs us that he had dug in several places in order to unearth the child's grave. He then tried to convince the Apache women at the camp to tell him where they had buried the child. These women had to be diligent in burying the child clandestinely so that Palmer could not steal the body; their forethought to hide the grave suggests that this was not the first time the women had dealt with this situation. Palmer's description of the interaction comprises one day's entry in a journal that reads like a field research log, the pages scattered with sketches of plants and geologic rock formations amidst everyday observations of life at the Arizona military camp. For Palmer, this child was another scientific specimen to study, not a life worth grieving.

In addition to providing medical care to soldiers, Palmer considered himself an amateur archaeologist; he frequently dug up the grave sites of Native-American peoples and collected their remains to send to research institutions for the purpose of scientific study.[2] During the mid-nineteenth century, Palmer worked as an army surgeon in a number of military camps across the territory comprising what is now the state of Arizona. These new territorial boundaries (acquired through the Treaty of Guadalupe Hidalgo in 1848 and then expanded by the Gadsden Purchase of 1853) were authoritatively claimed by the United States through the establishment of military encampments, especially along the newly re-defined borderlands shared with Mexico. These military forts marked the formative days of modern United States-Mexico border militarization. A quotidian occurrence in these military camps was the excavation of Native-American burial sites and the theft of Native-American dead by medical officers. As army surgeon Emile Cyrus Houle related to a friend, he had developed "an accidental interest in archaeology" while stationed in Arizona, stating that "I vaingloriously confess to being a grave-robber."[3]

While the Native American Graves and Repatriation Act (NAGPRA) of 1990 established legal measures to protect Native-American burial sites, these desecrations and excavations continue today, particularly during projects of construction and development.[4] In May of 2007, during the erection of a border security fence on Tohono O'odham Nation lands, workers dug up and removed the bodies of buried Tohono O'odham ancestors in order to complete the project.[5] The Tohono O'odham homelands were divided in half by the border, as established through the Gadsden Purchase of 1853. The Tohono O'odham, on both sides of the border, have since experienced extensive encroachment onto their homelands, severe mobility restrictions, and ongoing surveillance. Over the last twenty years, this situation has especially escalated due to the policies and tactics of the Department of Homeland Security (DHS). Due to immigration policies in the late twentieth century, undocumented migration traffic was largely funneled into the southern Arizona Tucson Sector, which stretches across the southern Arizona state boundary and contains the northern half of the Tohono O'odham homelands.[6] More undocumented migrants have died crossing through the Tucson Sector than any other segment of the border, while thousands more remain missing. Between 2002 and 2017, approximately 6,548 people have died crossing the entirety of the border, with 3,175 of these deaths occurring along the Arizona-Sonora border of the Tucson Sector.[7] The excavation of Tohono O'odham burial sites in service of the enforcement of border security raises questions about how the excavation and desecration of these sites may correlate with the militarized tactics of the Border Patrol.

This chapter examines how the excavation and desecration of Native-American burial sites in the nineteenth century have influenced the formation of militarized borderlands with a narrow focus on the southern Arizona region. Tracing the settler-colonial institutional practices of stealing and containing Native-American dead reveals how theft fundamentally enabled and sustained the country's military and policing power.[8] Settler archaeologists, army medical officers, and researchers laid the foundations for contemporary border militarization through surveillance and containment strategies over Indigenous dead.[9] While settler theft of this nature has been a widespread practice across North America, focusing on the southern Arizona borderlands will reveal how this practice correlates with the development of policing infrastructure and state disciplinary techniques in more recent decades. This framing will expose how state violence against the dead is critical to the maintenance of United States authority in the borderlands region. An examination of the politics of undocumented migration and border security will also show how the excavation of these burial places has facilitated the spatial transformation and militarization of the desert landscape into a deathly space utilized by the Border Patrol against undocumented border crossers.[10] By reading a genealogical history of the border through violence against the dead, we will be able to consider how the dead influence and disrupt the nation's power as participants within the complex shaping of the borderlands.

As the United States continentally expanded its westward claims during the nineteenth century, the southwestern borderlands had to be ideologically and authoritatively transformed into United States territory. At the end of the Civil War (1861–1865), most of the western territories acquired through the Treaty of Guadalupe Hidalgo had not yet achieved statehood due to the strength of Indigenous resistance to settler occupation.[11] Following the war's conclusion, the country focused its sights on the war "to win the West" by heightening military efforts to appropriate Indigenous lands and to suppress and eliminate Indigenous resistance to the occupation of their lands.[12] The establishment of army forts throughout these western territories supported the goal of opening up land to Anglophone settlement, and transitioning the territories into statehood, all of which was facilitated by the Homestead Act of 1866 and the Dawes Act of 1887. The Homestead Act allotted settlers 300 million acres of Indigenous lands west of the Mississippi. The Dawes Act, also known as the General Allotment Act, dissolved Indigenous communal land holdings by allotting 160 acres to each native family and selling off the leftover land. Indigenous communal lands decreased from 138 million acres in 1887 to 48 million acres by 1934.[13] Many native peoples then unintentionally lost their allotted acres of land without realizing that they had done so, as the concept of private property (along with the culture of titles and deeds to authorize individual ownership of land) was unfamiliar among Indigenous nations.

A significant tactic used by the country's military to clear the land of Indigenous claims was the mass excavation and containment of Indigenous dead during the nineteenth and early twentieth centuries. Army doctors stationed in western military forts were encouraged by authorities in Washington to excavate as a way to pass the time: "Superiors in Washington worried that doctors grew bored during peaceful and healthy months, when no soldiers came by complaining about diarrhea or conjunctivitis, when there were no bullet wounds or snake bites."[14] As a solution, the surgeon general recommended some possible hobbies, including the study and measurement of Native-American skulls.[15] Following this advice, many medical officers used their leisure hours to collect native skulls and skeletons.[16]

Initially started as a Civil War project, the Army Medical Museum (AMM) was established to amass a catalog of different kinds of human physical injuries and diseases. At the end of the war, the AMM shifted its focus and began collecting specimens of the so-called natural world, within which the AMM included Indigenous peoples. Collecting and ordering these biological specimens worked to establish authoritatively western lands as possessions of the United States by mapping and cataloging these territories through the language of scientific expertise.[17] In 1867, army surgeon general Joseph Barnes instructed medical officers to send various flora and fauna, including Native-American crania (as scientists categorically considered these be the same), to assist the AMM in growing its collections.[18] In 1868, Barnes issued a memorandum to both medical officers and army surgeons in which he requested that they collect and send in these skulls and skeletons.[19] The memorandum stated that these bodies were needed to promote "the progress of anthropological science by obtaining measurements of a large number of skulls of the aboriginal races of North America."[20] The AMM collected an estimated 4,500 Native-American skulls, which were later transferred to the Smithsonian Institute. The Smithsonian Institute held around 34,000 skeletal remains, the majority of which were Native American.[21] By the time that NAGPRA legislation was passed in 1990, scholars estimate that between 300,000 to 2.5 million Native-American bodies were held in museum, federal, and private collections around the world.[22]

In addition to these excavation activities, a common practice of settler warfare was to disinter the heads of the Indigenous people that they had killed during battles, massacres, and executions, to be sent along to the AMM and other researchers.[23] While stationed in southwestern Arizona in 1875, army surgeon William Henry Corbusier described a graphic military massacre of an Apache community, after which he removed the heads from fourteen of the dead and sent them to the AMM, as he considered the skulls to be exemplary specimens.[24] The actions of Corbusier firmly situate the pursuit of skull-collecting as a tactic of genocidal military warfare, while also demonstrating carceral modes of occupation enacted upon Indigenous dead. These activities in the pursuit of scientific research situate the historical function of American museums as settler-colonial institutions of militarization, while also regularizing the institutional containment of Indigenous bodies. Because ongoing Indigenous dispossession is necessary to sustain the settler occupation of territories, the ideological and institutional production of settler-colonial power is anchored to carceral formations that work to displace and contain Indigenous presence.

Building on the work of Angela Davis and Michel Foucault, carcerality relates to the logics of dispersed power that structure and maintain the reproductivity of state disciplinary techniques.[25] This framework will allow us to interpret settler-colonial projects of grave theft as a carceral technique that contains Indigenous peoples across space and time. As defined by Patrick Wolfe, settler colonialism is a project of genocidal invasion and distinct from colonialism in that settlers come to stay.[26] This concept differs from models of colonization in which colonial authority is enforced over Indigenous populations with the intent to exploit labor and resources, yet the goal is not to eliminate Indigenous peoples from the land for the purpose of colonial settlement. The term highlights the desire to claim and belong to Indigenous homelands in a way that naturalizes, necessitates, and benefits from ongoing Indigenous dispossession.[27] Settler colonialism has required the genocidal elimination and ongoing dispossession of Indigenous populations in order to maintain its claims to land and power. These narratives of Indigenous disappearance and demise are necessary to sustain ideological legitimacy to settler domination over land and life.

During the seventeenth and eighteenth centuries, British, French, and Spanish colonial authorities paid bounties for the heads, scalps, and ears of Indigenous peoples.[28] As historian Roxanne Dunbar-Ortiz observes, these "ghoulish trophies" were removed from Indigenous peoples and displayed prominently in colonial towns and governor's palaces.[29] While body parts were routinely displayed during the seventeenth and eighteenth centuries, the intent and context for the collection and display of Indigenous bodies in the nineteenth and twentieth centuries had changed to support the production of western scientific knowledge and to promote Indigenous inferiority as a biological fact. Amy Lonetree explains that during the height of museum collecting throughout the mid-nineteenth to early twentieth centuries, "Native people were believed to be 'vanishing,' and anthropologists at the turn of the twentieth century thought they were in a race against time. They saw themselves as engaged in 'salvage anthropology' to collect the so-called last vestiges of a dying race."[30] The height of museum collecting coincided with a period of tremendous dispossession, loss, forced relocation, genocidal policies, and extreme suffering of native peoples. As Lonetree notes, "this is precisely when most of the collecting took place."[31] By collecting and displaying these remains along with funerary objects and cultural items, museums informed public understandings of Indigenous peoples and cultures. Museums used the bones of Native-American dead as "evidence of Indian demise" while proclaiming settler society to have brought civilization and modernity, thus claiming both rightful and inevitable inheritance over Indigenous lands.[32] The divine right of Manifest Destiny had grown to become a secular scientific right of racial superiority, a biological fact, and the evolutionary inevitability of modern man.

Jean O'Brien's concept of firsting describes how settlers erase Indigenous existence by narrating it into a vanished past. Settlers first themselves onto Indigenous lands by proclaiming themselves the harbingers of civilization and order to an uncultivated wilderness.[33] As O'Brien argues, modernity is produced through "the purification of the landscape of [the] Indians" while subsuming Native-American existence as an inherited part of settler history; "doing so enabled [settlers] to establish unambiguously their own modernity. Non-Indians narrated their own present against what they constructed as the backdrop of a past symbolized by Indian peoples and their cultures."[34] Museum displays, imbued with the power of scientific rationality and empirical objectivity, inscribe settler narratives onto the bones of the dead, confining them to a vanished past that can only be studied and known through expert observations. Displacing Indigenous peoples from the present also allows for what O'Brien calls lasting, which she defines as "a rhetorical strategy that asserts as a fact the claim that Indians can never be modern;" thus, settlers last themselves onto land through ensuring that native claims could never be legitimate.[35] Living Indigenous peoples are depicted as either being "doomed to extinction" or as being assimilated and thus no longer truly native.[36] As Joanne Barker has defined through her discussions of authenticity politics, settler society imagines nativeness to be a material quality, traceable through blood quantum or DNA, and as being tied to fixed, static, unchanging locations in space and time.[37] Thus, settler society considers ostensibly authentic native peoples to be extinct or in a state of disappearance.[38] Federal Indian Policy then legally controls the boundaries used to federally recognize Indigenous nations by defining what constitutes authentic native identity. The country maintains its possession and control over land and resources by ensuring that proof of authentic nativeness is increasingly difficult to attain, enabling it to deny land and resource rights to unrecognized nations.[39]

The authority of western scientific expertise to contain and displace native peoples in both life and death crosses time and space. This positioning is central to the function of broader networks of carceral power, as the displacement of Indigenous peoples is necessary to allow for the very foundations from which the settler country's power can be exerted. By physically removing native dead from land, their connections to place may be erased and displaced, demonstrating a mode of settler surveillance. As a result, settler carceral power extends into death, or rather, the afterlife in a general spiritual and material sense of the term, converting the dead into lively beings who actively shape the world we inhabit. By foregrounding the significance and impact of state violence against the dead, we can understand how state power is authorized through the violation of, and control over, the dead, revealing how the settler-colonial world is ordered and arranged through these processes.

The rapid increase in the demand for Native-American skeletal remains during the nineteenth and early twentieth centuries was due also to the popularity of craniometry in formulating theories of race, along with the growth of physical anthropology and American archaeology.[40] Samuel Morton has been credited with establishing the discipline of American physical anthropology, which he developed through his racializing studies of skull size and cranial capacity.[41] In order to conduct these studies, Morton paid soldiers, government agents, and laborers to excavate native and African-American grave sites to collect human skulls and skeletons for his research.[42] This project coincided with the long national process of reburying the hundreds of thousands of soldiers who died in the Civil War.[43] The disturbance of Indigenous dead must be understood as a tactic of warfare, as these acts of violence entail a severing of the spiritual connection between the dead, their descendants, and the land, constituting a genocide that eliminates the landscape of Indigenous ancestral presence, place knowledge, and place relationship. By claiming Indigenous dead and their sacred burial sites as scientific objects belonging to American researchers, the legitimacy of the country's power is affirmed as the presence of Indigenous peoples is ideologically erased.

Through the practice of craniometry, experimentation upon native skulls supported the development of western theories of racial science. Through experimentations such as those conducted by Morton, western researchers demarcated and racialized the boundaries of the so-called modern human as an object of knowledge. Ideas of an evolved, universal and modern humanity were equated with the logics of private property, capitalist labor systems, and the taming of nature into ordered plots of agricultural production, resource extraction, and development. Foucault argues that in order to create the human or the body as an object of knowledge, the body must then be subjugated to carceral techniques of power. Foucault theorizes that the normalization of exploitative labor required humanity to concede their bodies as an exploitable resource through the mechanism of disciplinary power.[44] The necessity of rendering the human body into a raw material to be exploited for capital accumulation is central to all systems of colonial power, especially in the United States. Foucault traces the formation of the body into something capable of being controlled and regulated through the ideological emergence of sexual deviance and sin in seventeenth-century Christian Europe.[45] Once sexual desire became a sin that could control the body, the material body as an object of knowledge could become separate from the soul and, like matters unrelated to the faith, be regulated by the state. This authoritative management and control over the body allows for the state regulation of sexual reproduction, population, and life itself, and is a phenomenon that Foucault calls biopower or biopolitics.[46] This phenomenon marks Europe's shift into the modern era, in that biological life begins to be included in the mechanisms and calculations of state power. The growth of capitalism would not have been possible without the disciplinary techniques exercised by the state and thus ensured a supply of docile bodies that capitalism demanded.[47] In this way, Foucault argues that the modern state's sovereign power is exerted through the state's authority to grant "the right to the social body to ensure, maintain, or develop its life."[48]

Silvia Federici theorizes that Europe's obsession with the body as a mutual source of evil and passion is what drove the seventeenth-century development of anatomy as a scientific discipline.[49] Federici observes that the invention of the anatomy theater (where corpses were dissected to teach anatomy) transformed the body into a raw material; by divorcing the soul from the body, the secularized and controllable medical body could emerge: "once [the body's] devices were deconstructed and it was itself reduced to a tool, the body could be opened to an infinite manipulation of its powers and possibilities."[50] The desire, then, to dissect and dismember the anatomical body echoes the desire to control and conquer sin in ways that reveal that the knowledge of the soul, or more so, a preoccupation with the afterlife and its fate, is embedded within the creation of the secular medical body. In the United States, the human sciences were greatly formed through the dissection of and experimentation on the bodies of Native Americans and African Americans. Those who collected their corpses, including Morton and Aleš Hrdlicka, proclaimed to be above superstitious attitudes about respecting the dead. Yet, as Ann Fabian concludes, "they did not apply those new attitudes to the corpses of families and friends. The living Morton had been a thinking subject, and he did not leave behind a body as an object to be collected or displayed."[51]

James Riding In describes the post-Enlightenment formation of the western medical body as greatly impacting the mass detainment and excavation of native dead, which he refers to as "a spiritual holocaust."[52] Riding In exemplifies a tension between notions of the dead as sacred, as opposed to western secular notions of the dead as scientific objects of study, through an analysis of the British Murder Act of 1752. This act exempted executed criminals from the sacred protection of their bodies in death, which "impaired if not eliminated, the hapless criminals' ascension to heaven. In this sense, medical dissection and autopsy served as a form of spiritual punishment for the wicked and evil."[53] Riding In traces how western post-Enlightenment medical knowledge was informed by the understanding that dissection and dismemberment were forms of spiritual punishment, and thus only deviants, criminals, or less-than-humans could be dissected because of the infinite punishment and spiritual incarceration that would come in the afterlife. Federici describes dissection in these contexts as a "second and greater death," one that ensured that "the condemned spent their last days making sure that their body should not be abandoned into the hands of surgeons."[54] In the United States, Native and African-American dead were stolen for scientific purposes intended to improve settler vitality, lives, and thus futures. These experiments also protected settler afterlives, as the erasure of Native Americans and African Americans as sacred beings, and the denial of their sacred protection in death, contrasted with settler society's protection of its own sacred death. Denying rest and burial for these dead makes their bodies legible as ungrieveable scientific property, laboring in service of the sustainment of settler futures and afterlives.

Building upon Foucault's biopolitics, Achille Mbembe's theory of necropolitics contends that the sovereign power of the modern state involves more than the state's right to decide who may live and who must die by emphasizing the role of state terror within spaces of colonial occupation.[55] Under colonial occupation, warfare is purposeless, unending, and not subject to any rules.[56] Jason De León builds on Mbembe's necropolitics to consider how the power of the modern state is accessed through the violent treatment of the dead in his study of how the United States relies upon the Sonoran Desert to kill and then erase the remains of undocumented border crossers. De León terms the violent treatment of the dead by the state as "necroviolence [which] is specifically about corporeal mistreatment and its generative capacity for violence."[57] This practice is used elsewhere by the country to assert its right to and power, especially over native homelands. As Jodi Byrd theorizes, the state "enacts sovereignty as ontological possession, delineating what is and is not possessed."[58] By delineating Indigenous dead as possessions belonging to the United States, the country affirms and validates its own sovereign power over the dead. Sharon Holland further problematizes this treatment of non-settler dead and looks to Benedict Anderson's discussion of the tomb of the Unknown Soldier as cohering a sense of national identity.[59] In her view, the nation-state speaks for the dead at this memorial site, creating a narrative of service and sacrifice for the sake of the nation, for "it is not the *actual* dead but an *idea* of them that holds the nation together."[60] Holland determines that the nation exists because of its voicing of the dead, that "the nation exists precisely because the dead *do not speak*."[61] The nation speaks as an entity through its ability to use the dead in service to its creation: "Here the dead are the most intimate 'enemy' of the changing and growing nation. Should they rise and speak for themselves, the state would lose all right to their borrowed and/or stolen language."[62] For the United States, maintaining cohesion as a nation requires ongoing control of victim narratives, whose presence threatens the state's legitimacy. Holland importantly concludes that it is anonymity that divests death of its power: "if we cannot recall a face that looks like our own, then we cannot fear our own death in quite the same way."[63] In this way, through settler imaginaries that position native and black deaths as ungrieveable, their deaths remain anonymous to the settler nation. Retaining control over the settler populace then requires maintaining anonymity over those dead whose presence demands a reckoning with the ongoing genocidal violence upon which the United States is built. Byrd demonstrates how the notion of the ungrieveable Indian is necessary to both cohere the United States as a nation and to spread its settler empire.[64] Byrd demonstrates that settler imaginaries of Indianness function as a way for the country's colonialism and imperialism to travel, facilitating the global ascendency of its empire abroad.[65] Byrd argues that the idea of the Indian is "left nowhere and everywhere within the ontological premises through which US empire orients, imagines, and critiques itself;" the settler imaginary of the Indian forms the ontological grounds from which the country's imperialism can propel and reproduce itself.[66]

Along its southern border, the United States has militarized the desert over the last twenty-five years into a terrain of occupation, where it relies upon the desert both to kill and then erase the dead.[67] In 1994, the Immigration and Naturalization Service (INS) department launched a national protocol of "Prevention Through Deterrence" (PTD), which effectively redirected most undocumented migration traffic into the harsh and sparsely populated desert terrain of southern Arizona. Within ten years, migrant deaths due to border crossing increased more than 100 percent, with three quarters of these deaths occurring in the Sonoran Desert of the Tucson Sector. As Marta Caminero-Santangelo observes, "by knowingly 'forcing' people to cross risky terrain, the INS is contributing to the numerous deaths that have resulted. The border zone is now a 'landscape of death.'"[68]

Many border crossers are Indigenous peoples from southern Mexico and Central America who have been displaced due to the neoliberal economic policies of the United States and CIA-backed military interventions in their homelands.[69] The remains of hundreds of people who have perished crossing this region are found each year while thousands more remain missing. Volunteer search-and-rescue teams look for their bodies, yet many remain unfound. As revealed by De León's study of how bodies decompose in the Sonoran Desert, a human body can completely decompose and be erased—the bones picked clean and scattered into hundreds of tiny pieces by wildlife—in a matter of days.[70] He asserts that because many border crossers are Roman Catholic, the destruction and disappearance of their corpses violates religious practices in that the absence of the body prevents carrying out their burial customs: "a destroyed or incomplete corpse is seen as a threat to the afterlife in that it may stop people from rising from the dead to be judged at the end of time."[71] This situation results in erasing the presence of Latinx and Indigenous peoples in both life and death; their lives are considered expendable by the state, who through these carceral practices denies relatives and the community a sacred place of burial that imbues place with meaning and connection. Instead, loss and grief remain in indefinite suspension.

In 1994, in Arizona's Buenos Aires National Wildlife Refuge located within the Sonoran Desert, a birdwatcher stumbled upon five exposed skeletons eroding from the wall of a wash near the Arivaca Creek, what would become one of the most heavily trafficked areas for border crossers following the passage of PTD earlier that year. A Fish and Wildlife

Service archaeologist determined that the bodies should be excavated as they were in danger of being damaged by their location next to the wash.[72] The bodies were removed and subjected to thorough forensic study and examination by archaeologists.[73] The intention of these excavations was seemingly to protect the skeletons from destruction, yet the studies conducted on the dead make clear that they were being protected as scientific objects from which valuable information could be derived. In a map drawn by archaeologists to detail the location of the burial sites and positions of the dead (Figure 8.1), Arizona archaeologists detailed the precise location and position of the dead, along with the surrounding layers of rock sediment extending deep into the ground.[74] The map exemplifies what Donna Haraway calls "the conquering gaze from nowhere," wherein the gaze of its maker is seemingly detached and objective, imbued with the authority to "represent while escaping representation."[75] Building upon Simone Browne's work on surveillance, mapping the layers of earthen underground allows for the western gaze to surveil everything while remaining unseen.[76] The map makes the bodies seem as though they belong to, and are part of, the natural world. By mapping the dead and their burial places, these archaeologists partake in a colonial mode of surveillance as the map reifies the boundaries of colonial occupation; it becomes the venue where native dead and their burial places are made into sites of scientific study that may be excavated, exposed, and made knowable.

In 1906, the United States passed the Antiquities Act, which was intended to protect Native-American burial sites and material culture from common looters while claiming these sites as archaeological possessions. The act's passage ushered in the modern era of North American archaeological excavation, which was particularly prominent in the southwestern borderlands.[77] The act defined Indigenous human remains as archaeological resources and effectively "converted these dead persons into 'federal property.'"[78] James Riding In argues that the act allowed federal surveillance and control over the excavation of native dead as it granted "scientific authority" to "legitimate" grave robbers (that is, professional archaeologists).[79] As Clayton Dumont notes, "The legislation made no distinction between graves that were thousands of years old and the internment of one's mother at a tribal cemetery a week or even day prior."[80]

Historic and ongoing settler projects of burial desecration and excavation inscribe western colonial ontologies of life, death, body, and land onto place, structuring material and immaterial boundaries, while disrupting Indigenous ontologies that threaten the legitimacy of colonial claims. As Gloria Anzaldúa and Linda Tuhiwai Smith have concluded, colonial western orderings of the world necessitate a definitive separation and categorization of life from death, land from body, and body from spirit.[81] As Tuhiwai Smith has demonstrated, western scientific frameworks are built

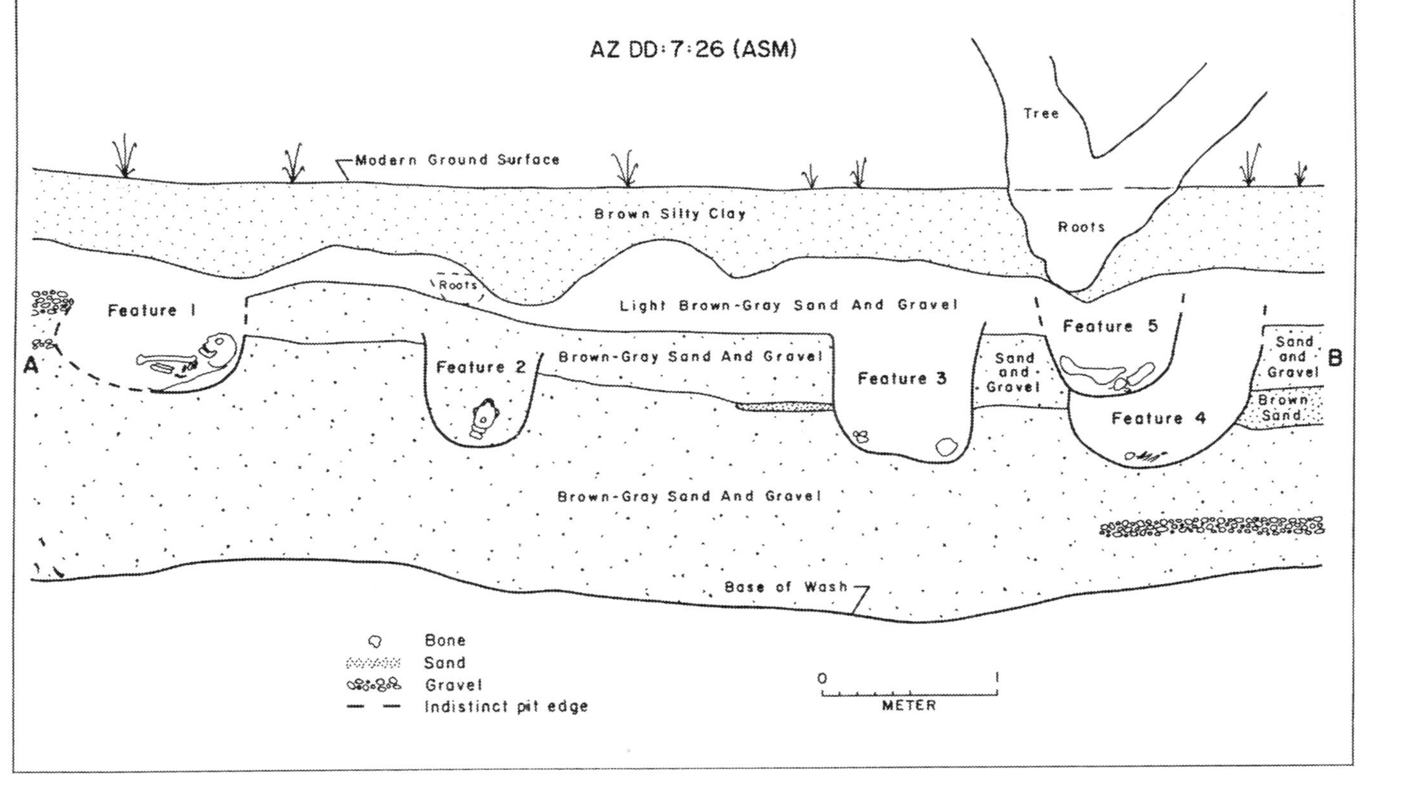

Figure 8.1 Archaeologist's map of the Arivaca Creek 1994 excavation site. The original caption reads: "A profile of the south wall of a wash running into Arivaca Creek. The cemetery, AZ DD:7:26 (ASM), has been cut by the wash, exposing portions of four burials. A fifth burial (Burial 5) was encountered during excavations." J. Homer Thiel, Penny Dufoe-Minturn, and Lorrie Lincoln-Babb, "Archaeological Excavations at the Arivaca Wash Cemetery, AZ DD:7:26 (ASM), Buenos Aires National Wildlife Refuge," *Center for Desert Archaeology*, Technical Report 94-17 (April 1995), pp. 1–38: 4.

Source: Courtesy Archaeology Southwest.

upon a secular understanding of a world in which Indigenous epistemologies are categorized as mythical, traditional, irrational, and as standing in the way of, or outside of, the legitimate pursuit of scientific rationality. Tuhiwai Smith critiques western scientific paradigms of empiricism and positivism by addressing the ways that western science reduces the understanding and interpretation of the world to issues of measurement.[82] Western spatial thinking arranges space so that it consists of lines and grids; this spatial ordering of the world undergirds the epistemological foundations of western scientific disciplines. Tuhiwai Smith posits that this spatial ordering and mapping have been integral to the colonization of Indigenous space:[83]

> For the indigenous world, Western conceptions of space, of arrangements and display, of the relationship between people and the landscape, of culture as an object of study, have meant that not only has the indigenous world been represented in particular ways back to the West, but the indigenous world view, the land and the people, have been radically transformed in the spatial image of the West. In other words, indigenous space has been colonized.[84]

In this way, land could be conceived of as something to be tamed, controlled, and rendered into a measurable, quantifiable object to be extracted for resources.[85] Mbembe also theorizes how colonial occupation spatially orders and demarcates the landscape into an unending battlefield, such that "The underground as well as the airspace are transformed into conflict zones. There is no continuity between the ground and the sky. Even the boundaries in airspace are divided between lower and upper layers. Everywhere, the symbolics of the top (who is on top) is reiterated."[86] This spatial ordering is militarization: the conditions that enable the separation of body from earth, and land from sky, are borne from the colonial imagination whose version of reality mediates the subjective positioning of racialized others.[87] In the Arizona borderlands, archaeological excavation becomes colonial surveillance by making known the space of the underground, the location of the dead, and thus enabling surveillance over the afterlife of the dead. Archaeological excavation maps colonial occupation over space by extending surveillance into the ground itself, and over the dead by removing and rooting out native presence. By digging into the ground and physically disconnecting Indigenous dead from place, the boundaries of land, body, life, and afterlife are demarcated and re-arranged, structuring a western spatial order of place. Through the disciplining and ordering of land, body, life, and death, the United States outlines and transforms space into terrains of colonial occupation, establishing the grounds from which military technologies and warfare may be enacted.

In 2016, two Tucson-based organizations released a thorough report on the Border Patrol's widespread and intentional use of the "extreme heat and bitter cold, scarce and polluted water sources, treacherous topography, and near-total isolation from possible rescue" as everyday weapons of border policing.[88] The report documents that the Border Patrol's routine and widespread destruction of thousands of gallons of water left on desert trails for border crossers, along with other sabotage and interference with humanitarian aid efforts, is an integral part of the PTD strategy to increase migrants' suffering and the likelihood of death.[89] Border Patrol flies helicopters low to the ground to terrorize border crossers through a technique called dusting. Dusting uses rotor wash from helicopter blades to create strong wind clouds of dust, gravel, and debris to cause "spatial disorientation, separation from one's guide and companions, loss of supplies and belongings, and exposure to the hazards of hostile terrain. In the remote wilderness, this directly leads to death and disappearance."[90] As De León notes, the United States depends upon the desert landscape to erase the bodies of the dead, along with the lives that they lived.[91] In this way, the country both reasserts power over its border territories while simultaneously evading culpability for these deaths as the desert terrain is deemed responsible for them.[92]

The DHS justifies its continued harassment and surveillance of Tohono O'odham peoples along the border as necessary to secure the nation as a whole from terrorism and trafficking.[93] Tribal elder and social justice activist Ofelia Rivas describes living on her nation's reservation as existing in a police state: "We are always under scrutiny, and always suspect in our own land as criminals, either drug traffickers or human traffickers."[94] Since the attacks on the World Trade Center and the Pentagon on 11 September 2001, the United States has experienced increased surveillance and policing practices especially in regard to immigration and border security, which include Tohono O'odham lands: "Helicopters clatter by in the night, Border Patrol vehicles race through on a patchwork of new roads that scar the land, portable spy cameras are posted on a nearby mountain, and drones periodically survey the landscape from the sky."[95] The Arizona Border Control Initiative of 2004 increased the numbers of Border Patrol officers and helicopters deployed above the reservation, including unmanned aerial spy-planes, electronic ground sensors, and remote-controlled video cameras.[96] Throughout the late twentieth and early twenty-first centuries, Tohono O'odham nation members have faced increasingly restricted mobility across their homelands, and especially across the United States-Mexico border. DHS expects them to carry identification at all times, subjects them to frequent stops and searches, seizes their vehicles, and threatens them with prosecution, incarceration, and even deportation.[97] Many members have reported being held at gunpoint by Border Patrol officers during random stops and searches. Tohono O'odham on either side of the border are routinely unable to access necessary services such as medical care, nor are they able to visit family on either side of the border due to fear of being unable to return home. The restriction of travel to attend ceremonies has impacted the cohesion of the Tohono O'odham nation across the border. As Jeffrey Schulze assesses, "these ceremonial migratory patterns represented the last of the tribe's transnational networks, or the last link between the two halves of the divided Tohono O'odham nation."[98]

The American Civil Liberties Union has stated that the Tohono O'odham nation is ground zero for Border Patrol abuses against United States citizens. Yet, it is precisely the imposition and requirement of United States or Mexican citizenship that lies at the root of this abuse. As Eric V. Meeks and Jeffrey Schulze have observed, it was the establishment and enforcement of the border that required Indigenous nations such as the Tohono O'odham, the Akimel O'odham, the Yaqui, and the Kickapoo, to define themselves as distinct national identities to protect themselves from further displacement and the dispossession of lands and resources by settlers on both sides of the border.[99] By being non-consensually subject to either and both countries' laws, groups such as the Yaqui found that they had to either face erasure as Indigenous peoples, evade state authority and lose all access to land and resources, or try to prove the legitimacy of their Indigenous background according to federal definitions.

In order to be granted sovereign status in the United States, the Tohono O'odham and the Yaqui had to shift their governance practices from decentralized modes of governance to a centralized, federally sanctioned form of governance.[100] For this reason, while the Tohono O'odham's national government approved the construction of fifteen new surveillance towers in 2017, and has historically worked with the DHS, these actions do not reflect the consent of Tohono O'odham people as a whole.[101] Their resistance to border militarization has involved cutting down and removing border fences, illegally leaving water and food for border crossers, participating in search and rescue teams, and defending the rights of border crossers. On 21 May 2010, Indigenous Arizona activists occupied the Border Patrol headquarters at Davis-Monthan Airforce Base in Tucson to protest border militarization and anti-immigrant policy.[102] The activists made a list of demands, including an end to border militarization and the respect of Indigenous peoples' right to migrate upon their traditional lands.[103] Their position rejects the spatial ordering and militarization of all colonial nations, and the surveilling and disciplining categorizations of race, nationality, and citizenship that the border imposes upon them.

The militarization of Tohono O'odham borderlands began with the desecration of their burial sites and continues today as a part of border enforcement.[104] On 1 April 2008, DHS secretary Michael Chertoff announced that the DHS would no longer be subject to NAGPRA law, meaning that the DHS was legally exempt from respecting Tohono O'odham ancestors and burial sites.[105] Workers dug up the human remains of their ancestors during the construction of a border security fence along the nation's Gu-Vo District. According to that nation's legislative council, the United States violated no laws and followed protocol.[106] However, Tohono O'odham women representing five families claimed the remains of the dead as their own and requested their immediate return. After widespread support, the ancestors were returned to their relatives.[107] The advocacy of these matriarchs, which went against agreements established between the DHS and the Tohono O'odham tribal government, reflects the ability of both the dead and living to resist and reject United States colonial occupation and authority.

In this chapter, I have begun to examine how colonial occupation extends carceral formations over the dead, enacting a spiritual violence that seethes and perpetuates through all forms of border surveillance technology. Archaeological excavation of native burial sites functions to subsume space into United States colonial possession; by severing and extracting native ancestral presence, the country firsts itself onto the land by projecting narratives of scientific authority onto the soil and the bones of the dead. Through carceral techniques such as excavation, experimentation, and surveillance, the United States restructures native lands and afterlife into a secularized spatial order of occupation, which is used to secure the border zone and the country as a whole. In turn, the dead and their living relatives demand a reckoning as they disrupt, resist, and reshape temporal cycles and spatial formations of settler-colonial violence. Border space can be remapped and reconceptualized through the destruction of border fences, the efforts to return, rebury, and reunite the dead with their relatives, and the construction of memorials, altars, and shrines along migrant paths. The sacred center of the Tohono O'odham universe is the Baboquivari Peak, which has also become an important point of reference for undocumented migrants crossing into central Arizona.[108] Indigenous peoples living and passing through the borderlands affirm other ontologies of being through the acknowledgment and honoring of sacred places, along with the proliferation of resistant knowledges that reshape place through acts of caring, mutual survivance, subterfuge, and decolonial anti-border activism.[109] By reading the formation of the United States-Mexico militarized borderlands through necroviolence, we can question how early-modern and modern settler-coloniality authorizes its power through the violence it extends over the dead and spiritual afterlife.

Notes

1. Edward Palmer Manuscripts 1831–1911, "Notes and Description of Life and Events at Old Camp Lincoln Arizona and at New Camp Lincoln on the Rio Vird in 1865 and 1866," February 1866, AZ 197, box 1, fol. 2, p. 10.
2. Edward Palmer Manuscripts 1866–1885, box 1, fols. 1–3.
3. Houle also describes "another enthusiastic 'Grave Robber'" named Matthews, the Wells Fargo Manager at Nogales. Emile Cyrus Houle Collection, box 10, fol. 2, pp. 1–4.

4. Examples of this practice include the deliberate and tactical bulldozing of Standing Rock burial sites during the construction of the Dakota Access Pipeline, and continued construction throughout the San Francisco Bay Area (Muwekma Ohlone homelands) that involves the excavation of Ohlone burial sites.
5. Gaynor, "Indians Complain Graves Dug up for Border Fence."
6. Levy, "There's No O'odham Word for Wall."
7. The actual number is likely much higher; see Ortega, "Border Patrol Failed to Count Hundreds of Migrant Deaths."
8. Following Indigenous feminist theories, I understand settler colonialism as a material system of ongoing dispossession sustained through gendered formations of Indigenous elimination. See Tuck and Yang. "Decolonization Is Not a Metaphor," pp. 1–40; Simpson and Smith, eds., *Theorizing Native Studies*; and Barker, *Critically Sovereign*.
9. Throughout this chapter, the term settler as defined by activist scholar Waziyatawin refers to colonizers who participate in the ongoing displacement of Indigenous peoples in order to live on Indigenous lands while continuing to reap and reproduce the benefits of conquest and settlement. Waziyatawain, "Understanding Colonizer Status," in Unsettling Minnesota Collective, ed., *Unsettling Ourselves*, pp. 152–155.
10. I use the term border crossers as defined by undocumented migrant advocacy organizations, which more broadly encompasses the myriad reasons and contexts that inform why people cross the border. See La Coalición de Derechos Humanos and No More Deaths, "The Disappeared Report." Anthropologist Jason De León theorizes the use of the desert as a weapon against border crossers; see De León, *The Land of Open Graves*.
11. Dunbar-Ortiz, *An Indigenous Peoples' History*, p. 141.
12. Ibid., p. 139.
13. See Ibid., pp. 11 and 157–161; and Lonetree, *Decolonizing Museums*, p. 11.
14. Fabian, *The Skull Collectors*, p. 184.
15. Ibid., p. 255.
16. Taking this advice, assistant surgeon George Kober explains that he decided to devote "some of my leisure hours [. . .] to the exploration of Indian burial grounds, and the collection of crania and skeletons;" see Kober, *Reminiscences of George Martin Kober*, p. 236.
17. Fabian, *The Skull Collectors*, p. 183.
18. Ibid.
19. Ibid. Also see (no author) "Indians Seek Burial of Smithsonian Skeletons."
20. Quoted in Fabian, *The Skull Collectors*, p. 185, from Crane, "Memorandum for the Information of Medical Officers," 1 September 1868, National Archives, RG 112, box 4.
21. (no author) "Indians Seek Burial of Smithsonian Skeletons."
22. Ibid.
23. Riding In, "Six Pawnee Crania," pp. 101–119; and Redman, *Bone Rooms*.
24. "On my way back to Camp Verde I disinterred the heads and sent the skulls to the Army Medical Museum, as they showed the so-called explosive action of a bullet passing through the skull which it broke into many pieces;" see Record of William Henry Corbusier, "Record of William Henry Corbusier, Colonel, U.S. Army Retired," box 2, fol. 4, p. 33.
25. Foucault describes the shift of disciplining power from a sovereign authority, whose power is asserted through the "ceremony of punishment" as an "exercise of terror," to an "equitably distributed social body, that is individualized and normalized" or rather, a complicit self-disciplining public. In describing this shift, Foucault traces the power to punish and the power to

judge. The emergence of judgment depends not on sovereignty but on the distributed effects of public power; the power to punish becomes embedded into the everyday workings of the social body and, in this way, discipline is socially dispersed and self-regulating; see Foucault, *Discipline and Punish*, p. 28; and Davis, *Are Prisons Obsolete?*

26. Wolfe, *Settler Colonialism and the Transformation of Anthropology*, p. 3.
27. For Scott Morgensen, building on Waziyatawin's definition, settler is "a way to refer to colonizers that highlights their desires to be emplaced on Indigenous land;" see Scott Lauria Morgensen, "Unsettling Settler Desire," in Unsettling Minnesota Collective, ed., *Unsettling Ourselves*, p. 3.
28. See Dunbar-Ortiz, *An Indigenous Peoples' History*, pp. 38 and 52–65; and Blackhawk, *Violence Over the Land*.
29. For more on scalping in this context, see Dunbar-Ortiz, *An Indigenous Peoples' History*, p. 146.
30. Lonetree, *Decolonizing Museums*, p. 10.
31. Ibid., p. 11.
32. O'Brien, *Firsting and Lasting*, p. 94.
33. Ibid., p. 6.
34. Ibid., p. xxi. For a thorough examination of how colonial America desires and imagines nativeness and Indianness as the substance of its national identity, see Deloria, *Playing Indian*.
35. O'Brien, *Firsting and Lasting*, p. 107.
36. Trope and Echo-Hawk, "The Native American Graves Protection and Repatriation Act," p. 42.
37. For further discussion of DNA and blood quantum, see TallBear, *Native American DNA*.
38. Barker, *Native Acts*.
39. For further discussion of the politics of federal recognition and refusal, see Simpson, *Mohawk Interruptus*.
40. Lonetree, *Decolonizing Museums*, p. 12.
41. Redman, *Bone Rooms*.
42. Ibid., p. 13. The theft of African-American dead for use in anatomical study and medical school instruction was also helped to develop the human sciences and modern medical technologies. See Washington, *Medical Apartheid*.
43. Fabian, *The Skull Collectors*, p. 5.
44. Foucault, *Discipline and Punish*, p. 28.
45. Foucault, *The History of Sexuality*, vol. 1, p. 20.
46. Ibid., vol. 1, p. 25. Foucault observes that "One of the great innovations in the techniques of power in the eighteenth century [is] the emergence of 'population' as an economic and political problem" (vol. 1, p. 136).
47. Ibid., p. 3.
48. Ibid., p. 136.
49. Federici, *Caliban and the Witch*, p. 139.
50. Ibid., p. 139.
51. Fabian, *The Skull Collectors*, p. 11.
52. James Riding In, "Our Dead Are Never Forgotten: American Indian Struggles for Burial Rights and Protections," in Weeks, ed., *They Made Us Many Promises*, pp. 291–323: 292.
53. Ibid., p. 294.
54. Federici, *Caliban and the Witch*, p. 145.
55. Mbembe, "Necropolitics," pp. 11–40.
56. Ibid., p. 25. Necropower describes the everyday of colonial occupation and enacts an "absolute domination over the inhabitants of the occupied territory [. . .]. The state of siege is itself a military institution [. . .]. Entire

populations are the target of the sovereign [. . .]. Daily life is militarized. Freedom is given to local military commanders to use their discretion as to when and whom to shoot. Movement between the territorial cells requires formal permits [. . .]. Invisible killing is added to outright executions;" see ibid., p. 30.

57. De León, *The Land of Open Graves*, p. 69.
58. Byrd, *The Transit of Empire*, p. 22.
59. This tomb serves as a monument to those who have died serving in that country's military and whose remains have never been identified.
60. Holland, *Raising the Dead*, p. 22.
61. Ibid., p. 28.
62. Ibid.
63. Ibid., p. 28.
64. Jodi Byrd, *The Transit of Empire.*
65. Byrd, *The Transit of Empire.*
66. Ibid., p. xix.
67. De León details how the Border Patrol relies upon the desert to erase the dead in *In the Land of Open Graves.*
68. Caminero-Santangelo, "The Lost Ones," p. 307. Jason De León also has demonstrated that the United States has intentionally pushed migration traffic into a landscape that can be utilized to kill border crossers through PTD, which itself states that "one way for the government to measure the efficacy of PTD is via a migrant body count;" see De León, *The Land of Open Graves*, p. 34.
69. This reality is evidenced by the recent caravans of Central American refugees seeking asylum in the United States at the Texas's southern border. The country's economic and military influence in Central America stretches back to the nineteenth century. Key military interventions include the 1954 CIA-funded overthrow of the democratically-elected government of Guatemalan President Jacobo Árbenz, as his policies threatened their holdings of the United Fruit Company. This action resulted in decades of military dictatorship, civil war, and the genocide of Indigenous Guatemalans. The United States has provided hundreds of millions of dollars in economic and military support to back right-wing militaries in El Salvador, Nicaragua, and Honduras, whose tactics involved violently repressing labor unions and social movements through wars, massacres, electoral fraud, and corruption. Through these military and economic interventions, Central Americans, and especially Indigenous Central Americans, have suffered extreme poverty, violence, and genocide, the conditions of which have resulted in Central Americans seeking asylum in the United States. See Culpepper, "The Debt We Owe Central America;" Levitz "We Owe Central American Migrants;" Bonner, "Time for a US Apology to El Salvador;" and Weiner, "Role of C.I.A."
70. De León, *In the Land of Open Graves.*
71. Ibid., p. 83.
72. Thiel, Minturn, and Lincoln-Babb, "Archaeological Excavations at the Arivaca Wash Cemetery, AZ DD:7:26 (ASM), Buenos Aires National Wildlife Refuge," in Center for Desert Archaeology Technical Report 94–17, pp. 1–38.
73. One body was left in the ground. Ibid.
74. Ibid.
75. Haraway, *Simians, Cyborgs and Women*, p. 188.
76. Browne, *Dark Matters.*
77. In Arizona, archaeologist Nels Christian Nelson has been accredited with the first so-called scientific excavation in the southwestern United States in

1914, ushering in the period of modern southwestern archaeological methods. Edward Twitchell Hall, "Methods of Excavation in the Southwest," in Papers of Edward Twitchell Hall, box 18, part II, fol. 9, p. 5. Mishuana Goeman also describes how the photography of Edward S. Curtis informed an American colonial imaginary of native peoples and the southwestern frontier; see his "Disrupting a Settler-Colonial Grammar of Place: The Visual Memoir of Hulleah Tsinhnahjinnie," in Simpson and Smith, eds., *Theorizing Native Studies*, pp. 235–265.

78. Trope and Echo-Hawk, "The Native American Graves Protection and Repatriation Act," p. 42.
79. Riding In, "Six Pawnee Crania," p. 307.
80. Dumont, "The Politics of Scientific Objections to Repatriation," p. 117.
81. Western culture's definition of that which is rational, civilized, and the most developed can be viewed as the consciousness of duality: "In trying to become 'objective,' Western culture made 'objects' of things and people when it distances itself from them, thereby losing 'touch' with them. This dichotomy is the root of all violence;" see Anzaldúa, *Borderlands/La Frontera*, p. 59.
82. Engaging Stuart Hall's theorization of concepts that make up and define the west, Tuhiwai Smith shows how societies are classified into systems of representation through a standard model of comparison and criteria of evaluation through which societies can be ranked; in this way, Indigenous peoples are coded into a western system of knowledge. See Tuhiwai Smith, *Decolonizing Methodologies*, p. 43.
83. Mishuana Goeman's concept of a settler-colonial grammar of place reveals how settler-colonial carceral practices become embedded within western language and place-naming in ways that contain Indigenous peoples within certain spaces by making bodies "legible or illegible as Indigenous peoples." Goeman uses this term to think about the spatial logics at work in settler colonialism, revealing a project of containment that spatially restructures bodies, while spatially restructuring the settler nation-state. Colonial violence is physically mapped onto both space and native bodies through colonial memory, narrative production, and imagined geographies. Goeman explores how colonial spatial structures constrict native mobilities and pathologizes mobile native bodies through scientific disciplines such as colonial map-making, which worked to eliminate, absorb, contain, and sever Indigenous connections to place. Goeman, "Disrupting a Settler Colonial Grammar of Place: The Visual Memoir of Hulleah Tsinhnahjinnie," in Simpson and Smith, eds., *Theorizing Native Studies*, pp. 235–265: 235.
84. Tuhiwai Smith, *Decolonizing Methodologies*, p. 51.
85. Ibid., p. 53.
86. Mbembe, "Necropolitics," p. 29.
87. Ibid.
88. La Coalición de Derechos Humanos and No More Deaths, "The Disappeared Report."
89. Ibid., part 2, p. 2.
90. Ibid., part 2, p. 3.
91. Ibid.
92. Ibid.
93. Hendricks, "Immigration, Imperialism and Cultural Genocide."
94. Boswell, "Caught in the Crossfire."
95. Ibid.
96. (no author) "Sonoran Desert Storm."
97. Schulze, *Are We Not Foreigners*, p. 200. Also see Boswell, "Caught in the Crossfire."

98. Schulze, *Are We Not Foreigners*, p. 146.
99. Meeks, *Border Citizens*; and Schulze, *Are We Not Foreigners*.
100. Schulze, *Are We Not Foreigners*, p. 193.
101. Innes, "Tohono O'odham Leaders."
102. Norrell, "Native Americans."
103. Ibid.
104. On the Mexico side of the Tohono O'odham nation, the town of Sonoita was constructed by bulldozing O'odham burial sites and building the town in their place. Boswell, "Caught in the Crossfire."
105. Archibold, "Border Fence Work Raises Environmental Concerns."
106. Gaynor, "Indians Complain Graves Dug up for Border Fence."
107. Rivas, "O'odham Remains Returned."
108. Schulze, *Are We Not Foreigners*, p. 55.
109. Some examples of decolonial anti-border activism include the activist groups O'odham Solidarity Across Borders Collective and O'odham Voice Against the Wall, who resist the ongoing colonization of traditional O'odham lands.

Bibliography

Anzaldúa, Gloria, *Borderlands/La Frontera: The New Mestiza* (San Francisco, CA: Aunt Lute Books, 1987).

Archibold, Randal C., "Border Fence Work Raises Environmental Concerns," *The New York Times*, 21 November 2007.

Barker, Joanne, *Native Acts: Law, Recognition, and Cultural Authenticity* (Durham, NC: Duke University Press, 2011).

———, *Critically Sovereign: Indigenous Gender, Sexuality, and Feminist Studies* (Durham, NC: Duke University Press, 2017).

Blackhawk, Ned, *Violence Over the Land: Indians and Empires in the Early American West* (Cambridge, MA: Harvard University Press, 2008).

Bonner, Raymond, "Time for a US Apology to El Salvador," *The Nation*, 15 April 2016.

Boswell, Tom, "Caught in the Crossfire: Border Crisis Threatens Traditional Way of Life for Sovereign Tohono O'odham Nation," *National Catholic Reporter*, 20 December 2010.

Browne, Simone, *Dark Matters: On the Surveillance of Blackness* (Durham, NC: Duke University Press, 2015).

Byrd, Jodi, *The Transit of Empire: Indigenous Critiques of Colonialism* (Minneapolis: University of Minnesota Press, 2011).

Caminero-Santangelo, Marta, "The Lost Ones: Post-Gatekeeper Border Fictions and the Construction of Cultural Trauma," *Latino Studies* 8 (2010), pp. 304–327.

Center for Desert Archaeology Technical Report 94–17, Arizona State Museum Library, Tucson, ACC 96216.

Culpepper, Miles, "The Debt We Owe Central America," *Jacobin Magazine*, 15 October 2018.

Davis, Angela, *Are Prisons Obsolete?* (New York: Seven Stories Press, 2003).

De León, Jason, *The Land of Open Graves: Living and Dying on the Migrant Trail* (Oakland: University of California Press, 2015).

Deloria, Philip, *Playing Indian* (New Haven, CT: Yale University Press, 1998).

Dumont, Clayton, "The Politics of Scientific Objections to Repatriation," *Wicazo Sa Review* 18.1 (2003), pp. 109–128.

Dunbar-Ortiz, Roxanne, *An Indigenous Peoples' History of the United States* (Boston, MA: Beacon Press, 2014).

Edward Palmer Manuscripts, University of Arizona Libraries (UAL), Tucson, University of Arizona Special Collections (SC): 1831–1911, AZ 197; 1866–1885.

Emile Cyrus Houle Collection 1896–2010, UAL, Tucson, SC, MS 478.

Fabian, Ann, *The Skull Collectors: Race, Science, and America's Unburied Dead* (Chicago: University of Chicago Press, 2010).

Federici, Silvia, *Caliban and the Witch: Women, the Body, and Primitive Accumulation* (Brooklyn, NY: Autonomedia, 2004).

Foucault, Michel, *The History of Sexuality*, vol. 1: *An Introduction* (New York: Random House, 1978).

———, *Discipline and Punish: The Birth of the Prison* (New York: Vintage Books, 1995).

Gaynor, Tim, "Indians Complain Graves Dug up for Border Fence," *Reuters*, 24 June 2007.

Haraway, Donna, *Simians, Cyborgs and Women: The Reinvention of Nature* (New York: Routledge, 1991).

Hendricks, Jeff, "Immigration, Imperialism and Cultural Genocide: An Interview with O'odham Activist Ofelia Rivas Concerning the Effects of a Proposed Wall on the US/Mexico Border," *O'odham Solidarity Project*, 2006. www.tiamat-publications.com/docs/imperialism_interview_article.pdf

Holland, Sharon, *Raising the Dead: Readings of Death and (Black) Subjectivity* (Durham, NC: Duke University Press, 2000).

Innes, Stephanie, "Tohono O'odham Leaders: Trump's Wall Won't Rise on Tribal Borderland," *Arizona Daily Star*, 20 February 2017.

Kober, George M., *Reminiscences of George Martin Kober, M.D. LL. D., Emeritus Dean and Professor of Hygiene of the School of Medicine, and Member of the Board of Regents, Georgetown University, Washington D.C.* (Washington, DC: Kober Foundation, 1930).

La Coalición de Derechos Humanos and No More Deaths, "The Disappeared Report: How the US Border Enforcement Agencies Are Fueling a Missing Persons Crisis," 2016. www.thedisappearedreport.org

Levitz, Eric, "We Owe Central American Migrants Much More Than This," *New York Magazine*, 21 June 2018.

Levy, Taylor, "There's No O'odham Word for Wall: Tribal Sovereignty, Resistance, and Acquiescence to the Militarization of the Border and the U.S.-Mexico Broder Wall," unpublished.

Lonetree, Amy, *Decolonizing Museums: Representing Native America in National and Tribal Museums* (Chapel Hill: University of North Carolina Press, 2012).

Mbembe, Achille, "Necropolitics," *Public Culture* 15.1 (2003), pp. 11–40.

Meeks, Eric V., *Border Citizens: The Making of Indians, Mexicans, and Anglos in Arizona* (Austin: University of Texas Press, 2007).

No author, "Indians Seek Burial of Smithsonian Skeletons," *New York Times*, 8 December 1987.

———, "Sonoran Desert Storm: Homeland Security Ramps up the War at Home," *Earth First! Journal*, July–August 2004.

Norrell, Brenda, "Native Americans Lock Down Occupy Border Patrol Headquarters Tucson," *Narcosphere*, 23 May 2010. https://narcosphere.narconews.com/notebook/brenda-norrell/2010/05/native-americans-lock-down-occupy-border-patrol-headquarters-tucson

O'Brien, Jean, *Firsting and Lasting: Writing Indians out of Existence in New England* (Minneapolis: University of Minnesota Press, 2010).

Ortega, Bob, "Border Patrol Failed to Count Hundreds of Migrant Deaths on US Soil," *CNN*, 15 May 2018.

Papers of Edward Twitchell Hall 1930–1979, UAL, Tucson, SC, MS 196.

Record of William Henry Corbusier, Colonel, U.S. Army 1844–1930, UAL, Tucson, SC, AZ 116.

Redman, Samuel J., *Bone Rooms: From Scientific Racism to Human Prehistory in Museums* (Cambridge, MA: Harvard University Press, 2016).

Riding In, James, "Six Pawnee Crania: Historical and Contemporary Issues Associated with the Massacre and Decapitation of Pawnee Indians in 1869," *American Indian Culture and Research Journal* 16.2 (1992), pp. 101–119.

Rivas, Ofelia, "O'odham Remains Returned," *O'odham Voice against the Wall*, 11 November 2007.

Schulze, Jeffrey M., *Are We Not Foreigners Here? Indigenous Nationalism in the U.S.-Mexico Borderlands* (Chapel Hill: University of North Carolina Press, 2018).

Simpson, Audra, *Mohawk Interruptus: Political Life across the Borders of Settler States* (Durham, NC: Duke University Press, 2014).

Simpson, Audra, and Andrea Smith, eds., *Theorizing Native Studies* (Durham, NC: Duke University Press, 2014).

TallBear, Kim, *Native American DNA: Tribal Belonging and the False Promise of Genetic Science* (Minneapolis: University of Minnesota Press, 2013).

Thiel, J. Homer, Penny Dufoe-Minturn, and Lorrie Lincoln-Babb, "Archaeological Excavations at the Arivaca Wash Cemetery, AZ DD:7:26 (ASM), Buenos Aires National Wildlife Refuge," *Center for Desert Archaeology, Technical Report* 94–17 (April 1995), pp. 1–38.

Trope, J. F., and Walter Echo-Hawk, "The Native American Graves Protection and Repatriation Act: Background and Legislative History," *Arizona State Law Journal* 24.1 (1992), pp. 35–77.

Tuck, Eve, and K. Wayne Yang, "Decolonization Is Not a Metaphor," *Decolonization: Indigeneity, Education & Society* 1.1 (2012), pp. 1–40.

Tuhiwai Smith, Linda, *Decolonizing Methodologies: Research and Indigenous Peoples* (London: Zed Books, 1999).

Unsettling Minnesota Collective, ed., *Unsettling Ourselves: Reflections and Resources for Deconstructing Colonial Mentality* (Minneapolis: Unsettling Minnesota Collective, 2011).

Washington, Harriet, *Medical Apartheid: The Dark History of Medical Experimentation on Black Americans from Colonial Times to the Present* (New York: Doubleday Random House, 2006).

Weeks, Philip, ed., *They Made Us Many Promises: The American Indian Experience, 1524 to the Present* (Wheeling, IL: Harlan Davidson, 2002).

Weiner, Tim, "Role of C.I.A. in Guatemala Told in Files of Publisher," *The New York Times*, 7 June 1997.

Wolfe, Patrick, *Settler Colonialism and the Transformation of Anthropology: The Politics and Poetics of an Ethnographic Event* (New York: Bloomsbury Academic, 1998).

Part III

Un-Firsting the West

9 American Indian Discovery

Jonathan DeCoster

We are fast approaching the bicentennial of one of the most important moments in the development of Indian law in the United States. *Johnson v. McIntosh* (1823) was the first in a series of Supreme Court decisions, followed by *Cherokee Nation v. Georgia* (1831) and *Worcester v. Georgia* (1832), sometimes called the Marshall Trilogy, in which chief justice John Marshall (1755–1835) articulated what became known as the Doctrine of Discovery. *Johnson* centered on the question of whether land could be purchased directly from Indian tribes by individuals, or whether only the government had the right to extinguish native title. The court found that absolute land title belonged to European monarchs based on the Doctrine of Discovery, and thus the transfer of that title was a right possessed by the European empires and their successor, the United States, not by the Indian tribes. As formulated by Marshall, this doctrine was based on long-standing practices that European powers used to organize their claims on other peoples' lands. To avoid conflict among each other and dispossess Indigenous people with maximum efficiency, Marshall claimed that colonial powers had decided on the principle "that discovery gave title to the government by whose subjects or by whose authority it was made against all other European governments."[1] This legal doctrine, conceived in the Middle Ages and enshrined in American law nearly two centuries ago as "the original foundation of titles to land on the American continent," was explicitly reaffirmed by the Supreme Court as recently as 2005.[2]

The precise mechanism of discovery was left somewhat hazy by Marshall. Similarly, it remained a source of contention among European powers as they debated whose claims of discovery should take precedence. Nevertheless, they unanimously agreed upon the necessity of being first to discover any new land. Jean O'Brien coins the term "firsting" to describe the numerous ways in which New Englanders promoted minor and major firsts—first settlements, births, schools, prisons, and so on—all of which contributed to a narrative of increasing modernity. The fact that these firsts cataloged by English colonists were almost invariably non-Indian "implicitly argues that Indian peoples never participated in social, cultural, or political practices worthy of note, and that history began only with the gathering of English people."[3] This selective remembrance of firsts memorialized the creation of "institutions of value that constituted the modernity of a place that could not have reached its pinnacle of rationality under Indian regimes of tradition and nature."[4] Her observations also apply to the Doctrine of Discovery, which was defined as an exclusive firsting process in which first discovery preempted the possibility of further discoveries, and thus informed who had the right to claim land and its resources. The Doctrine of Discovery became an act through which Indians and non-Christians were rendered incapable based on the principle of *terra nullius*, or the notion that lands occupied by Indians were effectively vacant, as they were not being utilized in a productive and modern fashion.[5]

Despite the Doctrine's assumed association between discovery and firsting, the idea of discovery did not inherently involve firsting. Samuel Johnson defined "discover" in his 1755 dictionary with three possible meanings: "1. To shew; to disclose; to bring to light. 2. To make known. 3. To find out; to espy."[6] None of these definitions insist on discovery as an exclusive firsting process; information may be unknown to its discoverer but known to others, making discovery a relative concept that, in the early-modern period, expressed the revelation of new information. For instance, Bernal Díaz del Castillo (c. 1495–1584), in a book manifestly concerned with discovery as a process of European firsting, nevertheless used the verb "to discover" in the limited sense of simply relating information when he said that "they wrote to his majesty all that was happening [. . .] giving complaints of the bishop and discovering the dealings that he had."[7] The word itself certainly does not inherently exclude non-Europeans or non-Christians, and in fact it required a degree of mental gymnastics to specifically prohibit Indigenous people from the process of discovery, since they so clearly were the first humans to discover the lands of the Americas. But the ambiguity and hidden meanings of discovery served colonial interests, and the doctrine was fundamentally a tool for dispossession, so its adherents favored a definition of discovery that served the legal process by which land title traveled from native peoples to Europeans and not the reverse.[8] It occupies a prominent place among the legal apparatus that Robert A. Williams Jr. calls "the West's most vital and effective instrument of empire during its genocidal conquest and colonization of the non-Western peoples of the New World."[9]

Native people of course reject the Doctrine of Discovery. They did not participate in discovery; they suffered it and its aftermath, which together encompass "a devastating swathe [. . .] a permanent wound, on the societies and communities who occupied the lands named and claimed under imperialism."[10] As an attempt to undermine the persistent power of the Doctrine of Discovery, this chapter re-envisions discovery stripped of its Eurocentric assumptions, so that Indigenous people become the discoverers.[11] This act of imagining a non-colonialist discovery can be a tool for subverting the doctrine and other colonialist epistemologies while looking to Indigenous ways of knowing that are generally excluded from such discourses, in part because they contradict the doctrine. This chapter offers an exploration of the several ways in which native people discovered Europe and Europeans. It will consider literal claims of native discovery, examine spiritual journeys discounted by European modes of historical understanding, and reframe the notion of discovery to account for events described in the conventional historical record but not understood as discoveries. By reexamining the meaning of discovery and broadening our understanding beyond the traditional Eurocentric use of the term, we can better comprehend the true nature of the colonial encounter and the ways in which native people exerted agency even within an overall paradigm that was dominated by European power.

Marshall rationalized his Doctrine of Discovery with a historical mythology about the origins of European colonization in the Americas, despite the fact that European powers had not formally agreed on any such doctrine.[12] The absence of a standard procedure with respect to arriving at new lands often led to disagreement among the colonizing powers concerning the precedence of their various claims.[13] Marshall's doctrine was an *ex post facto* codification of what had been a messy and improvised arrangement over the preceding centuries. Nevertheless, it is true that European diplomacy recognized the notion of discovery, ill-defined as it was, as a means of granting certain territorial rights. The roots of the doctrine have been traced back to the Roman empire and its claims to universalism. By the first century, the conception of Roman imperial power had evolved from an institution associated with Roman territory into a universal law that ostensibly applied to the entire world. With the triumph of Christianity, the emperors' claim of universal dominion over the world now brought with it an obligation to bring Christianity along with imperial rule to pagans and barbarians. In the fifth century, Augustine of Hippo (354–430) built on this universalism to legitimize military action against those who threatened the faith simply by living in manifestly un-Christian ways in the form of a "just war."[14] Pope Gregory VII (c. 1015–1085) vigorously asserted the universal sovereignty of the Catholic church to support launching holy wars against several enemies in the eleventh century, including Muslims on the Iberian peninsula. This line of reasoning was furthered by Innocent IV (c. 1195–1254), who in 1240 justified crusades against non-Christians by arguing that they violated natural law and thereby compromised their sovereignty and property rights. The 1414 Council of Constance endorsed this view that non-Christians possessed natural rights, but that they could be conquered if they violated natural law, including the practice of so-called idolatry or the rejection of Christianity.[15] This, Robert J. Miller argues, was the first articulation of the Doctrine of Discovery.[16] It is worth noting that during this period the doctrine made no claims as to any discovery or revelation of new lands; it was simply a policy defining and regulating just war against non-Christians and the right to seize their lands.

The voyages of exploration in the fourteenth and fifteenth centuries led to a refinement of the doctrine. As the two Iberian kingdoms squabbled over the Canary Islands, Eugenius IV (1383–1447) issued a bull in 1436 arguing that the pope's paternal authority allowed him to grant the title of new lands to the Christian powers so that they might protect and convert Indigenous peoples. It was this logic that produced perhaps the most famous articulation of the proto-Doctrine of Discovery, the three Papal Bulls of Donation issued in 1493.[17] They awarded to the Spanish monarchs any lands resulting from Columbus's voyages, "With this proviso however that none of the islands and mainlands, found and to be found, discovered and to be discovered [. . .] be in the actual possession of any Christian king or prince."[18] This position firmly established in European international law the notion that a first discovery could grant European monarchs sovereign and property rights to native lands, while also affirming that discovery was an act perpetrated by Christians against non-Christians. The justification was based in part on the Roman tradition of the *terra nullius* or *vacuum domicilium*—land that is either unoccupied or occupied in a way that does not conform to European standards, or as Robert A. Williams, Jr. describes it in an American context, the "normatively deficient use of the 'unmanned wild country' of America."[19] Robert Cushman illustrated this mindset, writing of Virginia's Indians in 1622 that "there are few and doe but run over the grasse, as doe also the Foxes and wilde beasts: they are not industrious, neither have art, science, skill or facultie to use either the land or the commodities of it."[20] By reducing native people to the level of the wilderness, Cushman emphasizes the discovery element of the doctrine—Indians are part of the unknown and untamed landscape that is being uncovered for the first time by Europeans. Any Indigenous occupation of the land simply did not count. As O'Brien explains of the firsting process, "The end product of 'firsting,' then, is the successful mounting of the argument that Indian peoples and their cultures represented an 'inauthentic' and prefatory history."[21]

Edward Said made a similar observation about the role of history in imperialism, arguing that "The power to narrate, or to block other narratives from forming and emerging, is very important to culture and imperialism, and constitutes one of the main connections between them."[22] To question a hegemonic historical narrative, therefore, is to resist the basis of imperialism. There are numerous avenues for challenging the Doctrine of Discovery; one might contest the right of Christians to dominate non-Christians or dispute the claim that Indigenous people were uncivilized and in violation of natural law. We can undermine the historical claims that undergird the Doctrine of Discovery and the notion that Europeans undertook all of the discovering during the age of colonial encounters. This approach reasserts the authority of alternative narratives over the one Marshall constructed in support of his Doctrine of Discovery. Some of these alternative narratives challenge the notion that Indians did not discover, while others push us to rethink the meaning of the term discovery.

One way to challenge the firsting claim of the Doctrine of Discovery would be to demonstrate how American Indians discovered Europe, in just the way that Columbus's discovery of America has been traditionally understood. Historian Jack D. Forbes has strongly advocated for this argument, which rests mainly on a few ambiguous textual references. For example, ancient Roman writers, including Pliny, recorded an incident in 62 BCE, when a trading ship from India was blown off-course to Germany. Some scholars have speculated that this trajectory was geographically impossible and have asserted instead that the ship must have come from North America. Furthermore, the reference to India stokes confusion arising from these already sparse and ambiguous accounts, as the term was sometimes used generically to describe unfamiliar peoples from anywhere east of Europe. Its use in this case may not have been intended to refer to a specific place of origin, but rather may have served as a guess or even simply as a signifier of the newcomer's foreignness. This confusion is exacerbated by Columbus's misuse of the term to describe the Americas, which he believed to be part of Asia. This misnomer leads Forbes to argue that the passengers who arrived in Europe were misidentified as Asian Indians, when in fact they were American Indians, who are of course misnamed. Medieval chronicles record the arrival of another vessel from India arriving in Lubeck in 1153. Some early-modern writers, including António Galvao (c. 1490–1557), speculated that these newcomers had come from Newfoundland or Labrador.[23]

Marginal notes written by Christopher Columbus indicate that he paid close attention to these tales as evidence of the possibility of sailing between Europe and Asia. He further noted that he had seen two such travelers, a man and a wife, during a visit to Galway, Ireland, in the 1470s. This experience convinced him that Cathay, as he called China, could not be so far to the west of Europe. There is some ambiguity in Columbus's notes, compounded by his confused geographical speculations. Those who believe that these were Native Americans interpret Columbus's experience to signify that American Indians in canoes rode the Gulf Stream from North America to Europe, and that Columbus had witnessed as much. Columbus described them as two people hung on two pieces of wood, possibly in reference to two wrecked boats. Some scholars contend that the vehicles described by Columbus were two dugout canoes, a vessel unknown in Europe and indigenous to the Americas, and therefore liable to be misunderstood and poorly described.[24]

These incidents do not satisfactorily meet scholarly standards of historical evidence, and they raise more questions than answers. Do they indicate that American Indians landed in Europe and were there other journeys that went undocumented? Scholars interested in this line of reasoning have attempted to demonstrate that it was possible for Native-American vessels to accidentally catch currents and cross the Atlantic quickly enough to survive the journey.[25] This possibility seems entirely plausible. But it is also possible that the effort to prove the feasibility of such voyages merely replicates Eurocentric ideas about discovery by proving that Native Americans came to Europe before Europeans came to the Americas. Such a premise challenges the Doctrine of Discovery in that it considers non-Christians capable of discovery, but by attempting to prove that Indians went to Europe before Europeans went to America, the act of discovery itself is still interpreted as a firsting event, which is problematic. If these voyages truly happened, would that give Indigenous Americans claim to Europe under the Doctrine of Discovery, and does it count if they did not realize what they had discovered?

Not incidentally, this line of reasoning would put Columbus's discoveries in jeopardy, as he maintained that he had arrived in Asia and had not discovered a New World.[26] Even more damning, Columbus's voyages do not qualify under the principle of firsting, since the re-discovery of the Norse site L'anse aux Meadows in Newfoundland in 1960 has conclusively demonstrated that Columbus was not the first European to reach the Americas, or even to make the return journey.[27] So Columbus would seem to fail the standards of the Doctrine of Discovery on multiple accounts. Yet, it is indisputable that his voyages served as the basis for Spanish territorial claims, and in a broader sense, held greater significance to Europeans than the ship that arrived in Lübeck or even the Norse settlement of Vinland. What made Columbus's voyage significant was his ability to repeat the journey and everything that resulted from the opening of an ongoing connection between the Americas and Afro-Eurasia, for good and for ill. None of these potential examples of Native-American discovery in Europe pass this significance test, nor do they go far enough in challenging the Eurocentrism of the Doctrine of Discovery.

Clearly, the notion of discovery has Eurocentric assumptions and colonialist implications. That critique can be extended to the entire framework within which western scholars practice history. Indigenous people have a different way of understanding, recording, and interpreting the past, and this knowledge challenges the doctrine in several important ways.[28] Black Elk, from the Lakota people of the Upper Great Plains, in *Black Elk Speaks* shares the story of a vision experienced by a holy man named Drinks Water. Before the Lakotas had any contact with Europeans, Drinks Water had dreamed of the arrival of a "strange race" who would bind the Lakotas up in "barren land" and "gray houses," where the Lakotas would starve: "You can look about you now and see that he meant these dirt-roofed houses we are living in, and that all the rest was true," Black Elk says, "Sometimes dreams are wiser than waking."[29] Black Elk's grandfather orally passed on to him this prediction of the arrival of Europeans and the consequences thereof. A spiritual intercession had allowed Drinks

Water to learn pertinent information about the Europeans, despite their separation in time and space. This distinction from the western version of what Peter Nabokov calls "historical consciousness" is significant.[30] As Linda Tuhiwai Smith explains, "The negation of indigenous views of history was a critical part of asserting colonial ideology, partly because such views were regarded as clearly 'primitive' and 'incorrect' and mostly because they challenged and resisted the mission of colonization."[31]

In recognition of this resistance, alternative discoveries emerge—discoveries claimed by native people that do not conform to western standards or expectations—which are often overlooked because they are not textually recorded and contain spiritual or supernatural elements that western historians eschew. Premonitions, as in Black Elk's story, involve advance knowledge of Europeans provided through spiritual or magical means. The 1832 autobiography of Black Hawk, a Sauk from the Great Lakes region, includes a story in which the Great Spirit spoke to Black Hawk's grandfather and told him that in four years, a white man would arrive who would become like a father to him. Four years later, a white man did arrive. He said that he was the son of the king of France, sent there by the Great Spirit, and that the Sauk and other Indians would be his children, and he their father.[32] While western scholars likely would not put much faith in knowledge gained from dreams or spirits, such a stance is a product of a European cultural tradition that is not universally shared. Oral traditions may be considered unreliable by cultures that privilege the written word, but texts can also mislead or even commit fraud. In cases where history is contested, written accounts embody the perspective and the ambitions of their authors no less than oral memories, yet scholars favor textual truth, a propensity that some Indigenous people have referred to as "pen and ink witchcraft."[33]

Some native cultures possess a rich tradition involving journeys of discovery undertaken through spiritual means. A tale collected in the nineteenth century from the Passamaquoddy people of Maine and New Brunswick is clearly framed as such a discovery. The Wabanaki hero Glooskap (alternately spelled Kluskap, Glous'gap, and several other variations) was a supernatural figure sometimes seen as a trickster or as an intercessor on behalf of the people.[34] According to one tale, he once made a canoe of stone, with sails of buffalo skins, and sailed across the sea to Europe. To quote the teller of this story, "This was before the white people had ever heard of America. The white men did not discover this country first at all. Glooskap discovered England, and told them about it. He got to London. The people had never seen a canoe before. They came flocking down to look at it."[35] The teller of this tale was obviously aware of the power of discovery and sought to specifically upturn the notion that Native Americans were discovered by Europeans.

For western-trained scholars, these stories can be difficult to process. They come from cultures with different understandings about how the past relates to the present and how the spiritual and material worlds interact. Just as it was a mistake for European colonizers to assume that the lack of a Christian prince meant that a people were primitive, ignorant, and savage, we would be mistaken to gloss over these alternative discoveries without considering the possibility that they contain either metaphorical or literal truths. Through these narratives, native people assert their agency in the face of often overwhelming power; they counter the discovery discourse that has been used to silence and invalidate Indigenous perspectives in the service of exploitation and dispossession. While these alternative discoveries have the merit of asserting Indigenous claims of authority and historical narrative, their use in this context still subscribes to many of the implicit assumptions of the doctrine, including its emphasis on firsting and the importance of establishing Indigenous firsts.

Another approach to challenging the doctrine is to reframe the notion of discovery itself. As Margarita Zamora observes, we can "consider the Discovery, then, not as a single and unique event, but as a process defining how Europeans were to relate to the newly found peoples and the territories they inhabited."[36] We can understand the process of discovery not simply as a European process of knowledge formation, but instead follow Mary Louise Pratt and "foreground the interactive, improvisational dimensions of colonial encounters so easily ignored or suppressed by diffusionist accounts of conquest and domination. A 'contact' perspective emphasizes how subjects are constituted in and by their relations to each other."[37] In other words, we can consider colonial encounters as a form of mutual discovery, a practice that does away with the quality of firsting. The encounter between Europeans and Indigenous people did not take place in a single moment of contact; it took place at different times and places over the course of centuries. While we can think of Europeans as initiating these encounters by crossing the Atlantic, sailing American coasts, and traveling into the interior of the Americas, Native-American peoples nevertheless also initiated encounters by actively seeking out Europeans, their goods, and even news of them. Just as Europeans mapped new lands, described wondrous new things, flora, and fauna, and tried to make sense of them within their worldview, so too did Indigenous people engage in a process of discovery by gathering and processing information about these novel people and their culture, including their traditional homeland of Europe. We know that news of the Europeans traveled quickly.[38]

Most first encounters thus involved some degree of prior knowledge or contact. The famous case of the pilgrims provides a classic example. Even though scholars position their colony as one of the most prominent firsts in American history, it is equally well-known that its survival depended on the assistance of a Patuxet Wampanoag Indian, Tisquantum (Squanto, c. 1580–1622), who already spoke English. His linguistic prowess may have been gained after being captured in 1605 by George Weymouth

(c. 1585–c. 1612), who had visited the region for years, and taken to Plymouth, England. Ferdinando Gorges claimed that Squanto was among the five men captured by Weymouth, and that he then lived with Gorges in England.[39] We know for certain that Squanto was captured (if not recaptured) by Thomas Hunt in 1614, who sold him along with other Wampanoags in Spain. We know little about his time in Spain except that he learned about Christianity from friars who opposed slavery; Squanto made it back to England and lived in London with the London merchant John Slany (d. 1632) for a time, and was then sent to create a colony in Newfoundland in 1618.[40] There are many other instances of Indians captured to be trained as interpreters. If Squanto's experience was anything like the others, he may have been "shewed in London for a wonder" and had numerous opportunities to learn about the English and their culture.[41] Some responded like Squanto and used this knowledge to gain the trust and assistance of Europeans. Others, like Epenow, a Nauset from Cape Cod who lived with Gorges and may have accompanied Squanto to Spain, used what they had learned to resist colonization. Most importantly, these interactions took place several years before the pilgrims arrived in New England. Indians and the English had much to discover about each other, but we cannot imagine the encounter between the pilgrims and the Indigenous peoples of the region comprised any kind of a first contact for the Wampanoags. As the example of Squanto demonstrates, moreover, Indigenous peoples possessed knowledge about Europeans—language expertise, for instance—that undermines the Doctrine of Discovery in more than one way.

The Squanto example is also illustrative because the Wampanoag Indians did not respond passively to the arrival of the newcomers. Their leader Massasoit (c. 1580–1661) chose when to avoid or seek out the English, and he sent translators when he wanted to communicate. This was a common practice: when news of Europeans reached native leaders, rather than waiting to be approached, they often went to great lengths to uncover what they could about the strangers and to initiate contact. True first contacts were probably quite rare because there was significant interest in Europeans and their goods, and the interconnected nature of the Indian world made news and goods available even to those who could not meet Europeans face-to-face.[42]

Indirect encounters of this nature afforded opportunities to connect with and learn about Europeans without encountering them directly. Information is highly mobile and valuable, and exchange networks that transacted orally and communicated details and news radiated throughout North America, and beyond. The Spanish invasions launched by the likes of Hernando de Soto (c. 1500–1542) in the early sixteenth-century southeast and southwest revealed the rapidity with which important news could travel. Spanish accounts describe their first arrival in villages where the native people had already hung crosses on their homes, hoping in this way to ward off disease and danger, as they had heard the Europeans did.[43] Clearly, they had discovered something about the Europeans in advance of their arrival, even though Europeans and settlers interpreted this anticipation of European presence as providence as well as an indication of the populations' convertibility to Christianity. This re-perspectivization reveals who discovered whom first; as Alejandra Dubcovsky puts it, "Indians made it their business to learn about the foreigners."[44]

Information about Europeans was valuable because they were novel and exotic, sometimes to the extent that they were perceived as otherworldly beings. This last perception has at times been overstated in Euro-settler scholarship, such as the allegation that Cortés and the Spanish conquistadors were believed to be returning gods by the Nahuas of Mexico. Most scholars now consider this narrative to be a post-invasion explanation for the events of the Spanish conquest.[45] A more prosaic example of this practice can be found at the Roanoke Colony in North Carolina. The colony's sponsor, Walter Raleigh (c. 1552–1618), described how his colonists had asked the Algonquians the name of their country and received the answer "Wingandacoa," which the English dutifully inscribed on their maps. Only later did they learn that the phrase meant "you weare good clothes, or gay clothes."[46] Indigenous peoples nonetheless viewed material goods of any origin as having practical and spiritual value. In one striking case, the archaeological excavation of a Wendat (Huron) village named Mantle (located near present-day Toronto, Ontario) uncovered a Basque axe. Carbon dating places the village's last occupation in the early sixteenth century, and geography places it 1,000 miles west of the Atlantic coast. This date is a full century before any known face-to-face contact with Europeans took place.[47] The exchange of goods this far into the interior is clearly driven by native people, not Europeans, who transacted them as valued objects across space using distribution networks, and their reception and use embody a form of discovery.

There were also thousands of American Indians who traveled to Europe during the fifteenth and sixteenth centuries. The majority of these Native Americans in Europe were there involuntarily; scholars estimate that as many as 30,000 were enslaved by Spaniards alone in the sixteenth and seventeenth centuries, some of whom were brought to Europe.[48] Some native people were repatriated due to queen Isabella's opposition to enslavement, who could then relate what they apprized of European culture, technology, agriculture, animal husbandry, and metallurgy, even for those who were enslaved to live among Europeans in the Americas rather than set foot in Europe itself.[49] Some Indians were brought to Europe with the hope that they would serve as guides and translators. One example of this was the Algonquian-speaking Indian Paquiquineo (1543–1646), baptized Don Luis de Velasco by the Spaniards, who was likely kidnaped from the region of present-day Virginia, then brought before the king of Spain in 1561, where he was ordered to help establish a Dominican mission in Virginia. He seems to have also spent time from 1562 to 1566 in Mexico City, and then returned to Spain until 1570. Jesuits finally resurrected the dormant mission plan, and they landed in Virginia in 1570. It gradually became clear, however, that Paquiquineo was not interested in living as a Christian or supporting the mission. In February 1571, Paquiquineo and his Indigenous compatriots killed all the Spaniards excepting one boy.[50] Paquiquineo's story highlights how translators who transmitted knowledge to Europeans also transmitted information back to Indians, who used and interpreted it as they chose. This knowledge economy prompts us to meditate on the modern legal meaning of discovery, by which the prosecution is required to reveal their own evidence, much as they would prefer to keep it secret. At a fundamental level, the interpreters would need to discover information about European society to even begin the process of cultural interpretation and translation.

Some Indigenous people traveled voluntarily to Europe to pursue political and diplomatic ends. Numerous delegations from Tlaxcala went to Spain to secure special privileges pursuant to their aid in Cortés's conquest. As early as 1527, five representatives from Tlaxcala traveled in company with relatives of both Cortés and the recently deceased emperor, Moctezuma. In 1534, Charles V met with Diego Maxixcatzin, the local Indigenous governor in Tlaxcala. Other delegations went in 1540, 1562, and 1583–1585, upon their own initiative to use the Spanish legal and political system to protect their interests.[51] Similarly, the Virginia Company brought the famous Powhatan Indian Pocahontas, also called Matoaka (1595–1617), her husband John Rolfe (1585–1622), and their one-year-old son Thomas on a highly public visit to England in 1616 to build support for the fledgling colony. With them came around a dozen other Powhatan Indians, including Uttamatomakkin, also called Tomocomo, a son-in law and trusted councilor of Pocahontas's father, the Powhatan chief Wahunsonacock (c. 1547–c. 1618). The Company may have arranged the transportation, but the Powhatans took advantage of the opportunity to gather their own information about England. Pocahontas was received in London with the honors due a princess; the British sovereigns took note of her, and she made appearances on the London social circuit, including the masque balls, while engraved reproductions of her portrait publicized her visit (Figure 9.1).[52] While Pocahontas served as the image of Virginia for Londoners, Uttamatomakkin had been expressly chosen by Wahunsonacock as "an understanding fellow" tasked with assessing the numbers and strength of the English.[53] He had been ordered by Wahunsonacock to count the English population by cutting notches in a stick, a practice that reflected Indigenous record-keeping practices.[54] According to English observers the effort soon became overwhelming; in any case Uttamatomakkin apparently returned with a negative report that would help lead the Powhatans to revisit their war with the English.

Figure 9.1 Van de Passe's engraving of Pocahontas, the only image of Pocahontas made from life, helped the Virginia Company publicize their recently concluded alliance with her father, "the mighty Prince Powhatan Emperour of Attanoughkomouck [Tsennacommacah] als Virginia." From Simon van de Passe, *Matoaka Al[ia]s Rebecca Filia Potentiss. Prince: Powhatani Imp: Virginiae, engraving* (London: Compton Holland, 1616).

These kinds of diplomatic delegations made sensations in the imperial cities during the colonial period.[55] They perhaps best represent the reframing of discovery put forward here—a mutual, ongoing process of acquiring and making sense of new information. The Indians possessed agency as they came to Europe not as subjects called to pay tribute, but rather as representatives conducting reconnaissance, negotiating relationships, and sometimes making demands of the European monarchs and colonists. They took their new-found knowledge back with them and disseminated it among other Native Americans. And as much as these were voyages of discovery for the native diplomats, for most Londoners, Parisians, and Sevillians, these Indigenous representatives offered a rare opportunity to discover something about the New World for themselves. The process of discovery entailed the mutual need to discern a place for America in the European worldview, and Europe in the Native-American worldview.

This reframing of discovery is more than a semantic argument. As Linda Tuhiwai Smith objects, "It angers us when practices linked to the last century, and the centuries before that, are still employed to deny the validity of indigenous peoples' claim to existence, to land and territories, to the right of self-determination, to the survival of our languages and forms of cultural knowledge, to our natural resources and systems for living within our environments."[56] Those practices are ongoing not just in the United States, but also in Canada and Australia, as those countries have all recently affirmed the Doctrine of Discovery.[57] Yet, it is not only native people who disavow the doctrine. The UN Declaration of the Rights of Indigenous Peoples (UNDRIP) is seen by many as a repudiation of the doctrine, and the United Methodist Church, the Unitarian Universalist Association, the Episcopal Church, and numerous other churches and religious communities have all recently taken stances against the doctrine.[58] Popes John Paul II and Francis both have apologized for the actions of the Catholic church in the past and expressed support for Indigenous rights, though neither formally renounced the doctrine.[59] As we approach the bicentenary of *Johnson v. McIntosh*, we should consider how this legal principle is still an active part of American law and an obstacle to ongoing legal challenges to the dispossession of native people. In so doing, scholars can promote the mutualism inherent in the act of discovery so to de-center European discovery and activate Indigenous agency within early-modern Atlantic scholarship.

Notes

1. *Johnson & Graham's Lessee v. McIntosh*, 21 U.S. 543 (1823). Lindsay Gordon Robertson identified over 750 articles and books related to *Johnson v. McIntosh* alone in *Conquest by Law*, p. x. Some other important recent works related to Doctrine of Discovery include Banner, *How the Indians Lost Their Land*; Miller, *Native America*; Miller, Ruru, Behrendt, and Lindberg,

Discovering Indigenous Lands; and Watson, *Buying America from the Indians*.

2. *Johnson v. McIntosh; City of Sherill v. Oneida Indian Nation of N.Y.*, 544 U.S. 197 (2005). Title is a legally recognized right to property ownership, whereas a land claim (many of which are made by Indian tribes) is an assertion of the right of ownership that is not yet legally recognized.
3. O'Brien, *Firsting and Lasting*, p. 6.
4. Ibid.
5. For *terra nullius*, see Banner, "Why Terra Nullius," pp. 95–131; Banner, *Possessing the Pacific*; and Benton and Straumann, "Acquiring Empire by Law," pp. 1–38.
6. Johnson, *A Dictionary of the English Language*, vol. 1, n.p.
7. "[Y] escribieron a su majestad todo lo que pasaba [. . .] dando quejas del obispo y descubriendo sus tratos que tenía," in del Castillo, *Historia Verdadera*, ch. 23, n.p. Unless otherwise stated, all translations are my own.
8. For some classic articulations of the role of power, language, narrative, and history in the law, see Gordon, "Some Critical Theories of Law and Their Critics," pp. 641–661, and Baron and Epstein, "Language and the Law: Literature, Narrative, and Legal Theory," pp. 662–679, both in Kairys, ed., *The Politics of Law*.
9. Williams Jr., *The American Indian*, p. 6.
10. Tuhiwai Smith, *Decolonizing Methodologies*, p. 21.
11. This thought experiment is partly inspired by Axtell, "Colonial America without the Indians," pp. 981–996.
12. Robertson, *Conquest by Law*, pp. 100–103.
13. Seed, *Ceremonies of Possession*, pp. 9–11.
14. Pagden, *Lords of All the World*, pp. 11–30 and 94–98.
15. Williams, *The American Indian*, pp. 13–15, 23–24, 29–32, and 44–50.
16. Miller, *Native America*, pp. 12–13.
17. Ibid., pp. 13–14.
18. Alexander VI, "Inter Caetera."
19. Williams, *The American Indian*, p. 220; and Miller, *Native America*, pp. 17–21.
20. Mourt, *A Relation*, p. 68.
21. O'Brien, *Firsting and Lasting*, pp. 52–53.
22. Said, *Culture and Imperialism*, p. xiii.
23. Forbes, *The American Discovery of Europe*, pp. 113–118; López de Gómara, *La historia general de las Indias*, fol. 16; and Galvão, *Tratado*, fol. 14v.
24. The Biblioteca Colombina holds a copy of Pierre d'Ailly's *Ymago Mundi*, printed in Leuven sometime between 1477 and 1483, which was owned and annotated by Columbus. A critical edition, including Columbus's annotations, was prepared by Edmond Buron; see *Ymago Mundi*, vol. 3, pp. 743–744. Columbus's relationship with d'Ailly's *Imago Mundi* is discussed throughout Wey Gómez, *The Tropics of Empire*. For an extensive dissection of the issues of translating Columbus's Latin notes, see Forbes, *American Discovery of Europe*, pp. 5–8.
25. Riley, Kelley, Pennington, and Rands, eds., *Man across the Sea*, pp. 277 and 301; Cooper, "Eskimo Voyages to Europe," p. 21; Quinn, "Columbus and the North," p. 284; and Jett, *Ancient Ocean Crossings*, pp. 48–49 and 52–53.
26. It has commonly been argued that Columbus failed to comprehend the nature of his discovery; for a classic version of this position, see O'Gorman, *La idea del descubrimiento de América*. A strong argument in favor of Columbus's understanding of his discovery appears more recently in Fernández-Armesto, *Columbus*, pp. 102 and 130–131.

27. Kolodny, *In Search of First Contact*, p. 5.
28. For Indigenous ways of thinking about history, see Nabokov, *A Forest of Time*; and Tuhiwai Smith, *Decolonizing Methodologies*. For the ways in which this has affected land claims, see McMillen, *Making Indian Law*; Miller, *Oral History on Trial*; Babcock, "'[This] I Know from My Grandfather';" and Borrows, *Recovering Canada*, pp. 111–123.
29. Neihardt, *Black Elk Speaks*, pp. 6–7.
30. Nabokov, *A Forest of Time*, p. 66.
31. Tuhiwai Smith, *Decolonizing Methodologies*, p. 29.
32. Nichols, ed., *Black Hawk's Autobiography*, pp. 9–12.
33. Calloway, *Pen and Ink Witchcraft*, pp. 35–40. Miller discusses the shift in the western legal attitude toward oral testimony in *Oral History on Trial*, pp. 1–3.
34. For detailed analyses of Kluskap and Charles G. Leland's ethnographic work, see Parkhill, *Weaving Ourselves into the Land*; RunningWolf and Clark Smith, *On the Trail of Elder Brother*; Hornborg, "'Readbacks' or Tradition;" and Reid, *Finding Kluskap*.
35. Leland, *The Algonquin Legends of New England*, p. 128.
36. Zamora, *Reading Columbus*, p. 7.
37. Pratt, *Imperial Eyes*, p. 6.
38. Kolodny, *In Search of First Contact*, p. 67; and Weaver, *The Red Atlantic*, p. 47.
39. Squanto and the sources for his history are discussed further in Baxter, *Sir Ferdinando Gorges*, vol. 1, pp. 104–106.
40. Details of Squanto's life can be found in Council for New England's *A Briefe Relation*, n/p; Mourt, *A Relation*, pp. 33 and 35; and Bradford, *History of Plymouth Plantation*, pp. 203–204. Also see Sweet and Nash, eds., *Struggle and Survival*, pp. 228–237.
41. "[S]hewed in London for a wonder;" see Baxter, *Sir Ferdinando Gorges*, vol. 2, p. 19.
42. Cohen, *The Networked Wilderness*; Dubcovsky, *Informed Power*; and Loewen and Chapdelaine, eds., *Contact in the 16th Century*.
43. de la Vega, *The Florida of the Inca*, pp. 482–483. There are also descriptions of native people sending emissaries to the Spaniards requesting crosses in Barrientos, *Pedro Menéndez De Avilés*, pp. 106, 119, and 121.
44. Dubcovsky, *Informed Power*, pp. 33–35.
45. The myth of Quetzalcoatl has been heavily studied by scholars. A comprehensive examination can be found in Townsend, "Burying the White Gods," pp. 659–687. Also see Restall, *When Montezuma Met Cortés*, pp. 43–46, 99–102, and 110–111.
46. Raleigh, *The History of the World*, pp. 175–176. Wingandacoa is used as a geographic label in Ortelius, *Americae Sive Novi Orbis*.
47. Birch and Williamson, *The Mantle Site*, pp. 63 and 149–152; and Weaver, *Red Atlantic*, p. 56.
48. A comprehensive if dated and inconsistently documented treatment of Indians who traveled to Europe and other places can be found in Foreman, *Indians Abroad, 1493–1938*. More recently Jace Weaver provides a broad view in *Red Atlantic*, while the experience of Indians in England has been studied in more detail by Vaughan, *Transatlantic Encounters*; also see Thrush, *Indigenous London*. The French experience is highlighted in Dickason, *Myth of the Savage*, pp. 203–229. Also see Forbes, *American Discovery of Europe*, p. 170.
49. Reséndez, *The Other Slavery*, pp. 22–28 and 48–61. Also see Gallay, *The Indian Slave Trade*; Snyder, *Slavery in Indian Country*; and Newell, *Brethren by Nature*.
50. Brickhouse, *The Unsettlement of America*, pp. 47–78.

51. Jaramillo, *Litigious Paupers*, pp. 33–34, 71, and 93.
52. Smith, *The Generall Historie of Virginia*, pp. 122–123; Hamor, *A True Discourse of the Present Estate of Virginia*, pp. 55–56 and 61–68; and John Chamberlain to Dudley Carleton, 18 January 1617, in National Archives of the United Kingdom State Papers, nos. 25 and 146. The engraved portrait, after Simon van de Passe, is titled "Matoaka als Rebecca," and dates from 1616. British Museum, 1863, 0509.625.
53. Smith, *The Generall Historie of Virginia*, p. 123; and Purchas, *Purchas His Pilgrimes*, book 4, pp. 1773–1774.
54. A system employed by the Pomo of California uses beads and sticks to easily manipulate numbers in the tens of thousands. The knotted strings of the Inca quipus were also used to track the population. See Closs, "Native American Number Systems," in Closs, ed., *Native American Mathematics*, pp. 3–43: 35–41. Farrell describes both Uttamatomakkin's use of notched sticks and Guaman Poma's use of quipus to count the population; see Farrell, *Counting Bodies*, pp. 1–2, 23–25, and 98–99. See also Aveni, "Native Numerals."
55. See, for example, Ellis and Steen, "An Indian Delegation in France, 1725," pp. 385–405; Hinderaker, "The 'Four Indian Kings'," pp. 491–505; and Vilches, "Columbus's Gift," pp. 201–202.
56. Tuhiwai Smith, *Decolonizing Methodologies*, p. 1.
57. Robertson, *Conquest by Law*, p. 144.
58. (no author) "'Doctrine of Discovery';" and Rotondaro, "Doctrine of Discovery."
59. Swan, "Doctrine of Discovery;" and Hill, "Pope Says Indigenous People Must Have Final Say."

Bibliography

Alexander VI, "Inter Caetera: Division of the Undiscovered World between Spain and Portugal," 1493. www.papalencyclicals.net/Alex06/alex06inter.htm

Aveni, Anthony F., "Native Numerals: Among American Indians, Numbers Counted for Morethan Math," *Colonial Williamsburg* (Autumn 2007). www.history.org/Foundation/journal/Autumn07/math.cfm

Axtell, James, "Colonial America without the Indians: Counterfactual Reflections," *The Journal of American History* 73.4 (1987), pp. 981–996.

Babcock, Hope M., "'[This] I Know from My Grandfather': The Battle for Admissibility of Indigenous Oral History as Proof of Tribal Land Claims," *American Indian Law Review* 37.1 (2012), pp. 19–61.

Banner, Stuart, *How the Indians Lost Their Land: Law and Power on the Frontier* (Cambridge, MA: The Belknap Press of Harvard University Press, 2005).

———, "Why Terra Nullius? Anthropology and Property Law in Early Australia," *Law and History Review* 23.1 (2005), pp. 95–131.

———, *Possessing the Pacific: Land, Settlers, and Indigenous People from Australia to Alaska* (Cambridge, MA: Harvard University Press, 2007).

Barrientos, Bartolomé, *Pedro Menéndez de Avilés, Founder of Florida*, trans. Anthony Kerrigan (Gainesville: University of Florida Press, 1965).

Baxter, James Phinney, *Sir Ferdinando Gorges and His Province of Maine: Including the Brief Relation* (Boston: Prince Society, 1890).

Benton, Lauren, and Benjamin Straumann, "Acquiring Empire by Law: From Roman Doctrine to Early Modern European Practice," *Law and History Review* 28.1 (2010), pp. 1–38.

Birch, Jennifer, and R. F. Williamson, *The Mantle Site: An Archaeological History of an Ancestral Wendat Community* (Lanham, MD: AltaMira Press, 2013).
Borrows, John, *Recovering Canada: The Resurgence of Indigenous Law* (Toronto: University of Toronto Press, 2015).
Bradford, William, *History of Plymouth Plantation, 1620–1647* (Boston: The Massachusetts Historical Society, 1912).
Brickhouse, Anna, *The Unsettlement of America: Translation, Interpretation, and the Story of Don Luis de Velasco, 1560–1945* (New York: Oxford University Press, 2015).
Buron, Edmond, *Ymago Mundi* (Paris: Librarie Oriental et Américaine, 1930).
Calloway, Colin, *Pen and Ink Witchcraft: Treaties and Treaty Making in American Indian History* (Oxford: Oxford University Press, 2013).
Castillo, Bernal Díaz del, *Historia verdadera de la conquista de la Nueva España* (Barcelona: Linkgua Historia, 2018).
Closs, Michael P., ed., *Native American Mathematics* (Austin: University of Texas Press, 1986).
Cohen, Matt, *The Networked Wilderness: Communicating in Early New England* (Minneapolis: University of Minnesota Press, 2010).
Cooper, Richard, "Eskimo Voyages to Europe: Evidence the Inuits Canoed the Atlantic," *Oceans* 17.5 (1984), pp. 20–22.
Council for New England, *A Briefe Relation of the Discouery and Plantation of Nevv England and of Sundry Accidents Therein* (London: John Haviland, 1622).
Dickason, Olive Patricia, *Myth of the Savage and the Beginnings of French Colonialism in the Americas* (Edmonton: University of Alberta Press, 1984).
Dubcovsky, Alejandra, *Informed Power: Communication in the Early American South* (Cambridge, MA: Harvard University Press, 2016).
Ellis, Richard N., and Charlie R. Steen, "An Indian Delegation in France, 1725," *Journal of the Illinois State Historical Society* 67.4 (1974), pp. 385–405.
Farrell, Molly, *Counting Bodies: Population in Colonial American Writing* (Oxford: Oxford University Press, 2016).
Fernández-Armesto, Felipe, *Columbus and the Conquest of the Impossible* (London: Phoenix Press, 2000).
Forbes, Jack D., *The American Discovery of Europe* (Urbana: University of Illinois Press, 2007).
Foreman, Carolyn Thomas, *Indians Abroad, 1493–1938* (Norman: University of Oklahoma Press, 1943).
Gallay, Alan, *The Indian Slave Trade: The Rise of the English Empire in the American South, 1670–1717* (New Haven, CT: Yale University Press, 2002).
Galvão, António, *Tratado que compós o nobre & notauel capitáo Antonio Galuáo, dos diuersos & desuayrados caminhos* (Lisbon: Joam da Barreira, 1563).
Hamor, Ralph, *A True Discourse of the Present Estate of Virginia* (London: William Welby, 1615).
Hill, David, "Pope Says Indigenous People Must Have Final Say about Their Land," *The Guardian*, 20 February 2017.
Hinderaker, Eric, "The 'Four Indian Kings' and the Imaginative Construction of the First British Empire," *William and Mary Quarterly* 53.3 (1996), pp. 491–505.

Hornborg, Anne-Christine, "'Readbacks' or Tradition? The Kluskap Stories among Modern Canadian Mi'kmaq," *European Review of Native American Studies* 16.1 (2002), pp. 9–16.

Jaramillo, Alejandra, *Litigious Paupers: Natives and Colonial Demands in Tlaxcala, 1545–1800* (PhD dissertation) (Houston, TX: University of Houston, 2014).

Jett, Stephen C., *Ancient Ocean Crossings: Reconsidering the Case for Contacts with the Pre-Columbian Americas* (Tuscaloosa: University of Alabama Press, 2017).

Johnson, Samuel, *A Dictionary of the English Language* (London: W. Strahan, 1755).

Kairys, David, ed., *The Politics of Law: A Progressive Critique*, 3rd ed. (New York: Basic Books, 1998).

Kolodny, Annette, *In Search of First Contact: The Vikings of Vinland, the Peoples of the Dawnland, and the Anglo-American Anxiety of Discovery* (Durham, NC: Duke University Press, 2012).

Leland, Charles G., *The Algonquin Legends of New England; or, Myths and Folk Lore of the Micmac, Passamaquoddy, and Penobscot Tribes* (Boston: Houghton, Mifflin and Company, 1885).

Loewen, Brad, and Claude Chapdelaine, eds., *Contact in the 16th Century: Networks among Fishers, Foragers and Farmers* (Ottawa: Canadian Museum of History and University of Ottawa Press, 2016).

López de Gómara, Francisco, *La historia general de las Indias, y todo lo acascido enellas dende que se ganaron hasta agora. Y la conquista de Mexico, y dela nueua España* (Antwerp: Martín Nucio, 1554).

McMillen, Christian W., *Making Indian Law: The Hualapai Land Case and the Birth of Ethnohistory* (New Haven, CT: Yale University Press, 2007).

Miller, Bruce Granville, *Oral History on Trial: Recognizing Aboriginal Narratives in the Courts* (Vancouver: UBC Press, 2011).

Miller, Robert J., *Native America, Discovered and Conquered: Thomas Jefferson, Lewis & Clark, and Manifest Destiny* (Westport, CT: Praeger, 2006).

Miller, Robert J., Jacinta Ruru, Larissa Behrendt, and Tracey Lindberg, *Discovering Indigenous Lands: The Doctrine of Discovery in the English Colonies* (New York: Oxford University Press, 2010).

Mourt, G., *A Relation or Iournall of the Beginning and Proceedings of the English Plantation Setled at Plimoth in New England* (London: John Bellamie, 1622).

Nabokov, Peter, *A Forest of Time: American Indian Ways of History* (New York: Cambridge University Press, 2002).

National Archives of the United Kingdom, Kew, State Papers, Domestic, James I, SP 14/90.

Neihardt, John, *Black Elk Speaks: Being the Life Story of a Holy Man of the Oglala* (Lincoln: University of Nebraska Press, 2004).

Newell, Margaret Ellen, *Brethren by Nature: New England Indians, Colonists, and the Origins of American Slavery* (Ithaca, NY: Cornell University Press, 2015).

Nichols, Roger L., ed., *Black Hawk's Autobiography* (Ames: Iowa State University Press, 1999).

No author, "'Doctrine of Discovery', Used for Centuries to Justify Seizure of Indigenous Land, Subjugate Peoples, Must Be Repudiated by United Nations,

Permanent Forum Told," United Nations Meeting Coverage and Press Releases, 8 May 2012. www.un.org/press/en/2012/hr5088.doc.htm

O'Brien, Jean M., *Firsting and Lasting: Writing Indians out of Existence in New England* (Minneapolis: University of Minneapolis Press, 2010).

O'Gorman, Edmundo, *La idea del descubrimiento de América* (Mexico City: Centro de Estudios Filosóficos, 1951).

Ortelius, Abraham, *Americae Sive Novi Orbis, Nova Descriptio* (Antwerp: Christopher Plantin, 1587).

Pagden, Anthony, *Lords of All the World: Ideologies of Empire in Spain, Britain and France c. 1500–c. 1800* (New Haven, CT: Yale University Press, 1995).

Parkhill, Thomas, *Weaving Ourselves into the Land: Charles Godfrey Leland, "Indians," and the Study of Native American Religions* (Albany: State University of New York Press, 1997).

Pratt, Mary Louise, *Imperial Eyes: Travel Writing and Transculturation* (New York: Routledge, 1992).

Purchas, Samuel, *Purchas His Pilgrimes: In Five Bookes* (London: Henrie Fetherstone, 1625–1626).

Quinn, David B., "Columbus and the North: England, Iceland, and Ireland," *William and Mary Quarterly* 49.2 (1992), pp. 278–297.

Raleigh, Walter, *The History of the World* (London: Walter Burre, 1614).

Reid, Jennifer, *Finding Kluskap: A Journey into Mi'kmaw Myth* (University Park: Pennsylvania State University Press, 2013).

Reséndez, Andrés, *The Other Slavery: The Uncovered Story of Indian Enslavement in America* (Boston: Houghton, Mifflin and Harcourt, 2016).

Restall, Matthew, *When Montezuma Met Cortés: The True Story of the Meeting That Changed History* (New York: HarperCollins, 2018).

Riley, Carroll L., J. Charles Kelley, Campbell W. Pennington, and Robert L. Rands, eds., *Man across the Sea: Problems of Pre-Columbian Contacts* (Austin: University of Texas Press, 1971).

Robertson, Lindsay Gordon, *Conquest by Law: How the Discovery of America Dispossessed Indigenous Peoples of Their Lands* (New York: Oxford University Press, 2005).

Rotondaro, Vinnie, "Doctrine of Discovery: A Scandal in Plain Sight," *National Catholic Reporter*, 5 September 2015.

RunningWolf, Michael B., and Patricia Clark Smith, *On the Trail of Elder Brother: Glous'gap Stories of the Micmac Indians* (New York: Persea Books, 2000).

Said, Edward W., *Culture and Imperialism* (New York: Alfred A. Knopf, 1993).

Seed, Patricia, *Ceremonies of Possession in Europe's Conquest of the New World, 1492–1640* (New York: Cambridge University Press, 1995).

Smith, John, *The Generall Historie of Virginia, New-England, and the Summer Isles* (London: John Dawson and John Haviland for Michael Sparkes, 1624).

Snyder, Christina, *Slavery in Indian Country: The Changing Face of Captivity in Early America* (Cambridge, MA: Harvard University Press, 2010).

Swan, Michael, "Doctrine of Discovery First Repudiated in 1537," *The Catholic Register*, 2 October 2014.

Sweet, David G., and Gary B. Nash, eds., *Struggle and Survival in Colonial America* (Berkeley: University of California Press, 1981).

Thrush, Coll, *Indigenous London: Native Travelers at the Heart of Empire* (New Haven, CT: Yale University Press, 2016).

Townsend, Camilla, "Burying the White Gods: New Perspectives on the Conquest of Mexico," *The American Historical Review* 108.3 (2003), pp. 659–687.

Tuhiwai Smith, Linda, *Decolonizing Methodologies: Research and Indigenous Peoples* (London: Palgrave, 2001).

Vaughan, Alden T., *Transatlantic Encounters: American Indians in Britain, 1500–1776* (New York: Cambridge University Press, 2006).

Vega, Garcilaso de la, *The Florida of the Inca*, trans. Jeannette Johnson Varner and John Grier Varner (Austin: University of Texas Press, 1951).

Vilches, Elvira, "Columbus's Gift: Representations of Grace and Wealth and the Enterprise of the Indies," *MLN* 119.2 (2004), pp. 201–225: 201–202.

Watson, Blake A., *Buying America from the Indians: Johnson v. McIntosh and the History of Native Land Rights* (Norman: University of Oklahoma Press, 2012).

Weaver, Jace, *The Red Atlantic: American Indigenes and the Making of the Modern World, 1000–1927* (Chapel Hill: University of North Carolina Press, 2014).

Wey Gómez, Nicolás, *The Tropics of Empire: Why Columbus Sailed South to the Indies* (Cambridge, MA: MIT Press, 2008).

Williams, Robert A., Jr., *The American Indian in Western Legal Thought: The Discourses of Conquest* (New York: Oxford University Press, 1990).

Zamora, Margarita, *Reading Columbus* (Berkeley: University of California Press, 1993).

10 Unsettling Spanish Atlantic History

Experiences of the Colonized Through Visual and Material Culture

Lauren Beck

This chapter takes as its basic premise that the early-modern written word colonizes our way of knowing Atlantic history and ensures that white, masculine voices predominate throughout the historical record. The western cultural protection of text as an authoritative source for knowledge furthermore perpetuates this problem in scholarship of all periods, which tends to circulate in written form. While eschewing the written word as a vehicle for knowledge is not within the scope of this chapter, we must meditate on the ways that written documents continue the firsting ideology explored throughout this book. This task gives us pause to consider how we can broaden the sources upon which we rely for our scholarship in order to draw out and study new voices and experiences and allow them to inform the historical record, particularly when cultural intermediaries provide inter-modal (text-image, text-object) forms of record. Valuing and engaging with sources from the realms of visual and material culture that involve non-European informants and creators could comprise a significant contribution to un-firsting the west within early-modern Atlantic-world scholarship.

Let us first problematize verbal culture as an instrument of colonization with gendered and racial implications. Stanley Fish in *Is There a Text in This Class* establishes that readers form an interpretive community within which no one person determines the binary of subjectivity and objectivity, and that this binary may not even exist. Rather, readers possess a collective consciousness guided by conventional notions that allow them to interpret conventionally seen objects.[1] Communities of readers subscribe to Benedict Anderson's concept of an imagined community with which Anderson sought to understand the creation of national identity in the minds of citizens of the western world. Both forms of community rely upon a sense of shared values, points of view, and experiences, all of which might define what Fish calls conventional notions.[2] It is within this framework that we can understand how Native Americans have been consistently seen as inferior to settler-colonizers by a community of readers because the readers themselves are implicated in terms of their identity as either settlers or colonizers. The rhetoric that permits this objectivity has existed since Columbus's letters to Isabel and Ferdinand, published and quickly translated into several languages in 1493, none of which included any authentic or meaningful engagement with Native-American languages and knowledges.

One of the conventional notions expressed by Columbus during his first voyage to the Americas is that unfamiliar language (*lengua*), and in later periods orality in general as opposed to textuality, is incomprehensible on the one hand and unauthoritative on the other. For this reason, he relied upon signs (*señas*) to communicate with individuals who he viewed as otherwise without language (*sin lengua*).[3] He and his successors leave the reader not knowing the voice, in either textual or oral form, of the individuals he encountered along his travels or, when vocalized, their expression is confined by the cultural limitations of European languages and rendered through the pen and from the press of a person possessing an entirely distinct worldview. Evidence of these limitations resides in the fact that traditional Andean chronicles, quipu, were comprised of knotted strings through which the knots, and their relationship to each other, relayed the story of a king's life, his nature, the clothing he wore, and so on, perhaps by serving as mnemonic devices that were related orally or consumed silently by the quipu user. While settler-colonists debated whether quipus could be considered texts, the way they were used disappeared and today the 600 or so quipu known to exist cannot be read.[4]

Native-American identities and voices are constrained when they become dispossessed of their language, whether by the likes of Columbus who view their languages as incomprehensible or by the suppression of Indigenous languages and ways of knowing. This last objective was one of the many consequences of residential school systems across the Americas. Indigenous youngsters were punished for speaking in their community's tongue rather than in the settler-colonial one; they were placed in situations where they studied alongside youth from other tribes, making the *lingua franca* of the classroom the colonial one of the region.[5] Indigenous people's knowledge becomes transubstantiated through the colonizer's language, either when settler-colonizers write about Indigenous peoples and become authorities on their history, or when Indigenous peoples express themselves in colonial languages.[6] This situation problematizes textuality as an instrument of colonization. Put another way, the Indigenous use of settler-colonial languages, including English, French, Portuguese, and Spanish, ensures that they transact their knowledge in terms that non-Indigenous people understand, which makes their knowledge obtainable and consumable by these sometimes-unintended audiences. Many scholars dismiss oral history and forms of literature as being corrupted by the passage of time and less reliable than sources that exist in textual form, the former characterized as unstable and the latter as dependable. Ironically, other scholars dismiss sources by Indigenous authors in colonial languages or that use western textual genres as inauthentic texts precisely because they are not Indigenous forms of storytelling. From more than one direction, Indigenous expression has been and continues to be devalued, qualified, and defined by non-Indigenous peoples who constantly interrogate who is Indigenous, how their work reflects ideals of western literature and sources for history, and what comprises an authoritative source of information.[7] On the subject of authority, and unlike in settler-colonial works in which information is authored and authorship is ascribed or claimed, Indigenous stories are often communal and in this way communitarian; for this reason, they are sometimes viewed as less authoritative because they can lack any one creator or author and exist as more than one version.

Further complicating this verbal framework is the western relationship between orality and textuality. Print during the early-modern period resulted in the petrification of previously orated information, such as sermons and theatrical works, which in turn led to the devaluation of the oral and the visual within western culture. Documenting oral information, whether with scribal recordings of Inquisition interviews with witnesses or parliamentary Hansard, meant that the text was appraised as an authority of information originally in oral form.[8] Such a view is echoed in the cultural importance given to key religious texts, such as the bible and the koran, in which God's words were almost always delivered through the pen of a man. Both Christianity and Islam view these books as inalienable and endowed with power; translating these works has aroused concerns about maintaining the legitimacy of God's words. Verbal culture became the vehicle for this knowledge and is what gives some religions their shape, rationale, and authority. And in the case of Spanish towns and cities during the colonial period, scholars have crafted the term lettered cities to describe the degree to which those cities were shaped by verbal culture and administrated through the written word.[9] Verbal culture also impacted Indigenous literacy and ways of knowing within the context of colonial authority and the city in ways that gave rise to expressions such as *el papelito manda* (the paper commands).[10] Moreover, literature of all genres includes speech, whether in the form of dialog and quotations or as a one-sided, monologed statement on the part of an interviewee. These forms of re-verbalizing oral speech also point to the fact that print, whether handwritten or published, almost always has a patron who commissions, makes money from, supports the creation of, or even publishes, the text. Contracts commissioning authors, invoices for printing materials, and other forms of text document the creation of textual works.[11] In scholarship, the notion of patronage grows complex when nation-states fund publications, sometimes with the requirement that they are peer reviewed, which involves another layer of authority in the process of creating printed works, especially through the bibliographic apparatus that lends legitimacy to works of scholarship by citing the research of other authorities. Thus, print is political, and it is also gendered, which is why the western literary canon and historical forms of scholarship are nearly entirely composed by men.

Yet, western orality continues despite the dominance of textuality. The seventeenth- and eighteenth-century textual recording of oral gestures using italics for words that the European speaker emphasized is one way through which orality continued alongside and within textual culture. This practice nonetheless demonstrates how verbal expression remains dominated by textuality and, when viewed in light of contemporary writing practices, particularly in scholarly contexts, these gestures are less welcome in peer-reviewed publications, which are also moving away from conference proceedings recording a meeting's activities.[12] Orality within western culture nonetheless points to authority in various ways: medieval *juglares* sang the most recent news as well as popular folklore; communities gathered in churches to listen to sermons meant to influence their worldviews and lives; and scholars convened for lectures delivered by masters in their fields. Literacy and the reformation of Christianity in Europe reduced the reliance upon oral expression as a source of authoritative information, but nonetheless venues beyond churches and universities where individuals could gather to listen, whether in the theater or via the television, continue to exist. Oral sources of information, often from non-white populations and people who were impoverished or disadvantaged in some way, including women, became increasingly valued by western scholars in the latter third of the twentieth century.[13] While oral history has been recognized as a valuable source of knowledge in some fields, in others—such as environmental studies—this realization is only happening in the twenty-first century. In one environmental scientist's view, oral history brings to her discipline different types of information and critical approaches; it allows her to incorporate environmental knowledge from outside of the western world.[14] This observation emphasizes the reality that textual expression remains a privileged domain and suggests that oral sources often come from less privileged parts of the world.

What this brief treatment of orality and textuality has exposed is that, in western culture, verbality brings with it the entrapments of colonialism, gender and racial inequity, and hierarchies of power. Incan chronicler Felipe Guamán Poma de Ayala (1534–1615), born in post-invasion Peru (known to him as Tawantinsuyo, which in Quechua means the four regions or divisions), understood the power of writing. He endeavored to serve as a translator between his people and the Spanish who had imposed themselves upon the region.[15] Guamán Poma harnessed text in order to craft a message for Philip III (1578–1621) in Spain because he believed that the king did not know about the violence and losses experienced by the Incan people. This was the purpose of his *Primer nueva corónica y buen gobierno* (First New Chronicle and Good Government, c. 1615), which not only remained unpublished but also undelivered to the king, as its author had desired to deliver it in person. Organized along the lines of a medieval Spanish chronicle, it is structured in a way that provides a history of the Incan people and their governance models, a history of Christianity, and a history of Incan-Spanish contact, all told through Incan eyes by appropriating a European language and genre of document. One quarter of its 1,200 pages contains illustrations that enable us to understand Guamán Poma's experiences in ways that are not confined by verbal culture, and this content deviates from traditional chronicles produced in Spain, which were not commonly illustrated.

Like others before and after him, Guamán Poma illustrated his concerns while making use of his linguistic prowess and asserting his own agency as a person knowledgeable of more than one culture and worldview. As a cultural intermediary, Guamán Poma shared his experiences and knowledge while ensuring that they were accessible to his target readership by preparing his work in the colonial language, while nonetheless employing and defining terms in Quechua and other Indigenous languages. By including an extensive illustrated component, moreover, the author provides Indigenous ways of viewing colonial Peru that are not necessarily available in the textual component. The allegorical representation of the six most feared animals within his people's lands exposes the typologies of European that Guamán Poma viewed as most destructive to his people (Figure 10.1).[16] The allegory represents the Andean concept of perpetual incarceration, *sankhu*, by surrounding a pleading Incan with the *corregidor* (Spanish colonial administrator), as the serpent; the *comendero* (Spanish plantation or labor manager), as the lion; the *cacique principal* (appointed Indigenous authority who imposed Spanish rule over an Indigenous community) as the rat; the Spanish traveler or inhabitant as the tiger; the missionary as the fox; and the *escribano* (scribe) as the cat. He explains that the scribe is feared because "the cat is a hunter that stalks and pushes and catches his prey and he doesn't let the rat get away. That's how he stalks the lands of the poor Indians until he catches them, too;" Guamán Poma views these Spanish interlocuters as criminals who are "mortal enemies of this kingdom."[17] In the section of his chronicle about Incan history, he relates that these wild animals were considered by some to be idols and worshiped for no other reason than to entice them to no longer kill Incans.[18] Additional context not provided by Guamán Poma illuminates the figural incarceration of the author and his people. Animals such as these ones were placed in an enclosure, *samka* (house or building), along with criminals, which was conceived as a place of perpetual incarceration that Guamán Poma and his contemporaries aligned with the Christian concept of hell.[19] The illustration depicts the Incas living within *sankhu* and pursued by Spaniards in ways that the text does not explore, while it also problematizes the written record as responsible for the violence experienced by his people. The pen of the scribe transubstantiated possibility into reality in ways that dispossessed Guamán Poma of

Figure 10.1 Allegory of an Incan surrounded by the animals that he most feared, from Felipe Guamán Poma de Ayala, *Nueva corónica y buen gobierno*, c. 1615. Copenhagen, Det Kongelige Bibliotek, GKS 2232 4°, p. 708.

his lands and titles. Importantly, Guamán Poma shares with his Spanish reader Incan ways of structuring and knowing his world in a format that his intended reader could understand, although it seems unlikely that the Spanish king would have detected the Andean concept of perpetual incarceration.

Guamán Poma's text exposes a problem facing scholars with respect to syncretic storytelling through which Indigenous stories and concepts become entangled with European ones, resulting in a colonized story through which perceptions and myths generated by Europeans make their way into Indigenous accounts. Scholars later assess this Indigenous knowledge as unauthoritative and corrupt rather than dismiss the Euro-settler components of the story as inaccurate. Disarming Indigenous writers of their textually expressed authority and knowledge ensures that settler-colonial scholars perpetuate the predominance of western epistemology in lands and about peoples who are not western. There is value in studying colonized information to understand how the colonized exert agency and deviate from the textually expressed record in meaningful ways; narrativizing the invasion of the Americas through the perspective and experiences of Indigenous people will transform our way of knowing the early-modern Atlantic world.[20] As Jo-Ann Episkenew concludes, "By studying an image of the colonized that the colonized, themselves, have created, settlers learn that the national collective myth of their country, and by extension its societal foundation, is flawed and that its prosperity is built upon the suffering of others."[21] One example of this practice comes from the apotheosis myth believed across the western world in which Indigenous peoples viewed the Spanish as their gods returning to their ancestral homeland in Mexico. This belief, and others that maintain Indigenous peoples as weak and dispossessed of their lands and cultures by Spanish strength and brutality, was machined by Spanish colonizers and later by the Black Legend.[22] The *leyenda negra* comprised an anti-Spanish propaganda campaign critical of Spanish culture, Catholicism, and international activities; it circulated throughout Europe in the early-modern period in text and image and has greatly infected scholarship about this period of Atlantic history. British and North American scholars in particular sustained the image of the degraded Native American as a means of criticizing Spanish activities by perpetuating their seeming superiority over Indigenous peoples through the architecture of colonization. Indigenous weakness became emblematic of Spanish domination in ways that excluded the possibility that native peoples were strong, knowledgeable, and capable; this perception extends to the preservation of knowledge and the historical record.[23] While the Spanish missionary and historian of New Spain (Mexico), Toribio de Benavente Motolinía (c. 1482–1569), appears to be among the first scholars to claim that the Spanish were viewed as gods in Mexico, which he does likely for syncretic purposes that enabled the project of conversion, for non-Spanish scholars the claim fits into the wider framework of the Black Legend and is intended to other Spaniards.[24]

Many illustrations originating from Indigenous sources in sixteenth-century Mexico were created decades after Tenochtitlan fell in 1521 and, while valuable for understanding the Native-American perception of the newcomers, they are sometimes undergirded by legends generated and embraced by Europeans. The Florentine Codex was compiled during the latter half of the sixteenth century by Franciscan Bernardino de Sahagún (1499–1590) in conjunction with Indigenous artists who studied at the school run by the Franciscan missionary; this work was one of the first to develop the apotheosis myth under the guise of Indigenous authorship. These artists prepared illustrations and provided sometimes revisionist or otherwise Sahagún's own historical information about their peoples, often in Nahuatl.[25] The memory of Indigenous artists for years had been impacted by the administration and installation of European educational institutions.[26] Camilla Townsend speculates that "The children of the Aztec elites—who were those the Spanish taught to write—probably wanted to come up with a reasonable explanation as to why their previously awe-inspiring fathers and uncles had been so roundly defeated."[27] The apotheosis myth served that end. Perhaps not surprising is another historian's claim that Indigenous peoples elsewhere, for instance in Peru, also viewed the Spanish as gods, and we have already seen this relationship tangentially expressed by Guamán Poma.[28]

It cannot be presumed that representations of intercultural contact crafted later in the sixteenth century reflected Indigenous lived experience or their perspective of the events relating to the Spanish arrival to and dispersal throughout Mexico and later Peru, even when those sources are written in Nahuatl and Quechua. The authority of the text remains at the crux of how scholars choose to value Indigenous knowledge, and in many ways, colonized stories such as the apotheosis myth arise out of text in ways not experienced in the visual and material realms. Certainly, had the Aztec god Quetzalcoatl been returning to his ancestral lands, the illustrators of both Moctezuma Xocoyotzin (1466–1520), who will be explored in due course, and those from Sahagún's school, would have characterized him using the feather (*quetzal*) and serpent (*coatl*) that iconize this god in Aztec visual culture, pre- and post-invasion. Rather, neither group of artists appears to question the humanity of the Spaniards who arrived on their shores; in the codices, Spaniards are not depicted with Quetzalcoatl's iconography upon arriving to Mexico, and the god is visualized traditionally in several other places within these chronicles.[29] It is, after all, in western culture that humans can become gods, as exemplified by Christ, whereas in many Indigenous cultures, gods are anthropomorphized flora, fauna, and geographic features capable of human-like agency.[30] Indigenous cultures often invest agency and life into flora, fauna, and objects that Europeans and settlers view as inanimate, a practice demonstrated by the belief that letters could speak to and interact with humans.[31]

Textual sources used as primary sources have perpetuated the colonized version of the first encounter between Cortés and Moctezuma's people, whereas the visually related narrative generated by Indigenous artists contains no mention of the apotheosis myth. Spanish interest in Indigenous print and visual culture resulted in the creation of a cohort of chronicle-like codices that weaved together both European and Indigenous versions of these first encounters. Many codices incorporated traditional visual material in synthetic ways; they extracted pre-conquest glyphs and situated them on blank pages, inserting them into European-style illustrations, as opposed to the complex documents containing interconnecting and dynamic glyphs from earlier in the century, and they filled the remainder of the page with text relating the episode of history depicted in the image.[32] The effect of this transposition is one of simplifying Indigenous visual discourse, making it seem inanimate, stark, and alien, while restructuring Indigenous knowledge so that it is expressed using the western chronicle genre. In tandem, native artists acquired European skillsets that allowed for the representation of three-dimensional objects on the printed page, a practice not seen before the Spanish invasion in Indigenous illustration practices. Their mastery of three-dimensional and traditional western modes of representation, including writing, at first accentuates the primitive skein attributed by Europeans to their work and to them as a people.[33] At the same time, however, this visual material gives agency to Indigenous artists who, despite supporting a colonized story in textual form, share in visual form their perception of Spaniards much in the same way that Guamán Poma would a few decades later.

Having questioned the validity of the apotheosis myth and its presence in textual but not visual culture, we must revisit this moment of intercultural encounter by considering the earliest exchanges between Europeans and Indigenous peoples in Mexico. The Durán Codex exemplifies a transformation of the Indigenous narrative later in the sixteenth century while also demonstrating the authority that the native peoples of New Spain invested in visual sources of information, which underlines the cultural complexity of this form of paratextual material. The codex was curated by Diego Durán (1537–c. 1588), yet much of its content comes from unnamed Indigenous informants who had been educated at Durán's school.[34] As Guamán Poma did in his chronicle, this illustrated book purports to provide the story of Indigenous contact with Spaniards, in this case Hernán Cortés (1485–1547), from a non-European perspective.[35] For example, after sighting Cortés's ships approaching the shore in 1519, Aztec ruler Moctezuma was told that an *altepetl* (hill of water) had appeared in the water off the coast.[36] Altepetls, not unlike the gothic church topped with a cross in the European cartographical tradition, visually symbolized the location of a settlement in pre-Hispanic

Mexican visual culture, which tended to be founded on hills if at all possible and assigned a tutelar god who was commemorated or worshiped on a neighboring hill; this practice continued in Indigenous visual culture well into the seventeenth century and was usually visualized with a hill, although the Durán codex contains other visualizations that include a castle.[37] Altepetls as socio-political entities were believed to contain wealth and nourishment for inhabitants, and by the second half of the sixteenth century, the term had become synonymous with the Spanish term *ciudad* (city). Earlier in the Durán Codex, the authors detail the foundation myth of the Mexica people, who were told by Huitzilopochtli (god of war and the sun, which shares a relationship with corn as the substance of life) to go to the lake where the eagle perches upon a cactus while devouring a snake; this would be their promised land where the Mexica flourished and built what became their capital city.[38] An illustration accompanies the textually related myth and relies upon western representations of humans codified nonetheless with ideograms that narrate the myth—including the lake from which sprouts a cactus, upon which rests the eagle with the snake ensnared in his beak. These characteristics for the foundational settlement inform their conceptualization of the city as a "floating house," and real cities—Tlatelolco and Tenochtitlan—emerged from the water. When the Spaniards invaded Mexico, the population believed that Aztlan, an ancestral city legended to contain incredible wealth located in a hitherto unknown place, existed and had launched expeditions to locate it; some scholars have argued that the appearance of the Spanish may have at first have given the Aztec ruler pause to consider whether Aztlan had appeared.[39] As James Lockhart has shown, altepetls each contained "radically separate people," which helps us understand how the Spanish were viewed when they arrived.[40] Ascribing this concept to a Spanish boat reminds us of how large the ships seemed and, due to their size, the brimming possibility appraised by Moctezuma about the wealth contained within those ships. Following in the footsteps of his father, Moctezuma I (c. 1398–1469), who had also breeched an altepetl located within a lake thought to contain ancestral wealth, the younger ruler ordered a painting to be prepared of the newcomers so that he may know them and the secret behind any wealth that they might possess.[41] Moctezuma saw not wonder, but rather opportunity.

The text ekphrastically describes the painting produced by the old artisan called upon to complete this task, and through this process, emphasizes the essentialized differences exhibited by the Spanish in the eyes of the Indigenous artist and author: "The painter painted the ship as he had seen it, and next to it he painted the Spanish with their long beards and their white faces and their bodies covered with different colors, and with their hats on their heads, capes, and belted swords."[42] Moctezuma summoned more artists from the region, one of whom described the Spanish boat as a house (*calli* in Nahuatl) where "they eat and sleep, and they cook food on their backs, and in them they walk and play as if on land [. . .] they are bearded and white men dressed in different colors and on their heads they wear round coverings [. . .] and they have deer-like beasts with them."[43] The author also records Moctezuma's positive response to the painting, claiming that Moctezuma, whose empire included many altepetls, admired the one that had appeared off the coast and wanted to gain access to it.[44] It also bears noting that Moctezuma and his contemporaries used color in material ways tied to the world around them and that influenced their worldview. Many white things, for example, linguistically developed into words relating to the culturally centralizing substance of corn (*textli*) and bone (*omitl*). The Aztecs honored their captives by painting their bodies white prior to exposing them to sacrificial rituals to the god Huitzilopochtli, prompting us to imagine how the appearance of white bodies may have been appraised by the ruler.[45] Certainly, Moctezuma viewed the newcomers and their altepetl as an opportunity for profit. Cortés established their interest in European textiles and quickly set about using these items in trade and as remuneration for cooperation. He had demonstrated his prowess in this regard in Cuba prior to coming to Mexico. While pre-invasion Mexico had well-established trade and tribute networks, the Aztec ruler instead used gift-giving to develop relationships, a traditional practice exercised throughout this part of the world; he also would have heard about European people-to-people relationships through his networks, which radiated throughout the Americas. Moctezuma, like other Indigenous leaders elsewhere, already knew what the European visitors desired. He sent Cortés jewelry, gold, precious stones, and cotton textiles that were subsequently sent to Spain.[46]

These exchanges documented within the chronicles, codices, and scholarship from and about this period tend to be characterized as either trade or gift exchanges; rarely is any critical attention given over to the material significance of these textually related exchange practices and how material culture can provide insight into Indigenous experiences. Moctezuma's gifts tend to iconize what westerners envision when the subject of wealth stolen by Spaniards from Mexico arises, and as objects of exchange, their material value should be appraised from more than one cultural perspective. By studying material objects and understanding the cultural significance of them in both Indigenous and European contexts, we can make use of European documentation practices in new ways that allow us to learn about Indigenous experiences. A material history of Cortés's mixed-blood son's experiences in Spain—and in this chapter, we are only scratching the surface of what is a complex undertaking—allows us to understand his lived experience in a foreign land in the absence of visual and textual sources of information created by him.

When Cortés sent jewels to Spain from Mexico in 1528 along with his mixed-blood son, Martín Cortés, we should not envision unpolished rocks but rather sophisticated pieces of art by Indigenous creators, some of whom used their craft to make European objects such as rosaries.[47] The textually cataloged inventory of these objects in both archival and published historical documents gives us pause to consider how material culture can inform us about Martín Cortés's reception in Spain. Accompanying Martín Cortés to court were jewels that were cataloged by the king's treasurer, Diego de la Haya, which include stones worked into animal figures; a gold chain with the face of a Huasteca, a shrimp, and two owl heads; a golden rosary; a golden scorpion-like lizard with a green insert; an eagle; and figurines of a tiger, a shrimp, and some owl heads.[48] The scorpion-like lizard would have been viewed by Martín's Nahua mother as a signifier of sexuality; they believed that the fertility goddess Xochiquetzal (flower-feather) protected them against scorpion stings. When one suffered a sting, the curer in the guise of Xochiquetzal would simulate sexual intercourse with the victim as a means of fighting against the scorpion's poison with her curative powers.[49] Martín would also have known the context for this golden lizard's creation from his father's perspective: this *alarcón* was created in Mexico to tell the story about how Cortés survived a scorpion sting; he had this piece created with a container inside for the body of the scorpion-like lizard that had attacked him. He offered the golden lizard to Nuestra Señora de Guadalupe at her shrine in Extremadura, Spain, as an acknowledgment of her protection over him.[50]

Martín wore, displayed, and distributed these items to residents and visitors of court, which materially confirmed his own exoticness in the eyes of those present; he interacted with the flora and fauna that his father had brought to court. Archival documentation detailing the materiality of Martín's trip also illuminates his quality of life. Joined by several Nahua noblemen and an Otomí nobleman, when Martín arrived in Spain in 1528, the group was sent to live at the Monastery of San Francisco in Madrid (now the royal basilica) before settling shortly thereafter at the court of Charles V (1500–1558) in Toledo, where he remained for several years. While at court, the people who collaborated with Cortés in his invasion of the Aztec empire, the Tlaxcalans, negotiated privileges for their own towns in New Spain as well as individual privileges in the form of titles and properties; Martín rubbed shoulders with the nation who helped the Spaniards invade his mother's people.[51] Recent arrivals at court included peoples from other parts of the Americas, including some Tupi, and this synthetic admixture of American indigeneity was replicated in the courts of other European monarchs where those in attendance could view, appraise, and interact with an array of objects and peoples originating from the Americas. Collected at court thusly, the monarch employed his acquisitive gaze with respect to these individuals and the flora, fauna, and objects that arrived with them as projections of the territories newly incorporated into his empire.

Cortés, himself of low-noble birth and unaccustomed to the gallantries of the court, accompanied this retinue along their journey and presented them and Mexico's wealth at court in what has been characterized as a pageant that attracted the gaze of the nation. Illustrations of Martín's retinue performing for the king were executed in 1528 by a German artist.[52] These illustrations demonstrate how some of the aforementioned objects sent by Cortés to accompany his entry into court were worn by his Indigenous companions as regalia. Charles V provisioned each of them with a salary as well as goods that ensured their comfort while in Toledo, including new clothing on a regular basis. The Casa de la Contratación in 1529 procured blue velvet for sleeveless coats and caps, and by some estimates the party's first year in Spain cost the crown as much as 408,013 maravedis, much of which came from the revenues generated from slave licenses paid to the crown.[53] To contextualize that amount, five sets of black breeches for this group cost 2,040 maravedis.[54] Velvet, moreover, was valued by Spanish contemporaries as a luxurious fabric and the color blue was popular at court during Martín Cortés's time in Spain, thus suggesting that Martín and his Indigenous companions dressed in fashionable attire.[55] Charles V also provided 4 ducats to cover the costs of medical care for one of the men's wives and furnished the husband with an annual salary of 25,000 maravedis to cover the cost of food for each year that he was in the country, and the king also paid for their travel to and from Seville, and the return trip to New Spain.[56] This insight into the king's treatment of a member of Martín's party allows us to imagine the man's experience while at court.

Cortés also worried about his son's welfare in his correspondence with his cousin, Francisco Núñez, who attended to Cortés's affairs on the peninsula. In 1530, Martín had secured a tutor, who provided him with a Spanish education, and he had entered the service of the prince.[57] Cortés sent 400 ducats for Martín's living costs while at court where his father believed his son was developing important relationships that could benefit both his son and the family. None of Cortés's other sons borne to European women were afforded the opportunity to be at court and Martín, and by extension his father, could capitalize on the son's exotic ethnicity as a prominent mixed-blood youth early in Mexico-Spanish intercultural relations.[58] To wax Martín's entry into court life, Cortés also sent, in addition to the funds, a gold chain and 33 silver marks with which to commission silver pieces encrusted with jewels for Martín's house and to give as gifts at court.[59] In this respect, Cortés sheds some light on how he believed his son was received and viewed in Spain as not only a young man, and thus inexperienced in society and at court, but also as a cultural outsider who required advising about protocols and mores.

Martín Cortés, as an intermediary between two cultures, had at his disposal two ways of looking at gift-giving as a means of accomplishing his objectives. The provision of gifts within the European world dovetails with gift-giving practices within many Indigenous cultures of the Americas, yet with some differences. In the Aztec world, gift-giving allowed the giver to grow in consequence when the receiver was unable to reciprocate with a gift of similar or greater value.[60] There is no record of Charles V reciprocating any of these gifts, although Martín may have viewed Charles V's patronage of him as a form of reciprocal gift. Indigenous leaders repeatedly noted the poor gifts they received from Europeans in the Americas compared to the highly valued gifts that they extended to the newcomers; they looked down upon Europeans for being unable or unwilling to reciprocate.[61] In the European world, however, gifts transitioned into valued possessions to be displayed, a practice that extended as well to people; in this sense, Charles V possessed part of Mexico and the presence of Martín affirmed this possession.[62]

Like Martín Cortés, the Mexican codex artist-authors and Guamán Poma also played the role of cultural intermediary that was often exercised by nonwhite individuals, as opposed to the clergy who acquired Indigenous languages in order to spread Christianity. Language acquisition and multilingualism characterize this period of Spanish imperialism and, beyond Spanish, Indigenous languages remained a lingua franca that allowed individuals from different backgrounds to communicate while working in a mine or on a plantation. As Robert C. Schwaller has shown, mixed-blood peoples and particularly mestizos and mulattos played a fundamental role as cultural bridges between peoples. Their understanding of how concepts would be manifested in more than one cultural context allowed them to create synchronicities that enabled the sharing of knowledge and understandings across cultures.[63]

Guamán Poma, like his Mexican counterparts, presses the advantage of possessing Spanish to engage directly with a claim made by most Spanish chroniclers about the first meetings between peoples who did not share a common language. He dismisses the possibility that his people viewed the Spanish as gods, which allows us to understand his allegory of Incan gods and perpetual incarceration in this context; he also takes advantage of the reality that without a common language they were left to exchanges comprised of signs and gestures. Guamán Poma depicts the first meeting between an ancestor of his, Incan ruler Huayna Capac (from the Quechua name *Wayna Qhapaq*, young king) Inga (c. 1467–c. 1527), and Greek artillery captain Pedro de Gandía (1494–1542), who Guamán Poma characterizes as "Columbus's associate" (Figure 10.2). News of the Europeans' arrival had come as early as 1526 after Francisco Pizarro (1478–1541) and company arrived. Guamán Poma also pauses to comment, perhaps comically, on how the name Indias descended not from his own people but from the fact that these lands were discovered during the day (*en días*, Indias).[64] In the illustration of the encounter, Guamán Poma shows the Incan enthroned, as opposed to the Spaniard who kneels. The former extends a bowl to the Spaniard who then claims that "We eat this gold."

Figure 10.2 The Inka asks what the Spaniard eats, "Cay coritacho micunqui [?]" and he replies "Gold." From Felipe Guamán Poma de Ayala, Nueva corónica y buen gobierno, 1615. Copenhagen, Det Kongelige Bibliotek, GKS 2232 4°, p. 371.

The textual description depicts the leader speaking Quechua, the traditional language of Cusco, transliterated into Roman characters, whereas the Greek soldier responds in Spanish. Guamán Poma therefore synthesizes the linguistic issues inherent to the intercultural encounter experienced from both cultural perspectives. In reality, they communicated via hand gestures, and this is described by the author on the following page, but here the claim that Spaniards eat gold is meant to other and render Europeans monstrous, and to take advantage of a language barrier to depict a European exhibiting his gluttonous greed. The illustration examples the unidirectional nature of gift-giving as well, which from an Indigenous perspective increases the power and authority of the Incan leader. Also notable is that the term *español* to represent the Greek invader is used by Guamán Poma as a homogenous term for all European invaders. This illustration populates a list of Incan- and European-produced objects with which viewers may be familiar, including the regalia worn by the Inca, which along with the furniture and vessels help to characterize him as the king, as well as an ideographic expression of his people's visualization of him located above the man's head. Guamán Poma informs the reader, for instance, that the ruler's cape is blue, and in this way his record exceeds the limitations of the visual form, which remains uncolored.[65] The detail spreading across the chest of his tunic is green and orange, and below this area the tunic has a blue and white checkered pattern, and four tassels tie each of his sandals onto his feet; around his head, he wears the sign of the Incan empire, called the *mascapaicha* (from the Quechua terms *mask'ay*, to seek, and *pacha*, time and earth), which consists of several cords wrapped in the style of a crown around the head.[66]

These details about the Incan leader's regalia come to the author from traditional sources. From a material perspective, Guamán Poma's pre-contact history of his people was based, he tells us, upon quipu reading. He points to pre-textual sources as a way of legitimizing the information shared in his chronicle as "unwritten histories, nothing more than quipus and memories and stories from ancient Indian men and women, wise witnesses of their time."[67] He adds that his sources originate from many languages, including Spanish, Quechua, and Aymara, among others. Guamán Poma at once appropriates a European genre of text while basing his chronicle upon a preexisting Andean genre of material record in ways that both Indigenous and western individuals would find familiar. We can be certain that he had exposure to European-style chronicles because he worked on and provided illustrations for a Spanish-authored chronicle in the late sixteenth century. It was his disagreement over how Martín de Murúa (1525–1618) represented his people that gave rise to Guamán Poma initiating his own chronicle.[68] Like the Mexican codices, his chronicle comprises a hybrid document composed of material, visual, and verbal (both oral and textual) ways of knowing from both the Indigenous and European worlds.

Being a cultural intermediary, however, did not signify that mixed-blood people could evade trouble with Spanish authorities, and one particularly interesting example involving a mestizo man highlights an increasing tension between visual and verbal culture of this period. The mixed-blood Juan Luis (Otomí?-Spaniard) claimed during his 1601 Inquisition trial for sorcery that the tattoo on his arm did not portray an owl, as he had first asserted; rather, he argued that the tattoo represented Jesus and thus comprised a Christian portrait. He tried to hide his Indigenous knowledge and practices with the guise of Christianity while hoping that his interrogators would not possess the visual literacy required to recognize the non-Christian meaning of his tattoo. In fact, the entire codices project developed around the need, on the part of missionaries, to understand Indigenous ideographic expressions that did not conform to Christianity; they were created as bi-modal, interpretive tools.[69] The owl in Indigenous Mexico forewarned impending death and might fetch a person's soul away from the gods, and thus the owl is associated with witchcraft and death.[70] After being further pressed, the mestizo man admitted to having Mantelillos (the devil) on his forearm.[71] Mantelillos, he explained, served Lucifer and had two heads—the front head looked like a man with a dark red beard (*barbas bermejas*) and the rear head was a ball of fire with horns and claws for feet; missionaries had linked Tlacatecólotl (the man-owl and bringer of death) to demons and the devil, which is how these concepts became syncretically related.[72] The Nahua looked to this god's wisdom and sorcery to solve problems, provide cures, and answer prayers. Despite the tattoo's post-invasion connection with European visualizations of the devil, the mestizo claimed that Indigenous informants had shown him the power of Mantelillos and provided him with the tattoo because in the post-invasion Spanish Americas, Indigenous gods had become categorized by Spaniards as devils; thus, so-called devils were considered helpful when one found themselves in difficult situations, which was his way of acknowledging the continued observance of Indigenous deities.[73] The presence of the tattoo also recalls the Christian belief that devil-worshipers' bodies would be marked in some way.

Tattooed images such as this one demonstrate how visual sources of information are discredited or made illegitimate, particularly when their meanings remain unknown to western peoples. In contrast, when golden and jewel-encrusted figurines of owls arrived at court along with Martín Cortés, their ceremonial and spiritual purposes did not concern the king and his companions; rather, they transformed into objects to be displayed. Tattoos became a way of telling stories and knowing a people's past within Indigenous North America, but as a practice, tattooing was increasingly not welcome throughout the colonial Americas.[74] As C. Stephen Jaeger documents, throughout European colonized space, settler-colonists repeatedly attempt to read tattoos and to subject them to their discerning gaze as legible, consumable objects. Increasingly, images such as tattoos could no longer exist in the visual realm alone; rather, a verbalized story had to be extracted from them in some way. As Jaeger observers, "Tribal wisdom is recorded on the most precious mediums available: the chieftain's flesh," which underlines the significant difference in values between western and non-western peoples and their epistemological practices, such that we cannot "Imagine Americans demanding that the Constitution, Bill of Rights, and Gettysburg Address be carved onto the body of the president because mere paper and ink are cheap and contemptible."[75] By regulating the bodies of Indigenous peoples through the prohibition of tattoos, visual modes of expression become silenced while their bearers are forced to make these images legible to western eyes.

Another consideration that must be explored further is how visual and material cultures give scholars new ways to access women's voices and their experiences. As Laura L. Peers and Carolyn Podruchny note with respect to Indigenous people, rarely do historians use material culture as a source of knowledge for their scholarship. As we have demonstrated in this chapter, material culture provides scholars with new inroads into the geographic, temporal, and thematic scope of their existing research program and inspires new questions about objects: who created them, how were they used and valued, what techniques and skills were required to produce them, and how they change over time and across cultural lines.[76] As we saw with respect to Martín Cortés, the consideration of material life, even when basing this research on the written record's description of materiality, gives scholars the opportunity to understand the lives of individuals who left no written record or memoire. This practice easily extends to women, whose voices are rarely recorded in the early-modern Atlantic world. A material reading of women's lives can demonstrate that they were authoritative over and agents of wealth, a conclusion usually unavailable in verbal culture.[77]

Whenever possible this chapter has taken a two-eyed seeing approach, as articulated by Albert Marshall and later developed within many disciplinary contexts, to viewing the early-modern Atlantic world.[78] By performing scholarly inquiry through the lens of both Indigenous and non-Indigenous perspectives, we encourage non-western knowledge and ways of knowing to inform our scholarship. Works that attempt to provide non-European perspectives on the invasion and colonization of Mexico and Peru by Spaniards are not mainstream sources compared to the chronicles prepared and published by Spaniards, some of whom had never been to the Americas. Accounts by the likes of Columbus and Cortés continue to be relied upon by scholars as sources of authority whereas Guamán Poma and the creators of the Mexican codices are much less cited and comparatively few modern critical editions exist of these materials, which went unpublished for centuries. When cited, the visual material is usually unexplored compared to the textual contents of these sources, and as we have demonstrated in this chapter, visual sources created by Indigenous people provide new information often not available in textual form. Unfirsting the early-modern Atlantic world will thus entail reevaluating the quality of our sources and a deliberate re-positioning of Indigenous perspectives at the top of our list of sources. Between the Mexican codices and Guamán Poma's chronicle, we have highlighted ways of seeing the Spanish invasion that elevate the agency and voices of Native-American peoples, particularly those who served some role as a cultural intermediary. This material has also exposed how Indigenous peoples, whether in Mexico or Peru, recognized the impact that western writing was having on their lives and in some cases problematized textual culture. By turning to visual and material sources of knowledge, scholars can unsettle the text as an instrument of colonialism.

Notes

1. Fish, *Is There a Text in this Class*, p. 332.
2. Anderson, *Imagined Communities.*
3. This characterization is common throughout Columbus's work and is reproduced by later authors. See his *Carta a Luis Santangel* (Barcelona: Pedro Posa, 1493). In his diary entry 24 October 1492, the Genovese explorer shares how "por señas que me hizieron todos los indios destas islas y aquellos que llevo yo en los navíos, porque por lengua no los entiendo [all the Indians of these islands and those that I'm bringing in the boats use signs because I do not understand their language];" see Columbus, *Los cuatro viajes*, p. 47. Unless otherwise noted, all translations are my own.
4. Brokaw, "The Poetics of *Khipu* Historiography," p. 112.
5. Gonzalbo Aizpuru, *Historia de la educación en la época colonial.* See the chapters exploring Indigenous education and school environments in Woolford, Benvenuto, and Hinton, eds., *Colonial Genocide in Indigenous North America.* Also see Trafzer, Keller, and Sisquoc, eds., *Boarding School Blues.*
6. Weaver, *That the People Might Live*, p. 13.
7. Ibid., pp. 21–24.
8. Collinson, Hunt, and Walsham, "Religious Publishing in England, 1557–1640," in Barnard and McKenzie, eds., *The Cambridge History of the Book in Britain*, vol. 4, pp. 29–66: 52–53.
9. Rappaport and Cummins, *Beyond the Lettered City.* Also see the chapters devoted to this topic in Beverley, *Subalternity and Representation*; and Campa, *Latin Americanism.*
10. See Niño-Murcia and Salomon, *The Lettered Mountain.* Also see Ong, *Orality and Literacy.*
11. Roland Barthes calls this form of text lexia that inform the creation of a work; see his *S/Z*, pp. 11–12.
12. See Birrell, "Sir Roger L'Estrange: The Journalism of Orality," in Barnard and McKenzie, eds., *The Cambridge History of the Book in Britain*, vol. 4, pp. 657–661.
13. Dougherty, "From Anecdote to Analysis," pp. 712–723.
14. Endres, "Environnemental Oral History," pp. 485–498. Also see Alexander, "Africana Studies and Oral History: A Critical Assessment," in Davidson, ed., *African American Studies*, pp. 171–193; Eynon, "Cast Upon the Shore," pp. 560–570; and Murphy, Pierce, and Ruiz, "What Makes Queer Oral History Different," pp. 1–24.

15. For more on the importance of mixed-blood translators and interpreters, see Puente Luna, "The Many Tongues of the King," pp. 143–170.
16. Guamán Poma de Ayala, *Nueva corónica*, p. 708.
17. Ibid., p. 709.
18. Ibid., p. 270.
19. Husson, "La poesía quechua prehispánica," p. 70. Also see the illustration of this perpetual incarceration within his history of the Incan people in Guamán Poma de Ayala, *Nueva corónica*, p. 304.
20. Tuhiwai Smith, *Decolonizing Methodologies*, pp. 2–3.
21. Episkenew, *Taking Back Our Spirits*, p. 73.
22. See Restall, *Seven Myths*, pp. 108–114.
23. On this topic, see Greer, Mignolo, and Quilligan, eds., *Rereading the Black Legend*, especially the chapter devoted to the Spanish invasion, by Silver-Moon and Michael Ennis, "The View of the Empire from the *Altepetl*: Nahua Historical and Global Imagination," pp. 150–166.
24. Motolinía, *Historia de los indios de la Nueva España*, pp. vi and 143.
25. Titled *La historia universal de las cosas de Nueva España*, it is housed at the Biblioteca Medicea-Laurenziana, Florence, Palat. 218–220.
26. Jackson and Castillo, *The Impact of the Mission System*.
27. Townsend, *Malintzin's Choices*, pp. 45–46.
28. This positioning seems to have arisen first in Cieza de León, *Parte primera de la Chronica del Peru*. An exception among these authors is the mixed-blood Garcilaso de la Vega Inca; see his *Historia general del Peru*, fol. 12v. Also see Restall, *Seven Myths*, pp. 115–116.
29. For more on the relationship between oral and ideographic culture in Mexico, as well as the authority undergirding the composite form of knowledge found in the codices, see Stone, *In Place of Gods and Kings*.
30. Gruzinski, *Man-Gods in the Mexican Highlands*; and Read and González, *Mesoamerican Mythology*.
31. See chapter 4 of this book.
32. Townsend, *Malintzin's Choices*, pp. 63–65.
33. Boone, "Introduction: Writing and Recording Knowledge," in Boone and Mignolo, eds., *Writing without Words*, pp. 3–26; and Brotherston, *Book of the Fourth World*, p. 41.
34. For more on the context of the codex's production, see Paloma Vargas Montes, "The Durán Codex: A Content Analysis," in López de Mariscal, Kabalen de Bichara, and Vargas Montes, eds., *Print Culture through the Ages*, pp. 62–79.
35. Durán, *Historia de las Indias*, fol. 197r.
36. Ibid., fol. 197v. These water hills were also conceived of as "water houses." See Mundy, *Death of Aztec Tenochtitlan*, p. 10.
37. Ramírez Ruiz, "La más alta parte del mundo," p. 20. Also see James Lockhart's chapter on this subject, in *The Nahuas after the Conquest*, pp. 14–58.
38. Durán, *Historia de las Indias*, fol. 14v.
39. Levin Rojo, *Return to Aztlan*, pp. 126–129.
40. Lockhart, *The Nahuas after the Conquest*, p. 15.
41. Durán, *Historia de las Indias*, fol. 200v.
42. Ibid.
43. Ibid., fol. 201r.
44. Ibid., fol. 200v.
45. Dupey García, "The Materiality of Color," pp. 72–88. Whiteness also characterized Aztlan in many of the codices, a connection that requires further investigation; see Herren Rajagopalan, *Portraying the Aztec Past*, p. 107.

46. These items are described in his second letter as well as related documentation, published for the first time by Gayangos, *Cartas y relaciones de Hernán Cortés*, pp. 1–34. The reception of the first shipment sent from the Yucatan to Spain is documented in a letter from the king held at the Archivo General de Indias, Indiferente, 420, fol. 173v–175r.
47. Martínez Martínez, *Hernán Cortés*, p. 230.
48. Archivo General de Indias, Justicia, 1005.
49. Sigal, *The Flower and the Scorpion*, p. 3–7.
50. The creation also involved 43 emeralds and 9 pearls; it now resides at the Instituto de Valencia de Don Juan, Madrid. See Gómez de Orozco, "¿El exvoto de don Hernando Cortés?," p. 52; and Oktavec, *Answered Prayers*, p. 4.
51. Johnson, *Cultural Hierarchy in Sixteenth-Century Europe*, pp. 88–89.
52. Drawings of members of Martín Cortés's retinue—possibly of Martín himself—performing at court can be found in Weiditz, *Trachtenbuch*, fol. 7r. Also see Cline, "Hernando Cortés," pp. 70–90.
53. Cline, "Hernando Cortés," p. 84.
54. Archivo General de Indias, Indiferente, 422, leg. 16, fol. 52v.
55. Context for this popularity can be found in Cox-Rearick, "Power-Dressing at the Courts of Cosimo de Medici and François I," pp. 39–69; and O'Malley, "A Pair of Little Gilded Shoes," pp. 45–83.
56. The definition of these relationships using European terminology associated with Christian marriage is a common practice in this era and we simply may not know if the couples were married or even romantically involved. See Archivo General de Indias, Indiferente, 422, leg. 17, fol. 17; Indiferente, 422, leg. 16, fol. 231 and 267v. Also see Indiferente, 422, leg. 17, fols. 103r and 105v–106r.
57. Archivo Real de la Chancillería de Valladolid, fols. 56v–58r, cited in Martínez Martínez, *Hernán Cortés*, p. 201.
58. Archivo Real de la Chancillería de Valladolid, fols. 27v–30v and Archivo General de Simancas, fols. 11r–12v, cited in Martínez Martínez, *Hernán Cortés*, p. 215.
59. Archivo Real de la Chancillería de Valladolid, fols. 24r–27v, cited in Martínez Martínez, *Hernán Cortés*, p. 212.
60. Weber, *Bárbaros*, pp. 191–192.
61. Frederic Hicks, "Gift and Tribute: Relations of Dependency in Aztec Mexico," in Claessen and van de Velde, eds., *Early State Economics*, pp. 199–213.
62. Findlen, *Possessing Nature*, p. 294.
63. Schwaller, "The Importance of Mestizos and Mulatos," pp. 721–722.
64. Guamán Poma, *Nueva corónica*, p. 370.
65. Ibid., p. 113.
66. Ibid., p. 114. Also see Arnold and Yapita, *The Metamorphosis of Heads*.
67. Guamán Poma, *Nueva corónica*, p. 8.
68. Murúa's chronicle is partly illustrated by Guamán Poma. See Murúa, *Historia general del Piru*.
69. Domínguez Torres, *Military Ethos and Visual Culture*, pp. 48–49.
70. Read and González, *A Guide to the Gods*, p. 165.
71. Baudot, "Sociedad colonial y desviaciones," in Baudot, ed., *Poder y desviaciones*, pp. 63–102: 93.
72. María de Lourdes Somohano Martínez, "La figura del diablo en el imaginario colectivo de la sociedad novohispana," in Jiménez Gómez, ed., *Creencias y prácticas religiosas*, pp. 183–232: 204–205. Also see Schwaller, "The Importance of Mestizos and Mulatos," pp. 728 and 732.

73. Schwaller, "The Importance of Mestizos and Mulatos," p. 730.
74. Deter-Wolf and Díaz-Granados, eds., *Drawing with Great Needles*.
75. Jaeger, *Enchantment*, pp. 52 and 58.
76. Peers and Podruchny, eds., *Gathering Places*, p. 23.
77. Beck, "Women's Power and Material Exchange," pp. 35–55.
78. See, for example, Bartlett, Marshall, and Marshall, "Two-Eyed Seeing and Other Lessons," pp. 331–340.

Bibliography

Anderson, Benedict, *Imagined Communities: Reflections on the Origin and Spread of Nationalism* (London: Verso, 1983).

Archivo General de Indias, Seville: Indiferente, 420, leg. 8; Indiferente, 422, leg. 16 and leg. 17; Justicia, 1005, núm. 2, r. 1.

Archivo General de Simancas, Consejo Real, 588–7.

Archivo Real de la Chancillería de Valladolid, Pleitos civiles, Zarandona y Balboa, Pleitos olvidados, Caja 145–2.

Arnold, Denise Y., and Juan de Dios Yapita, *The Metamorphosis of Heads: Textual Struggles, Education, and Land in the Andes* (Pittsburgh: University of Pittsburgh Press, 2006).

Barnard, John, and D. F. McKenzie, eds., *The Cambridge History of the Book in Britain,* vol. 4: *1557–1695* (Cambridge: Cambridge University Press, 2002).

Barthes, Roland, *S/Z* (Paris: Éditions du Seuil, 1970).

Bartlett, Cheryl, Murdena Marshall, and Albert Marshall, "Two-Eyed Seeing and Other Lessons Learned within a Co-Learning Journey of Bringing Together Indigenous and Mainstream Knowledges and Ways of Knowing," *Journal of Environmental Studies and Sciences* 2.4 (2012), pp. 331–340.

Baudot, Georges, ed., *Poder y desviaciones: Génesis de una sociedad mestiza en Mesoamérica* (Toulouse: Presses Universitaires du Mirail, 1998).

Beck, Lauren, "Women's Power and Material Exchange in Early Modern Transatlantic Spain," *Journal of Women's History* 30.1 (2018), pp. 35–55.

Beverley, John, *Subalternity and Representation: Arguments in Cultural Theory* (Durham, NC: Duke University Press, 1999).

Boone, Elizabeth Hill, and Walter D. Mignolo, eds., *Writing without Words: Alternative Literacies in Mesoamerica & the Andes* (Durham, NC: Duke University Press, 1994).

Brokaw, Galen, "The Poetics of *Khipu* Historiography: Felipe Guaman Poma de Ayala's *Nueva corónica* and the *Relación de los quipucamayos*," *Latin American Research Review* 38.3 (2003), pp. 111–147.

Brotherston, Gordon, *Book of the Fourth World: Reading the Native Americas through Their Literature* (New York: Cambridge University Press, 1992).

Campa, Román de la, *Latin Americanism* (Minneapolis: University of Minnesota Press, 1999).

Cieza de León, Pedro, *Parte primera de la Chronica del Peru* (Antwerp: Casa de Juan Steelsio, 1554).

Claessen, Henri J. M., and Pieter van de Velde, eds., *Early State Economics* (London: Transaction, 1991).

Cline, Howard F., "Hernando Cortés and the Aztec Indians in Spain," *Quarterly Journal of the Library of Congress* 26.2 (1969), pp. 70–90.

Columbus, Christopher, *Carta a Luis Santangel* (Barcelona: Pedro Posa, 1493).
———, *Los cuatro viajes*, ed. Ignacio B. Anzoátegui (Madrid: Espasa-Calpe, 1991).
Cox-Rearick, Janet, "Power-Dressing at the Courts of Cosimo de Medici and François I: The 'moda alla spagnola' of Spanish Consorts Eléonore d'Austriche and Eleonora di Toledo," *Artibus et Historiae* 30.60 (2009), pp. 39–69.
Davidson, Jeanette R., ed., *African American Studies* (Edinburgh: Edinburgh University Press, 2010).
Deter-Wolf, Aaron, and Carol Díaz-Granados, eds., *Drawing with Great Needles: Ancient Tattoo Traditions of North America* (Austin: University of Texas Press, 2013).
Domínguez Torres, Mónica, *Military Ethos and Visual Culture in Post-Conquest Mexico* (Burlington, VT: Ashgate, 2013).
Dougherty, Jack, "From Anecdote to Analysis: Oral Interviews and New Scholarship in Educational History," *Journal of American History* 86.2 (1999), pp. 712–723.
Dupey García, Élodie, "The Materiality of Color in the Body Ornamentation of Aztec Gods," *RES: Anthropology and Aesthetics* 65/66 (2014/2015), pp. 72–88.
Durán, Diego, *Historia de las Indias de Nueva España e islas de la tierra firme*, 1579. Biblioteca Nacional de España, Madrid, Vitr/26/11.
Endres, Danielle, "Environnemental Oral History," *Environnemental Communication* 5.4 (2011), pp. 485–498.
Episkenew, Jo-Ann, *Taking Back Our Spirits: Indigenous Literature, Public Policy, and Healing* (Winnipeg: University of Manitoba Press, 2009).
Eynon, Bret, "Cast Upon the Shore: Oral History and New Scholarship on the Movements of the 1960s," *Journal of American History* 83.2 (1996), pp. 560–570.
Findlen, Paula, *Possessing Nature: Museums, Collecting, and Scientific Culture in Early Modern Italy* (Berkeley: University of California Press, 1994).
Fish, Stanley, *Is There a Text in This Class? The Authority of Interpretive Communities* (Cambridge, MA: Harvard University Press, 1980).
Gayangos, Pascual de, *Cartas y relaciones de Hernán Cortés al emperador Carlos V, colegidas é ilustradas* (Paris: Imprenta Central de los Ferro-Carriles, 1866).
Gómez de Orozco, Federico, "¿El exvoto de don Hernando Cortés?," *Anales del Instituto de Investigaciones Estéticas* 8 (1842), pp. 51–54.
Gonzalbo Aizpuru, Pilar, *Historia de la educación en la época colonial. El mundo indígena* (Mexico City: Colegio de México, Centro de Estudios Históricos, 1990).
Greer, Margaret R., Walter D. Mignolo, and Maureen Quilligan, eds., *Rereading the Black Legend: The Discourses of Religious and Racial Difference in the Renaissance Empires* (Chicago: University of Chicago Press, 2008).
Gruzinski, Serge, *Man-Gods in the Mexican Highlands: Indian Power and Colonial Society, 1520–1800* (Stanford, CA: Stanford University Press, 1989).
Guamán Poma de Ayala, Felipe, *Nueva corónica y buen gobierno*, c. 1615. Det Kongelige Bibliotek, Copenhagen, GKS 2232 4°.
Herren Rajagopalan, Angela, *Portraying the Aztec Past: The Codices Boturini, Azcatitlan, and Aubin* (Austin: University of Texas Press, 2019).
Husson, Jean-Philippe, "La poesía quechua prehispánica: sus reglas, sus categorías, sus temas, a través de los poemas transcritos por Waman Puma de Ayala," *Revista de Crítica Literaria Latinoamericana* 19.37 (1993), pp. 63–85.

Jackson, Robert H., and Edward Castillo, *The Impact of the Mission System on California Indians* (Albuquerque: University of New Mexico Press, 1995).

Jaeger, C. Stephen, *Enchantment: On Charisma and the Sublime in the Arts of the West* (Philadelphia: University of Pennsylvania Press, 2012).

Jiménez Gómez, Juan Ricardo, ed., *Creencias y prácticas religiosas en Querétaro, siglos XVI–XIX* (Querétaro: Universidad Autónoma de Querétaro, 2004).

Johnson, Carina L., *Cultural Hierarchy in Sixteenth-Century Europe: The Ottomans and Mexicans* (Cambridge: Cambridge University Press, 2011).

Levin Rojo, Danna A., *Return to Aztlan: Indians, Spaniards, and the Invention of Nuevo México* (Norman: University of Oklahoma Press, 2014).

Lockhart, James, *The Nahuas after the Conquest: A Social and Cultural History of the Indians of Central Mexico, Sixteenth through Eighteenth Centuries* (Stanford, CA: Stanford University Press, 1992).

López de Mariscal, Blanca, Donna M. Kabalen de Bichara, and Paloma Vargas Montes, eds., *Print Culture through the Ages: Essays on Latin American Book History* (Newcastle upon Tyne: Cambridge Scholars Publishing, 2016).

Martínez Martínez, María del Carmen, *Hernán Cortés: Cartas y memoriales* (León: Junta de Castilla y León, Universidad de León, 2003).

Motolinía, Toribio de Benavente, *Historia de los indios de la Nueva España* (Barcelona: Herederos de Juan Gili, 1914).

Mundy, Barbara E., *The Death of Aztec Tenochtitlan, the Life of Mexico City* (Austin: University of Texas Press, 2015).

Murphy, Kevin P., Jennifer L. Pierce, and Jason Ruiz, "What Makes Queer Oral History Different," *Oral History Review* 43.1 (2016), pp. 1–24.

Murúa, Martín de, *Historia general del Piru*, c. 1583–1616. J. Paul Getty Museum, Los Angeles, Ms. Ludwig XIII 16.

Niño-Murcia, Mercedes, and Frank Salomon, *The Lettered Mountain: A Peruvian Village's Way with Writing* (Durham, NC: Duke University Press, 2011).

Oktavec, Eileen, *Answered Prayers: Miracles and Milagros Along the Border* (Tucson: University of Arizona Press, 1998).

O'Malley, Michelle, "A Pair of Little Gilded Shoes: Commission, Cost, and Meaning of Renaissance Footwear," *Renaissance Quarterly* 63.1 (2010), pp. 45–83.

Ong, Walter J., *Orality and Literacy: The Technologizing of the Word* (New York: Routledge, 1982).

Peers, Laura L., and Carolyn Podruchny, eds., *Gathering Places: Aboriginal and Fur Trade Histories* (Vancouver: UBC Press, 2010).

Puente Luna, José Carlos de la, "The Many Tongues of the King: Indigenous Language Interpreters and the Making of the Spanish Empire," *Colonial Latin American Review* 23.4 (2014), pp. 143–170.

Ramírez Ruiz, Marcelo, "La más alta parte del mundo: señales de la sacralidad hispana en Mesoamérica," *Tzintzun: Revista de Estudios Históricos* 31 (2000), pp. 9–28.

Rappaport, Joanne, and Tom Cummins, *Beyond the Lettered City: Indigenous Literacies in the Andes* (Durham, NC: Duke University Press, 2012).

Read, Kay Almere, and Jason J. González, *A Guide to the Gods, Heroes, Rituals, and Beliefs of Mexico and Central America* (New York: Oxford University Press, 2000).

———, *Mesoamerican Mythology: A Guide to the Gods, Heroes, Rituals, and Beliefs of Mexico and Central America* (New York: Oxford University Press, 2002).

Restall, Matthew, *Seven Myths of the Spanish Conquest* (New York: Oxford University Press, 2003).

Schwaller, Robert C., "The Importance of Mestizos and Mulatos as Bilingual Intermediaries in Sixteenth-Century New Spain," *Ethnohistory* 59.4 (2012), pp. 713–738.

Sigal, Pete, *The Flower and the Scorpion: Sexuality and Ritual in Early Nahua Culture* (Durham, NC: Duke University Press, 2011).

Stone, Cynthia L., *In Place of Gods and Kings: Authorship and Identity in the Relación de Michoacán* (Norman: University of Oklahoma Press, 2004).

Townsend, Camilla, *Malintzin's Choices: An Indian Woman in the Conquest of Mexico* (Albuquerque: University of New Mexico Press, 2006).

Trafzer, Clifford E., Jean A. Keller, and Lorene Sisquoc, eds., *Boarding School Blues: Revisiting American Indian Educational Experiences* (Lincoln: University of Nebraska Press, 2006).

Tuhiwai Smith, Linda, *Decolonizing Methodologies: Research and Indigenous Peoples* (New York: Zed Books, 1999).

Vega, Garcilaso de la, *Historia general del Peru* (Cordoba: Viuda de Andrés Barrera, 1617).

Weaver, Jace, *That the People Might Live: Native American Literatures and Native American Community* (New York: Oxford University Press, 1997).

Weber, David J., *Bárbaros: Spaniards and Their Savages in the Age of Enlightenment* (New Haven, CT: Yale University Press, 2005).

Weiditz, Christoph, *Trachtenbuch*, c. 1530s. Germanisches Nationalmuseum, Nurnberg, Hs 22474.

Woolford, Andrew John, Jeff Benvenuto, and Alexander Laban Hinton, eds., *Colonial Genocide in Indigenous North America* (Durham, NC: Duke University Press, 2014).

11 "This Is an Indigenous City"

Un-Firsting Early Representations of Vancouver

Ashley Caranto Morford

> Our understandings of the city must be truly, honestly, fully Indigenous. And that means the Indigenous people themselves are front and centre, visible, heard, included. No longer written out of the story [. . .] [T]his is an Indigenous City [. . .] Stop saying that the pioneers settled this place [. . .] Start acknowledging that this is an ancient place [. . .] Contrary to the colonial propaganda, this has never been a land free for the taking. The [P]eople are still here.
>
> Kamala Todd (Métis-Cree)[1]

Illuminating the challenge posed to settlers by Kamala Todd, and drawing on the words of Allison Hargreaves, I recognize that I, like many of my readers, am "a perpetual visitor—both to the [Indigenous] literatures I teach, and to the [Indigenous] homelands in which I teach them."[2] Non-Indigenous scholars have the responsibility to engage with and write about Indigenous stories, histories, territories, and knowledge systems in ways that are guided by the principles of respect and restitution, that foreground and actively listen to Indigenous voices and perspectives, and that recognize the inability of settlers to be experts or authorities of Indigenous cultures, histories, knowledges, and experiences.[3] This chapter attempts to un-first how non-Indigenous scholars approach, conceptualize, and discuss early print materials related to the territories colonially known as the city of Vancouver.[4]

Douglas Sanderson (Opaskwayak Cree) has emphasized that, when Europeans began their imperial travels to and colonization of Turtle Island (North America), the territory was a continent of well-established empires, an international and cosmopolitan space made up of a diverse array of Indigenous nations.[5] Relatedly, John Borrows (Anishinaabe) has asserted that Indigenous nations "have laws [. . .] that precede the Crown."[6] For instance, the Haudenosaunee (Iroquois) Confederacy—from which the United States took inspiration for its own, much younger, government—formed its empire and governmental system long before the European arrival to Turtle Island.[7]

Yet, Indigenous civilizations, knowledge systems, legal structures, worldviews, stories, and perspectives remain silenced within mainstream settler society by scholarship, media, and western education. Linda Tuhiwai Smith (Ngati Awa and Ngati Porou) observes that the west is often seen as "the centre of legitimate knowledge, the arbiter of what counts as knowledge and the source of 'civilized' knowledge."[8] The oppressive and pervasive domination of western thought, and the silencing and erasure of Indigenous thought within mainstream spaces, is a result of ongoing settler colonialism and colonization. Colonial powers physically and violently invade space while simultaneously forcing their own worldviews, names, languages, knowledge systems, and cultural and religious beliefs onto and into the lands and waters. This imposition violently normalizes and privileges western systems and naming practices over the existing systems and names of the Indigenous peoples. The most populous city of the colonially known province of British Columbia derives its name from the British colonialist, George Vancouver (1757–1798). This commemorative naming serves as a mechanism of multiple erasures. It obscures the colonial movements and acts of the Spanish colonizer José María Narváez (1768–1840), who sailed throughout and surveyed the territories in 1791 (a year prior to Vancouver) and whose expedition named the lands and waters through a Spanish lens, as indicated in the cartographic documents produced by Juan Carrasco; indeed, Vancouver himself would heavily rely on these cartographic records in his own travels.[9] The place name Vancouver also obfuscates the fact that the city illegally occupies the Coast Salish territories of the Musqueam, Squamish, and Tsleil-Waututh nations. Due to colonial mechanisms of erasure such as these ones, most Vancouverites know the lands and waters of the area through settler-colonial understandings.

Euro-settler material culture has played a key role in perpetuating colonial domination and dispossession, and the critical study of this material from an anti-colonial framework enables us to better comprehend and address how, in Tonawanda Seneca scholar Mishuana Goeman's words, colonial "space is produced and productive" so as to "unbury the generative roots of spatial colonization and lay bare its concealed systems."[10] In *Network Sovereignty* (2017), Marisa Elena Duarte (Pascua Yaqui/Chicana) draws on the nineteenth-century painting *American Progress* (1872) by John Gast (1842–1896) to assert that Euro-settler material culture has been a primary means of colonization. In this painting, a white female angel with the "star of Empire" shining on her forehead, who is followed by light and represents progress and Manifest Destiny, watches over Native Americans being removed from the unfolding phenomenon of so-called civilization.[11] The angel figure pulls a telegraph wire along as a marker of incoming civilization, and carries a school book from Euro-American print culture, thereby linking telegraph wiring, Euro-American education, and western print culture and, in so doing, legitimizing western knowledge, power, and enlightened education as signifiers of civilization.[12] *American Progress* also features trains as markers of civilization; the depicted trains push Indigenous peoples and the wilderness, represented by a herd of bison, out of the way of civilization.[13]

The construction and expansion of the railway throughout Turtle Island in the nineteenth-century encouraged colonial mapping as well as increased colonization in the west. Far from being the glorious technology that Gast's painting portrays, the railroad has been a settler-colonial weapon of extermination and destruction, one that forced Indigenous peoples off their own lands and aided the settler-colonial project of destroying the buffalo, with whom many Indigenous peoples share an intimate relationship and upon which they relied for their livelihoods. In the context of Canada, the construction of the Canadian Pacific Railway (CPR) entailed clearing the land for sale and its subsequent settlement by white people, who built the power of the nation-state by possessing land "from sea to sea."[14] James Daschuk adds that "Canadian officials used food, or rather denied food, as a means to ethnically cleanse a vast region [. . .] as the Canadian Pacific Railway took shape. For years, government officials withheld food from aboriginal people until they moved to their appointed reserves, forcing them to trade freedom for rations."[15] *American Progress* portrays a romanticized version of colonial expansion and railroad technology, with a smiling angelic figure leading the way—but, in reality, Duarte observes,

> At the time of this painting, Native peoples of the southwest were enduring removal along the Trail of Tears, the people of the Plains were being confined by military force to reservations, federal authorities and missionaries were kidnapping children and sending them to boarding schools, and in the burgeoning US-Mexico borderlands, former Confederate soldiers were being paid government money for Indian scalps and captives.[16]

John Gast's *American Progress* is a clear and violent example of the firsting propaganda all-too-often embedded within and forcefully asserted through settler-made material culture.

Un-firsting within and through print culture related to Vancouver and published shortly after the city was founded under the Act of Incorporation in 1886 can be performed using cartographic and literary documentation published between 1887 to 1922, during which time the railroad was established in this region.[17] White Earth Ojibwe scholar Jean M. O'Brien documents the erasure of Indigenous peoples in the name of so-called progress and civilization, as if "non-Indians were the first people to erect the proper institutions of a social order worthy of notice."[18] Such firsting has led much of settler society to view Indigenous peoples as "alien[s] within [their] own territory."[19] Un-firsting will challenge, undo, and deconstruct firsting narratives while striving toward the recognition and assertion of a living and ongoing Indigenous presence, as encompassed by Indigenous peoples, nations, cultures, identities, laws, systems, and ways of knowing.

The map, *City of Vancouver, Canadian Pacific Town Site* (Figure 11.1), by CPR chief surveyor L.A. Hamilton (1852–1941) was published shortly after the city's official founding; it highlights how Euro-settler colonialists were attempting to envision and represent the territory during the early conceptualization of the city. The belief that settlers are entitled to this land undergirds the very premise of the city of Vancouver, and is an

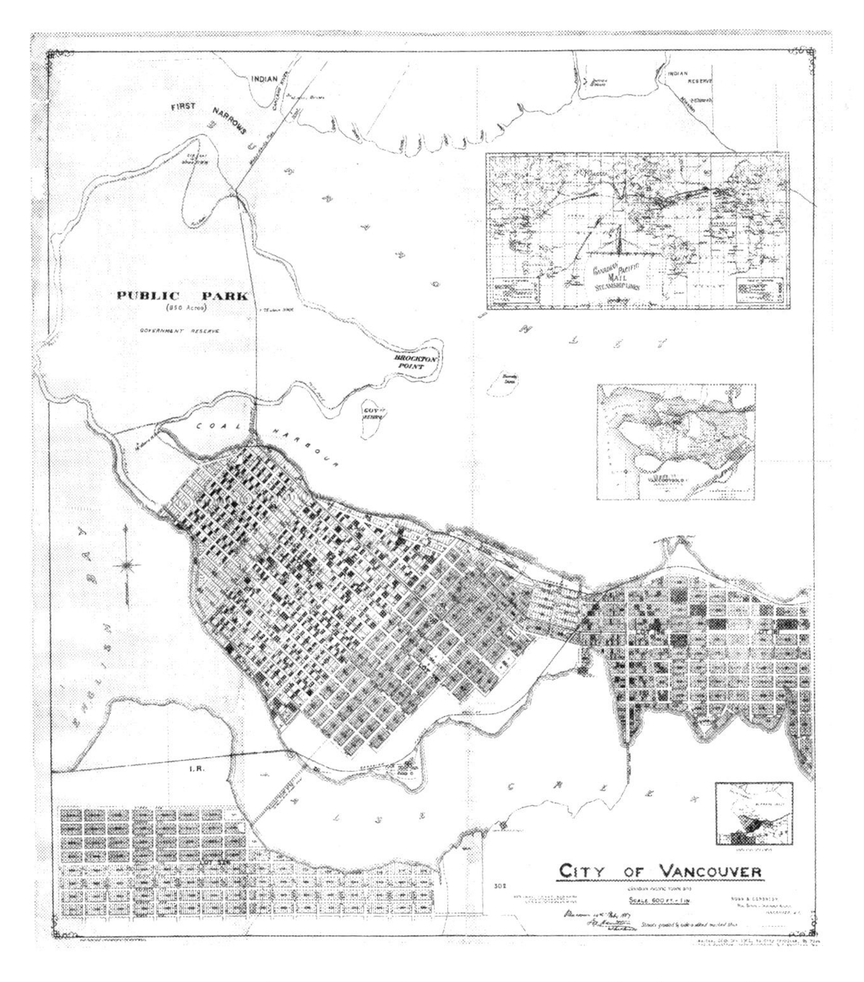

Figure 11.1 L.A. Hamilton, *City of Vancouver, Canadian Pacific Town Site* (Vancouver: Ross & Ceperley, 1887).

underlying assumption of this map, which labels the territory a "Canadian Pacific Town Site," and divides up land in colonial and objectifying ways that promise a new pathway for the railroad. The map was created as a result of Vancouver becoming the terminus of the CPR, which was a key technology of settler-colonial nation-building. The map responds to the hope that the railroad would attract more settlers to the area and increase profits; for this reason, the government of British Columbia granted the CPR over 6,000 acres, this in addition to acreage from private owners.[20] As the chief surveyor, Hamilton had the task of preparing these lands for the railway and its colonial enterprises, and this map is a projection of these efforts.[21] The real estate company Ross & Ceperley seems a fitting publisher for this map given the rail- and land-based interests of its partners, Arthur Wellington Ross (1846–1901) and Henry Tracy Ceperley (c. 1850–1929).[22] By mid-1884, Ross was working to make Granville the CPR's terminus in Vancouver, purchasing town site lots from the railway, and in 1886 opened a real estate business with Ceperley.[23] The map makes room for these settler-colonial developments by erasing Indigenous presence from the area in key ways. This is one way in which this map can be interpreted.

The map can also be read in light of another representation of Vancouver, the book *Legends of Vancouver* (1911). Mohawk artist E. Pauline Johnson (1861–1913) remains one of the most well-known and beloved Indigenous artists in Canada despite, in Cherokee scholar Daniel Heath Justice's words, "how pervasive the miasma of white settler colonial supremacy was in Johnson's time. 'Indians' were simply not humans to most Canadians [. . .] and, if they were, their status was of a decidedly lower order."[24] This settler-colonial supremacy would be even more heightened for Johnson, as she was not only Indigenous, but was also a woman inserting her voice and presence into heteropatriarchal spaces. Though Johnson was from Six Nations (colonially known as southern Ontario), she spent her final years in Vancouver; *Legends of Vancouver* remains one of the most popular books associated with her career. This collection of stories was a best-seller from its first printing and has continued to be widely printed ever since, with each edition containing its own unique paratextual features.[25] Gerard Genette asserts that paratexts, which adorn, reinforce, and accompany pieces of a story-text, can play a significant role in how we interpret a piece of literature. Alix Shield observes that each of the editions published since it first appeared exhibits a distinct character that reflects the views of more than a century of editors and publishers, which together demonstrates how a book's paratext shifts over time.[26] An example of this paratext, to be studied in due course, is the cover sleeve of the 1922 McClelland & Stewart edition of *Legends of Vancouver* (Figure 11.2); this particular edition and its design was reissued between that year and 1949 nine times.[27] The visual character lent to the book from its cover art, and which remained with each of these

Figure 11.2 Cover sleeve for the 1922 McClelland & Stewart edition with illustrations by J.E.H. MacDonald. Johnson, E. Pauline, *Legends of Vancouver* (Toronto: McClelland & Stewart, 1922).

nine editions, left a lasting impression on how readers imagine Vancouver, and the visual elements of the work will allow us to perform a rereading of the 1887 map.

A third method through which the map can be read is by considering Indigenous ways of viewing the land, exemplified by Bonnie Devine (Anishinaabe) in her mixed-media installation *Battle for the Woodlands* (2014–2015). Indigenous peoples have always had rich and complex mapping practices and technologies, and Indigenous cartographies deconstruct the violent firsting narratives of Euro-settler maps. In *Battle for the Woodlands*, Devine paints Anishinaabe worldviews overtop of a colonial nineteenth-century map of Upper and Lower Canada to reclaim the territories and their histories from an Anishinaabe perspective and to emphasize that lands and waters are our living relations. For instance, she depicts the Great Lakes as animals painted in a color reflective of blood.[28] Another challenge to Euro-settler maps, *The Shadow King* (2013), comprises an Indigenous re-envisioning of William Shakespeare's *King Lear* staged by Malthouse Theater and starring Murrungan artist Tom E. Lewis. The work teaches audiences

> the folly of believing you can own land [. . .] For millennia, [Indigenous] people have lived and existed with the land and on the land without claiming to own the land, but this story is about a man who believes he can own land and therefore divide it and give it to his three daughters. It's a folly that becomes a tragedy.[29]

These Indigenous engagements with territory, embedded in Indigenous epistemologies, point to some shortcomings of mainstream and official maps, which represent land and water as objects, rather than as relatives, broken apart into grids of land that can be sold, owned, developed, and mined for resources.

Mainstream maps have a deeply entrenched history of promoting colonialism and notions of European superiority and they exclude Indigenous knowledge in critical ways. The 1569 world map by Gerardus Mercator (1512–1594) presents a two-dimensional rectangular view of the globe and was meant for European navigation. It asserts white control over non-European lands through its portrayal of cannibalism and monstrosity in areas of North America that were unexplored by Europeans.[30] Mercator's cartographic projection of the world, known as the Mercator projection, continues to be used on maps, despite the inaccuracies it introduces by distorting space in firsting ways, for instance by making Europe look larger than it is while making Africa look smaller.[31] The projection exemplifies how, as Mark Rifkin recognizes, colonial regimes and their cartographic traditions naturalize Eurocentric perspectives of land within the mainstream psyche, "enacting a particular kind of figuration of territory and political authority as if it were simply empirical truth."[32] Barbara Belyea is critical of the Eurocentrism embedded within the field of cartographic studies and observes that many approaches to Indigenous mapping technologies, including the scholarship of June Helm (1989) and G. Malcolm Lewis (1979), "rely on the assumptions and standards of European cartography as universal measures of accuracy. Like European explorers of the eighteenth and early-nineteenth centuries, Helm and Lewis translate [Indigenous] maps into European terms."[33] Mainstream cartographic studies, then, have been complicit in normalizing European mappings as accurate and ideal by making them the standard by which other complex cartographic technologies are compared.

While the normalization of maps may make them seem apolitical, they must always be considered at once political and incomplete, and thus subject to revision. Leslie Main Johnson, while sharing her experiences working and learning with the Gitksan, Witsuwit'en, Kaska Dene, and Gwich'in nations, emphasizes the limitations imposed by the aerial and ichnographic perspectives of land that have become normalized within mainstream cartography. Such a bird's eye view "may or may not be 'natural' to the community whose knowledge is being represented; a traveller's path mediated by known landmarks may better represent the emic perspective."[34] She concludes that the aerial and ichnographic views privileged within mainstream mapping "cannot replace the landscape of experience."[35] Coming to know territory through a mainstream map rather than through lived experience renders one a passive and disconnected audience member rather than someone who has established a relationship with the territory.[36] Mainstream maps often fail to account for the living and breathing soul of a territory that shifts and changes with the seasons and which has relationships with both human and other-than-human beings, including weather, plants, stones, animals, and spirit beings.[37] Because mainstream maps cannot incorporate the sensory experiences and knowledge of being on and with territory, our relations with the spirit, plant, water, rock, and animal lives of a territory go unacknowledged.

Perhaps the most overt signal that the 1887 map firsts the Canadian state's systems and structures on Indigenous territories is through the document's place nomenclature, which is settler-colonial. By not acknowledging the original and living Indigenous names of the mapped territories, colonial names become legitimized and normalized within this document; they portray the colonial ownership and control of the land and endure to this day. For instance, the coastal fjord documented in the map as Burrard Inlet continues to be known by this name, though these territories also bear the Hun'qumyi'num name səl̓ilw̓ət.[38] The name for the inlet documented by the map as False Creek persists today, although an ancient village site known to the Musqueam nation as sən'aʔqʷ and to the Squamish nation as Sen'ákw existed in the same location.[39] The lasting hold of colonial place names within the mainstream imagination reveals the pervasive power that the Euro-settler cartographic tradition has had in firmly embedding colonial understandings of place into mainstream identity and culture.

The map makes use of its margins in order to contain Indigenous peoples along the periphery. Hugh Brody cultivates the argument that, as colonial powers forced their way through Indigenous territories and stole what they capitalistically deemed the most resource-rich lands and waters, "the Indians were progressively restricted to the edges, and even to pockets at the edges, of the territory that had always been theirs."[40] This act of placing Indigenous peoples on the periphery is often perpetuated through western maps. As Tuhiwai Smith writes, "Maps of the world reinforced our place on the periphery of the world," as figures literally placed in the margins of the document.[41] Such peripheralization is reenacted in and through the 1887 map. Hamilton places the majority of the Indigenous spaces acknowledged on this map—that is, those spaces that were sanctioned by the colonial government, marked here by the terms "Indian," "Indian houses," and "Indian reserve"—along the top of the map. These moments of marginalization deny Indigenous peoples' inherent belonging to and central place within these territories and articulate the false idea that Indigenous peoples are on the brink of physically vanishing from the landscape in the face of the so-called civilizational projects of, in this case, the railway. The "Indian reserve" lands located in the False Creek area are marginalized not spatially but onomastically with the ambiguous term "I.R.," an abbreviation that denies the central, historical, and ongoing Indigenous presence in the area.[42] Settler-colonial ambiguity continues on the map with the refusal to acknowledge the distinct nationhoods of the Indigenous peoples and the use of the generalizing and homogenizing blanket term "Indians." This ambiguity erases the political sovereignties of each of the Coast Salish nations of these territories. As Sliammon Elder Elsie Paul acknowledges with respect to the distinctiveness of each of these nations, "I'm a Coast Salish person. But all Coast Salish people are not all the same. We're different. We all have our unique language, our dialect, from other Coast Salish people."[43] Glen Coulthard (Yellowknives Dene) views this homogenization as "the ultimate goal" of Indigenous "elimination [. . .] as cultural, political, and legal peoples distinguishable from the rest of Canadian society."[44]

Firsting narratives are also apparent in how the map documents a church and mission located on the "Indian reserve" land. The presence of the church in one of the only Indian spaces granted on this map draws attention to the role that the Christian institution has played in colonization and in the perpetuation of firsting discourse. O'Brien identifies this institutional problem when she asserts that "Indian history appears in local narratives in fairly patterned ways," one of which is the mission.[45] Because Christianity was not a part of Indigenous cultures prior to colonization, settler conversion of Indigenous peoples to Christianity was portrayed as a civilizing act, "an espoused justification for colonialism in the first place."[46] The map's framing of indigeneity as under the guardianship and within the confines of the church and mission implies that settler civilization has been brought to and is somehow bettering the Indigenous peoples of these territories. That the Christian church and mission are located on reserve land on this map serves as a reminder of the complex and often fraught colonial history between the Christian institution and Indigenous communities. As O'Brien concludes, many settler-colonial documents have "produced narratives that failed to understand and account for Indian persistence [. . .] exposing cracks in their facade of New England modernity purified of Indians."[47] Settler-colonial documents often intend to first; but the undeniable presence of Indigenous peoples comes through nonetheless, revealing narratives of Indigenous resistance that un-first settler-colonizers.[48] Furthermore, post-colonial and Indigenous artistic works and scholarship have a long history of engaging with and responding to colonial archives.[49] These approaches deconstruct and disempower Eurocentric imaginings, and recognize and honor "lived Indigenous histories of resistance under colonization."[50]

It is in this light that an anti-colonial reading of the 1887 map de-emphasizes its firsting ideologies by recognizing Indigenous presence, survival, and resistance. Daniel Heath Justice reflects on the stories told by Cherokee allotment maps and argues that these maps made by colonialists do not merely chronicle Cherokee displacement from their homelands; they also document the story of Cherokee survival.[51] Taking up Justice's anti-colonial approach, the 1887 map's acknowledgment of Indigenous presence evidences colonialism's inability to erase Indigenous peoples from the landscape and from ongoing history. Gerald Vizenor (Anishinaabe) defines survivance as "an active sense of presence, the continuance of [N]ative stories [. . .] Native survivance stories are renunciations of dominance, tragedy, and victimry."[52] By reading a narrative of survivance within this map, firsting narratives are invalidated. This map is ultimately unable to hide the presence of Indigenous people in the past, present, and future of these territories. To assist us in a survivance reading of the 1887 map, we can turn to Indigenous stories to challenge settler-colonial narratives presented in Canadian documents to invalidate the ways in which such documents view and claim territory. Mishuana Goeman argues that Indigenous storytellers "mediate and refute colonial organizing of land, bodies, and social and political landscapes."[53] Furthermore, Justice asserts that Indigenous stories are good medicine in that they "remind us of the greatness of where [Indigenous peoples] came from as well as the greatness of who [they are] meant to be" and, as such, Indigenous stories begin to undo the bad medicine and harmfulness of colonial documentation and its accompanying narratives.[54]

A challenge to this approach is the fact that non-Indigenous editing practices and paratextual elements created by non-Indigenous people have a history of re-mapping settler-colonial narratives onto or overtop of nineteenth and early twentieth-century Indigenous texts.[55] For instance, the archives of nineteenth-century Ojibwe writer Jane Johnston Schoolcraft (1800–1842) have been understudied within Indigenous studies, in part due to her settler husband's editorship and acts of authorial theft that have concealed the depth of her contributions to the nineteenth-century literary scene.[56] We find another example in Okanogon author Mourning Dove (c. 1884–1936), who rejected the notion of the vanishing Indian and ended her novel *Cogewea* (written in the 1910s, published in 1927) with the marriage of two mixed-blood natives as a means of signifying Indigenous futures. Sara Humphreys's research engaging with the current edition of *Cogewea* analyses how settler-created paratexts—including notes by Lucullus Virgil McWhorter, cover art by Arlene Hooker Fay, and an introduction by Dexter Fisher—end up framing the novel by openly asserting that Indigenous peoples and ways are vanishing.[57] The paratexts of early editions of *Legends of Vancouver* feature settler-colonial imaginings too, such as stereotypical headdress imagery.[58] Indigenous studies scholars Humphreys, Shield, Treena Chambers (Métis), and Deanna Reder (Cree-Métis), and new media projects such as *The People and the Text*, are drawing attention to the impacts non-Indigenous editors and publishers have had on Indigenous literature and art. These editorial and publishing practices, including the incorporation of paratextual elements into Indigenous texts, can perpetuate settler-colonial and firsting ideologies. Shield argues that such settler-colonial practices have "marginalized the authorial roles of Indigenous storytellers and thus reinforced colonial conceptions of race and status throughout the text's publishing history."[59] Johnson learned the stories that make up the majority of *Legends of Vancouver* from her Squamish friends chief Joe Capilano/Sahp-luk (d.1910) and Mary Agnes Capilano/Lixwelut (d.1940), and the story-text of *Legends of Vancouver* is primarily focused on Squamish oral histories.[60] As Shield asserts, chief Joe and Mary must be recognized as coauthors alongside Johnson for the essential ways that their voices and perspectives have shaped this work of literature. Shield argues that the "destructive editing practices common throughout Canada's twentieth century" have led to the undermining or downright "erasure of Chief Joe and" particularly of Mary's authorship roles "from the paratext."[61]

Another important consideration is that, between the publication of the 1887 map and the 1922 McClelland & Stewart edition of *Legends of Vancouver*, Canada as a young nation-state was negotiating its identity and agency in relation to the metropole of Britain. The occupation of Indigenous territories added to the nation-state's consistent and forceful attempt to affirm its legitimacy. The cover sleeve of the 1922 edition can be viewed as another means through which this discourse of Canadian authenticity and independence was perpetuated. The Canadian character of this edition may first be indebted to its publisher. Carl Spadoni and Judy Donnelly observe that

> In the case of M&S, the record of imprints follows the path from agency publishing to a genuine commitment to the publication of books by Canadian authors [. . .] it is the publisher's story of an emerging nation, formerly in the shadows of a mother country [. . .] that broke away and celebrated its cultural diversity and literary vitality. [. . .] '[W]e might say that we are specializing as far as possible on the works of Canadian writers,' McClelland informed J. Murray Gibbon in 1918 regarding his company's publishing programme.[62]

Indeed, the back sleeve of this edition advertises "the Livest Book List in Canada," which includes the representative titles *Canadian Cities of Romance* and *Our Prairie Trails*, described as depicting "The Charm, the Beauty, the Romance of Canada."

In the 1920s, the company began to engage well-known Canadian artists to illustrate their publications, another declaration of their commitment to helping to establish an independent Canadian identity. This edition of *Legends of Vancouver* employed settler artist J. E. H. MacDonald (1873–1932), one of the founding members of the Group of Seven, which was comprised of influential Canadian artists who shaped early twentieth-century perceptions of the nation-state. They are arguably most well-known for their landscape paintings, which consolidated the narrative of settler right to and belonging on the territories by portraying them as an uninhabited, virginal wilderness characterized by untouched mountains of snow and ice. In line with this narrative of settler belonging, MacDonald's paintings, as with other paintings from the Group of Seven, broke away from European practices and portrayed Canada and the lands it occupies "not as an extension of Europe, but as a separate physical entity."[63] MacDonald depicted objects and scenes that settler society has commonly associated in generalizing and homogenizing ways with native cultures and identities. Settler Canada has simultaneously co-opted and misappropriated these objects and scenes to assert a unique North American origin story and identity. Viewed thusly, MacDonald's images of the canoe, the carved pole, and unclothed human figures projected upon a seemingly uninhabited and vast wilderness articulate this edition's self-fashioning as an independent Canadian text.[64] Settler appropriation and use of perceived representations of indigeneity to assert, portray, and characterize American and Canadian identities is problematic, especially as Indigenous nations are distinct and separate from the American and Canadian nation-states and have existed longer than either the United States or Canada. But, settlers wanted to claim and feel Indigenous to these lands. As O'Brien observes, they "insisted on origin stories of the nation that were rooted in that place [where they had settled] and its Indian history."[65] Dakota scholar Philip J. Deloria examines how settlers have dressed up as and enacted fictional perceptions of the so-called Indian—a practice he terms playing Indian—to assert independence from Britain and to claim the right to and identity associated with the lands they had colonized.[66]

Playing Indian occurred on both sides of the colonial border. The participants of the 1773 Boston Tea Party dressed in the colonial imaginings of the Indian to create and assert an American self-image that was distinct from British imagery and identity. To American settlers, Deloria concludes, "Indians represented instinct and freedom [. . .] the 'spirit of the continent,'" traits that starkly contrasted with Europe, which was viewed as being aligned with logic and social order.[67] Settlers imagined a rupture between the so-called New World and Britain, in which the "New World" had a spirit "rooted in nature" that was in opposition to Britain's immersion in civilization.[68] The imagery on the cover sleeve of this edition of *Legends of Vancouver*—with its focus on the all-encompassing wilderness and its subsuming objects and landscapes that were selected and appropriated to inform Canadian identity—arguably functions in a similar way, particularly when packaged together with the book's Canadian publisher and illustrator in light of their respective agendas for representing Canada. Colonialist and settler-made representations of indigeneity reveal far more about settler beliefs, desires, epistemologies, and ideologies than they do about Indigenous peoples, identities, histories, lived experiences, cultures, and traditions. Once attached as paratexts to an Indigenous literary work, these settler-made images risk perpetuating colonial stereotypes and committing acts of firsting even when the story-text itself anti-colonially un-firsts settler narratives.

At the same time, however, limiting analysis of the cover sleeve's images to critiques of how they reinforce settler colonialism elides the potential of reading the un-firsting possibilities that these illustrations also offer. Whereas the 1887 map of Vancouver marginalizes Indigenous presence, the illustrations on the cover sleeve of this edition use so-called native imagery in a way that bolsters the text's Canadian character and thereby reinforces that Indigenous peoples and cultures are legitimate and integral parts of Vancouver. By attaching Vancouver to these images, MacDonald links these territories, their histories and origins, to Indigenous rather than British identities, stories, and histories. In this way, these illustrations can be seen to challenge firsting ideas in that they acknowledge rather than overlook the fact that Indigenous peoples are a central part of this land. In so doing, these illustrations de-legitimize firsting narratives designed for the settler-colonial realm.

Nevertheless, the settler artist's work perpetuates colonial narratives that white people are more qualified to speak to and represent Indigenous cultures than Indigenous communities. A non-Indigenous artist in this way profits from appropriating the artistic traditions of Indigenous peoples, particularly as MacDonald was commissioned for the project at a time when the Canadian nation-state's Potlatch Ban (1885–1951) was in effect and Indigenous communities were prohibited from practicing their ceremonies and traditions (although they resisted the government's attempts at extermination by finding ways to continue these practices). Contemporary editions of *Legends of Vancouver* have sought to rectify the violence and cultural theft of non-Indigenous artists by commissioning Coast Salish artists to create the illustrations. Two examples are the 1991 Quarry Press edition, which features illustrations by Salish/Kwakwaka'wakw artist Laura Wee Láy Láq, and the Midtown Press 100th anniversary edition, which features a cover design by Musqueam artist Raymond Sim. These issues of cultural appropriation and intellectual property rights dovetail with issues surrounding the practices of publishing and profiting from these works, and allow non-Indigenous people to become profiters from, key contributors to, and perceived authorities of these Indigenous stories. As Shield's scholarly work articulates and as was briefly recognized earlier in this chapter, chief Joe and Mary's authorial contributions are often overlooked in the various editions of and scholarly contributions about *Legends of Vancouver*. Johnson is consistently attributed as the single author of this book, although most of the stories in this book are living histories and narratives from and of the Squamish nation and thus are not Johnson's.

Beyond the authorship of the book, we can also point to problems arising from its title. Daniel Heath Justice reflects on how Indigenous literatures teach us to be good kin to everything in creation.[69] In many ways, *Legends of Vancouver* may comprise a kinship text. Johnson's intimate relationship with the Capilanos and their ancestral homelands is honored in the book through various kinship scenes shared between Johnson and the Capilano family, the wider Squamish community, and especially chief Joe, together on the land. Johnson wished to honor these kinships by titling the work *Legends of the Capilano*. Evidently, the publishers believed that the book would be more eye-grabbing and marketable if it bore a name more recognizable in their eyes.[70]

Two forthcoming community-centered and collaborative works will provide scholars with new ways of acknowledging, addressing, and undoing the harm caused by western literary practices, which have perpetuated settler-colonial violence, control, and domination with respect to *Legends of Vancouver*. They strive to recognize and honor the communities who have lived in the territories of Vancouver since time immemorial, whose living stories are integral to *Legends of Vancouver* and crucial today.[71] Alix Shield is preparing a new edition of this book as a means of honoring and renewing the kinship of Johnson, chief Joe Capilano, and Mary Agnes; it will appear under the title that Johnson had initially chosen: *Legends of the Capilano*. This edition is a community-centered one that will feature interviews with members of the Squamish and Mohawk nations; it has been created in collaboration with these communities, including the relatives of chief Joe and Mary. The second work is *The New Legends of Vancouver*, which is being developed by Mohawk/Tuscarora poet Janet

Rogers through a Canada Council Creating, Knowing and Sharing Grant. Johnson and Rogers both found a home in Vancouver (Johnson adopting Vancouver in the last four years of her life and Rogers being born there) and fostered strong kinship connections with the territories and their ancestral communities. As Johnson's book is a kinship text, Rogers is collaboratively developing and creating this collection with members of the Coast Salish nations as a celebration of the strong kinship connections that she has fostered with the lands, waters, and peoples of the region, past, present, and future. *The New Legends of Vancouver* will comprise a collection of interviews, poems, stories, and more, shared by various Coast Salish community members, including relatives of chief Joe Capilano and Mary Agnes. And, while *Legends of Vancouver* has been seen to obscure the voices and contributions of the Squamish nation, the community members whose stories are shared in this new collection will speak from their own voices and will be given full credit for their contributions. These examples demonstrate the valuable ways that scholars and Indigenous artists and storytellers are dismantling the firsting architecture that influenced works published and edited decades ago (and that all-too-often continues to influence Canadian print culture) so that Indigenous authors' intentions and the ongoing cultures, identities, peoplehoods, and lived experiences of Indigenous communities become visible, valued, and honored.

Those of us who live on these territories as settlers have the responsibility to understand that we are complicit in settler colonialism and colonization; we must always challenge, interrogate, and work to dismantle firsting discourse in respectful ways while remembering and recognizing that all cities, territories, and waters in and of Turtle Island are Indigenous. We must understand the ways in which documentation such as cartography is highly political and, when created by settler-colonial powers and systems, how it perpetuates Canada's dispossession of Indigenous lands to legitimize firsting narratives supporting Canada's right to these lands. We have the responsibility to know and honor the original and living Indigenous laws, protocols, treaties, and agreements of the territories that we inhabit. Métis writer Cherie Dimaline's novel *The Marrow Thieves* (2017) emphasizes that Indigenous stories are woven into the very marrow of Indigenous peoples' bones. So, too, are Indigenous stories woven into the marrow of Indigenous territories. Indigenous oral histories are complex, nuanced, intricate, and living teachings that help us understand the ongoing histories and laws of these lands, and the protocols and peoples we are accountable to as we move on these lands. The most significant un-firsting power of *Legends of Vancouver* is the Squamish oral histories that it celebrates and shares. These oral histories invalidate the territory as represented in the 1887 map and elsewhere in mainstream culture. They evince the complex, respectful, responsible, and reciprocal relationship between Indigenous peoples and the territories since time immemorial. These oral histories reveal and dismantle the settler-colonial narrative of firsting, allowing us to anti-colonially re-first and re-map the lands and waters, emphasizing that these territories have always been and will continue to be Indigenous lands.[72]

Notes

1. Todd, "Vancouver Is an Indigenous City."
2. Allison Hargreaves, "Final Section Response: 'The Lake Is the People and Life that Come to It': Location as Critical Practice," in Reder and Morra, eds., *Learn, Teach, Challenge*, pp. 107–110: 109.
3. For a critical reflection on settler refusal of the authority position, see Eigenbrod, *Travelling Knowledges*.
4. Mitcholos Touchie (Nuu-chah-nulth) advocates the use of c.k.a. as an acronym for "colonially-known as" to acknowledge the Eurocentrism of many of the place names privileged within western society. See Touchie's post "Feel Free to Use the Term 'CKA' (Colonially Known As)."
5. Sanderson, "Wampum Diplomacy."
6. Borrows, "Ethics."
7. Sanderson, "Wampum Diplomacy."
8. Tuhiwai Smith, *Decolonizing Methodologies*, p. 63.
9. McDowell, *Uncharted Waters*, pp. 232–233.
10. Goeman, "Notes Toward a Native Feminism's Spatial Practice," p. 171.
11. This piece was commissioned by the travel guide publisher George Croffut, who used the image in travel materials; see Duarte, *Network Sovereignty*, p. 111. Also see Gast, *American Progress*. For more on *American Progress*, see Greenberg, *Manifest Destiny*; and by the same author, *Manifest Manhood*.
12. Duarte, *Network Sovereignty*, pp. 111–112.
13. Ibid., pp. 111–112.
14. Canada's first prime minister, John A. MacDonald, dreamed of creating a nation-state that stretched from the Atlantic Ocean to the Pacific Ocean through the construction of a railway. It is both emphasized and romanticized—the land presented as vast and uninhabited rather than as occupied by a diversity of Indigenous nations—in the Canadian Heritage Minute about this prime minister. This video features MacDonald stating that the Canadian nation-state will be "made one by a railway, from sea to sea;" see Historica Canada, "Heritage Minutes: Sir John A. MacDonald," 0:27–0:40. Indeed, "a mari usque ad mare" (from sea to sea) is featured on the Canadian coat of arms adopted in 1921. This statement reflects a verse from Psalm 72: "he shall have dominion from sea to sea;" see Royal Heraldry Society of Canada, "Arms & Badges."
15. Daschuk, "When Canada Used Hunger to Clear the West." For more on the relationship between Canadian railways and colonization, see Daschuk, *Clearing the Plains*.
16. Duarte, *Network Sovereignty*, p. 112.
17. The Act of Incorporation has since been superseded by the Vancouver Charter, a provincial statute under which the city is now regulated. See City of Vancouver Archives, "Vancouver (B.C.)--Incorporation Act." The petition to found the city sent to the provincial legislature and which led to the Act of Incorporation has been reproduced by the Vancouver Public Space Network, "Blog."
18. O'Brien, *Firsting and Lasting*, ibid., p. xii.

19. Duarte, *Network Sovereignty*, p. x.
20. MacDonald, "Vancouver in the Nineteenth Century," p. 52.
21. Ibid., pp. 52–53.
22. Scholefield, *British Columbia*, vol. 3, p. 30; Brissenden and Loyie, "The History of Metropolitan Vancouver's Hall of Fame."
23. Burley, "Ross, Arthur Wellington." For more on Ross, see Kerr, *Biographical Dictionary of Well-Known British Columbians*; and McKee, "The Vancouver Park System, 1886–1929," pp. 33–49.
24. Heath Justice, *Why Indigenous Literatures Matter*, p. 62.
25. Here I honor how Alix Shield and the digital Indigenous literary studies project *The People and the Text* have chosen to categorize *Legends of Vancouver*. The categorization of archival materials is often Eurocentric and colonial; the project's research team has carefully and critically recognized this issue and works to respectfully and anti-colonially approach engaging with archival materials. See Shield, "The People and the Text."
26. Shield, "Rethinking the Paratext," p. 107.
27. Quirk, "Labour of Love," p. 216.
28. Devine, "Claims, Names, and Allegories."
29. Melbourne International Arts Festival, "The Shadow King Trailer," 2:06–2:21.
30. Presner, Shepard, and Kawano, *Hypercities*, p. 95. For more about the history of cartography, see Harley, Woodward, Lewis, Edney, Pedley, Kain, and Monmonier, eds., *The History of Cartography*.
31. For more about the inaccuracies of the Mercator Projection, see *The True Size*.
32. Rifkin, *The Erotics of Sovereignty*, p. 14.
33. Belyea, "Amerindian Maps," p. 267. Also see Helm, "Matonabbee's Map," pp. 28–47; and Lewis, "The Indigenous Maps and Mapping," pp. 145–167.
34. Johnson, *Trail of Story, Traveller's Path*, p. 185.
35. Ibid., p. 200.
36. Ibid., pp. 188–189 and 201.
37. Ibid., p. 186.
38. The Tsleil-Waututh pe̓oples receive their name from this territory; see Simon Fraser University, "*səlilw̓ət* (Sleilwaut): Burrard Inlet and Indian Arm."
39. Roy, "Mapping Tool."
40. Brody, *Maps and Dreams*, p. 97.
41. Tuhiwai Smith, *Decolonizing Methodologies*, p. 33.
42. For more about the Kitsilano reserve lands, see Roy, "Mapping Tool."
43. Paul, *Written as I Remember It*, p. 68.
44. Coulthard, *Red Skin, White Masks*, p. 4.
45. O'Brien, *Firsting and Lasting*, p. 26.
46. Ibid., p. 29.
47. Ibid., p. xxiv.
48. Ibid.
49. There are various ways of understanding colonial archives, their materials, the ethics surrounding them (including who has control over and access to them), and how researchers epistemologically approach and treat archives. *The People and the Text* recognizes colonial archives as those made up of materials that neglect or appropriate Indigenous knowledges, assert a narrative of Euro-settler right to Indigenous territories, and create a Euro-settler and especially a British-settler historical and national canon. This project strives to create an Indigenous literary archive that challenges the ethical problems of mainstream archives, and re-imagines and concretely transforms archives in anti-colonial ways; see *The People and the Text*. Dallas Hunt (Cree) presents

colonial archives as "those archives that are constructed according to colonial logics of history, settlement, and knowledge production" and "that [. . .] consolidate claims over space in a macropolitical context;" Hunt "call[s] upon an Indigenous archive of memories, including those held by elders and the land itself, beyond what settler histories allow;" see "Nikîkîwân 1," pp. 26–27. For more on confronting colonial archives, see Stoler, "Colonial Archives and the Arts of Governance," pp. 87–109; Million, "Felt Theory," pp. 53–76; and Luker, "Decolonising Archives," pp. 108–125.

50. Hunt, "Nikîkîwân 1," p. 36. Also see the following representation of anti-colonial interventions into colonial archives: Monkman, *The Triumph of Mischief*; Philip, *Zong*; Abel, *The Place of Scraps*; and by the same author, *Un/inhabited* and *Injun*; and Whitehead, *Full-Metal Indigiqueer*.
51. Justice, *Why Indigenous Literatures Matter*, pp. 195–197.
52. Vizenor, *Manifest Manners*, p. vii.
53. Goeman, *Mark My Words*, p. 3.
54. Justice, *Why Indigenous Literatures Matter*, p. 5.
55. The publication history of *Legends of Vancouver* exposes the lack of control an author can have over the editing and paratexts of their works because so many editions have been published after Johnson's death and, thus, have been published outside of her control. Even during her life, Johnson did not appear to have much control over the text. For instance, as Linda Quirk observes, Johnson had originally wanted to honor chief Joe Capilano and Mary Agnes by having the title of the collection bear the name Capilano, but the first publishers of the book deemed it would be more marketable under the title *Legends of Vancouver*; see Quirk, "Labour of Love," p. 205.
56. For more on Schoolcraft, see Parker, "Introduction: The World and Writings of Jane Johnston Schoolcraft," in Parker, ed., *The Sound the Stars Make*, pp. 1–84.
57. Mourning Dove, *Cogewea*. Also see Humphreys, "Cogewea."
58. While settler society continuously and harmfully appropriates headdress imagery, headdresses are nation-specific, sacred, and living items that only certain people earn the right to wear and that come with great responsibility. See Cherokee scholar Keene, "But Why Can't I Wear a Hipster Headdress." *Native Appropriations*.
59. Shield, "Rethinking the Paratext," p. 108.
60. Shield, "Mary Agnes Capilano (Lixwelut)."
61. Shield, "Rethinking the Paratext," pp. 107 and 114–115. The 1922 McClelland & Stewart edition of *Legends of Vancouver* recognizes in the bottom right of the cover sleeve and in the author's foreword that chief Joe shared most of the stories in this book with Johnson, but Mary and her contributions are not mentioned.
62. Spadoni and Donnelly, *A Bibliography of McClelland and Stewart Imprints*, pp. 11 and 29.
63. Robertson, *J.E.H. MacDonald*, p. 5.
64. For more on the settler co-option of the canoe, see Dean, *Inheriting a Canoe Paddle*. Quirk acknowledges that the title, *Legends of Vancouver*, is misleading, as the story-text is not about George Vancouver, and the cover sleeve imagery, which uses images that settlers often co-opt and appropriate to signify "nativeness," may be seen as misleading. Indigenous pole carving traditions have been and continue to be culturally appropriated by settler society and settler corporations. Quirk recognizes that "MacDonald['s . . .] illustrations seem to connect" the book "to contemporary Native cultures of the Northwest Coast," yet MacDonald's illustrations may arguably still

be seen as homogenizing and generalizing: the carving on the front sleeve, for instance, appears to be appropriated from Haida carving traditions, although the majority of the story-text itself is focused on Squamish rather than Haida stories (one exception is the story, "The Grey Archway," that features members of the Haida nation), and the landscape of Vancouver—the territory of primary focus in the book—does not occupy Haida territories (which include the islands of Haida Gwaii and parts of what is now called southern Alaska). See Quirk, "Labour of Love," pp. 205 and 217. It is important to recognize that, in response to settler-colonial appropriations of and fascinations with carved poles, as well as the city of Vancouver's erecting of non-Salish carvings in Stanley Park in the 1920s, a pole carved by Squamish chief Mathias Joe Capilano was raised in Stanley Park's Prospect Point in 1936. Aldona Jonaitis and Aaron Glass observe that this "pole represents the first recorded large-scale Salish totem pole" as, historically, "many Salish people had carved interior house posts [. . .] but they had erected no tall, multifigured 'totem poles' such as the Prospect Point Carving." This pole, reflective of Kwakwaka'wakw pole carving traditions and imbued with Squamish histories and epistemologies, was "a quiet, legal mechanism to proclaim Squamish rights to the Vancouver region using a recognizable northern-style marker." This pole is an innovation that some might read as an appropriation in response to settler-colonial appropriations. Counter to settler-colonial imaginings that Indigenous cultures and traditions are static relics of the past, Capilano's pole is an example of how Indigenous nations, cultures, identities, and traditions are ongoing and living, and are always shifting and changing. See Jonaitis and Glass, *The Totem Pole*, pp. 224–245.

65. O'Brien, *Firsting and Lasting*, p. xiii.
66. Deloria, *Playing Indian*, pp. 2–3.
67. Ibid., p. 3.
68. O'Brien, *Firsting and Lasting*, p. xxi. This settler fascination, based in part on the erroneous colonial binaries of nature versus civilization or nature versus urbanity, incorrectly assumed and posited that nature is apart from civilization, urbanity, innovation, and modernity. Glen Coulthard terms the erroneous settler-colonial conception that urban spaces are not Indigenous and are devoid of Indigenous peoples, nationhoods, cultures, and presence "urbs nullius;" see Coulthard, *Red Skin, White Masks*, p. 176.
69. Justice, *Why Indigenous Literatures Matter*, pp. 74–75.
70. Quirk, "Labour of Love," p. 205. It is important to recognize that Quirk states that Johnson had originally wanted the book to be entitled *Legends of Capilano*; it was Shield who emphasized to me that Johnson had actually wanted the book to be entitled *Legends of the Capilano*.
71. As well, the *SquamishAtlas.com* project is an online Squamish place name map "curated by Sḵwx̱wú7mesh language-speaker and teacher Khelsilem, of Sḵwx̱wú7mesh-Kwakwa̱ka̱'wakw descent, in collaboration with web developer Victor Temprano and curriculum developer Nicki Benson [. . .]. Many of the names on this map were collected from a 1937 Sḵwx̱wú7mesh place names map developed by the City of Vancouver and August Jack Khatsalano of the Squamish nation." Some of the significant places and oral histories shared in *Legends of Vancouver* are also shared in the digital project. See Khelsilem, Temprano, Benson, and Keeling, "About." The *Cultural Journey* online project created by and through the Squamish Lil'Wat Cultural Center in map and audio forms shares various oral histories of the Squamish and Lil'Wat nations, including many of the ones that chief Joe and Mary shared with Johnson and which are featured in *Legends of Vancouver*; and the various exhibits, texts, and multimedia pieces that the community has made for

the Squamish Lil'Wat Cultural Centre also share many of these stories and landscapes with visitors. See "Cultural Journey."

72. Acknowledgements: There are many people—human and other-than-human—to extend salamat (thanks) to, including: the Indigenous activists, community members, scholars, writers, researchers, aunties, youth, and Elders with whom I have had the honor and privilege of learning and working; Alix Shield and Janet Rogers, for their permission to include information about their respective forthcoming works in this chapter; Mitcholos Touchie, for his permission to cite his writings on challenging colonial place-naming through the use of c.k.a. in this chapter; Sara Humphreys, for her permission to cite her insightful blog writings in this chapter; Kira Baker, reference archivist for the City of Vancouver Archive, for her valuable insights regarding the 1887 map and the official founding of the city of Vancouver; the Department of First Nations Studies at Simon Fraser University and the Centre for Indigenous Studies at the University of Toronto; the Book History and Print Culture program at the University of Toronto, where I began working on this piece; the Thomas Fisher Rare Book Library, where I spent many hours looking at editions of *Legends of Vancouver*; Pamela Klassen, for her guidance and supervision throughout writing; Natalie Davis, who offered transformative insight during the beginning stages of writing; the territories where I have lived, worked, and written as an uninvited occupant; my Pilipinx ancestors and relations; and everyone who works to transform this world with decolonial love, and who pushes me to be better and to do better. I have, and will always have, so much to learn.

Bibliography

Abel, Jordan, *The Place of Scraps* (Vancouver: Talonbooks, 2013).

———, *Un/Inhabited* (Vancouver: Talonbooks, 2014).

———, *Injun* (Vancouver: Talonbooks, 2016).

Belyea, Barbara, "Amerindian Maps: The Explorer as Translator," *Journal of Historical Geography* 18.3 (1992), pp. 267–277.

Borrows, John, "Ethics: Aboriginal Rights, Bravery and Humility," presentation before the F.E.L. Priestly Memorial Lectures in the History of Ideas, University of Toronto, Toronto, 17 October 2017.

Brissenden, Constance, and Larry Loyie, "The History of Metropolitan Vancouver's Hall of Fame," *The History of Metropolitan Vancouver*, 2011. www.vancouverhistory.ca/whoswho_C.htm

Brody, Hugh, *Maps and Dreams: Indians and the British Columbia Frontier* (Middlesex: Pelican Books, 1983).

Burley, David G., "Ross, Arthur Wellington," in *Dictionary of Canadian Biography*. Vol. 13 (University of Toronto/Université Laval, 1994). www.biographi.ca/en/bio/ross_arthur_wellington_13E.html

City of Vancouver Archives, "Vancouver (B.C.): Incorporation Act," *City of Vancouver Archives*. https://searcharchives.vancouver.ca/vancouver-b-c-incorporation-act

Coulthard, Glen, *Red Skin, White Masks: Rejecting the Colonial Politics of Recognition* (Minneapolis: University of Minnesota Press, 2014).

"Cultural Journey," *SLCC Squamish Lil'Wat Cultural Centre*, 2018. https://slcc.ca/experience/cultural-journey/

Daschuk, James, *Clearing the Plains: Disease, Politics of Starvation, and the Loss of Aboriginal Life* (Regina: University of Regina Press, 2013).

———, "When Canada Used Hunger to Clear the West," *The Globe and Mail*, 19 July 2013.

Dean, Misoa, *Inheriting a Canoe Paddle: The Canoe in Discourses of English-Canadian Nationalism* (Toronto: University of Toronto Press, 2013).

Deloria, Philip J., *Playing Indian* (New Haven, CT: Yale University Press, 1998).

Devine, Bonnie, "Claims, Names, and Allegories," presentation at CHESS, Women's Art Association of Canada, Toronto, 31 May 2017.

Duarte, Marisa Elena, *Network Sovereignty: Building the Internet across Indian Country* (Seattle: University of Washington Press, 2017).

Eigenbrod, Renate, *Travelling Knowledges: Positioning the Im/Migrant Reader of Aboriginal Literatures in Canada* (Winnipeg: University of Manitoba Press, 2005).

Gast, John, *American Progress*, 1872. Library of Congress, Washington, DC, Prints and Photographs Division, Crofutt, American progress (B size) [P&P].

Goeman, Mishuana R., "Notes Toward a Native Feminism's Spatial Practice," *Wicazo Sa Review* 24.2 (2009), pp. 169–187.

———, *Mark My Words: Native Women Mapping Our Nations* (Minneapolis: University of Minnesota Press, 2013).

Greenberg, Amy S., *Manifest Manhood and the Antebellum American Empire* (New York: Cambridge University Press, 2005).

———, *Manifest Destiny and American Territorial Expansion: A Brief History with Documents* (Boston: St. Martin's, 2011).

Harley, J. B., David Woodward, G. Malcolm Lewis, Matthew H. Edney, Mary S. Pedley, Roger J. P. Kain, and Mark Monmonier, eds., *The History of Cartography*, 6 vols. (Chicago: University of Chicago Press, 1987-c. 2022).

Helm, June, "Matonabbee's Map," *Arctic Anthropology* 26.2 (1989), pp. 28–47.

Historica Canada, "Heritage Minutes: Sir John A. MacDonald," YouTube Video, 12 September 2014. www.youtube.com/watch?v=vBGNEJpznNE

Humphreys, Sara, "Cogewea," *The Expendable Citizen*, 2017–2018. https://expendablecitizen.wordpress.com/category/cogewea/

Hunt, Dallas, "Nikîkîwân 1: Contesting Settler Colonial Archives through Indigenous Oral History," *Canadian Literature* 230/231 (2016), pp. 25–42.

Johnson, Leslie Main, *Trail of Story, Traveller's Path: Reflections on Ethnoecology and Landscape* (Edmonton: Athabasca University Press, 2010).

Jonaitis, Aldona, and Aaron Glass, *The Totem Pole: An Intercultural History* (Seattle: University of Washington Press, 2010).

Justice, Daniel Heath, *Why Indigenous Literatures Matter* (Waterloo: Wilfrid Laurier University Press, 2018).

Keene, Adrienne, "But Why Can't I Wear a Hipster Headdress?," *Native Appropriations*, 2010. https://nativeappropriations.com/2010/04/but-why-cant-i-wear-a-hipster-headdress.html

Kerr, John Blaine, *Biographical Dictionary of Well-Known British Columbians* (Vancouver: The News-Advertiser Printing and Publishing Co., 1890).

Khelsilem, Victor Temprano, Nicki Benson, and Corrina Keeling, "About," *Squamish Atlas.com.* http://squamishatlas.com/

Lewis, G. Malcolm, "The Indigenous Maps and Mapping of North American Indians," *Map Collector* 9 (1979), pp. 145–167.

Luker, Trish, "Decolonising Archives: Indigenous Challenges to Record Keeping in 'Reconciling' Settler Colonial States," *Australian Feminist Studies* 32.91–92 (2017), pp. 108–125.

MacDonald, Norbert, "Vancouver in the Nineteenth Century," *Urban History Review* 1.75 (1975), pp. 51–54.
McDowell, Jim, *Uncharted Waters: The Explorations of José Narváez (1768–1840)* (Vancouver: Ronsdale Press, 2015).
McKee, William C., "The Vancouver Park System, 1886–1929: A Product of Local Businessmen," *Urban History Review* 3–78 (1979), pp. 33–49.
Melbourne International Arts Festival, "The Shadow King Trailer," YouTube Video, 26 September 2013. www.youtube.com/watch?v=d-UdrWqjxXU
Million, Dian, "Felt Theory: An Indigenous Feminist Approach to Affect and History," *Wicazo Sa Review* 24.2 (2009), pp. 53–76.
Monkman, Kent, *The Triumph of Mischief*, eds. David Liss and Shirley J. Madill (Montreal: ABC Art Books Canada Distribution, 2008).
Mourning, Dove, *Cogewea* (Lincoln: University of Nebraska Press, 1981).
O'Brien, Jean M., *Firsting and Lasting: Writing Indians out of Existence in New England* (Minneapolis: University of Minnesota Press, 2010).
Parker, Robert Dale, ed., *The Sound the Stars Make Rushing through the Sky: The Writings of Jane Johnston Schoolcraft* (Philadelphia: University of Pennsylvania Press, 2007).
Paul, Elsie, *Written as I Remember It: Teachings from the Life of a Sliammon Elder*, eds. Paige Raibmon and Harmony Johnson (Vancouver: UBC Press, 2014).
The People and the Text. http://thepeopleandthetext.ca/
Philip, NourbeSe M., *Zong!* (Middletown, CT: Wesleyan University Press, 2008).
Presner, Todd, David Shepard, and Yoh Kawano, *Hypercities: Thick Mapping in the Digital Humanities* (Cambridge, MA: Harvard University Press, 2014).
Quirk, Linda, "Labour of Love: *Legends of Vancouver* and the Unique Publishing Enterprise That Wrote E. Pauline Johnson into Canadian Literary History," *Papers of the Bibliographical Society of Canada* 47.2 (2009), pp. 201–251.
Reder, Deanna, and Linda M. Morra, eds., *Learn, Teach, Challenge: Approaching Indigenous Literatures* (Waterloo: Wilfrid Laurier University Press, 2016).
Rifkin, Mark, *The Erotics of Sovereignty: Queer Native Writing in the Era of Self-Determination* (Minneapolis: University of Minnesota Press, 2012).
Robertson, Nancy E., *J.E.H. MacDonald, R.C.A., 1873–1932* (Toronto: Rous & Mann Press Limited, 1965).
Roy, Susan, "Mapping Tool: Kitsilano Reserve," *Indigenous Foundations*, 2009. https://indigenousfoundations.arts.ubc.ca/mapping_tool_kitsilano_reserve/
Royal Heraldry Society of Canada, "Arms & Badges: Royal Arms of Canada, a Brief History," *The Royal Heraldry Society of Canada*, 2018. www.heraldry.ca/content/arms_badges_royal_arms.php
Sanderson, Douglas, "Wampum Diplomacy in the Early-Middle Encounter Period," presentation before The Forum on Canadian and Commonwealth Indigenous-Settler Development Relations, Trinity College, University of Toronto, Toronto, 14 September 2017.
Scholefield, E. O. S., *British Columbia From the Earliest Times to the Present*, vol. 3: *Biographical* (Vancouver: The S.J. Clarke Publishing Company, 1914).
Shield, Alix, "Mary Agnes Capilano (Lixwelut)," *Alix Shield*, 2018. http://alix-shield.com/people/mary-agnes-capilano-lixwelut
———, "The People and the Text Featured Authors: E. Pauline Johnson," *The People and the Text*, May 2018. http://thepeopleandthetext.ca/EPaulineJohnson

———, “Rethinking the Paratext: Digital Story-Mapping E. Pauline Johnson’s and Chief Joe and Mary Capilano’s *Legends of Vancouver* (1911),” *BC Studies* 197 (2018), pp. 107–121.

Simon Fraser University, “səl̓ilw̓ət (Sleilwaut): Burrard Inlet and Indian Arm.” www.sfu.ca/brc/imeshMobileApp/place-names/sleilwaut.html

Spadoni, Carl, and Judy Donnelly, *A Bibliography of McClelland and Stewart Imprints, 1909–1985: A Publisher’s Legacy* (Toronto: ECW Press, 1994).

Stoler, Ann Laura, “Colonial Archives and the Arts of Governance,” *Archival Science* 2 (2002), pp. 87–109.

Todd, Kamala, “Vancouver Is an Indigenous City,” *The Tyee*, 12 November 2015. https://thetyee.ca/Opinion/2015/11/12/Vancouver-Indigenous-City/

Touchie, Mitcholos, “Feel Free to Use the Term ‘CKA’ (Colonially Known As),” Facebook, 8 December 2016. www.facebook.com/mitcholos/posts/10153995894817536

The True Size, 2018. https://thetruesize.com/

Tuhiwai Smith, Linda, *Decolonizing Methodologies: Research and Indigenous Peoples* (New York: Zed Books, 1999).

Vancouver Public Space Network, “Blog: A PETITION for the Incorporation of the City of Vancouver,” 2013. http://vancouverpublicspace.ca/2011/04/06/a-petition-for-the-incorporation-of-the-city-of-vancouver/

Vizenor, Gerald, *Manifest Manners: Narratives on Postindian Survivance* (Lincoln: University of Nebraska Press, 1999).

Whitehead, Joshua, *Full-Metal Indigiqueer* (Vancouver: Talonbooks, 2017).

12 Native-American Contributions to Democracy, Marxism, Feminism, Gender Fluidity, and Environmentalism

Bruce E. Johansen

While Europe did not discover America, America was quite a discovery for Europe. For roughly three centuries before the American Revolution, the ideas that made the revolution possible were being discovered, nurtured, and embellished in the growing English and French colonies of North America, as images of America became a staple of European literature and philosophy. America provided a counterpoint for European convention and assumption; it existed in European and western eyes as both a dream and a reality, and in this sense Americans shaped European and settler identity in important ways. In order to appreciate the way in which European eyes first alighted upon the New World, we must take the phrase literally and with our first-hand experience and knowledge of the excitement aroused today by human exploration of and travel to outerspace. Unlike their contemporaries today, however, one electrifying difference remains evident: the voyagers of the so-called Age of Discoveries knew that their New World was inhabited. They had only to look and learn, to drink in the bewildering newness and enchanting novelty of seeing it all for the first time.

Native Americans also became a means of idealizing independence-seeking colonies vis a vis their European colonial administrators. American-born Benjamin Franklin (1706–1790) used his image of Indians and their societies to critique Europe. In his view, "The Care and Labour of providing for Artificial and fashionable Wants, the sight of so many Rich wallowing in superfluous plenty, while so many are kept poor and distress'd for want; the Insolence of Office [. . .] [and] restraints of Custom, all contrive to disgust [Indians] with what we call civil Society."[1] American Indians and their societies figured into Franklin's conceptions of life, liberty, and the pursuit of happiness. The same objectives also arose in the mind of Thomas Jefferson (1743–1826), who authored the phrase inspired by those conceptions in the Declaration of Independence published in 1776; Franklin functioned in many ways as Jefferson's revolutionary mentor. An important debate at the time resulted in the term "happiness" being substituted for "property," and it is in this light that we must consider the two so-called founders' description of American

Indian societies and the provocative role they played in influencing Franklin and Jefferson's thought. Both men sought to create a society that operated as much as possible on consensus and public opinion, while citing the same mechanisms in native societies. Both described Indians' passion for liberty while upholding liberty as a patriotic prinicple around which they mustered the masses; they admired Indians' notions of happiness while seeking a definition of happiness that suited the nascent nation. As Franklin makes clear,

> It is for the project of nation-building that Franklin sought help from all the Indians of North America not under the dominion of the Spaniards, who are in that natural state, being restrained by no Laws, having no Courts, or Ministers of Justice, no Suits, no prisons, no governors vested with any Legal Authority. The persuasion of Men distinguished by Reputation of Wisdom is the only Means by which others are govern'd, or rather led—and the State of the Indians was probably the first State of all Nations.[2]

The acknolwedgement on the part of Franklin that Indigenous peoples comprised a collective form of first nation within the context of international relations seems significant given his own objective to formulate a nation. Thus, he comes across as pro-national with respect to Indigenous peoples.

Also looking to Indigenous societies for inspriation when writing to Virginian statesman Edward Carrington (1748–1810) in 1787, Jefferson linked freedom of expression with public opinion as well as happiness, citing American Indian societies as an example to be emulated:

> The basis of our government being the opinion of the people, our very first object should be to keep that right; and were it left to me to decide whether we should have a government without newspapers or newspapers without a government, I should not hesitate for a moment to prefer the latter [. . .]. I am convinced that those [Indian] societies which live without government enjoy in their general mass an infinitely greater degree of happiness than those who live under European governments.[3]

The Haudenosaunee (Iroquois) are often thought to have influenced these two men's thought. This idea continues to receive endorsements from some well-known people outside of the United States, including the 14th Dalai Lama of Tibet, who decried the United Nations's ignorance of Tibet's oppression by China and compared the former country's plight to the subjugation of North American native peoples. Along the way, the Dalai Lama observed that

> The inspiration for the American founding forefathers, Thomas Paine and Benjamin Franklin, by their comprehensive studies of

> the Iroquois Confederacy and the thousand-year-old "Great Law of Peace" given by the Peacemaker [and] Hiawatha, provided them with the foundation stone for our United States Constitution and the Declaration of Independence! The early drafts of the American Constitution included some of the Iroquois language, for the English words were too limiting![4]

These ideas have been debated in several scholarly venues for history research and have spread across the world, as the comments of the Dalai Lama demonstrate. The ideas raised in these books have been integrated into a number of university courses, theses, and dissertations, as well as other school curricula at all levels.[5]

After ratification of the United States Constitution in 1788, the political ideas of the Haudenosaunee and their influence on the American mind persisted for most of the nineteenth century. Knowledge of Haudenosaunee and other Native-American societies and their political organizations appealed to the organizers of European and American social and political movements during the nineteenth century much as they had helped shape the ideals of some of the United States' most influential founders the preceeding century. Early feminists and Marxists, among others, used the Haudenosaunee as a counterpoint to what they described as European-bred oppressiveness at a time when mainstream America was preoccupied with westward expansion. No century has been more hostile to America's Indigenous peoples. But, even in that bleakest of centuries, impressions of native liberty continued to exert a powerful allure.

The Haudenosaunee's influence is apparent and clearly cited in an important book that participated what Sally R. Wagner calls the first wave of feminism, as represented by Matilda Joslyn Gage's *Woman, Church and State*, first published in 1893.[6] In that book, Gage (1826–1898) acknowledges that "the modern world [is] indebted for its first conception of inherent rights, natural equality of condition, and the establishment of a civilized government upon this basis" of the "Six Nations," meaning the Haudenosaunee.[7] Gage was one of the three most influential feminist architects of the nineteenth-century women's movement, along with Elizabeth Cady Stanton (1815–1902) and Susan B. Anthony (1820–1906). In the 1980s, scholars such as Wagner were among the first to provide a scholarly basis for a resurgent feminist movement in the late twentieth century. Gage prior to this time had been read out of the movement and its history by scholars because of her radical views, especially regarding the oppression of women by organized religion. Knowledge of the Haudenosaunee's matrilineal system of society and government was widespread among early feminists, many of whom lived in upstate New York in territory that traditionally belonged to the Haudenosaunee. The early feminists learned of the Iroquois not only through reading the works of Morgan, Schoolcraft, and others, but also through direct personal experience. Wagner asserts that "Nineteenth century radical feminist theoreticians, such as Elizabeth Cady Stanton and Matilda Joslyn Gage, looked to the Iroquois for their vision of a transformed world."[8] The feminist movement was significantly influenced by Haudenosaunee social and political thought and thus it is from Indigenous values and practices that feminism first emerges in nineteenth-century America.

Feminisim is not the only movement and body of thought that sprung from Indigenous sources of inspiration. Friedrich Engels (1820–1895) inherited copious notes authored by Karl Marx (1818–1883) on Morgan's *Ancient Society* (1877). After Marx's death, Engels authored *The Origin of the Family, Private Property and the State* in 1886.[9] Studying Morgan's account of so-called primitive societies, with the Haudenosasunee being his cornerstone, Engels provided what he believed to be an egalitarian, classless model of society that also ensured justice between the sexes. In this way, the feminist movement dovetailed with other movements pushing to create more egalitarian societies along the lines of gender, but also class and social status. In his work, Engels approvingly cited Morgan's assertion that

> Democracy in government, brotherhood in society, equality in rights and privileges, and universal education, foreshadow the next higher plane of society to which experience, intelligence, and knowledge are steadily tending. *It will be a revival, in a higher form, of the liberty, equality, and fraternity of the ancient gentes.* (Engels's emphasis)[10]

Engels's tone seems to indicate that he had seen a promising future reflected in the past. In this future, just as in Haudenosaunee society,

> [E]verything runs smoothly without soldiers, gendarmes, or police; without nobles, kings, governors, prefects, or judges; prisons, without trials. All quarrels and disputes are settled by the whole body of those concerned [. . .] not a bit of our extensive and complicated machinery of administration is required. [. . .] There are no poor and needy [. . .]. All are free and equal—including the women.[11]

Without citing him, Engels evoked an image of Native American (likely Haudenosaunee) society that was strikingly similar to Benjamin Franklin's vision expressed a century before him.[12] Franklin's contemporary, Thomas Paine (1737–1809), also teased out the advantages of looking to Native American ways of life in order to improve the future:

> To understand what the state of society ought to be, it is necessary to have some idea of the natural and primitive state of man; such as it is at this day among the Indians of North America. There is not, in that state, any of those spectacles of human misery which poverty and want present to our eyes in all the towns and streets of Europe.[13]

As contemporaries of Morgan, Engels, and Marx, the founding mothers of modern feminism in the United States shared their enthusiasm for establishing functioning societies that incorporated notions of sexual equality. All of these founding mothers seemed to believe that the native model held promise for the future. Gage and Stanton looked to the native model for a design of a "regenerated world."[14] To Gage, "Never was justice more perfect, never civilization higher than under the Matriarchate," and it was "Under [Haudenosaunee] women [that] the science of government reached the highest form known to the world."[15] In her 1891 speech before the National Council of Women, Stanton surveyed the research of Morgan and others, and stated that "Among the greater number of the American aborigines, the descent of property and children were in the female line. Women sat in the councils of war and peace and their opinions had equal weight on all questions;" in this regard, she specified the Haudenosaunee councils.[16] After surveying tribal societies in other parts of the world as well, Stanton closed her speech with a case for sexual equality:

> I would say that every woman present must have a new sense of dignity and self respect, feeling that our mothers, during long periods in the long past, have been the ruling power and that they used that power for the best interests of humanity. As history is said to repeat itself, we have every reason to believe that our turn will come again [. . .]. It may not be for woman's supremacy, but for, the as yet untried experiment of complete equality, when the united thought of man and woman will inaugurate a just government, a pure religion, a happy home, a civilization at last in which ignorance, poverty and crime will exist no more. Those who watch already behold the dawn of the new day.[17]

As Gage and Stanton's positions on gender equity demonstrate, Native-American practices have shaped all manner of gendered relationships, and reaching beyond feminism, Indigenous thought also plays a fundamental role in gay, lesbian, bisexual, and transgender (LGBT) peoples in our society today. LGBT peoples arise in at least 150 Native-American myths and stories and they have been a welcomed part of Indigenous cultures for ages.[18] Jim Elledge compiled an anthology that contains stories from many cultural contexts, including among others the Arapaho, Assiniboine, Chemehuevi, Comanche, Coos, Crow, Dakotas, Fox, Hopi, Kamia, Menomini, Mohave, Navajo, Ojibwa, Passamaquoddy, Pawnee, Sioux (Lakota), Tewa, Western Mono, Yokut, and Zuñi. The inclusion of LGBT people in foundational myths demonstrates how they have been an accepted and welcome part of Indigenous societies "since the dawn of time," according to Elledge, and "were often at least of equal standing with other members of their tribe, if not more powerful than those in whose midst they existed."[19]

Heterosexuals usually were not threatened by variations of gender and gender non-normativity. In fact, in this light normativity itself becomes unsettled; rather, they "saw the two-spirits as individuals with special talents which they offered the tribe for its continued existence, its prosperity, and its safety."[20] Cross-gender roles and labor also generally were respected. This point of view was echoed in more recent times by Erna Pahe, a Navajo community activist, who vocalized his understanding of gender roles:

> We're the one group of people that can really understand both cultures [. . .]. You go out there into the straight world and it's really amazing the stereotypes. Man can do this and women can't do that. Or women can do this and men can't do that. In our culture, in our little gay world, anybody can do anything.[21]

In 1982, a Crow tribal elder also affirmed the racial limitations imposed by the west that simply do not exist in the North American Indigenous world: "We don't waste people the way white society does. Every person has their gift."[22] One of those talents in many cases seems to have been match-making.

A minority of scholars dissent from these ideas. Chicano gender historian Ramón Gutiérrez criticized what he called the "queer-friendly" approach of Will Roscoe and others as "an unsubstantiated gay liberationist white projection of idealizing and projecting queer freedom onto Native-American pasts."[23] According to Elledge, however, "Typically, the two-spirit individual was a gay, lesbian, bisexual or transgendered person—in the western definition of gender variance—who often, but not always, adopted the clothing, habits, and/or social roles of the opposite sex."[24] Many assumed such roles in youth, aided by dreams or visions, and an individual's peers performed a ritual to recognize the change. Such roles had a valuable place in many native societies and were not morally condemned as a violation of a religious principle that dictated gender normativity and roles within European-American cultures. While some gay, lesbian, bisexual, and transgender people formed intimate relationships with others of similar orientation, more often two-spirited individuals formed relationships with heterosexual partners. As Elledge explains,

> Their partnerships were overwhelmingly with individuals who were comfortable with the roles assigned them by virtue of their gender. Thus, a male two-spirit formed a sexual relationship [. . .] with an individual who was, in terms of his social status, a heterosexual man; likewise, a female two-spirit would form a relationship with a heterosexual woman.[25]

Long-term, male two-spirits often were considered wives and husbands of their respective partners, and "for many Native Americans," continues

Elledge, "sexuality seems to have been more fluid than the polarized notion of heterosexuality at one extreme and homosexuality at the opposite extreme allows."[26] In recent years, western knowledge about gender has come to agree with the point of view that a person may have both attributes in varying proportions.

Will Roscoe, a prominent scholar of sexual orientation in Native-American cultures, notes that some people had criticized the use of the term berdache, which, like the word Indian when used to describe Native-American peoples, is now viewed as a western imposition (actually the word was appropriated by French anthropologists from the Persian word *barda* [captive or slave]). He had his doubts that "two spirit" was any less western and tended to use both terms, or to use "third gender" for male homosexuals and "fourth gender" for lesbians. Roscoe documented male same-sex relationships in at least 155 Native-American groups, and female relationships in a third as many.[27]

During the colonization of North America, the fluidity of gender and cultural roles among Native Americans confounded Europeans whose cultures confined behavior according to gender roles with a rigidity unknown today. Many native men not only blurred gender barriers, but crossed them, back and forth, many times during their lives. Some preferred the company of other men, but also married women and fathered children.[28] The same men also may have performed tasks usually identified with women, such as farming and dressing hides, until they shed their female roles and led other men in war. Some men (and a smaller number of women) were bisexual, and others abstained from sex altogether. The Lakota called men who affected women's roles *winkte*. Such people were not ostracized but generally respected as *wakan* and believed to possess powers that other men did not. Although winktes did not go to war, they sometimes were said to be able to foretell the future, so warriors consulted with them about upcoming battles. Sicangu and Oglala Lakota chief Luther Standing Bear (1868–1939) relates that "Everyone accepted the winktes with kindness and allowed them to choose their own work, be it either man's or women's, and one of the bravest men I ever knew was a winkte. They were scarce, however, and in my life I have not known more than half a dozen."[29] Standing Bear's observation that winktes had grown scarce allows us to consider the impact of the European notions of gender roles upon Native-American peoples.

Early in 1801, the trader Alexander Henry (1739–1824) encountered a young Anishinaabe (Ojibwa) man whose dress and mannerisms were feminine, but who was known as a superlative warrior whose feats of bravery were legendary; he had once, in fact, routed an entire Sioux war party with a bow and a single quiver of arrows. "This person," wrote Henry, "is a curious compound between a man and a woman. He is a man in every respect both as to members [sexual organs] and courage but still he seems to appear womanish, and dresses as such;" some of the young man's compatriots (including his own father) disapproved of his gender bending, but others admired it, Henry attests.[30] The Illinois singled out young boys who played with women's toys ("the spade, the spindle, the axe") and dressed them as girls, including tattoos on their cheeks and breasts. "They omit nothing that can make them like the women," an observer wrote.[31] The Hidatsa believed that effeminate men had been blessed by a female deity. They were believed to be favored as religious leaders. An Omaha man was described as having been commanded by the moon to shift gender roles—he was an outstanding husband and father, but also a woman in his dress and cultural behavior.[32]

European response to witnsssing non-binary sexual practices was negative. In 1513, the Spanish explorer Vasco Nuñez de Balboa (1475–1519) encountered forty male homosexuals dressed as women in present-day Panama. He ordered their murder by hunting dogs, an act that was praised by a Spanish historian a century later as "a fine action of an honorable and Catholic Spaniard."[33] Hernán Cortés (1485–1547), Spanish invader of the Aztecs and other peoples residing in present-day Mexico, regarded every man in the lands that he was authorized by his king to govern as a sodomite: "We have learnt and been informed for sure that they are all sodomites and use that abominate sin," he expounded, and his compatriot, Bernal Diaz del Castillo (1492–1584), thought that "all the rest were sodomites, especially those who live on the coasts and in warm lands; so much so that young men paraded around dressed in women's clothes in order to work in the diabolical and abominable role."[34] He assumed that cross-dressing signified homosexuality. Similarly, Álvar Núñez Cabeza de Vaca (1490–1559) shared his encounter with the Karankawa of present-day Texas in 1540, during which time he "saw a most brutish and beastly custom [. . .] a man who was married to another and these be certain effeminate and impotent men, who go clothed and attired like women, and perform the office of a woman."[35] Clearly, men performing women's work and inhabiting a women's way of life violated these sixteenth-century Europeans' sense of right and wrong, and these attitudes persist for centuries among European colonists and settlers who lived in the Americas.

Returning to the nineteenth century when the foundations for the feminist movement were emerging, settlers received non-binary demonstrations of gender in varying ways. Part of the first generation of ethnographers interested in describing Indigenous ways of life, Edwin T. Denig (1812–1858), arrived in Crow country in 1833 as a trader with the American Fur Company. For twenty-three years, he remarked at what he thought was the alien nature of native cultures. One aspect that often perplexed Denig was how the Crows regarded gender diversity. He found that some of the Crows' most highly regarded people were men who dressed as women and did women's work. Conversely, some women led men into battle. Denig noted that such behavior in European-American societies could lead to a person's jailing, persecution, and even execution once their sexual orientation was condemned as deviant, even satanic.[36] One prominent Crow, who was known as Woman Chief, had four wives, led men into battle, and was highly esteemed by her peers. Originally a Gros Ventre, she was captured at the age of 10 by the Crows. Denig described her as taller and stronger than most women, and that she "desired to acquire manly accomplishments."[37] The German prince Maximilian (1782–1867), who traveled on the northern plains between 1832 and 1834, also remarked on the "many bardaches, or hermaphrodities, among them."[38] Laguna Pueblo author Leslie Silko noted that "Pueblo men in sacred kiva spaces can become possessed by female spirits, momentarily and appropriately embodying mixed gender energy."[39]

Christianity, western law, and cultural biases often inhibit the expression of these fluid gender realities in public, but this mode of expression survives in oral history. Paula Gunn Allen, Silko's cousin (and also a Laguna Pueblo author), believes that such expressions have been repressed by Christianity.[40] As a result, many Indigenous groups now frown upon same-sex relationships. Western societies generally have become more accepting of gender fluidity as many native peoples practiced it. As support for same-sex marriage increased rapidly around the world early in the twenty-first century, members of many American Indian tribes found themselves caught up in the same debate. A few tribal councils had approved same-sex unions by 2013, but the vast majority had remained silent, pending a landmark ruling by the United States Supreme Court on the federal *Defense of Marriage Act* or DOMA; the court struck down DOMA in June of 2013. Some native governments (such as the Suquamish in Washington State) had approved nonetheless same-sex marriages in eleven states by May of 2013. In the meantime, the Navajos were standing by a ban on same-sex marriage between close blood relatives that their council had passed in 2005. Thus, not only does gender fluidity find a degree of origination from Native-American cultures, but also centuries of suppression by western peoples of non-binary practices has undermined Indigenous cultures in this respect. In contrast, settler-colonists in North America today are increasingly challenging gender normativities that existed during Cortés and Jefferson's times, and this is not the only example of Native-American practices later being embraced by settler societies.

Native-American philosophy often combines spiritual and environmental themes in ways that appeal to many non-Indian environmental activists today. A lively scholarly debate has flared regarding how Native Americans generally conceived of the earth. Some ethnohistorians maintain that Native Americans possessed little or no environmental philosophy, and that any attempt to assemble evidence to sustain a Native-American ecological paradigm is doomed to failure because the entire argument is an exercise in wishful thinking by environmental activists seeking sentimental support for their own views, and thus part of a recently concocted pan-Indian mythology. References to mother earth in Native-American cosmology are abundant, however, and as George Cornell observes, "Native peoples almost universally view the earth as a feminine figure. The Mother provides for the sustenance and well-being of her children: it is from her that all subsistence is drawn. The relationship of native peoples to the earth, their Mother, is a sacred bond with the creation."[41] Many native cosmologies conceive of the sky and the sun as a masculine counterpart to mother earth, who together form a loving couple that is sometimes prone to many of the failings of human relationships between men and women. In the Algonkian Ojibwe language, for example, "The words for Earth and the vagina, respectively *aki* and *akitun*, share the same root."[42] Each native people in the Americas has its own origin story, but many share common elements. The characterization of the earth as feminine, using kin terminology, is one of these elements. While the bible commands the subordination of the earth in Genesis 3:18, many native cosmologies place human beings in a web of interdependent relationships with all facets of the created world. In this web, all things are animate, even objects, such as the pebbles under one's feet, which European languages characterize as lifeless. In the web of Native-American experience, the landscape of life envelopes our entire existence and the existence of that which is not us; even the rocks upon which we walk possess spirit and animus.

Settler-colonists have been hearing Native Americans characterize the earth as mother since shortly after the Mayflower landed in 1620 at Plymouth in present-day Massachusetts. Wampanoag sachem Massasoit (c. 1581–1661), who invited the so-called pilgrims to share with him in their first Thanksgiving feast, faced European ideas of land tenure with a few questions of his own: "What is this you call property? It cannot be the earth, for the land is our mother, nourishing all her children, beasts, birds, fish, and all men. The woods, the streams, everything on it belongs to everybody and is for the use of all. How can one man say it belongs only to him?"[43] Similarly, characterizations of mother earth are usually metaphorical rather than human-centered in Native-American religions and their adaptation of Christianity. Native-American cosmology may be characterized as a church of the earth, even though the very idea of a church is a European concept; yet the hybridized structure makes sense within what some scholars have called a religion of nature.[44]

Scholars who dismiss a native ecological ethic as merely resulting in the invention of modern-day hippies and pan-Indianists are missing something much more significant than references to mother earth in nineteenth-century primary sources. Scholars who have failed to engage with Indigenous ecological criticism also fail to understand or see the fundamental nature of many Native-American traditions, and the terms within which native thought conceptualizes the land and the life it nurtures. To Roger Dunsmore, western thought creates hierarchies and categories that do not exist in Native-American thoughtways. The very cognitive map for conceptualizing life is different, as illustrated in recent times by the example of a Wasco Indian who fell trees; he decided to quit logging and to sell his chainsaw because "he couldn't stand hearing the trees scream as he cut into them."[45] His is a worldview in which all components of the earth are valued and respected. As Black Elk offers, "With all beings and all things, we shall be as relatives."[46] Native-American perspectives on the environment often contrasted and bumped up against those of many early settlers who sought to tame the so-called wilderness.

References to Indigenous affection for nature permeated the thoughts of Luther Standing Bear, who affirms that

> The Lakota was a true naturalist—a lover of Nature. He loved the earth and all things of the earth, the attachment growing with age. The old people came literally to love the soil and they sat or reclined on the ground with a feeling of being close to a mothering power [. . .]. In talking to children, the old Lakota would place a hand on the ground and explain: "We sit in the lap of our mother. From her, we, and all other living things, come. We shall soon pass, but the place where we now rest will last forever [. . .]." Our altars were built on the ground and were altars of thankfulness and gratefulness. They were made of sacred earth and placed upon the holiest of all places—the lap of Mother Earth.[47]

Standing Bear defined his people's relationship to everything else on earth, writing that in the native view everything is animate and "possessed of personality;" he compared the world to a library, with "the stones, leaves, grass, brooks [. . .], birds, and animals" as its books.[48] Many times, wrote Standing Bear, the Indian is embarrassed and baffled by the white man's alienation from nature, as reflected in allusions to nature in such terms as "crude, primitive, wild, rude, untamed, and savage;" to Standing Bear, many whites imagined Native Americans as savages to "salve [. . . their] sore and troubled conscience now hardened through the habitual practice of injustice."[49] Standing Bear, who watched large-scale Anglo-American immigration change the face of the Great Plains, contrasted settler-colonial and Native-American conceptions of the natural world of North America:

> We did not think of the great open plains, the beautiful rolling hills, and winding streams with tangled brush, as "wild." Only to the white man was nature "a wilderness" and only to him was the land "infested" with "wild" animals and "savage" people. To us it was tame. Earth was bountiful, and we are surrounded with the blessings of the Great Mystery. Not until the hairy man from the east came and with brutal frenzy heaped injustices upon us and the families we loved

> was it "wild" for us. When the very animals of the forest began fleeing from his approach, then it was for us that the "Wild West" began.[50]

Standing Bear severelly criticized white attitudes toward nature. He said he knew of no species of plant, bird, or animal that had been exterminated in America until the coming of the white man. For some years after the buffalo disappeared, there remained vast herds of antelope, but the white hunter's work was no sooner complete after the buffalo cull that his attention turn toward the deer populations. "The white man considered natural animal life just as he did natural [Native-American] life upon this continent, as 'pests,'" lamented Standing Bear, and "Plants which the Indian found beneficial were also 'pests.' There is no word in the Lakota vocabulary with the English meaning of this word."[51]

Like Shaunee Tecumseh (1768–1813), Sauk Black Hawk (1767–1838), Oglala Lakota (Sioux), and Black Elk (1863–1950), among others, Standing Bear invoked the image of mother earth in his writing and explicitly linked the extermination of species to white presence in North America. In addition to being rooted in their homelands, Native Americans maintain historical and spiritual bonds to the land that foster attention to environmental threats. Long-time fishing-rights activist Billy Frank, Jr. explains that this connection places the protection of the environment and its role in sustaining human and all other life "at the top of our priority list."[52] It is in this light that modern-day environmentalism can be seen to have grown out of—or adopted the values of—Indigenous relationships with the land and its contents.[53] Indigenous environmental activism (including visceral opposition to the development of extractive industry) stems from a long historical experience with resource colonization. Both work in synthesis with a spiritual ethos that invests animus in everything natural to reinforce devotion to an ecological ethos common among many native peoples. While European religions often restrict their blessings to humanity, many Native Americans interpret "all my relations" to mean all of nature. This respect for nature is fundamental and enduring, and at the root of traditional Native-American responses to economic development. Definitions of balance are couched in this context, countering the protection of mother earth with a colonial ethos that seeks instead the mother lode, as rooted in Genesis ("Go forward, multiply, and subdue the Earth"). Naomi Klein has recently condemned this ethos as well as the continuing activities of industrialists who persist in viewing "nature as a bottomless vending machine."[54] Awareness of economic development's costs also animates the non-Indian environmental movement and results in a settler-activist agenda being cleansed of non-Indigenous science rather than becoming informed by Indigenous knowledge and conservation practices.

Firsting has been a practice used since Europeans arrived to the Americas, yet it has demonstrated itself to be fluid with respect to more recent times as settlers began to embrace the values and practices that they encountered in these continents upon their arrival. It is in this respect that scholars need to re-perspectivize Native-American contributions to knowledge, philosphy, and values as innovations within western society. Traditionally, western scholars have valued western innovation or, as has been shown in this chapter regarding the development of democracy, the first wave of feminism, evolving gender normativities, and environmental activism, western peoples have appropriated Indigenous practices and made them their own, often without acknowledgment. Throughout this chapter I have also made room for nontraditional voices, whether women or Indigenous, on these subjects, with the hope that scholars continue to seek out these voices and include them as critical sources of knowledge about women's and gender studies, race studies, and environmental studies.

Notes

1. Labaree and Willcox, eds., *The Papers of Benjamin Franklin*, vol. 17, p. 381.
2. Allan Ramsey, *Thoughts on the Origin and Nature of Government* (London: T. Becket and P.A. de Hondt, 1769), as cited in Lynd, *Intellectual Origins of American Radicalism*, p. 85.
3. Jefferson to Carrington, 16 January 1787, in Boyd, ed., *The Papers of Thomas Jefferson*, vol. 11, p. 49.
4. See discussion of the Dalai Lama's position as well as context for this quotation, in Johansen, "Reaching the Grassroots."
5. See, for example, the works of Bruce E. Johansen, "Native American Democratic Traditions," in Isakhan and Stockwell, eds., *The Edinburgh Companion to the History of Democracy*, pp. 233–244, and two more works by the same author, "The Influence Issue Revisited," pp. 49–53, and "Native American Ideas of Governance," pp. 12–15. Also see Sanders, "Benjamin Franklin," pp. 143–162.
6. Roesch Wagner, "The Iroquois Confederacy," pp. 32–34.
7. Gage, *Woman, Church and State*, p. 10.
8. Roesch Wagner, "The Iroquois Confederacy," pp. 32–33.
9. Morgan, *Ancient Society*.
10. Ibid., p. 552, cited in Engels, *Origin of the Family, Private Property, and the State*, in Marx and Engels, *Selected Works*, p. 528.
11. Engels, *Origin of the Family*, in Marx and Engels, *Selected Works*, p. 528.
12. Staughton, *Intellectual Origins*, pp. 55 and 85.
13. Foner, ed., *Complete Writings of Thomas Paine*, vol. 1, p. 610. Also see Jefferson, *Notes on the State of Virginia*, p. 93.
14. Roesch Wagner, "The Root of Oppression," p. 11.
15. Gage, *Woman, Church and State*, pp. 9–10.
16. Stanton, "The Matriarchate," p. 1.
17. Ibid., p. 7.
18. Elledge, *Gay, Lesbian, Bisexual*, p. xix.
19. Ibid., p. xv.
20. Ibid., p. xviii.
21. Roscoe, *Changing Ones*, p. 65.
22. Ibid., pp. 4 and 9.

23. Estrada, "Two-Spirit Histories in Southwestern and Mesoamerican Literatures," in Slater and Yarbrough, eds., *Gender and Sexuality*, pp. 165–184: 171.
24. Elledge, *Gay, Lesbian, Bisexual*, p. xiv.
25. Ibid.
26. Ibid., p. xv.
27. Roscoe, *Changing Ones*, p. 7.
28. Carpenter, "Womanish Men and Manlike Women," in Slater and Yarbrough, eds., *Gender and Sexuality*, pp. 146–164: 148.
29. Standing Bear, *Land of the Spotted Eagle*, p. 93.
30. Carpenter, "Womanish Men and Manlike Women," in Slater and Yarbrough, eds., *Gender and Sexuality*, pp. 147–148.
31. Ibid., p. 151.
32. Ibid., p. 157.
33. Roscoe, *Changing Ones*, p. 4.
34. Sandra Slater, "'Nought But Women': Construction of Masculinities and Modes of Emasculation in the New World," in Slater and Yarbrough, eds., *Gender and Sexuality*, pp. 30–53: 47.
35. Roscoe, *Changing Ones*, p. 4.
36. Ibid., p. 3.
37. Ibid., p. 78.
38. Ibid., p. 25.
39. Estrada, "Two-Spirit Histories," in Slater and Yarbrough, *Gender and Sexuality*, p. 171.
40. Ibid., pp. 169–170.
41. Cornell, "Native American Perceptions," pp. 3–13.
42. Jordan Paper, "Through the Earth Darkly: The Female Spirit in Native American Religions," in Vecsey, ed., *Religion in Native North America*, pp. 3–19: 14.
43. Jace Weaver, "Introduction: Notes from a Miner's Canary," in Weaver, ed., *Defending Mother Earth*, pp. 1–28: 10.
44. See the essays in Vecsey and Venables, eds., *American Indian Environments*.
45. Dunsmore, *Earth's Mind*, p. 7.
46. Black Elk, *The Sacred Pipe*, p. 105.
47. Standing Bear, *Land of the Spotted Eagle*, pp. 192, 194, and 200.
48. Hughes, *American Indian Ecology*, p. 80.
49. Standing Bear, *Land of the Spotted Eagle*, pp. 196 and 251.
50. Ibid., p. 38.
51. Ibid., p. 165.
52. Grossman and Parker, *Asserting Native Resilience*, esp. pp. 38 and 45–46.
53. Berry, "Scholar Daniel Wildcat in Discussing the Environment."
54. Klein, *This Changes Everything*, p. 183.

Bibliography

Berry, Carol, "Scholar Daniel Wildcat in Discussing the Environment: Its Relatives, Not 'Resources'," *Indian Country Today Media Network*, 1 October 2011.

Black Elk, *The Sacred Pipe: Black Elk's Account of the Seven Rites of the Oglala Sioux* [1953], recorded and ed. Joseph Epes Brown (Norman: University of Oklahoma Press, 1967).

Boyd, Julian P., ed., *The Papers of Thomas Jefferson* (Princeton, NJ: Princeton University Press, 1950).

Cornell, George, "Native American Perceptions of the Environment," *Northeast Indian Quarterly* 7.2 (1990), pp. 3–13.
Dunsmore, Roger, *Earth's Mind* (Albuquerque: University of New Mexico Press, 1997).
Elledge, Jim, *Gay, Lesbian, Bisexual and Transgender Myths: From the Arapaho to the Zuñi* (New York: Peter Lang, 2002).
Foner, Philip S., ed., *Complete Writings of Thomas Paine* (New York: Citadel Press, 1945).
Gage, Matilda Joslyn, *Woman, Church and State* (Watertown, MA: Persephone Press, 1980).
Grossman, Zoltán, and Alan Parker, *Asserting Native Resilience: Pacific Rim Indigenous Nations Face the Climate Crisis* (Corvallis: Oregon State University Press, 2012).
Hughes, J. Donald, *American Indian Ecology* (El Paso: University of Texas Press, 1983).
Isakhan, Benjamin, and Stephen Stockwell, eds., *The Edinburgh Companion to the History of Democracy* (Edinburgh: Edinburgh University Press, 2012).
Jefferson, Thomas, *Notes on the State of Virginia* [1784], ed. William Peden (Chapel Hill: University of North Carolina Press, 1955).
Johansen, Bruce E., "Reaching the Grassroots: The World-Wide Diffusion of Iroquois Democratic Traditions," April 2002. https://ratical.org/many_worlds/6Nations/grassroots.html
———, "The Influence Thesis Revisited," *European Review of Native American Studies* 21.1 (2007), pp. 49–53.
———, "Native American Ideas of Governance and the United States Constitution," *Indigenous People Today: Living in Two Worlds* 14.6 (2009), pp. 12–15.
Klein, Naomi, *This Changes Everything: Capitalism vs. the Climate* (Toronto: Alfred A. Knopf Canada, 2014).
Labaree, Leonard, and William B. Willcox, eds., *The Papers of Benjamin Franklin* (New Haven, CT: Yale University Press, 1950 to present).
Lynd, Staughton, *Intellectual Origins of American Radicalism* (New York: Pantheon, 1968).
Marx, Karl, and Friedrich Engels, *Selected Works* (London: Lawrence & Wishart, 1968).
Morgan, Lewis H., *Ancient Society, or Researches in the Lines of Human Progress from Savagery, through Barbarism to Civilization* (New York: Henry Holt and Company, 1877).
Roesch Wagner, Sally, "The Iroquois Confederacy: A Native American Model for Non-Sexist Men," *Changing Men* 19 (1988), pp. 32–34.
———, "The Root of Oppression Is the Loss of Memory: The Iroquois and the Early Feminist Vision," *Akwesasne Notes* 21.1 (1989), pp. 11–13.
Roscoe, Will, *Changing Ones: The Third and Fourth Genders in Native North America* (New York: St. Martin's Press, 1998).
Sanders, J. T., "Benjamin Franklin and the League of the Haudenosaunee," *The Philosophical Age Almanac* 32 (2006), pp. 143–162.
Slater, Sandra, and Fay A. Yarbrough, eds., *Gender and Sexuality in Indigenous North America: 1400–1850* (Columbia: University of South Carolina Press, 2012).

Standing Bear, Luther, *Land of the Spotted Eagle* [1933] (Lincoln: University of Nebraska Press, 1978).
Stanton, Elizabeth Cady, "The Matriarchate or Mother-Age: An Address of Mrs. Stanton before the National Council of Women, February 1891," *The National Bulletin* 1.5 (1891), pp. 1–12.
Staughton, Lynd, *Intellectual Origins of American Radicalism* (New York: Pantheon, 1968).
Vecsey, Christopher, ed., *Religion in Native North America* (Boise: University of Idaho Press, 1990).
Vecsey, Christopher, and Robert W. Venables, eds., *American Indian Environments: Ecological Issues in Native American History* (Syracuse, NY: Syracuse University Press, 1980).
Weaver, Jace, ed., *Defending Mother Earth: Native American Perspectives on Environmental Justice* (Maryknoll, NY: Orbis Books, 1996).

Contributors

Lauren Beck specializes in the visual culture of the early-modern Atlantic world, with interests in text-and-image relations, historical cartography, and marginalized voices. She holds the Canada Research Chair in Intercultural Encounter, the rank of Professor of Hispanic Studies at Mount Allison University, and has served as editor of *Terrae Incognitae* since 2013. Her recent publications include *Visualizing the Text: From Manuscript Culture to Caricature* (co-edited with C. Ionescu, University of Delaware Press, 2017); *Canada before Confederation: Maps from the Exhibition* (co-authored with C. Van Duzer, Vernon Press, 2017); *Mapping North America: Early Modern Narratives of Discovery and Exploration* (with C. Ionescu, Mount Allison University, 2015); and *Transforming the Enemy in Spanish Culture: The Conquest through the Lens of Visual and Textual Multiplicity* (Cambria Press, 2013). She has recently held fellowships at the Library of Congress and the James Ford Bell Library.

Rachel Bryant is a settler-Canadian researcher and an uninvited guest who divides her time between the traditional and unceded territories of the Mi'kmaq and Wolastoqiyik peoples. She is a Social Sciences and Humanities Research Council Postdoctoral Fellow in the Department of English at Dalhousie University in K'jipuktuk. Her first book, *The Homing Place: Indigenous and Settler Literary Legacies of the Atlantic* (Wilfred Laurier University Press, 2017), demonstrates how settler-Canadian literary criticism can function diplomatically, helping to transform heavily fortified Euro-western understandings of history and of place. Bryant's current scholarship restores British and pre-Revolutionary American contexts to the study of Canadian culture and literature, revealing the deep roots of "CanLit" as a settler-colonial institution, one that long predates confederation, and one that continues to actively and systematically minoritize Indigenous and black voices.

Jonathan DeCoster is Assistant Professor of History at Otterbein University in Westerville, Ohio. His research focuses on rivalries and alliances among native peoples and Europeans in the colonial period. In 2013, he published "Entangled Borderlands: Europeans and Timucuans in 16th-Century Florida" in the *Florida Historical Quarterly*. He is currently working on a book manuscript about rivalries and alliances among southeastern Indians and their effect on French, English, and Spanish colonies, titled *Intimate Enemies: Native Rivalry and Imperial Competition in the Southeastern Borderlands, 1562–1614*, which was funded by research fellowships from the American Historical Society, the American Philosophical Society, the Council for European Studies, and the Mellon Foundation. Jonathan is also interested in history pedagogy. He participated in a project through the Council of Independent Colleges to explore online humanities instruction and will soon publish an online textbook module about the Pueblo revolt of 1680 with Oxford University Press.

Jorge M. Escobar received his doctorate in human and social sciences from the National University of Colombia, a master's degree in history and the philosophy of science from the University of Notre Dame, a master's degree in philosophy from the University of Manitoba, and a bachelor's degree in philosophy from the University of Antioquia. He is currently a member of the research group Science, Technology, and Society Studies at the Instituto Tecnológico Metropolitano (Medellin, Colombia) and director of the master's program in STS Studies at the same institution. He is interested in early-modern history and the philosophy of science on both sides of the Atlantic, as well as contemporary issues in science policy and the public understanding of science.

Manuel Lucena Giraldo holds the appointment of Research Scientist at the Concilio Superior de Investigaciones Científicas (CSIC) in Spain and is Professor of Humanities at the IE Business School attached to IE University in Madrid. He has also held the appointment of Visiting Scholar at Harvard University, Lecturer at the Bing Overseas Studies Program at Stanford University, and Visiting Professor at Tufts University, Javeriana University, Instituto Venezolano de Investigaciones Científicas, Colegio de México, Universidad de los Andes, and St. Antony's College at Oxford. He was the Education Attaché to the Spanish Embassy in Colombia. He served as CSIC's representative at the European Science Foundation, and as manager and research project consultant at the Fundación Carolina, the agency responsible for building ties between researchers across the Spanish-speaking world. He has authored several books, co-authored *The Oxford Illustrated History of the World*, and serves on the editorial board of *Revista de Occidente*, the advisory committee of *National Geographic*, and as member of the European Academy.

Nicolas Haisell is a doctoral candidate at Queen's University, Kingston. His current work focuses on the output of Nova Scotian public intellectuals and historians, examining the processes through which Indigenous, Acadian, and other so-called problematic groups were reckoned with in local printed material as competing regional and national identities coalesced in the mid- to late nineteenth century. His other research projects have included an examination of the British-Canadian study of the Beothuk, a group whose extinction at the hands of settlers problematized the liberal rhetoric of paternalistic settler colonialism. As a result, local writers turned to novel anthropological theories of race and unilinear human evolution to polemically explain the decline as a natural process. Broadly, his work seeks to understand the intersections between race and the construction of liberal modernity in nineteenth-century Canada through settler-colonizer enumerations and taxonomies. He also holds a master's degree in history from Queen's and a bachelor's degree (honors) in social anthropology from Dalhousie University.

Bruce E. Johansen is Frederick W. Kayser Professor of Communication and Native American Studies at the University of Nebraska in Omaha, where he has been teaching and writing since 1982. He has authored forty-seven books, most recently a three-volume set, *Climate Change: An Encyclopedia of Science, Society, and Solutions* (ABC-Clio, 2017). Johansen holds the University of Nebraska award for Outstanding Research and Creative Activity (ORCA), the state system's highest faculty recognition. Johansen's first academic specialty was the influence of Native-American political systems on United States political and legal institutions; his best-known books in this area are *Forgotten Founders* (Gambit, 1982) and *Exemplar of Liberty* (with Donald A. Grinde, Jr.; American Indian Center, 1991). Johansen has described the debate over Indigenous influence on American politics in *Debating Democracy* (Clear Light, 1998), and *Native American Political Systems and the Evolution of Democracy: An Annotated Bibliography* (Greenwood, 1996; volume 2, 1999).

Vivien Kogut Lessa de Sá is Teaching Associate in Portuguese Studies at the University of Cambridge. Her main teaching and research interests are in early-modern travel writing, especially in connection to the New World, and comparative studies in Brazilian, Portuguese, and English literatures. She has previously taught at the University of Essex, the State University of Rio, and the Pontifical Catholic University of Rio, in Brazil. In 2015, she published a critical edition of one of the earliest English descriptions of Brazil, *The Admirable Adventures and Strange Fortunes of Anthony Knivet: an English Pirate in Brazil* (Cambridge University Press, 2015). More recently she translated and co-edited (with Sheila Moura Hue) twelve accounts of English travelers to colonial Brazil. Vivien is presently researching a rare Jesuit manuscript taken from Brazil in 1592 conserved in Oxford.

Ashley Caranto Morford is a queer of color scholar. She is currently pursuing her doctorate in English and Book History at the University of Toronto, where she is an uninvited occupant on Wendat,

Haudenosaunee, and Anishinaabe territories. Her research is supported by the Social Sciences and Humanities Research Council. She is a member of the Visayan and Luzonese diasporas on her mother's side and is British on her father's side. Her work centers on the intersections of Indigenous studies, digital humanities, and sexuality studies. She has facilitated scholarly and grassroots classes, workshops, and reading groups on asexuality, de-colonialism, and the digital humanities.

Nate Probasco is Assistant Professor of History and Director of the Honors Program at Briar Cliff University in Sioux City, Iowa. He teaches courses in Atlantic, European, and world history, and his research centers on the roles of gender, technology, and the domestic landscape in colonization and exploration. In 2017, his co-edited (with Estelle Paranque and Claire Jowitt) collection *Colonization, Piracy, and Trade in Early Modern Europe: The Roles of Powerful Women and Queens* was published by Palgrave Macmillan. He also has published articles in *Renaissance Quarterly*, *The Journal of Military History*, *Literature Compass*, and *Explorations in Renaissance Culture*, as well as a chapter in *The Foreign Relations of Elizabeth I* (Palgrave Macmillan, 2011). He has held short-term fellowships at the Huntington and John Carter Brown Libraries.

Julián Díez Torres is an independent scholar and holds doctorates in History (Universidad de Navarra, 2010) and Romance Studies (University of North Carolina, Chapel Hill, 2017). During 2017, he was a postdoctoral fellow at the Universidad de Salamanca (Cátedra de Altos Estudios del Español). His publications include a critical edition of Diego de Aguilar's *El Marañón* (a late sixteenth-century Peruvian chronicle about Lope de Aguirre's voyage in the Amazon basin) and academic papers dealing with Aguirre's rebellion against Philip II, Iberian ethnography, and Inca Garcilaso's colonial historiography. He is currently preparing a book on Garcilaso's historiographical rhetoric; conceived as a transatlantic study, the book will explore Garcilaso's significance in terms of the intellectual, literary, and social status of historiography around 1600.

Claire Urbanski is a doctoral candidate in Feminist Studies and Critical Race and Ethnic Studies at the University of California, Santa Cruz. As a scholar and social justice activist invested in collective liberation, her work centers on the topics of belonging, home, memory, and sexuality to unveil and elaborate the ways that settler-colonial ideologies of Indigenous dispossession, anti-blackness, capital extraction, and gendered violence structure and inform relationships between places, bodies, identities, and lands. Her doctoral research examines the entanglements of United States settler colonialism, sexuality, and spirituality through the lenses of space, incarceration, and formations of the human. Her research has been funded by fellowships from the Princeton University Library and the Institute for Humanities Research.

Index

Note: Page numbers in italic indicate a figure and page numbers in bold indicate a table on the corresponding page.

Printed in the United States
by Baker & Taylor Publisher Services